The United States
in Africa

The United States in Africa

A Historical Dictionary

DAVID SHAVIT

Greenwood Press
NEW YORK · WESTPORT, CONNECTICUT · LONDON

Library of Congress Cataloging-in-Publication Data

Shavit, David.
    The United States in Africa : a historical dictionary / David
Shavit.
        p. cm.
    Bibliography: p.
    Includes index.
    ISBN 0–313–25887–2 (lib. bdg. : alk. paper)
        1. Africa—Relations—United States—Dictionaries. 2. United
States—Relations—Africa—Dictionaries. I. Title.
DT38.1.S53 1989
303.4′8273′06—dc19   88–7707

British Library Cataloguing in Publication Data is available.

Library of Congress Catalog Card Number: 88–7707
ISBN: 0–313–25887–2

First published in 1989

Greenwood Press, Inc.
88 Post Road West, Westport, Connecticut 06881

Printed in the United States of America

The paper used in this book complies with the
Permanent Paper Standard issued by the National
Information Standards Organization (Z39.48–1984).

10 9 8 7 6 5 4 3 2 1

For Rebecca and Rachel

Contents

Preface

Contacts between the United States and Africa began in the seventeenth century when American slavers arrived in West Africa. They were followed by colonists, ships, and officers of the United States Navy, sea captains and traders, missionaries, diplomats, explorers, travelers and adventurers, soldiers, educators, authors and artists, scientists, mining engineers, hunters, and other Americans and American institutions, organizations, and business firms, which established a whole gamut of relationships between the United States and Africa. This dictionary provides in one alphabetical format information about the persons, institutions, and events that affected the relations between the United States and Africa, persons who actually have been in Africa, and particularly those who have left written or visual records of their stay; organizations and institutions that functioned in Africa itself; and events that occurred in that area.

The term Africa includes all the countries south of the Sahara and the adjacent islands. Geographical names have been modernized, but the names used in a specific entry are the ones relevant to the period covered by that entry.

The dictionary attempts to be comprehensive, including persons, institutions, and events that brought the United States into contact with Africa. The choice of entries in a historical dictionary is always difficult. Only those diplomats who contributed to U.S.-African relations in some significant way are included; such contributions may consist of only a book of memoirs of their service in the area. A complete list of all chiefs of American diplomatic missions in Africa is included at the end of this book.[1]

Only a limited number of travelers, government agencies, and business firms are included. With regard to travelers, only those whose travel reports are of particular interest and influence are covered.[2] Although many governmental agencies, in addition to the U.S. Department of State, were involved with Africa, only a few had establishments in the area.[3] Finally, as regards business, only a few business firms are covered in this dictionary. For those who are interested, lists of firms that sold their products in Africa are available in several sources.[4]

The references at the end of each entry note whether the subject is listed in the general biographical dictionaries, such as the *Dictionary of American Biography*, *National Cyclopaedia of American Biography*, *Appleton's Cyclopaedia of American Biography*, *Notable American Women*, *Who's Who in America*, *Who Was Who in America*, and *Contemporary Authors*. The references also attempt to list every book and article written about the subject, but references that appear in the *Dictionary of American Biography* and *Notable American Women* have not been duplicated. Volume and page numbers are provided only for the *National Cyclopaedia of American Biography* and the *Biographie Coloniale Belge*, because they are not arranged in alphabetical order, and volume numbers are given for the *Dictionary of South African Biography*. Asterisked names indicate that the subject is covered in a separate entry in this volume.

Efforts have been made to include complete and accurate information, but this was not always possible because some information is no longer available and other information could not be located. Unfortunately, mistakes are inevitable in a work of this scope. The author would appreciate receiving corrections and emendations.

Many individuals provided valuable assistance, especially librarians, archivists, and officials of missionary societies. The dictionary would have been far less complete without their help. Special thanks are again due to the staff of the Interlibrary Loan Office of Northern Illinois University, DeKalb, Illinois.

NOTES

1. A complete list is available in U.S. Department of State, *United States Chiefs of Mission 1778–1986* (Washington, D.C., 1987). A complete list of consuls who served in Africa is available only through 1865 in Walter B. Smith II, *America's Diplomats and Consuls of 1776–1865: A Geographic and Biographic Directory of the Foreign Service from the Declaration of Independence to the End of the Civil War* (Washington, D.C., 1986).

2. A list of travel accounts of the nineteenth century is included in Harold F. Smith, *American Abroad: A Bibliography of Accounts Published Before 1900* (Carbondale, Ill., 1969).

3. A comprehensive list of current governmental agencies involved with Africa is available in Purnima Mehta Bhatt, *Scholars' Guide to Washington, D.C., for African Studies* (Washington, D.C., 1980), pp. 193–244. Missionary societies are listed in Jean E. Meeh Gosebrink, comp. and ed., *African Studies Information Resources Directory* (Oxford, 1986), pp. 394–481; and the ones in Zaire can be found in Cecilia Irvine, comp., *The Church of Christ in Zaire: A Handbook of Protestant Churches, Missions and Communities, 1878–1978* (Indianapolis, 1978).

4. Comprehensive lists are Jacqueline S. Mithun, comp., *African Programs of U.S. Organizations: A Selective Directory* (Washington, D.C., 1965); *AF: LOG: African Interests of American Organizations* (Washington, D.C., 1975); and *Directory of American Firms Operating in Foreign Countries* (New York, 1955/56–).

Abbreviations

AA	*American Anthropologist*
ACAB	*Appleton's Cyclopaedia of American Biography* (New York, 1888–1901)
ACWW	*American Catholic Who's Who*
Amherst	*Amherst College Biographical Record, 1973: Biographical Record of the Graduates and Nongraduates of the Classes of 1822–1971 Inclusive* (Amherst, Mass., 1973)
AMWS	*American Men and Women of Science*
AndoverTS	*General Catalogue of Andover Theological Seminary* (Boston, 1908)
BCB	*Biographie Coloniale Belge* (Bruxelles, 1948–)
BDAC	*Biographical Directory of the American Congress 1774–1971* (Washington, D.C., 1971)
BDAE	*Biographical Dictionary of American Educators*, ed. John F. Ohles (Westport, Conn., 1978)
BE	*Brethren Encyclopedia* (Philadelphia, 1983–1984)
BMNAS	*Biographical Memoirs of the National Academy of Science*
CA	*Contemporary Authors* (Detroit, 1962–).
CB	*Current Biography*
CBAA	*Current Bibliography on African Affairs*
Christmas	*Negroes in Public Affairs and Government*, ed. Walter L. Christmas (Yonkers, N.Y., 1966)
DAB	*Dictionary of American Biography* (New York, 1928–)
DADH	*Dictionary of American Diplomatic History*, John E. Findling (Westport, Conn., 1980)
DAMB	*Dictionary of American Medical Biography*, Howard A. Kelly (Boston, 1928)
DAMB 1984	*Dictionary of American Medical Biography*, ed. Martin Kaufman, Stuart Galishoff and Todd L. Savitt (Westport, Conn., 1984).
DAMIB	*Dictionary of American Military Biography*, ed. Roger J. Spiller (Westport, Conn., 1984)
DANB	*Dictionary of American Negro Biography* (New York, 1982)

DANFS	*Dictionary of American Naval Fighting Ships* (Washington, D.C., 1959–1981)
DARB	*Dictionary of American Religious Biography*, Henry W. Bowden (Westport, Conn., 1977)
DAS	*Directory of American Scholars*
Davis	*This Is Liberia*, Stanley A. Davis (New York, 1953)
Dirty Work 2	*Dirty Work 2: The CIA in Africa*, ed. Ellen Ray et al. (Secaucus, N.J., 1979)
DLB	*Dictionary of Literary Biography* (Detroit, 1978–)
DSAB	*Dictionary of South African Biography* (Cape Town, 1968–)
DSB	*Dictionary of Scientific Biography* (New York, 1970–1976).
EAJ	*Encyclopedia of American Journalism*, Donald Paneth (New York, 1983)
Ebony 1	*The Ebony Success Library, Vol. I: 1,000 Successful Blacks* (Nashville, Tenn., 1973)
EIHC	*Essex Institute Historical Collections*
EM	*Encyclopaedia of Missions* (New York, 1891–1904)
EMCM	*The Encyclopedia of Modern Christian Missions: The Agencies*, ed. Burton L. Goddard (Camden, N.J., 1967)
Engle	*There Is No Difference: God Works in Africa and India*, Anna R. Engle (Nappanee, Ind., 1950)
ESB	*Encyclopedia of Southern Baptists* (Nashville, Tenn., 1958–1982)
EWM	*Encyclopedia of World Methodism* (Nashville, Tenn., 1974)
GSAB	*Geological Society of America Bulletin*
Hewitt	*Williams College and Foreign Missions*, John M. Hewitt (Boston, 1914)
Huberich	*The Political and Legislative History of Liberia*, Charles H. Huberich (New York, 1947)
IAB	*Indiana Authors and Their Books*, R. E. Banta and Donald R. Thompson (Bloomington, Ind., 1949–1974)
IJAHS	*International Journal of African Historical Studies*
JAH	*Journal of African History*
JNH	*Journal of Negro History*
LC	*Lutheran Cyclopedia*, rev. ed. (St. Louis, 1975)
Leete	*Methodist Bishops: Personal Notes and Bibliography*, Frederick D. Leete (Nashville, Tenn., 1948)
MBEP	*Macmillan Encyclopedia of Photography*, Turner Browne and Elaine Partnow (New York, 1983)
NAW	*Notable American Women* (Cambridge, Mass., 1971–1980)
NCAB	*National Cyclopaedia of American Biography* (New York, 1898–).
NHB	*Negro History Bulletin*
NYT	*New York Times*
OAB	*Ohio Authors and Their Books*, ed. William Coyle (Cleveland, 1962)
PGSA	*Proceedings of the Geological Society of America*

Richardson	*Liberia's Past and Present*, Nathaniel R. Richardson (London, 1959)
SADNB	*South African Dictionary of National Biography*, comp. Eric Rosenthal (London, 1966)
SDAE	*Seventh-Day Adventist Encyclopedia*, rev. ed. (Washington, D.C., 1976)
SESA	*Standard Encyclopedia of Southern Africa* (Cape Town, 1972)
S	Supplement
Tabler/Natal	*Pioneers of Natal and Southeastern Africa 1552–1878*, Edward C. Tabler (Cape Town, 1977)
Tabler/Rhodesia	*Pioneers of Rhodesia*, Edward C. Tabler (Cape Town, 1966)
Tabler/South West Africa	*Pioneers of South West Africa and Ngamiland 1738–1880*, Edward C. Tabler (Cape Town, 1973)
TWTA	*They Went to Africa: Biographies of Missionaries of the Disciples of Christ* (Indianapolis, 1952)
WAMB	*Webster American Military Biographies* (Springfield, Mass., 1978)
Wright	*The Bishops of the African Methodist Episcopal Church*, Richard R. Wright, Jr. (Nashville, Tenn., 1963)
WWA	*Who's Who in America*
WWAP	*Who's Who in American Politics*
WWBA	*Who's Who Among Black Americans*
WWCR	*Who's Who of the Colored Race*, ed. Frank L. Mather (Chicago, 1915)
WWE	*Who's Who in the East*
WWG	*Who's Who in Government*
WWPNL	*Who's Who Among Pastors in All the Norwegian Lutheran Synods of America 1843–1927* (Minneapolis, 1928)
WWS	*Who's Who in the South and Southwest*
WWW	*Who's Who in the West*
WWWA	*Who Was Who in America*

Place Names

Since geographical names in Africa appear in several versions, the following list provides the names that have been used in the dictionary. In those cases where names have changed, the dictionary has followed the usage of the times.

Current Name	Former Name
Benin	Dahomey
Botswana	Bechuanaland
Burkina Faso	Upper Volta
Burundi	Ruanda-Urundi
Central African Republic	Oubangui-Chari
Ethiopia	Abyssinia
Harrare	Salisbury
Kenya	British East Africa
Kinshana	Léopoldville
Kisangani	Stanleyville
Lesotho	Basutoland
Lubumbashi	Elisabethville
Malawi	Nyasaland
Mauritius	Isle de France
Namibia	Southwest Africa
Rwanda	Ruanda-Urundi
Shaba	Katanga (Province)
Somalia	Somaliland
Tanzania	Tanganyika/Zanzibar
Zaire	Belgian Congo/Congo Free State
Zambia	Northern Rhodesia
Zimbabwe	Southern Rhodesia

Chronology

1517	Regular establishment of the slave trade
1595	Dutch establish themselves on the Guinea Coast
1626	French establish themselves at the mouth of the Senegal River
1652	Cape Town founded by the Dutch
1662	British establish themselves at the mouth of the Gambia River
1672	Royal African Company established
1768–1773	James Bruce explored Ethiopia
1787	British acquired Sierra Leone
1795–1796	Mungo Park explored the Gambia and reached the Niger River
1799	Sierra Leone made a British colony
1805	Mungo Park explored the Niger River
1817	American Colonization Society founded
1820	First American black immigrants arrived in Africa
1821	First American missionaries arrived in Africa
1822	Liberia founded as colony for freed American slaves
1835	American Zulu mission founded
1835–1837	Great Trek of the Boers in South Africa
1838	Commonwealth of Liberia established
1847	Independent Republic of Liberia established
1849	David Livingstone's first expedition
1853–1856	David Livingstone's second expedition
1858–1859	Richard Burton and John Speke discovered lakes Tanganyika and Victoria Nyanza
1858–1861	David Livingstone's third expedition
1860–1863	John Speke and James Grant explored Uganda
1861	British annexed Lagos
1862	The United States recognized the Republic of Liberia
1867	Discovery of diamonds on the Orange River
1871	Henry Morton Stanley found David Livingstone
1872–1889	Johannes IV, King of Abyssinia
1873–1874	Anglo-Ashanti War
1874–1877	Henry Morton Stanley explored Lake Victoria Nyanza
1879	Zulu War

1880–1881	Revolt of the Transvaal Boers
1885	Founding of the Congo Free State
1886	Discovery of gold on the Witwatersrand
1887–1890	Emin Pasha Relief Expedition
1889–1911	Menelek, Emperor of Abyssinia
1890	British protectorate over Zanzibar; American Presbyterian Congo Mission founded
1893	French conquest of Dahomey
1894	British protectorate over Uganda; French occupation of Timbuktu
1894–1896	French conquest of Madagascar
1895	Jameson raid in the Transvaal; British occupation of Ashanti; Africa Inland Mission founded
1895–1896	Italo-Abyssinian War
1896–1897	Revolts in Matabeleland and Mashonaland
1899–1902	South African (Boer) War
1900–1903	British occupation of Northern Nigeria
1904–1908	Hererro Revolt in Southwest Africa
1905–1907	Maji-Maji uprising in German East Africa
1908	Congo Free State annexed by Belgium
1909	United States Commission investigated Liberia
1911	Congo Inland Mission founded
1912	African National Congress formed in South Africa
1914	British conquest of German colonies
1920	British East Africa renamed Kenya; German East Africa renamed Tanganyika
1923	Southern Rhodesia became a crown colony
1925	Agreement between the Liberian government and Firestone Rubber Plantation Company
1930–1974	Haile Selassie I, emperor of Ethiopia
1930	League of Nations investigated conditions of native labor in Liberia
1935–1936	Italian-Ethiopian War
1936–1941	Italian occupation of Ethiopia
1943–1971	William V. S. Tubman, president of Liberia
1945	Fifth Pan-African Congress held in Manchester, England
1950	Apartheid laws passed in South Africa
1952	Eritrea was federated with Ethiopia
1952–1960	Mau Mau revolt against white settlers in Kenya
1953–1963	Federation of Rhodesia and Nyasaland
1956–1961	Treason trials in South Africa
1957	The Gold Coast became independent as Ghana
1958	Guinea became independent
1958–1984	Ahmed Sékou Touré, president of Guinea
1960	Year of Africa—Belgian Congo, Cameron, Central African Republic, Chad, Dahomey, French Congo, Gabon, Ivory Coast, Madagascar, Mali, Mauritania, Niger, Nigeria, Senegal, Somalia, Togo, and Upper Volta became

	independent; African National Congress banned in South Africa; Sharpeville massacre in South Africa
1960–1963	Secession of Katanga Province, Republic of the Congo
1960–1966	Kwame Nkrumah, president of Ghana
1960–1967	Conflict in the Congo
1961	Sierra Leone and Tanganyika became independent; South Africa became a republic
1962–	Julius K. Nyerere, president of Tanzania
1962	Uganda, Burundi, and Rwanda became independent
1963	Kenya and Zanzibar became independent; Organization of Africa Unity set up in Addis Ababa
1963–1975	Guerrilla war in Portuguese colonies
1964	Nyasaland became independent as Malawi; Northern Rhodesia became independent as Zambia; Tanganyika and Zanzibar united as Tanzania; Nelson Mandela sentenced to life imprisonment
1964–1978	Somali-Ethiopian conflict over the Ogaden desert
1964–1980	Ian Smith, premier of Rhodesia
1965–	Gambia became independent; white minority government in Rhodesia unilaterally declared independence
1966	Bechuanaland became independent as Botswana; Basutoland became independent as Lesotho; military coup in Ghana deposed Nkrumah; military coup in Nigeria
1967–1970	Civil war in Nigeria
1968	Rio Muni and Fernando Po became independent as Equatorial Guinea; Mauritius and Swaziland became independent
1968–	Guerrilla war in Rhodesia
1971	Republic of the Congo renamed Zaire; military coup in Uganda
1971–1979	Idi Amin, president of Uganda
1972–1973	Tribal warfare in Burundi and Rwanda
1974	Military coup in Ethiopia; Guinea-Bissau became independent
1975	Angola, Cape Verde Islands, Comoro Islands, Mozambique, and São Tomé and Principe became independent; Ethiopia proclaimed a republic
1975–	Civil war in Angola; conflict in Western Sahara
1976	Seychelles became independent; Soweto riots in South Africa
1977	Djibouti became independent
1977–1978	Invasion of Shaba Province in Zaire
1980	Military coup in Liberia; Rhodesia became independent as Zimbabwe
1984	Upper Volta renamed Burkina Faso
1985	Military coups in Nigeria and Uganda
1986	State of emergency imposed in South Africa

Introduction

American slave traders appeared on the west coast of Africa in the middle of the seventeenth century and, until the American Civil War, continued to go there and bring back slaves into the United States. Even after the United States formally abolished the slave trade in 1808, American slave smugglers continued their illegal trade. The efforts of the United States Navy to eliminate the illegal trade were unsuccessful. Legal trade in other items of commerce with West and East Africa began in the last years of the eighteenth century.

Missionaries began to arrive in Africa in the 1820s when the interest in returning freed slaves to Africa and creating a refuge for them also began. This interest led to the establishment of several colonies of black Americans on the west coast of Africa, which were merged eventually to become the Republic of Liberia, one of the few enduring direct links between the United States and Africa.

Missionary activities expanded after the Civil War and the number of missionary societies working in Africa increased greatly. Thousands of American missionaries, including many Afro-Americans, went to Africa and operated in most of its areas.

Economic contacts during the nineteenth century were slight, but the discovery of gold and diamonds in South Africa increased these contacts somewhat. Furthermore, most of the mining engineers who have helped to exploit the mineral resources of South Africa were Americans.

Antedating and following in the footsteps of Henry Morton Stanley, an increasing number of American explorers and travelers arrived in Africa and began to penetrate its interior. Americans went on safari to Africa to hunt big game with gun and camera and to bring specimens to natural history museums in the United States.

The only political ties of any significance before World War II were with Liberia, with which the United States had a special involvement. The United States showed little interest or involvement in African affairs. It refused to participate in the partition of Africa by the colonial powers, and declared its neutrality in the South African War and later in the Italo-Ethiopian War. It showed marginal interest in Africa even after World War I, when it refused to accept a mandate over the conquered German territories, and after World War II, when it refused to accept a trusteeship over the conquered Italian territories. Diplomatic and consular services before World War II were very limited; the first American ambassador to an African country was appointed in 1949.

The United States' only concern in the period between the world wars was in economic matters, and specifically in assuring access to African markets. Africa has also been an important source for a number of strategic metals and minerals. Before 1960, however, Africa accounted for less than 2 percent of United States foreign trade. Trade and investment were concentrated in the Firestone operations in Liberia and in mineral industries in Southern Africa.

American foundations contributed substantially to the educational and health services in Africa, but scholarly interest in Africa was minimal prior to the 1950s. The United States' interest and programs in Africa and its involvement in African affairs increased only after the Gold Coast attained independence in 1957. While the United States avoided direct engagement of American military personnel, it has played a significant role in the 1960s crisis in the Congo and in the Civil War in Angola in the 1970s. The United States' relations with Rhodesia during the 1970s, and with South Africa since the 1970s, have been of great concern to the U.S. government and the American public.

A

ABBOTT, WILLIAM LOUIS (1860–1936). Naturalist and explorer, born February 23, 1860, in Philadelphia. Abbott graduated from the University of Pennsylvania and studied in London, but did not practice medicine. He inherited a considerable fortune, and being financially independent, devoted his time to studying natural history. From 1887 to 1889 he collected natural history specimens in East Africa and ascended Mount Kilimanjaro; he then collected in the Seychelles Archipelago and in Madagascar in 1890, 1892, and 1894. He later collected in the Himalayas, in Southeast Asia, and in the islands of the South China Sea, and explored Santo Domingo and Haiti. Died April 2, 1936, in North East, Maryland. *References*: William Louis Abbott Papers, Smithsonian Institution Archives, Washington, D.C.; *NCAB* 27:312.

ADAMS, NEWTON (1804–1851). Medical missionary, born August 4, 1804, in East Bloomfield, Ontario County, New York. Adams graduated from Hamilton College (N.Y.), and was ordained in 1844. He then practiced medicine in New York City. He was missionary under the American Board of Commissioners for Foreign Missions (ABCFM)* in South Africa, working among the Zulus and the Matabeles from 1836 until his death. He traveled overland to Natal in 1836 and opened the first mission station, school, and mission press at Umlazi. He was received by the Zulu king, Dingane, who allowed him to practice medicine and to print the first booklets in the Zulu language. In 1847 he moved his mission station to Amanzimtoti, Natal. He was later a member of the first Natal Land Commission, which was instrumental in setting up the Natives Reserves in Natal. Died September 16, 1851, in Adams Mission, Amanzimtoti, Natal, South Africa. *References*: *DSAB* 2; *SADNB*; and *Tabler/Natal*.

ADAMS COLLEGE. Established in 1836 by missionaries of the American Board of Commissioners for Foreign Missions (ABCFM)* as a school in the Amanzimtoti Mission Reserve, south of Durban, Natal, under the name Amanzimtoti Institute. It began teacher training in 1909. It was closed down in 1957

2 AFRICA INLAND MISSION

and liquidated in accordance with the Bantu Education Act, which transferred the control and administration of native education to the Native Affairs department of the government of the Union of South Africa. The campus was sold to the government which opened the Amanzimtoti Zulu College on the site. The Adams United Theological School was established in 1957 in Modderspoort, Orange Free State, by the ABCFM and the Bantu Presbyterian Church of South Africa, to replace the Theological Training department of Adams College. *References*: George C. Grant, *The Liquidation of Adams College* (Amanzimtoti, South Africa, 1957); and *SESA*.

AFRICA INLAND MISSION. An international interdenominational mission, founded in 1895 by Peter Cameron Scott* in the United States. The largest part of the money and the personnel have always come from the United States. Scott began missionary work in 1895 in British East Africa. In 1909 the Church Missionary Society transferred to it part of its mission in Tanganyika. It entered the Congo in 1912, Uganda in 1918, the Central African Republic in 1924, and the Sudan in 1949. In the 1970s it also began missionary work in Reunion, the Comoro Islands, the Seychelles, Madagascar, and Namibia. *References*: Africa Inland Mission Records, Billy Graham Center Archives, Wheaton College, Wheaton, Ill.; *EMCM*; and Kenneth Richards, *Garden of Miracles: The Story of the Africa Inland Mission* (London, 1976).

AFRICAN EDUCATION COMMISSIONS. Two commissions organized by the Phelps-Stokes Fund to study educational conditions and needs in several African territories. The first commission visited West and South Africa in 1920–1921, and the second commission visited East, Central, and South Africa in 1924. The reports of both commissions, written by Thomas Jesse Jones*, were a catalyst in the creation of a British colonial educational policy for Africa. *References*: Edward H. Berman, "American Influence on African Education: The Role of the Phelps-Stokes Fund's Education Commissions," *Comparative Education Review* 15 (1971): 132–45; Edward H. Berman, "Educational Colonialism in Africa; The Role of the American Foundations, 1910–1945," in *Philanthropy and Cultural Imperialism: The Foundations at Home and Abroad*, ed. Robert F. Arnove (Bloomington, Ind., 1982), pp. 179–201; Kenneth J. King, *Pan-Africanism and Education: A Study of Race, Philanthropy and Education in the Southern States of America and East Africa* (Oxford, 1971), ch. 4; and L. J. Lewis, *The Phelps-Stokes Reports on Education in Africa* (London, 1962).

AFRICAN METHODIST EPISCOPAL CHURCH: DEPARTMENT OF HOME AND FOREIGN MISSIONS. Founded in 1844, although African Methodist Episcopal Church missionaries began working in Sierra Leone in 1821. The first mission was organized in Sierra Leone in 1866. Missionary work began in Liberia in 1891, in South Africa in 1892, in Nyasaland and Northern and Southern Rhodesia in 1900, in Bechuanaland in 1901, in Basutoland in 1903, in Swaziland in 1904, in Tanganyika in 1920, in the Gold Coast in 1935, in Southwest Africa in 1953, and in Nigeria in 1956. The name was changed later to the Department of Missions. *References*: Lewellyn L. Berry, *A Century of the African Methodist Episcopal Church 1840–1940* (New York, 1942); Josephus R. Coan, "The Expansion of the Missions of the African Methodist Episcopal Church in South Africa, 1896–1908." Ph.D. diss., Hartford Seminary Foundation, 1961; *EMCM*; and Artishia W. Jordan, *The African Methodist Episcopal Church in Africa* (n.p., 1964).

AFRICAN METHODIST EPISCOPAL ZION CHURCH: DEPARTMENT OF FOREIGN MISSIONS. Organized in 1892, it began missionary work in Liberia in 1876, in the Gold Coast in 1896, and in Nigeria in 1930. The name was changed later to the Department of Overseas Missions. *References*: David H. Bradley, *A History of the A. M. E. Zion Church, 1872–1968* (Nashville, Tenn., 1970); *EMCM*; Hampton T. Medford, *Zion Methodism Abroad* (Washington, D.C., 1937); and William J. Walls, *The African Methodist Episcopal Zion Church: Reality of the Black Church* (Charlotte, N.C., 1974).

AFRICAN SOCIETY OF PROVIDENCE. See SIERRA LEONE EMIGRATION SCHEME

AFRICAN SQUADRON. See U. S. AFRICAN SQUADRON

AFRICA SPEAKS. The first all-sound film of African adventure, which resulted from Paul Louis Hoefler's* Colorado African Expedition of 1929.

AGNEW, G(EORGE) HARRY (1864–1903). Missionary, born October 17, 1864, in Sheerness, England; moved to Ireland in 1873. Agnew came to the United States in 1880. He was missionary under the General Missionary Board of the Free Methodist Church of North America* in Mozambique from 1885 until 1895 and founded the mission station at Inhambane, Mozambique. He went to South Africa in 1895 and worked in the Mines District of Transvaal. Died March 9, 1903, in Johannesburg, South Africa. *Reference*: Wilson T. Hogue, *G. Harry Agnew, a Pioneer Missionary* (Chicago, 1904).

AKELEY, CARL ETHAN (1864–1926). Taxidermist, naturalist, and explorer, born May 19, 1864, in Clarendon, Orleans County, New York. Akeley began working at Ward's Natural Science Establishment in Rochester, New York, in 1883. He worked in the Milwaukee Museum from 1887 until 1895, developing techniques of constructing habitat groups of animals, and moved to the Field Museum of Natural History in Chicago in 1895. He made his first expedition to Africa in 1896 and his second expedition in 1905, during which he collected the elephants now displayed at Stanley Field Hall of the Field Museum of Natural History. He went on his third expedition to Africa in 1911 for the American

Museum of Natural History. He wrote *In Brightest Africa* (Garden City, N.Y., 1920). He made his fourth expedition in 1921–1922, during which he collected gorillas and made the first motion pictures ever taken of wild gorillas in their natural environment. He was instrumental in securing the establishment of Parc National Albert in the Belgian Congo, the first wildlife sanctuary in Central Africa. He went on his fifth expedition to Africa in 1926. Died November 17, 1926, in Mount Mikeno, Kivu, Belgian Congo. *References*: Carl Ethan Akeley Papers, University of Rochester Library, Rochester, N.Y.; *BCB* 1; *DAB*; *NCAB* 26:130; *NYT*, December 1, 1926; and *WWWA*.

AKELEY, DELIA (DENNING) (1874–1970). Explorer, big-game hunter, and writer; first wife of Carl Ethan Akeley,* born in Beaver Dam, Wisconsin. Delia Akeley went with her husband on expeditions to Africa in 1905 and 1911. After her divorce in 1923, she made expeditions on her own to Africa on behalf of the Brooklyn Museum in 1924 and 1928, crossed Africa from coast to coast, did research among the BaMbuti pygmies of the Ituri Forest, in the Belgian Congo, and lived alone among the pygmies in 1930. She wrote *Jungle Portraits* (New York, 1930). Died May 22, 1970, in Daytona Beach, Florida. *References*: *NYT*, May 23, 1970; Elizabeth F. Olds, *Women of the Four Winds* (Boston, 1985), pp. 71–153; and Mignon Rittenhouse, *Seven Women Explorers* (New York, 1964), pp. 58–78.

AKELEY, MARY L(EE) JOBE (1878–1966). Explorer and photographer, second wife of Carl Ethan Akeley,* born Mary Leonore, January 29, 1878, in Tappan, Ohio. Mary Jobe Akeley graduated from Scio College (later Mt. Union College) in Alliance, Ohio, studied at Bryn Mawr College, and graduated from Columbia University. She taught history at Normal (later Hunter) College of the City of New York until 1916. She explored British Columbia from 1913 to 1916, and established Camp Mystic (Mystic, Conn.) in 1916 and presided over it until 1930. She accompanied her husband on the expedition to the Belgian Congo in 1926–1927, served as field assistant, safari manager, and photographer, and took over the expedition on his death. In 1935 she went to southern Africa on an expedition for the American Museum of Natural History and surveyed the wildlife in the Kruger National Park, and in 1947 made a survey of wildlife sanctuaries and national parks in the Belgian Congo for the Belgian government. She wrote *Carl Akeley's Africa* (New York, 1929); *Adventures in the African Jungle* (New York, 1930); *The Restless Jungle* (New York, 1936); *The Wilderness Lives Again: Carl Akeley and the Great Adventure* (New York, 1940); *Rumble of a Distant Drum, a True Story of the African Hinterland* (New York, 1946); and *Congo Eden: A Comprehensive Portrayal of the Historical Background and Scientific Aspects of the Great Game Sanctuaries of the Belgian Congo, etc.* (London, 1951). Died July 19, 1966, in Stonington, Connecticut. *References*: Mary L. Jobe Akeley Papers and diaries, American Museum of Natural History Library, New York City; *BCB* 7; *NAW*; *OAB*; and *WWWA*.

AKELEY-EASTMAN-POMEROY AFRICAN HALL EXPEDITION (1926). An expedition, led by Carl Ethan Akeley* and financed by Daniel Pomeroy, Detroit industrialist, and George Eastman (who joined the expedition), sent to the Congo by the American Museum of Natural History in 1926 to collect specimens for the African Hall in the museum. Martin and Osa Johnson* were the expedition's photographers. *References*: Mary L. Jobe Akeley, *Carl Akeley's Africa: An Account of the Akeley-Eastman-Pomeroy African Hall Expedition of the American Museum of Natural History* (New York, 1929); George Eastman, *Chronicles of an African Trip* ([Rochester, N.Y.], 1927).

ALABAMA, **C.S.S.** Confederate raider, built in England in 1862, and commanded by Raphael Semmes. It conducted raids on merchant ships of the Union in 1863, including raids in the neighborhood of the Cape of Good Hope in South Africa, in which it captured fourteen Union vessels. At that time, the Malays of Cape Town composed a folksong about it. It was sunk in 1864 near Cherbourg Harbor, France. *References*: Edward Boykin, *Ghost Ship of the Confederacy: The Story of the "Alabama" and Her Captain, Raphael Semmes* (New York, 1957); Edna and Frank Bradlow, *Here Comes the "Alabama"* (Cape Town, 1958); and *SESA*.

ALDEN, HAROLD LEE (1890–1964). Astronomer, born January 10, 1890, in Chicago. Alden graduated from Wheaton College (Ill.) and the universities of Chicago and Virginia. He was associated with the Yerkes Observatory at Williams Bay, Wisconsin, from 1912 to 1914, and with the Leander McCormick Observatory at the University of Virginia from 1914 to 1925. He was also assistant professor and associate professor of astronomy at the University of Virginia. From 1925 until 1945 he was astronomer in charge of the Astronomical Observatory of Yale University in Johannesburg, and photographed almost the entire southern heavens. He was professor of astronomy at the University of Virginia and director of their McCormick Observatory from 1945 until his retirement in 1960. Died February 3, 1964, in Charlottesville, Virginia. *References*: *DSAB* 4; *NCAB* 52:498; *SADNB*; and *Sky and Telescope* 27 (1964): 203.

ALEXANDER, DANIEL ROBERT (1859- ?). Blacksmith, born in Lincoln County, Missouri. In the early 1900s he escorted a shipload of Missouri mules to Liverpool, England, and in 1908 he traveled to Abyssinia and reached Addis Ababa. He married an Abyssinian woman and settled in Addis Ababa, the first permanent Afro-American settler in Abyssinia. He had a farm near the city and was involved in various trading activities, including a money-lending business. He returned to the United States after the Italian occupation of Ethiopia. *Reference*: William R. Scott, "A Study of Afro-American and Ethiopian Relations: 1896–1941," Ph.D. diss., Princeton University, 1971, pp. 45–50.

ALLEN, FRANCES GRACE (1864–1957). Missionary, born July 12, 1864, in Palmyra, Michigan, and grew up in Lawrence, Kansas. She taught in public schools in Kansas. She was missionary under the General Mission Board of the Free Methodist Church of North America* in Mozambique from 1888 to 1891, and was transferred to Natal in 1891. She founded a school for girls at Fairview, Natal, and served as its principal, and was in charge of the mission in Pondoland from 1926 until 1940. Died April 15, 1957, in Oklahoma City, Oklahoma. *Reference*: EWM.

ALLEN, GLOVER MERRILL (1879–1942). Naturalist, born February 8, 1879, in Walpole, New Hampshire, and grew up in Newton, Massachusetts. Allen graduated from Harvard University. He was secretary and librarian of the Boston Society of Natural History from 1901 to 1928, and became naturalist at the Museum of Comparative Zoology of Harvard University in 1907 and curator of mammals at the museum in 1925. He was lecturer, associate professor, and professor of zoology at Harvard University. He made collecting trips to East Africa in 1909 and again to Africa in 1912 and 1926, and prepared *A Checklist of African Mammals* (Cambridge, Mass., 1939). He also made collecting trips to the Bahamas, Labrador, British West Indies, Brazil, and Australia. Died February 15, 1942, in Cambridge, Massachusetts. *References*: Glover Merrill Allen Papers and journals, Museum of Comparative Zoology Archives, Harvard University, Cambridge, Mass.; *DAB S3*; *NCAB* 31:143; and *WWWA*.

ALLEYNE, CAMERON CHESTERFIELD (1880–1955). Clergyman, born September 3, 1880, in Bridgetown, Barbados, British West Indies. Alleyne graduated from Naprima College (Port of Spain, Trinidad), came to the United States in 1903, attended Tuskegee Institute, and was ordained in 1905. He was pastor in Anniston, Alabama; Elmo, Tennessee; Washington, D.C.; Providence, Rhode Island; Charlotte, North Carolina; and New Rochelle, New York; and was editor of the *Quarterly Review* from 1916 to 1924. He was consecrated a bishop in 1924 and became the first resident bishop of the African Methodist Episcopal Zion Church* in Africa. He wrote *Gold Coast at a Glance* (New York, 1931). He was superintendent of the Third Episcopal district of his church from 1928 until his death. Died March 24, 1955, in Philadelphia. *References*: *NYT*, March 26, 1955; and William J. Walls, *The African Methodist Episcopal Zion Church: Reality of the Black Church* (Charlotte, N.C., 1974).

ALVORD, EMORY DELMONT (1899–1959). Missionary and agriculturist, born March 25, 1899, in Utah. Alvord graduated from Washington State College. He was a teacher, specialized in agriculture after 1913, and joined the Extension Service of the United States Department of Agriculture in 1919. He was missionary under the American Board of Commissioners for Foreign Missions (ABCFM)* from 1919 to 1926, serving as an agriculturist to the Mount Silinda mission in the Chipinga District of Southern Rhodesia, teaching agricultural techniques to Africans. He was appointed by the Rhodesian government as Agriculturist for the Instruction of Natives in 1926, and was director of the Department of Native Agriculture of Southern Rhodesia from 1944 until his retirement in 1950. He was reinstated as missionary of the ABCFM in 1950, was principal of the Alvord Agricultural School in Chikore until 1954, and principal of the Marandelles School of Agriculture of the Methodist Mission from 1954 until his death. Died May 6, 1959, in Southern Rhodesia. *References*: *NYT*, May 9, 1959; L. Rope and C. W. Hall, "Man Who Founded a People," *Reader's Digest* 58 (March 1951): 51–55; and *SADNB*.

AMERICAN BAPTIST FOREIGN MISSION SOCIETY. See AMERICAN BAPTIST MISSIONARY UNION

AMERICAN BAPTIST MISSIONARY UNION. Organized in 1814, it was renamed American Baptist Foreign Mission Society in 1910. It began missionary work in Liberia in 1821, but transferred it later to the Southern Baptist Convention Foreign Mission Board.* In 1884 it took over from the Livingstone Inland Mission its stations in the Congo, which became part of the local Baptist church in 1966. The society was later renamed the International Ministries of the American Baptist Church USA. *References*: American Baptist Missionary Union Archives, Valley Forge, Pa.; *EMCM*; *Mission in Mid-Continent: One Hundred Years of American Baptist Commitment in Zaire: 1884–1984*, ed. Dean R. Kirkwood (Valley Forge, Pa., 1984); and Robert G. Torbet, *Venture of Faith: The Story of the American Baptist Foreign Mission Society and the Woman's American Baptist Foreign Mission Society 1814–1954* (Philadelphia, 1955).

AMERICAN BOARD OF COMMISSIONERS FOR FOREIGN MISSIONS (ABCFM). Founded in 1810, it began missionary work in South Africa in 1835, in Liberia from 1834 to 1842, in Gabon in 1842 (transferred in 1870 to the Presbyterian Church in the U.S.A.), in Angola in 1880, in Southern Rhodesia and Mozambique in 1893, and in the Gold Coast in 1947. It was superseded in 1961 by the United Church Board for World Ministries. *References*: American Board of Commissioners for Foreign Missions Archives, Houghton Library, Harvard University, Cambridge, Mass.; *EMCM*; Clifton J. Phillips, *Protestant America and the Pagan World: The First Half Century of the American Board of Commissioners for Foreign Missions* (Cambridge, Mass., 1968); *SESA*; Fola Soremekun, "A History of the American Board Mission in Angola, 1880–1940," Ph.D. diss., Northwestern University, 1965; William E. Strong, *The Story of the American Board. An Account of the First Hundred Years of the American Board of Commissioners for Foreign Missions* (Boston, 1910); and Mary A. Walker, "The Archives of the American Board for Foreign Missions," *Harvard Library Bulletin* 4 (Winter 1952): 52–68.

AMERICAN COLONIZATION SOCIETY (ACS). Formally the American
Society for Colonizing the Free People of Color of the United States, founded
in 1817 in Washington, D.C., to transport freeborn and emancipated American
blacks to Africa and help them start a new life. The society assumed responsibility
for transporting black emigrants to Africa and providing them with land, shelter,
and subsistence during their first six months there. The first expedition of black
immigrants went to West Africa in 1820. Between 1822 and 1867, the society
and its affiliates were responsible for the colonization of some 19,000 people
along the west coast of Africa. In 1839, it formed the various settlements into
the Commonwealth of Liberia and the society's agent was designated governor.
Liberia claimed independence in 1847, and the society became an emigration
society. After the Civil War, it stressed educational and missionary activities.
It ceased functioning as a colonizing society in 1904, and was finally dissolved
in 1963. *References*: American Colonization Society Papers, Manuscript Division, Library of Congress; Willis D. Boyd, "The American Colonization Society
and the Slave Recaptives of 1860–61: An Early Example of United States-African
Relations," *JNH* 47 (1962): 108–26; Early L. Fox, *The American Colonization
Society, 1817–1840* (Baltimore, 1919); Eli Seifman, "The Passing of the American Colonization Society," *Liberian Studies Journal* 2 (1969): 1–7; P. J. Stau-
denraus, *The African Colonization Movement 1816–1865* (New York, 1961);
and Werner T. Wickstrom, *The American Colonization Society and Liberia (An
Historical Study in Religious Motivation and Achievement) 1817–1867* (Monrovia, Liberia, 1960).

AMERICAN CONGO COMPANY. Formed in 1906 by a syndicate of American capitalists represented by financier Thomas Fortune Ryan (1851–1928) and
Senator Nelson Wilmarth Aldrich (1841–1915) as the result of King Leopold
II's efforts to stifle criticism of his administration of the Congo Free State. The
company was granted a mineral prospecting concession in an area that covered
more than 370,000 square miles of the state plus long-term lease arrangement
for any mine it chose to exploit. Initial investigations proved the concession to
be uneconomical, and the company became defunct by 1911. *Reference*: Jacob
Sternstein, "King Leopold II, Senator Nelson Aldrich, and the Strange Beginnings of American Economic Penetration in the Congo," *African Historical
Studies* 2 (1969): 189–204.

AMERICAN LUTHERAN CHURCH: DIVISION OF WORLD MISSIONS.
See EVANGELICAL LUTHERAN CHURCH and UNITED LUTHERAN
CHURCH IN AMERICA

AMERICAN MISSION TO THE ZULUS. *See* AMERICAN ZULU MISSION

AMERICAN MISSIONARY ASSOCIATION. Began missionary work in the
1840s in Mende country, later part of Sierra Leone (see Mende Mission*). In
1882 the mission was transferred to the United Brethren in Christ. *References*:

American Missionary Association Archives, Amistad Research Center, New Orleans; American Missionary Association, *Author and Added Entry Catalog of the American Missionary Association,* intro. Clifton H. Johnson (Westport, Conn., 1970); Augustus F. Beard, *A Crusade of Brotherhood: A History of the American Missionary Association* (Boston, 1909); and Clifton H. Johnson, ''The American Missionary Association, 1846–1861: A Study of Christian Abolitionism,'' Ph.D. diss., University of North Carolina, 1958.

AMERICAN PRESBYTERIAN CONGO MISSION (APCM). Established by the Board of Foreign Missions of the Presbyterian Church in the United States* in 1890 in the Kasai region of Congo Free State. *References*: Robert D. Bedinger, *Triumphs of the Gospel in the Belgian Congo* (Richmond, Va., 1935); Stanley Shaloff, *Reform in Leopold's Congo* (Richmond, Va., 1970); and Ethel T. Wharton, *Led in Triumph: Sixty Years of Southern Presbyterian Mission in the Belgian Congo* (Nashville, Tenn., 1952).

AMERICAN ZULU MISSION. Established in South Africa in 1835 by the American Board of Commissioners for Foreign Missions (ABCFM).* The first mission station was established in Umlazi (later renamed Amanzimtoti and Adams), Natal, in 1836. *References*: Arthur F. Christoferson, *Adventuring with God: The Story of the American Board Mission in South Africa*, ed. Richard Sales (Durban, 1967); Myra Dinnerstein, ''The American Board Mission to the Zulu, 1835–1900,'' Ph.D. diss., Columbia University, 1971; Myra Dinnerstein, ''The American Zulu Mission in the Nineteenth Century: Clash Over Customs,'' *Church History* 45 (1976): 235–46; Norman A. Etherington, ''An American Errand into the South African Wilderness,'' *Church History* 39 (1970): 62–71; Dorothy O. Kelly, ''The American Board for Foreign Missions in South Africa,'' *Quarterly Bulletin of the South African Library* 11 (June 1957): 129–43; C. Tsheloane Keto, ''Race Relations, Land and the Changing Missionary Role in South Africa: A Case Study of the American Zulu Mission, 1850–1910,'' *IJAHS* 10 (1977): 600–627; *Letters of the American Missionaries, 1835–1838*, ed. D. J. Kotze (Cape Town, 1950); *SESA*; *Tabler/Natal*; and James Dexter Taylor, *One Hundred Years of the American Board Mission in South Africa* (n.p., 193-).

ANDERSON, BENJAMIN J(OSEPH) K(NIGHT) (1834- ?). Surveyer and explorer, born in Baltimore, Maryland. Anderson came to Liberia at an early age, and was educated in Monrovia. He was secretary of the treasury in Liberia from 1864 to 1866. He made a journey into the hinterland of Liberia (the area not included in the coastal counties) in 1868–1869, visiting the western Mandingo city of Musardu in 1868, and wrote *Narrative of a Journey to Musardu, the Capital of the Western Mandingoes* (New York, 1870; 2d ed. with new introduction by Humphrey Fisher, London, 1971). He went on a second expedition in 1874, and wrote *Narrative of the Expedition Despatched to Musardu by the Liberian Government Under B. J. K. Anderson, Sr. Esquire in 1874* (Monrovia,

1912). In 1879 he worked with a survey party on the St. Paul River for a railway project that was never built, and in 1882 was tutor in mathematics in Liberia College. Died after 1905. *Reference*: *Davis*.

ANDERSON, GEORGE N(ATHANAEL) (1883–1958). Missionary, born August 8, 1883, in Morganville, Kansas. Anderson graduated from Bethany College and Augustana Theological Seminary, studied at the University of Minnesota and Union Theological Seminary, and was ordained in 1912. He served parishes in the midwest. He was missionary under the Board of Foreign Missions of the Augustana Lutheran Church* in Africa from 1924 until his retirement in 1956, and was president of the mission and general director of all Lutheran missions in Tanganyika from 1944 until 1952. He translated the New Testament into the Iramba language and wrote hymns and liturgies. Died October 8, 1958, in Minneapolis. *Reference*: George F. Hall, *The Missionary Spirit in the Augustana Church* (Rock Island, Ill., 1984), ch. 9.

ANDERSON, VERNON ANDY (1896-   ). Missionary, born in Illinois, and grew up in Alabama. Anderson graduated from Alabama Presbyterian College, Presbyterian Theological Seminary (Louisville) and Southern Baptist Theological Seminary. He was missionary under the Board of Foreign Missions of the Presbyterian Church in the United States* and served in the American Presbyterian Congo Mission (APCM).* He served in the Bibanga station near the Lubilashi River in the Kasai Province, and worked among the Baluba-Lubilashi from 1921 to 1946. He revised an early Tshiluba-English dictionary. He was the interim general secretary of the Congo Protestant Council at Leopoldville from 1942 to 1944, served on the Belgian government's Commission Pour la Protection des Indigènes in 1947, was the legal representative of the APCM in 1948, and the mission's inspector of schools from 1949 to 1959. He returned to the United States in 1959, and was associate pastor in Dallas, Texas, from 1960 until his retirement in 1966. He wrote *Still Led in Triumph* (Nashville, Tenn., 1959). *References*: Vernon Anderson Papers, Northwestern University Library, Evanston, Ill.; and James Sanders, "The Vernon Anderson Papers," *History in Africa* 8 (1981): 361–64.

ANDERSON, WILLIAM HARRISON (1870–1950). Missionary, born in Mexico, Indiana, and grew up in New Waverley, Cass County, Indiana. Anderson graduated from Battle Creek College and Emanuel Mission College, and was ordained in 1905. He went to Africa in 1895 to establish the first permanent mission of the Seventh-Day Adventists in Africa, and established the Solusi mission, near Bulawayo, Southern Rhodesia. He began missionary work in Bechuanaland in 1919, and commenced missionary work in Angola in 1922. He was member of the staff of the Africa Division of the Seventh-Day Adventists from 1930 until 1945. He wrote *On the Trail of Livingstone* (Mountain View,

Calif., 1919). He returned to the United States in 1945. Died June 26, 1950, in Claremont, North Carolina. *References*: *NYT*, June 27, 1950; and *SDAE*.

ANDERSON, WILLIAM SPENCER (ca. 1832–1872). Colonist, born in Wilmington, Delaware. Anderson immigrated to Liberia in 1853, and inherited a large sugar plantation on the St. Paul River in 1858. He was elected to the House of Representatives of Liberia in 1869 and became speaker of the house. In 1871 he was commissioned to negotiate a loan from British financiers in London. He was successful, but the terms of the loan caused dissatisfaction, and he was arrested when he returned to Liberia. Died September 27, 1872, in Monrovia, Liberia.

ARMITAGE, FRANK BENJAMIN (1864–1952). Missionary, born December 31, 1864, in Darlington, Wisconsin. Armitage attended Battle Creek College. He was missionary under the Seventh-Day Adventists in Southern Rhodesia from 1897 until 1906, stationed at the Solusi mission from 1897 until 1901 and at the Somabula mission from 1901 until 1906. He was in South Africa and Basutoland from 1906 until 1925. He returned to the United States in 1925 and did pastoral work in northern California until 1933. Died March 20, 1952, in Loma Linda, California. *References*: *Review and Herald*, April 24, 1952; and *SDAE*.

ASHMUN, JEHUDI (1794–1828). Colonial agent, born April 21, 1794, in Champlain, New York. Ashmun attended Middlebury College and graduated from the University of Vermont. He was principal of the Maine Charity School (Hampden, Me.) from 1816 to 1818, went to Washington, D.C., in 1818, and became editor of the *Theological Repertory*. In 1822 he was appointed agent of the United States government and the American Colonization Society* to accompany recaptured African slaves to Liberia. He led the defense of the colony against several attacks, and his leadership of Liberia from 1822 until 1828, first as assistant agent and then as agent, was an important factor in the colony's survival during one of its most critical periods. He wrote *History of the American Colony in Liberia, from December 1821 to 1823* (Washington, D.C., 1826). He returned to the United States in 1828 because of ill health. Died August 25, 1828, in New Haven, Connecticut. *References*: *ACAB*; *DAB*; *Davis*; *Huberich*; *NCAB* 6:195; S. C. Saha, "Jehudi Ashmun's Agricultural Policy: Organizing the Settlers for Self-reliance," *IJAHS* 18 (1985): 505–11; and *WWWA*.

ASSEMBLIES OF GOD, GENERAL COUNCIL: FOREIGN MISSIONS DEPARTMENT. First missionaries went to Sierra Leone in 1905 before the Assemblies of God was officially organized in 1914. Missionaries were sent to Liberia in 1908, to South Africa in 1910, to the Belgian Congo in 1918, to Upper Volta in 1921, to Nyasaland in 1930, to the Gold Coast in 1931, to Tanganyika in 1938, to Nigeria in 1939, to Togo in 1940, to Dahomey in 1950, to Basutoland in 1950, and to Senegal in 1956. *References*: Assemblies of God Archives, Springfield, Mo.; Joyce W. Booze, *Into All the World: A History of Assemblies of God Foreign Missions* (Springfield, Mo., 1980); *EMCM*; Gary B. McGee, *"This Gospel . . . Shall Be Preached": A History and Theology of Assemblies of God Foreign Missions to 1959* (Springfield, Mo., 1986); and Elizabeth A. G. Wilson, *Making Many Rich* (Springfield, Mo., 1955).

ATTWOOD, WILLIAM (1919-   ). Journalist and diplomat, born July 14, 1919, in Paris, France, to American parents. Attwood graduated from Princeton University and served in the army during World War II. He was foreign correspondent for the *New York Herald-Tribune* from 1946 to 1949, European correspondent for *Collier's* from 1949 to 1951, and European editor, national editor, and foreign editor of *Look* magazine from 1951 to 1961. He was U.S. ambassador to Guinea from 1961 to 1963 and U.S. ambassador to Kenya from 1964 to 1966. He described his experiences in *The Reds and the Blacks* (New York, 1967). He was editor-in-chief of Cowles Communications, Inc., from 1966 to 1970, and president and publisher of *Newsday* (Long Island, N.Y.) after 1971. *References*: *CA*; *CB* 1968; *WWA*; and *WWE*.

AUGUSTANA LUTHERAN CHURCH: BOARD OF FOREIGN MISSIONS. Established in 1923, the Augustana Church administered German missions in Tanganyika from 1922 to 1926, and then established its own mission in Tanganyika. Its name was changed in 1956 to the Board of World Missions, and it merged in 1962 with other Lutheran churches to form the Board of World Missions of the Lutheran Church in America. *References*: *EMCM*; George F. Hall, *The Missionary Spirit in the Augustana Church* (Rock Island, Ill., 1984); and S. Hjalmar Swanson, *Foundation for Tomorrow: A Century of Progress in Augustana World Missions* (Minneapolis, 1960).

AYRES, ELI (fl. 1821–1831). Physician and colonial agent from Baltimore. Ayres was agent of the American Colonization Society* and United States government agent for recaptured Africans from 1821 to 1824. With Lieutenant Robert F. Stockton,* he signed the Treaty of Mesurado in 1821, purchased the land at Cape Mesurado near the mouth of the St. Paul River, and brought the original settlers from Sierra Leone to Liberia. In 1831 he became resident agent of the American Colonization Society in Baltimore. *Reference*: *Huberich*.

AZORES MILITARY BASES. In 1943, the United States was permitted to establish military facilities in the Azores. The Azores bases agreement expired in 1962, and Portugal refused to renew it. The United States Navy and Air Force continued to use the facilities, and especially the Lajes Air Base, on an informal basis until 1971 when the agreement was renewed.

B

BABE, JEROME L. (fl. 1865–1873). Inventor and diamond miner, born in Louisiana. Babe came to South Africa about 1865 as representative of an American arms company, and also acted as special correspondent for the *New York World*. He went to the diggings in 1870 soon after the discovery of diamonds, and invented a machine for washing diamondiferous gravel, named "baby" after his surname, which was first used in the Vaal River diggings in 1871. He made a fortune which he subsequently lost. He wrote *The South African Diamond Fields* (New York, 1872). He returned to the United States in 1873. *References*: *SADNB*; and *SESA*.

BACON, DAVID FRANCIS (1813–1866). Physician and writer, born November 30, 1813, in Prospect, Connecticut. Bacon graduated from Yale University and the Yale Medical School. He was sent by the American Colonization Society* as principal colonial physician to Liberia. He wrote *Wanderings on the Seas and Shores of Africa* (New York, 1843). During the greater part of his life he lived in New York City and was actively interested in politics. Died January 23, 1866, in New York City. *References*: *ACAB*; *DAMB*; and *Huberich*.

BACON, SAMUEL (1781–1820). Clergyman, born July 22, 1781, in Sturbridge, Massachusetts. Bacon graduated from Harvard University and studied law. He practiced law in Pennsylvania, edited the *Worcester Aegis* and later the Lancaster (Pa.) *Hive*. He was ordained in the Protestant Episcopal Church. In 1819 he was appointed by the United States government as one of the agents that accompanied the first expedition of colonists on the *Elizabeth** in 1820, and settled on Sherbro Island in Sierra Leone. He later moved to Kent, Cape Shilling, and died May 3, 1820. His brother **EPHRAIM BACON** (fl. 1821) was assistant agent of the United States government who accompanied the colonists who sailed to Africa on the brig *Nautilus* in 1821. Interested in encouraging settlement in West Africa, he compiled detailed accounts of the region for use by potential emigrés, as well for the general public in America, and published *Abstract of a*

Journal of E. Bacon, Assistant Agent of the United States, to Africa (Philadelphia, 1821). Becoming ill, he fled to the West Indies. *References*: *ACAB*; and Jehudi Ashmun, *Memoir of the Life and Character of the Rev. Samuel Bacon, A.M.* (Washington, D.C., 1821; reprinted 1971).

BAILEY, ALBERT WILLIAM (1873–1955). Missionary, born in Maine. He was minister in New York and missionary under the Christian and Missionary Alliance in the lumber camps of Maine. He went to South Africa in 1909, served in the South African General Mission in Durban in 1909, established a mission station at Chisalala in 1910, opened the Lalafuta mission station in 1912, and transferred his activities permanently to Angola in 1913. He resigned from the mission in 1948. *References*: Albert William Bailey, "Commission and Conquest in South Africa: An Autobiographical Account of Pioneer Mission Work in Africa," ed. Metha D. Bailey, MS, Columbia Bible College, Columbia, S. C. (1928?); and James G. Kallam, "A History of the African Evangelical Fellowship from Its Inception to 1917," Ph.D. diss., New York University, 1978, ch. 10.

BAILEY, ALFRED M(ARSHALL) (1894–1978). Ornithologist, born February 18, 1894, in Iowa City, Iowa. Bailey graduated from the University of Iowa. He was curator of birds and mammals at the Louisiana State Museum, New Orleans, from 1916 to 1919; representative of the United States Biological Survey in Juneau, Alaska, from 1919 to 1921; representative of the Denver Museum of Natural History in Arctic Alaska in 1921–1922; curator of birds and mammals at the Chicago Academy of Sciences from 1922 to 1926; director of the Chicago Academy of Sciences from 1926 to 1936; and director of the Denver Museum of Natural History from 1936 to 1970. He was a member of the Field Museum of Natural History expedition to Abyssinia in 1926–1927 and wrote of his experiences in *The Living Bird* (Laboratory of Ornithology, Cornell University) of 1977. He was the leader of the Denver Museum of Natural History expedition to Botswana and South Africa in 1969. Died February 25, 1978, in Denver, Colorado. *References*: *AMWS*; *Auk* 98 (1981): 173–175; *CA*; and *WWWA*.

BAILEY, SOLON IRVING (1854–1931). Astronomer, born December 29, 1854, in Lisbon, New Hampshire, and grew up in Concord, New Hampshire. Bailey graduated from Boston University and studied at Harvard University. He became assistant professor of astronomy at Harvard University in 1893, associate professor in 1898, and was professor from 1912 until his retirement in 1925. In 1888 he went on tour of South America to select sites for astronomical observatories which led to the establishment of a station at Arequipa, Peru, and a chain of meterological stations in Peru. In 1906 he went to South Africa, erected the first American observatory near Hanover, Cape Province, and spent a year there. Died June 5, 1931, in Lisbon, New Hampshire. *References*: *ACAB*; *DAB S1*; *DSB*; *NCAB* 28:411; *NYT*, June 6, 1931; and *WWWA*.

BALDRIDGE, CYRUS LEROY (1889–1977). Cartoonist and illustrator, born May 27, 1889, in Alton, New York. Baldridge graduated from the University of Chicago. He worked as a cowpuncher in Texas, served with the United States Army on the Mexican border, and with the French and the U.S. armies in France during World War I, and was cartoonist with the *Stars & Stripes*. He then traveled all over the world. He was in West Africa and Abyssinia in 1927–1928, and co-authored *Boomba Lives in Africa* (New York, 1935). He wrote an autobiography, *Time and Chance* (New York, 1947). He settled in Sante Fe, New Mexico, in 1952. Died June 6, 1977, in Santa Fe. *References*: Cyrus Leroy Baldridge, prints and drawings, Fisk University Library and Media Center, Nashville, Tenn.; Doris O. Dawdy, *Artists of the American West: A Biographical Dictionary* (Chicago, 1981), 2:16; and Ruth H. Viguers, Marcia Dalphin, and Bertha M. Miller, comps., *Illustrators of Children's Books 1946–1956* (Boston, 1958).

BALDWIN, JOHN THOMAS, JR. (1910–1974). Botanist, born September 5, 1910, in Chase City, Virginia. Baldwin graduated from the College of William and Mary and the University of Virginia, and studied at Cornell University. He was associate cytologist of the Rubber Plant Investigations of the United States Department of Agriculture in the Amazon Valley from 1942 to 1944, manager of Blandy Experimental Farm and assistant professor at the University of Virginia from 1944 to 1946, and professor of biology at the College of William and Mary from 1946 to 1974. He made two collecting trips to Africa: as horticulturist of the United States Economic Mission to Liberia in 1947–1948, and as principal botanist of the Division of Plant Exploration and Introduction of the Department of Agriculture to survey the natural sources of cortisone in Africa in 1949–1950. Died September 3, 1974, in Williamsburg, Virginia. *References*: *AMWS*; *NYT*, September 5, 1974; and *WWWA*.

BALL, SYDNEY (HOBART) (1877–1949). Mining engineer, born December 11, 1877, in Chicago. Ball graduated from the University of Wisconsin. He was geologist for the Missouri Bureau of Mines and Geology in 1901–2, instructor in geology at the University of Wisconsin in 1902–3, and assistant geologist with the United States Geological Survey from 1903 to 1907. He became the technical head of an expedition to survey the Forminière mineral concessions in the Belgian Congo in 1907, and the Belgian Congo-Angola diamond field was an outgrowth of this expedition. He was in charge of an expedition exploring for minerals in the Belgian Congo for the Ryan-Guggenhein Group from 1907 to 1909. He co-authored *Economic Geology of the Belgian Congo, Central Africa* (Lancaster, Pa., 1914). He was a member of the firm Rogers, Mayer & Ball, consulting engineers, from 1917 until his death, and was consulting mineralogist to the United States Bureau of Mines and mining consultant to the War Production Board from 1942 to 1944. Died April 3, 1949, in New York City. *References*:

Geological Society of America *Proceedings* 1949: 113–14; *NCAB* 40:181; *NYT*, April 10, 1949; and *WWWA*.

BANE, HOWARD T. (1927-   ).Government official, born August 5, 1927, in Virginia. Bane graduated from Georgetown University. He was research analyst with the Department of the Army from 1951 to 1955, assistant attaché and political officer, and later second secretary and vice consul in Bangkok, Thailand, from 1955 to 1958, and second secretary and political officer in New Delhi, India, from 1959 to 1962. He was Central Intelligence Agency (CIA) chief of mission in Accra, Ghana, from 1964 to 1967, and CIA chief of operations in Nairobi, Kenya, from 1969 to 1974. He served in The Hague from 1974 to 1978, became chief of the Office on Terrorism of the CIA in 1978, and was later chief of operations for the Africa Division of the CIA. *Reference*: *Dirty Work 2*.

BAPTIST MID-MISSIONS. Independent Baptist organization, organized in 1920 and began missionary work in Oubangui-Chari, French Equatorial Africa. It expanded its work to Chad in 1925, to Liberia in 1938, to the Gold Coast in 1946, and to the Belgian Congo in 1953. The mission in Zaire was closed in 1973. *References*: *EMCM*; Polly Strong, *Burning Wicks* (Cleveland, 1984).

BARNES, JAMES (1866–1936). Author, born September 19, 1866, in Annapolis, Maryland. Barnes graduated from Princeton University. He served on the staff of *Scribner's Magazine* from 1891 to 1893, and was assistant editor of *Harper's Weekly* in 1894–1895. He was war correspondent for *The Outlook*, the McClure Syndicate, and the *London Daily Mail* in South Africa from 1899 to 1901, and wrote of his experiences in *The Great War Trek with the British Army of the Veldt* (New York, 1901). He was literary editor of D. Appleton & Co. from 1905 to 1908. He served in the Spanish-American War and in the aviation section of the Signal Corps in World War I organizing aviation photographic work in France. He wrote histories, biographies, and historical novels for young readers, including *Rifle and Caravan; or, Two Boys in East Africa* (New York, 1912). In 1913 he conducted a photographic expedition across British East Africa and the Belgian Congo for the American Museum of Natural History, and wrote *Through Central Africa from Coast to Coast* (New York, 1915). He wrote his reminiscences, *From Then to Now: Anecdotal Portraits and Transcript Pages from Memory's Tablets* (New York, 1934). Died April 30, 1936, in Princeton, New Jersey. *References*: *NCAB* 14:437; *NYT*, May 1, 1936; and *WWWA*.

BARNS, T(HOMAS) ALEXANDER (1880–1930). Settler and traveler. Barns was plantation agent in Nyasaland and a settler in Northern Rhodesia. After 1919 he was associated with several exploring expeditions in Central Africa and wrote *Tales of the Ivory Trade* (London, 1923); *The Wonderland of Eastern Congo* (London, 1922); *Across the Great Craterland to the Congo* (New York,

1924); *An African Eldorado, the Belgian Congo* (London, 1926); and *Angolan Sketches* (London, 1928). Died March 1930 in Chicago. *Reference*: *BCB* 3.

BARRETT, OTIS W(ARREN) (1872–1950). Agriculturist, born April 18, 1872, in Clarendon, Vermont. Barrett graduated from the University of Vermont. He was entomologist and botanist to the Puerto Rico Agricultural Experiment Station from 1901 to 1905, and plant introducer for the Office of Seed and Plant Introduction and Distribution of the U.S. Department of Agriculture from 1905 to 1908. He was director of agriculture for Mozambique from 1908 to 1910, and there established a scientific agriculture program. He was chief of the divisions of experimental stations and horticulture in the Bureau of Agriculture in Manila, the Philippines, from 1910 to 1914; horticulturist of the Panama Canal Zone from 1914 to 1917; agricultural adviser to Liberia in 1920–1921; served with the Department of Agriculture of Puerto Rico from 1923 to 1929; and was horticulturist of the University of Hawaii in 1929–1930. Died October 6, 1950, in Clarendon, Vermont. *References*: *NYT*, October 11, 1950; and *WWWA*.

BARRON, EDWARD WINSTON (1801–1854). Missionary, born June 28, 1801, in Ballyneale, County Waterford, Ireland. Barron studied at Trinity College and was ordained in 1829. He came to the United States in 1837 and was pastor and vicar-general of Philadelphia until 1840. In 1842 he went to Liberia as prefect apostolic of Upper Guinea. His jurisdiction was extended to Sierra Leone, and he was consecrated bishop in 1842. He was discharged as vicar apostolic in 1844 and returned to the United States in 1845 because of ill health. He later served in St. Louis, Missouri, and Florida. Died September 13, 1854, in Savannah, Georgia. *References*: *Catholic Encyclopaedia* (New York, 1967), 2:124–25; *DACB*; and Richard K. MacMaster, "Bishop Barron and the West African Missions, 1841–1845," *United States Catholic Historical Society Historical Records and Studies* 50 (1964): 83–129.

BASCOM, WILLIAM R(USSEL) (1912–1981). Anthropologist, born May 23, 1912, in Princeton, Illinois. Bascom graduated from the University of Wisconsin and Northwestern University. He did fieldwork in Nigeria in 1937–1938 and again in 1950–1951. He served with the Office of Strategic Services (OSS) in World War II and was later chief of the French West African Section of the Board of Economic Warfare. He was assistant professor, associate professor, and professor of anthropology at Northwestern University from 1946 to 1957. He was chief economist for the United States Commercial Company at Ponape in the Caroline Islands in 1946 and studied the Yoruba in Cuba in 1948. He was professor of anthropology at the University of California at Berkeley from 1957 until his retirement in 1970. He again visited in Nigeria in 1960 and 1965. He collected African art and became the owner of an important collection. He wrote *The Sociological Role of the Yoruba Cult-Group* (Menasha, Wis., 1944); *The Yoruba of Southwestern Nigeria* (New York, 1969); *Ifa Divination: Communi-*

cation between God and Men in West Africa (Bloomington, Ind., 1969); *African Art in Cultural Perspective: An Introduction* (New York, 1973); and *African Dilemma Tales* (The Hague, 1975). Died September 11, 1981, in Berkeley, California. *References*: William R. Bascom Papers, the General Library, University of California, Berkeley; *African Arts* 16 (February 1983): 26–27; *CA*; *Journal of American Folklore* 95 (1982): 465–67; Simon Ottenberg, ed., *African Religious Groups and Beliefs: Papers in Honor of William R. Bascom* (Meerut, India, 1982); *Research in African Literature* 13 (Winter 1982): 537–41; and *WWA*.

BASSA COVE. A colony established in 1835 at the mouth of the Saint John River, Liberia, by the Young Men's Colonization Society of Pennsylvania in cooperation with the Colonization Society of New York. In 1838 it merged with the American Colonization Society's* colony to become the Commonwealth of Liberia. *References*: *Huberich*; and Kurt L. Kocher, "A Duty to America and Africa: A History of the Independent African Colonization Movement in Pennsylvania," *Pennsylvania History* 51 (1984): 118–53.

BAUM, JAMES (EDWIN) (1887–1955). Journalist and explorer, born November 15, 1887, in Lincoln, Nebraska. Baum attended Princeton University. He was reporter for the *Omaha Bee* from 1908 to 1914, was employed in 1914 by an investment firm in Boston, and served as an aviator in World War I. He was engaged in cattle ranching in Wyoming from 1919 to 1922, became president of the Chicago Brick Company in 1923, and was reporter for the *Chicago Evening Journal* until 1925 and for the *Chicago Daily News* in 1925–1926. In 1926 he went with Louis Agassiz Fuertes* on an exploring and collecting expedition to Abyssinia for the Field Museum of Natural History, and wrote *Savage Abyssinia* (New York, 1927) and *Unknown Ethiopia* (New York, 1935). He later was a big-game hunter in various parts of the world. Died November 28, 1955, in Palm Beach, Florida. *Reference*: *NCAB* 57:403.

BECKER, CARL K. (1894–). Medical missionary, born in Manheim, Pennsylvania. Becker graduated from Hahnemann Medical College. He practiced medicine in Boyertown, Pennsylvania, from 1922 to 1929. He was missionary under the Africa Inland Mission in Oicha, Belgian Congo, after 1929. *Reference*: William J. Peterson, *Another Hand in Mine: The Story of Dr. Carl K. Becker of Africa Inland Mission* (New York, 1967).

BECKER, GEORGE FERDINAND (1847–1919). Geologist, born January 5, 1847, in New York. Becker graduated from Harvard and Heidelberg universities and the Royal Academy of Mines in Berlin. He was instructor in mining and metallurgy at the University of California from 1874 to 1879, United States geologist-in-chief both from 1879 to 1892 and after 1894, and special agent for the Tenth U.S. Census from 1879 to 1883. In 1896 he visited the Witwatersrand,

South Africa, examined its gold and diamond mines, and wrote *The Witwaters-rand Banket, with Notes on Other Gold-bearing Pudding Stones* (Washington, D.C., 1897) and an article on the Jameson Raid in the November 1896 issue of *National Geographic Magazine*. He served as geologist with the army in the Philippine Islands in 1898–1899, and was later in charge of the division of chemistry and physical research of the United States Geological Survey and geophysicist at the Carnegie Institution. Died April 20, 1919, in Washington, D.C. *References*: George Ferdinand Becker Papers, Manuscript Divison, Library of Congress; *BMNAS* 21 (1926): 1–13; *DAB*; *DSB*; and *NYT*, April 22, 1919.

BEDINGER, ROBERT DABNEY (1889–1970). Missionary, born June 1, 1889, in Fulton, Kentucky. Bedinger graduated from Hampden-Sidney College (Va.) and the Union Theological Seminary of Virginia, and was ordained in 1911. He was missionary under the Board of Foreign Missions of the Presbyterian Church in the United States from 1911 to 1929, serving in the American Presbyterian Congo Mission (APCM).* He wrote *Triumphs of the Gospel in the Belgian Congo* (Richmond, Va., 1920). He returned to the United States in 1930, was pastor in Jackson, Mississippi, from 1930 to 1934, and superintendent of home missionary evangelists from 1934 until his retirement in 1960. Died January 21, 1970. *Reference*: E. D. Witherspoon, comp., *Ministerial Directory of the Presbyterian Church, U.S.* (Doraville, Ga., 1967).

BELL, WILLIAM C(LARK) (1872–1942). Agricultural missionary, born July 27, 1872, in Lockport, New York. Bell graduated from Cornell University and was ordained in 1907. The first graduate agriculturist ever sent into foreign field, he was agricultural missionary in Benguela, Angola, under the PhilAfrican League from 1897 until 1904, and under the American Board of Commissioners for Foreign Missions (ABCFM)* from 1907 until his retirement in 1934. He edited *African Bridge Builders* (New York, 1936). Died February 19, 1942, in Claremont, California.

BENDER, CARL JACOB (1869–1935). Missionary, born December 20, 1869, in Eschelbach, Baden Baden, Germany. He came to the United States in 1881, where he grew up in Buffalo, New York, and became an American citizen. Bender graduated from the German Baptist Seminary (Rochester, N.Y.), and was ordained in 1899. He was a missionary under the German Baptist Missionary Society of Berlin in the Cameroon mission from 1899 until 1919, first in Duala and later in Soppo. He returned to the United States in 1919, and was district missionary in the eastern part of the United States in 1919–1920, and pastor in Watertown, Wisconsin, and in Chicago from 1921 to 1929. He returned to the Cameroon in 1929 and was missionary under the North American Baptist Conference in Soppo until his death. He wrote *African Jungle Tales* (Girard, Kans., 1924); *Proverbs of West Africa* (Girard, Kans., 1924); *Twenty Years Among African Negroes* (Girard, Kans., 1925); and *Religious and Ethical Beliefs of*

African Negroes; Duala and Wakweliland (Girard, Kans., 1925). Died November 8, 1935, in Soppo, Cameroon. *Reference*: Carl F. H. Henry, *Bender of the Cameroons: The Story of Missionary Triumph in a Dark Region of the World's Darkest Continent* (Cleveland, 1936–1940).

BENEDICT, BURTON (1923-   ). Anthropologist, born May 20, 1923, in Baltimore, Maryland. Benedict graduated from Harvard University and the University of London. He was assistant lecturer, lecturer, and senior lecturer in social anthropology at the London School of Economics and Political Science from 1958 to 1968, and became professor of anthropology at the University of California, Berkeley, in 1968. He did field-work in Mauritius from 1955 to 1957 and in Seychelles in 1960. He wrote *Indians in a Plural Society* (London, 1961); *Mauritius: The Problems of a Plural Society* (London, 1965); and *People of the Seychelles* (London, 1966; 3d ed., 1970) and he was coauthor of *Men, Women and Money in Seychelles: Two Views* (Berkeley, Calif., 1982). *References*: *AMWS*; and *CA*.

BENEDICT, SAMUEL (ca. 1808–1854). Colonist, born a slave in Savannah, Georgia. Benedict immigrated to Liberia in 1835 and was minister of the Baptist Church in Liberia. He was president of the Constitutional Convention of 1847, and chief justice of the Republic of Liberia from 1847 to 1854. In 1852 he was an unsuccessful candidate for the presidency there. Died February 25, 1854, in Monrovia. *References*: *African Repository* 30 (1854): 229; and *Huberich*.

BENNETT, HUGH HAMMOND (1881–1960). Soil conservationist, born April 15, 1881, in Wadesboro, North Carolina. Bennett graduated from the University of North Carolina. A pioneer in the field of soil conservation, he joined the Bureau of Soils of the U.S. Department of Agriculture in 1903, was superviser of soil surveys from 1909 until 1928, director of the Soil Erosion Service from 1933 to 1935, and chief of the Soil Conservation Service from 1935 until his retirement. In 1944 he was invited by the government of the Union of South Africa to advise it on how to deal with soil erosion. He spent two months in South Africa and prepared a report entitled *Soil Erosion and Land Use in the Union of South Africa* (Pretoria, 1945). The result of his visit was South Africa's Soil Conservation Act of 1946. Died July 7, 1960, in Falls Church, Virginia. *References*: *DAB S6*; *NYT*, July 8, 1960; and *WWWA*.

BENSON, STEPHEN ALLEN (1816–1865). Colonist, born free March 16, 1816, in Cambridge, Maryland. Benson immigrated with his parents to Liberia in 1822. He served in the militia and took part in a military expedition in 1832. He was a local preacher of the Methodist Church, secretary to governor Thomas Buchanan, member of the Colonial Council of Grand Bassa County from 1842 to 1847, vice president of Liberia in 1854, and president of Liberia from 1856 to 1864. He was responsible for a number of boundary surveys and established the first hospital in Liberia. Died January 12, 1865, in Grand Bassa County, Liberia. *References*: *Davis*; and *Richardson*.

BERGSMA, STUART (1900-   ). Medical missionary and psychiatrist, born November 15, 1900, in Grand Rapids, Michigan. Bergsma graduated from Calvin College and the University of Chicago and studied at the London School of Tropical Medicine and Hygiene. He was medical missionary, surgeon, and hospital superintendent under the Board of Foreign Missions of the United Presbyterian Church of North America* in its mission in Ethiopia from 1928 to 1934. He wrote *Rainbow Empire: Ethiopia Stretches Out Her Hands* (Grand Rapids, Mich., 1932) and *Sons of Sheba* (Grand Rapids, Mich., 1933). He returned to the United States in 1934; practiced medicine in Passaic, New Jersey, from 1935 to 1938; was medical missionary under the United Presbyterian Church in India from 1939 to 1943; practiced in Grand Rapids from 1943 to 1949; and was medical missionary, surgeon, hospital superintendent, and associate professor of surgery at the Ludhiana Christian Medical College in the Punjab, India, from 1949 to 1953. He was a resident in psychiatry from 1955 until 1957, and then practiced psychiatry in Grand Rapids from 1958 until 1972. *Reference*: *WWA*.

BEST, JACOB (1823–1898). Missionary, born February 3, 1823, in Livingston, New York. Best graduated from Williams College and was ordained in 1848. He was a missionary under the American Board of Commissioners for Foreign Missions (ABCFM)* in Gabon from 1849 to 1861, serving in Olandebenk and Baraka. He returned to the United States in 1861 and was pastor in Waymond and Brooklyn, Pennsylvania, until his retirement in 1895. Died April 16, 1898, at Coventry, New York. *Reference*: *Hewitt*.

BICKHAM, MARTIN (ca. 1780- ?). Merchant, born in New Jersey. Bickham was apprenticed to Stephen Girard, the Philadelphia merchant, and then established a firm of importers and exporters that went bankrupt. In 1796 he was supercargo on *Sally II*, which opened the trade with Ile de France (Mauritius). He was agent for Girard on Ile de France from 1798 to 1825, and consul in Port Louis from 1816 until 1825. He returned to the United States in 1825. *References*: Martin Bickman Correspondence in Girard papers, Girard College, Philadelphia; and Harry E. Wildes, *Lonely Midas: The Story of Stephen Girard* (New York, 1943).

BIDDLE, HARRY N(ICHOLAS) (1872–1898). Medical missionary, born January 1, 1872, in Cincinnati. Biddle attended Pulte Medical College and Chicago Medical Mission Institute. He went to Africa with Ellsworth Faris* in 1897 for the Foreign Christian Missionary Society of the Disciples of Christ (see United Christian Missionary Society*) to search for a location for its mission. Died October 8, 1898, at Las Palmas, Grand Canary Island, on his way back to the United States. *References*: *BCB* 4; and *TWTA*.

BIGELOW, HARRY A(UGUSTUS) (1874–1950). Lawyer, big-game hunter, and explorer, born September 22, 1874, in Norwood, Massachusetts. Bigelow graduated from Harvard College and Harvard Law School. He taught law at Harvard University and practiced in Honolulu, Hawaii, from 1900 to 1903. He joined the faculty of the University of Chicago in 1904, became professor in 1908, and was dean of the law school from 1929 until his retirement in 1939. He accompanied Herbert E. and Mary Hastings Bradley* in 1924 and 1925 on their African hunting expeditions, and was one of the first to cross the unexplored Belgian Congo west of Lake Edward. Died January 8, 1950, in Chicago. *References*: *BDAE*; *DAB* S4; *NYT*, January 9, 1950; and *WWWA*.

BILLINGS, KATHARINE STEVENS (FOWLER-LUNN) (1902–   ). Geologist, born June 12, 1902, in North Hampton, New Hampshire. Billings graduated from Bryn Mawr College, the University of Wisconsin, and Columbia University. She was in Africa from 1929 to 1935, prospecting for iron, gold, and molybdenum in the Gold Coast and Sierra Leone and wrote *The Gold Missus: A Woman Prospector in the Sierra Leone* (New York, 1938). She was later instructor of geology at Wellesley College from 1935 to 1939 and at Tufts College in 1942, and associate in geology at the New England Museum of Natural History from 1938 to 1948. *Reference*: *WWAW*.

BINGHAM, HAROLD C(LYDE) (1888–1964). Psychologist, born January 21, 1888, in Rowan, Iowa. Bingham graduated from Ellsworth College, and Harvard and Johns Hopkins universities. He was professor of education and psychology and coach of baseball and track at Ellsworth Junior College from 1912 to 1927, served in the army during World War I, was member of the Research Information Service of the National Research Council from 1920 to 1923, research associate at Wesleyan University from 1923 to 1925, and research associate and associate professor of psychology at Yale University from 1925 to 1930. He was the leader of the Carnegie Institution-Yale University expedition to the Belgian Congo to study the social behavior of the mountain gorillas in 1929–1930, the first planned field research of gorillas. He wrote *Gorillas in a Native Habitat* (Washington, D.C., 1932). He was supervisor of research and education director for the Civil Works Administration, the Emergency Relief Administration, and the Works Progress Administration in New Hampshire from 1931 to 1933, and director of the National Youth Administration for New Hampshire from 1934 to 1941. He served in the army during World War II, and was senior psychologist with the Veterans Administration in Washington, D.C., from 1946 until his retirement in 1955. Died August 26, 1964, in Laconia, New Hampshire. *References*: *NCAB* 51:367; and *NYT*, August 27, 1964.

BLAKE, JOHN Y. FILMORE (1856–1907). Military officer, born in Missouri and grew up in Texas. Blake attended Arkansas State University, graduated from the United States Military Academy in 1880, and was commissioned second lieutenant. He served with the Sixth Cavalry in the western United States. He resigned in 1889 and went into business in Grand Rapids, Michigan, but failed. He came to South Africa in 1895 and was in Rhodesia in 1896, helping to quell the Matabele uprising. He was then in the Witwatersrand from 1896 to 1899. With the outbreak of the South African War, he offered his services to the Boers and was given the rank of colonel. He formed an Irish Brigade, consisting mainly of Irish Americans living in the Transvaal. He fought with the Boers to the end of the war and lost the use of a hand at the Battle of Modderspruit in 1899. At the end of the war, he returned to the United States. He wrote *A West Pointer with the Boers* (Boston, 1903). Died January 24, 1907, in New York City. *References*: *DSAB* 3; and *SESA*.

BLANCKÉ, WILTON WENDELL (1908–1971). Diplomat, born June 29, 1908, in Philadelphia. Blancké graduated from Haverford College and studied painting in Paris. He joined the advertising agency of N. W. Ayer and Son, Inc., in 1929, and was its art director in Buenos Aires from 1933 to 1942. He served as foreign service auxiliary officer at the embassy at Buenos Aires from 1942 until 1945, and served in the office of the Allied Military Government in Berlin in 1945–1946. He entered the foreign service in 1946; was second secretary in Havana; consul and principal officer in Hanoi, Vietnam; counselor of embassy at Vientiane, Laos; and consul general in Frankfurt until 1960. He was the first ambassador to Congo (Brazzaville) from 1960 until 1963, and was also accredited as ambassador to the Central African Republic, Chad, and Gabon from 1960 until 1961. He was senior inspector in the foreign service from 1963 to 1965, and consul general in Mexico City from 1965 until his retirement in 1966. Died March 14, 1971, in Washington, D.C. *References*: *DADH*; *NYT*, March 15, 1971; and *WWWA*.

BLISS, ANNA ELVIRA (1843–1925). Educator, born January 14, 1843, in Jericho, Vermont, and grew up in Amherst, Massachusetts. Bliss graduated from Mount Holyoke College. She went to South Africa with Abbie Park Ferguson* in 1873 and began teaching at the Huguenot Seminary* girls' school in Wellington, Cape Province, in 1874. She became principal of the primary school in 1874, was principal of the high school from 1899 to 1910, and president of Huguenot College from 1911 until her retirement in 1920. Died June 25, 1925, in Wellington, Cape Province. *References*: *DSAB* 2; *NAW*; and *SADNB*.

BLOWERS, GEORGE ALBERT (1906–1969). Banker, born March 5, 1906, in Pineville, Kentucky. Blowers graduated from Harvard University. He was with the National City Bank of New York from 1928 to 1937 and general manager of the Bank of Monrovia in Liberia from 1938 to 1943; he changed Liberian currency from the pound sterling to the dollar. He was governor of the Bank of Ethiopia from 1943 until 1948 and introduced a new Ethiopian currency in place of the East African shilling. He was deputy director for finance of the Economic

Cooperation Administration in Paris in 1948–1949, head of the United Nations Mission on currency and banking to Libya in 1950, governor of the Saudi Arabian Monetary Agency in 1952–1953, director of the Export-Import Bank from 1954 to 1961, and vice president for finance of the United States Beryllium Corporation after 1961. Died October 19, 1969, in Hempstead, Long Island, New York. *Reference*: *NYT*, October 20, 1969.

BOHANNAN, LAURA (M. SMITH) (1922-   ). Anthropologist, wife of Paul James Bohannan,* born July 1922 in New York City. Bohannan graduated from the University of Arizona and Oxford University and studied at Brown University. She was lecturer in anthropology at Northwestern University from 1959 to 1962, lecturer in social sciences at the University of Chicago from 1962 to 1965, associate professor at the University of Illinois, Chicago Circle, from 1965 to 1970, and professor there after 1970. She wrote, under the name Elenore Smith Bowen, *Return to Laughter* (New York, 1954). Under her own name she wrote *Tiv of Central Nigeria* (London, 1953) and coauthored *Tribes without Rulers, Studies in African Segmentary Systems* (London, 1958) and, with Paul Bohannan,* *Tiv Economy* (Evanston, Ill., 1968). *References*: *AMWS*; *WWA*; and *WWWA*.

BOHANNAN, PAUL (JAMES) (1920-   ). Anthropologist, born March 5, 1920, in Lincoln, Nebraska. Bohannan graduated from the University of Arizona and Oxford University. He was lecturer in social anthropology at Oxford University from 1951 to 1956, assistant professor of anthropology at Princeton University from 1956 to 1959, professor of anthropology at Northwestern University from 1959 to 1975 and at the University of California at Santa Barbara from 1976 to 1982, and dean of social sciences and communications at the University of Southern California after 1982. He did field research among the Tiv of Nigeria from 1949 to 1953 and among the Wanga of Kenya in 1955, and wrote *Tiv Farm and Settlement* (London, 1954); *Justice and Judgment Among the Tiv* (London, 1957); *African Homicide and Suicide* (Princeton, 1960); and *Africa and Africans* (Garden City, N.Y., 1964). He coauthored (with Laura Bohannan*) *Tiv Economy* (Evanston, Ill., 1968). *References*: *AMWS*; *CA*; and *WWA*.

BOISE, CHARLES WATSON (1884–1964). Mining engineer, born in Lakota, North Dakota, and grew up in Hope, North Dakota. Boise graduated from the University of North Dakota. He worked with the Santa Rita Mining Company in New Mexico. He went to the Congo in 1911 as field engineer for the Société Internationale de Forestière et Minière, and was in charge of exploration, diamond mining, and research, developing diamond deposits in the Kasai district. He later became the company's chief engineer, and remained in the Belgian Congo through World War I. He then went to London and became an independent consultant and an authority on diamond mining. In 1920 he made the first examination of the diamond fields in the Gold Coast, which led to the formation of what later became Consolidated African Selection Trust Limited. He was actively involved with the opening up in 1934 of the diamond fields of Sierra Leone, and with the early exploration of Northern Rhodesia which led to the formation of copper mining companies; these were later included in the Rhodesian Selection Trust Group. He retired in 1959. Died November 15, 1964, in Kent, England. *Reference*: The *Times* (London), November 21, 1964.

BOOKER WASHINGTON INSTITUTE OF LIBERIA. Industrial school, patterned after Tuskegee Institute, established in 1929 by the Phelps-Stokes Fund with financial support from the Firestone Rubber Plantations Company.* It became the property of the Republic of Liberia in 1954 and served as the industrial arm of the University of Liberia. *References*: Louise Johnston, "Tuskegee in Liberia: The Politics of Industrial Education, 1927–1935," *Liberian Studies Journal* 9 (1980–1981): 61–68; Donald Spivey, "Education in Conflict: The Booker Washington Institute of Liberia," *History of Higher Education Annual* 1 (1981): 55–87; and Donald Spivey, *The Politics of Miseducation: The Booker Washington Institute of Liberia, 1929–1984* (Lexington, Ky., 1986).

BOONE, CLINTON C(ALDWELL) (1883–1939). Medical missionary, born May 9, 1883, in Winston, North Carolina. Boone graduated from Water Normal Institute (Winston) and Richmond Theological Seminary (later Virginia Union University). He was missionary under the American Baptist Foreign Mission Society (see American Baptist Missionary Union*) in the Belgian Congo mission from 1901 to 1906, working at Mpalabala, up the Congo River. He was missionary in Liberia under the Lott Carey Baptist Foreign Mission Convention* from 1913 to 1920, and pastor in Monrovia from 1920 until 1926. He returned to the United States in 1926 and wrote *Congo as I Saw It* (New York, 1927) and *Liberia as I Know It* (Richmond, 1929). Drowned July 1939, in the James River in Richmond, Virginia.

BOOTH, NEWELL SNOW (1903–1968). Missionary, born June 14, 1903, in Belchertown, Massachusetts. Booth graduated from Boston University and Hartford Seminary Foundation. He was a pastor in Bryntville, West Duxbury, New Bedford, and Freetown, Massachusetts. He was missionary under the Board of Foreign Missions of the Methodist Episcopal Church* in the Belgian Congo mission from 1930 to 1943, and served as principal of the Congo Training Institute and superintendent of the Belgian Congo mission until 1943. He was head of the Africa department at the Hartford Foundation Seminary in 1943–1944. He was elected bishop in 1944 and served as bishop in Africa from 1944 until 1964, in charge of Methodist activities in the Congo and southern Africa. He wrote *The Cross Over Africa* (New York, 1945) and *This is Africa South of the Sahara* (New York, 1959) and was coeditor of *Abundant Life in Changing Africa* (New York, 1946). He was bishop of the Harrisburg, Pennsylvania, area for the United Methodist Church from 1964 until his death. Died May 17, 1968, in Harrisburg, Pennsylvania. *References*: *EWM*; *Leete*; *NYT*, May 19, 1968; and *WWWA*.

BOULTON, LAURA (THERESA) (CRAYTOR) (1899–1980). Ethnomusicologist, born January 4, 1889, in Conneaut, Ohio. Boulton attended Western Reserve University, graduated from Denison University and the University of Chicago, and also studied at the Chicago Music School, the Sorbonne and the University of London. She was lecturer in primitive music at the University of Chicago from 1931 to 1933, served on the faculty of the University of California from 1946 to 1949, was director of the Laura Boulton Collection of traditional and liturgical music in the School of International Affairs of Columbia University from 1962 to 1972, and professor of fine arts and director of the Laura Boulton Collection of World Music and Musical Instruments at Arizona State University from 1972 to 1977. A music collector, she made seven trips to Africa. She was ethnologist and musicologist on the Straus Central African expedition for the American Museum of Natural History in 1929, the South African expedition for the Carnegie Museum in 1930, the Pulitzer Angola expedition of 1931, the Straus West African expedition for the American Museum of Natural History in 1934, the African expedition for the University of California in 1947–1948, and the Coptic music project from 1966 to 1968. She wrote *Music Hunter, the Autobiography of a Career* (Garden City, N.Y., 1969). Died October 16, 1980, in Bethesda, Maryland. *References*: *CA*; *NYT*, October 21, 1980; *WWAW*; and *WWWA*.

BOULTON, (WOLFRID) RUDYERD (1901–1983). Ornithologist, born April 5, 1901, in Beaver, Pennsylvania. Boulton attended Amherst College and graduated from the University of Pittsburgh. He was research assistant at the American Museum of Natural History from 1922 to 1925, assistant curator at the Carnegie Museum from 1927 to 1931, assistant curator at the Field Museum of Natural History from 1931 to 1936, and curator from 1937 until 1946. He was a member of the Vernay expedition to Angola in 1925, the Straus expedition to Africa in 1929, the Carnegie Museum expedition to Africa in 1929–1930, the Pulitzer expedition to Angola in 1930–1931, and the Field Museum–Straus expedition to West Africa in 1934. He also participated in expeditions to Panama, the West Indies, and the Galapagos Islands. He was in governmental service in Washington, D.C., from 1946 until 1959. In 1959 he moved to Southern Rhodesia and founded the Atlantica Foundation as a research base for naturalists studying African birds. Died January 24, 1983, in Zimbabwe. *References*: *AMWS*; *The Auk* 103 (April 1986): 420; and *Bokmakierie* 35 (1983): 96.

BOWEN, THOMAS J(EFFERSON) (1814–1875). Missionary, born January 2, 1814, in Jackson County, Georgia. Bowen served in the Indian wars and in the Texas War of Independence and was pastor and preacher in Georgia and Florida after 1840. He was a missionary under the Foreign Mission Board of the Southern Baptist Convention* from 1849 to 1856 and served in Nigeria. He founded the Baptist mission station at Ijaye in 1853 and then moved to Ogbom-osho in 1855 and founded a mission there. He returned to the United States in 1856 and wrote *Central Africa: Adventures and Missionary Labors in Several Countries in the Interior of Africa, from 1849 to 1856* (Charleston, S.C., 1857; 2d ed., ed. E. A. Ayandele, London, 1968); *Meroke; or, Missionary Life in Africa* (Philadelphia, 1858); and *A Grammar and Dictionary of the Yoruba Language* (Washington, 1858). From 1868 to 1874 he traveled in Texas and Florida. Died November 24, 1875, in Georgia. *References*: Thomas J. Bowen Papers, Southern Baptist Convention Historical Commission, Nashville, Tenn.; *ESB*; W. K. McNeil, "The First American Collectors of African Folklore," *Kentucky Folklore Record* 28 (1982): 40–47; Lysle E. Meyer, " T. J. Bowen and Central Africa: A Nineteenth-Century Missionary Delusion," *IJAHS* 15 (1982): 247–60; and Orville W. Taylor, "Thomas J. Bowen: A Man for All Seasons," *Viewpoints* 8 (1982): 51–61.

BOYCE, WILLIAM (DICKSON) (1858–1929). Newspaper publisher and big-game hunter, born June 16, 1858, in New Texas, Allegheny County, Pennsylvania. Boyce studied at the University of Wooster (Ohio). He was advertising solicitor in Chicago and later organizer and manager of the bureau of correspondence at the New Orleans Cotton Exposition of 1884. He founded and was publisher of two weeklies, the *Saturday Blade* and the *Chicago Ledger*, which were merged in 1924 to form a monthly, the *Blade-Ledger*. He launched the American Balloonograph Expedition in East Africa in 1909, taking the first aerial pictures of wildlife from a balloon suspended over the Rift Valley. He incorporated the Boy Scouts of America in 1910 in Washington, D.C., and founded the Lone Scouts in 1915. He later led a second expedition into Africa and wrote *Illustrated Africa, North, Tropical, South* (Chicago, 1925). Died June 11, 1929, in Chicago. *Reference*: *WWWA*.

BRADLEY, HERBERT EDWIN (1874–1961) and **BRADLEY, MARY (WILHELMINA) HASTINGS** (1882–1976). Herbert Edwin Bradley, lawyer, traveler, and big-game hunter, was born December 20, 1874, in Brooklyn, Ontario, Canada. Mary Hastings Bradley, author and traveler, was born April 19, 1882, in Chicago. Herbert Edwin attended the University of Michigan and Northwestern University and practiced law in Chicago after 1901. Mary Hastings graduated from Smith College. They were married in 1910. They accompanied Carl Ethan Akeley* on his expedition for the American Museum of Natural History to the Belgian Congo to find gorillas in 1921–1922. They made a second trip to the Belgian Congo in 1924, making the first expedition through the country west of Lake Edward. They made a third expedition to Africa in 1930–1931 to study pygmies and the Mangbetu tribes and a fourth trip in 1951. Herbert Edwin also made an expedition to Sumatra and Indochina in 1935 to hunt tigers. Mary Hastings wrote *On the Gorilla Trail* (New York, 1922) and *Caravans and*

Cannibals (New York, 1926). She was special correspondent for *Collier's* magazine in 1945. Herbert Edwin died April 22, 1961, in Chicago. Mary Hastings died October 25, 1976, in Chicago. *References*: *Chicago Tribune*, October 28, 1976; *WWWA*.

BRANCH, THOMAS H. (1856–1924). Missionary, born December 24, 1856, in Jefferson County, Missouri. Branch began missionary work in Pueblo, Colorado, in 1901. From 1902 until 1906 he was a missionary under the Seventh-Day Adventists in Nyasaland, the first black American in British Central Africa, stationed at Plainfield (renamed Malamulo in 1907). He was sent to Cape Town in 1906 and returned to the United States in 1908 because of ill health. He was later engaged in pastoral work among blacks in Denver, Colorado, until 1918 when he moved to Watts, California. Died November 24, 1924, in Los Angeles, California. *Reference*: *SDAE*.

BRANDER, NATHANIEL (ca. 1799- ?). Colonist, born in Petersburg, Virginia. Brander immigrated to Africa on the *Elizabeth** in 1820. He was vice agent of the colony of Liberia in 1834–1835, became judge of the superior court in 1843, and was the first vice president of the Republic of Liberia from 1848 to 1850. *Reference*: *Huberich*.

BRASS, LEONARD (JOHN) (1900–1971). Botanist, born May 27, 1900, in Toowoomba, Australia. Brass was in charge of the Arnold Arboretum expeditions to New Guinea in 1925–1926 and to the Solomon Islands in 1932–1933. He was botanist to the Archbold expeditions to New Guinea in 1933–1934, 1936–1937, and 1938–1939, and expedition leader in 1953, 1956–1957, and 1959. He served in the Canadian Army during World War II, and was consultant to the U.S. Army on the vegetation and ecology of the islands of the South Pacific. He became a U.S. citizen in 1947. He was a member of the staff of the American Museum of Natural History from 1940 to 1954, and associate curator and then curator of the Archbold collections of the American Museum of Natural History at the Archbold Biological Station, Lake Placid, Florida, from 1954 until his retirement in 1966. He was botanist of the American Museum of Natural History expedition to Nyasaland in 1946 and director of field operations of the Upjohn-Penick expedition for botanical exploration in Africa in 1949–1950. Died August 29, 1971, in Cairns, Queensland, Australia. *References*: *AMWS*; *NYT*, September 2, 1971; and Lily M. Perry, "Leonard J. Brass (1900–1971), an Appreciation," *Arnold Arboretum Journal* 52 (1971): 695–98.

BRETHREN CHURCH: FOREIGN MISSIONARY SOCIETY. Founded in 1900, it began missionary work in Oubangui-Chari, French Equatorial Africa, in 1921 and in Chad in 1965. The name was changed to the National Fellowship of Brethren Churches and later to the Fellowship of Grace Brethren Churches. *References*: *BE*; Orville D. Jobson, *Conquering Oubangui-Chari for Christ* (Winona Lake, Ind., 1957); and Homer A. Kent, Jr., *Conquering Frontiers: A History of the Brethren Church (The National Fellowship of Brethren Churches)*, rev. ed. (Winona Lake, Ind., 1972).

BRETHREN IN CHRIST FOREIGN MISSIONS. Organized in 1895, it began missionary work in Southern Rhodesia in 1898 and in Northern Rhodesia in 1906. It also conducted an independent mission in Johannesburg, South Africa. The name was changed later to Brethren in Christ Missions. *References*: Archives of the Brethren in Christ Church, Messiah College, Grantham, Pennsylvania; Anna R. Engle et al., *There is No Difference: God Works in Africa and India* (Nappanee, Ind., 1950); and Carlton O. Wittinger, *Quest for Piety and Obedience: The Story of the Brethren in Christ* (Nappanee, Ind., 1978).

BRIDGE, HORATIO (1806–1893). Naval officer, born April 8, 1806, in Augusta, Maine. Bridge graduated from Bowdoin College and the Northampton law school and was admitted to the bar. He practiced from 1828 to 1838 in Skowhegan and later in Augusta, Maine. Appointed in 1838 as purser in the United States Navy, he served on the *Cyane* in its cruise in the Mediterranean from 1838 to 1841, and on the *Saratoga* in the African squadron from 1843 to 1845. He published *Journal of an African Cruiser; Comprising Sketches of the Canaries, Cape Verde, Liberia, Madeira, Sierra Leone, and Other Places of Interest on the West Coast of Africa*, ed. (from Bridge's notes) by Nathaniel Hawthorne (New York, 1845). He subsequently served again in the Mediterranean, in the Portsmouth Navy Yard, and in the Pacific squadron. He was chief of the bureau of provisions and clothing from 1853 until 1869 and was chief inspector of provisions and clothing until his retirement in 1873. Died March 20, 1893, in Athens, Pennsylvania. *References*: Patrick Brancaccio, "The Black Man's Paradise: Hawthorne's Editing of the *Journal of an African Cruiser*," *New England Quarterly* 53 (1980): 23–41; and *NCAB* 4:358.

BRIDGMAN, BURT NICHOLS (1864–1951). Medical missionary, son of Henry Martyn Bridgman,* born December 31, 1864, at Ifumi, Natal, South Africa. Bridgman graduated from Amherst College and the New York University Medical College. He practiced medicine in New York City from 1889 to 1892. He was missionary under the American Board of Commissioners for Foreign Missions (ABCFM)* in Adams, Natal, from 1892 to 1898, and opened a medical department there. He returned to the United States in 1898 because of the ill health of his wife, and practiced in Jamaica Plains, Boston, from 1899 to 1916. He returned to South Africa in 1917, served in the South African Medical Corps in Pretoria from 1917 to 1921, and practiced medicine in Kenterton, Natal, from 1921 until his death. Died May 3, 1951, in Kenterton, Natal, South Africa. *References*: *Amherst*; *NYT*, May 24, 1951; and *SADNB*.

BRIDGMAN, FREDERICK BRAINERD (1869–1925). Missionary, son of Henry Martyn Bridgman,* born May 18, 1869, at Ifumi mission station in Natal, South Africa. Bridgman graduated from Oberlin College and Chicago Theological Seminary. He was a missionary under the American Board of Commissioners for Foreign Missions (ABCFM)* in South Africa from 1897 until his death. He first served at the Zulu mission in Ifumi, and was later in charge of missionary work in Durban and subsequently in Johannesburg. Died August 23, 1925, in Portland, Maine. *References*: *Amherst*; *NYT*, August 27, 1925; Charles N. Ransom, "Frederick B. Bridgman, of South Africa," *Missionary Review of the World* 49 (1926): 429–34; and *SADNB*.

BRIDGMAN, HENRY MARTYN (1830–1896). Missionary, born January 3, 1830, in Westhampton, Massachusetts. Bridgman graduated from Amherst College and Hartford and Union theological seminaries and was ordained in 1860. He was missionary under the American Board of Commissioners for Foreign Missions (ABCFM)* at Ifumi, Natal, South Africa, from 1861 to 1866, and at Umzumbi, Natal, from 1869 to 1896. Died August 29, 1896, at Amanzimtoti, Natal, South Africa. *Reference*: *Amherst*.

BRIDGMAN, HERBERT LAWRENCE (1844–1924). Newspaper publisher and explorer, born May 30, 1844, in Amherst, Massachusetts. Bridgman graduated from Amherst College. He began working on the *Springfield Republican* and became its city editor. He worked for the Associated Press, *Frank Leslie's*, *New York Press*, and *New York Tribune*, and was business manager of the *Brooklyn Standard Union* from 1887 until 1924. He was one of the founders of the American Newspaper Publishers Association. He was a patron of Arctic exploration, was associated with Robert Peary, and led several expeditions to the Arctic. In 1904 he penetrated the Congo from the headwaters of the Nile and described his impressions in the May 1906 issue of *National Geographic Magazine*. Died September 24, 1924, at sea on the way home from a vacation cruise. *References*: *DAB*; *NCAB* 22:51; and *NYT*, September 27, 1924.

BRIDGMAN, LAURA BRAINERD (NICHOLS) (1834–1923). Missionary, wife of Henry Martyn Bridgman,* born June 20, 1834, in East Haddam, Connecticut. Bridgman graduated from Mount Holyoke Seminary. She taught at Liverpool, Nova Scotia, and Canton, Connecticut. She was missionary under the American Board of Commissioners for Foreign Missions (ABCFM)* in South Africa from 1860 until her death. She was stationed first at Ifumi and later at Umzumbe in Zululand, where she opened the Umzumbe Home School. Died January 13, 1923, in Adams Mission Station, Natal, South Africa. *References*: Bridgman Family Papers, Forbes Library, Northampton, Mass.; and *The Natal Mercury*, January 22, 1923.

BROOKLYN, U.S.S. Wooden screw sloop-of-war. She made four cruises in South American waters between 1865 and 1889, a cruise in European waters from 1871 to 1873, and cruised in Asiatic waters from 1886 to 1889. She visited the coast of Africa in 1884. The trip was described by William Henry Beehler in *The Cruise of the Brooklyn. A Journal of the Principal Events of a Three Years' Cruise in the U.S. Flagship Brooklyn, in the South Atlantic Station. . . . Descriptions of Places in South America, Africa, and Madagascar* (Philadelphia, 1885). *Reference*: DANFS.

BROOKS, BERRY BOSWELL, JR. (1902-   ). Business executive and big-game hunter, born February 2, 1902, in Senatobia, Mississippi. Brooks attended Washington and Lee University. In 1923 he began a business career with the Farnsworth-Smithwick Company of Memphis, cotton brokers, and in 1936 established his own cotton firm, Berry B. Brooks Cotton Company, in Memphis. He owned land and farm property and raised cattle in Arkansas and Tennessee. In 1947 he made his first journey to Kenya and collected animals for the Berry B. Brooks African Hall of the Memphis Museum. He returned to Africa in 1949, in 1962, and in 1965. He also made hunting expeditions to Vietnam in 1961 and to India in 1967. His safari diary was serialized in *Outdoor Life* magazine in 1951, and was published as *Passport to Safariland* (Memphis, 1951?). *Reference*: NCAB M:285.

BROWN, WILLIAM HARVEY ("CURIO BROWN") (1862–1913). Naturalist, soldier and settler, born August 22, 1862, in Des Moines, Iowa. Brown graduated from the University of Kansas. He joined the staff of the natural history department of the Smithsonian Institution and was a naturalist on the eclipse expedition sent by the United States government in 1889 to the Congo. He came to South Africa to collect animals for the Carnegie Institute and joined the pioneer column, the British force sent to occupy Mashonaland in 1890. When the Matabele war broke out, he enlisted with the British. In recognition of his services he received 13,000 acres of land in what became Rhodesia. He remained there and became a naturalized British subject. He served on the Salisbury, Rhodesia, city council, was mayor of Salisbury in 1909–1910, and served on the Legislative Council from 1908 to 1911. He wrote *On the South African Frontier: The Adventures and Observations of an American in Mashonaland and Matabeleland* (New York, 1899). Died April 5, 1913, in Salisbury, Rhodesia. *References*: NYT May 15, 1913; and SADNB.

BROWNE, JOHN ROSS (1821–1875). Traveler and author, born February 11, 1821, in Dublin, Ireland, came to the United Sates with his parents in 1821, and grew up in Louisville, Kentucky. Browne was a porter in the United States Senate in 1841–1842; shipped as a sailor on a whaler from New Bedford, Massachusetts, in 1842–1843; visited Zanzibar; and wrote *Etchings of a Whaling Cruise with Notes of a Sojourn on the Island of Zanzibar* (New York, 1846; ed.

John Seelye, Cambridge, Mass., 1968). He traveled extensively for the next twenty years, was official reporter to the first Constitutional Convention of California in 1849, and later was a confidential agent for the Treasury Department in the western United States and minister to China in 1870–1871. He subsequently settled in Oakland, California. Died December 8, 1875, in Oakland, California. *References*: *ACAB*; Lina F. Browne, ed., *J. Ross Browne: His Letters, Journals and Writings*, (Albuquerque, N.M., 1969); *DAB*; *NCAB* 8:117; and *WWWA*.

BRYANT, JAMES CHURCHILL (1812–1850). Missionary, born April 8, 1812, in Easton, Massachusetts, and grew up in New Boston, New Hampshire. Bryant graduated from Amherst College and Andover Theological Seminary, and was ordained in 1840. He was pastor in Littleton, Massachusetts, from 1840 to 1845. He was a missionary under the American Board of Commissioners for Foreign Missions (ABCFM)* in South Africa from 1846 until his death. He established a mission station at Ifumi in Zululand. He became an authority on the Zulu language and published the first account of the Zulu language in the *Journal of the American Oriental Society* in 1849. Died December 23, 1850, in Inanda, Natal, South Africa. *References*: *Amherst*; *AndoverTS*; *DSAB* 1; Eleanor S. Reuling, *First Saint to the Zulus* (Boston, 1960); and *SESA*.

BUCHANAN, THOMAS (1808–1841). Colonist, born September 19, 1808, in Covington, Franklin County, New York. In 1835 he was appointed governor of Bassa Cove by the New York and Pennsylvania colonization societies and served in 1836–1837. He returned to the United States in 1837, but came back to Liberia in 1839, and was the first governor of the Commonwealth of Liberia from 1839 to 1841, the last white to serve as chief administrative officer of Liberia. He played an important role in the drafting of the Commonwealth Constitution of Liberia. Died September 3, 1841, at Bassa Cove, Liberia. *Reference*: *Huberich*.

BUCK, THERESA R(OBINSON) (1912–1964). Missionary nurse, born May 25, 1912, in Hartford, Connecticut. Buck attended Rollins College (Florida) and graduated from Bates College (Maine). She received nurses' training at the Peter Bent Brigham Hospital (Boston) and became a registered nurse and attended the Kennedy School of Missions (Hartford, Connecticut). She was missionary under the American Board of Commissioners for Foreign Missions (ABCFM)* in Southern Rhodesia from 1938 until her death. She served as nurse and nursing teacher at the Mount Silinda hospital, Southern Rhodesia, from 1938 to 1949, was administrator of the Mount Silinda hospital from 1949 to 1959, and of the Cottage Hospital and Dispensary at Chikore, Southern Rhodesia, from 1959 until her death. Died September 25, 1964, in Chikore, Southern Rhodesia. *Reference*: *Bates Alumnus*, January 1965.

BUELL, RAYMOND LESLIE (1896–1946). Educator and publicist, born July
13, 1896, in Chicago, and grew up in Wilmar, Minnesota, and Santa Paula,
California. Buell graduated from Occidental College (Los Angeles) and Princeton
University. He served in the army during World War I. He was instructor and
assistant professor of government at Harvard University from 1922 to 1927. He
went to Africa in 1925–1926, under the auspices of the Bureau of International
Research of Harvard University and Radcliffe College, to study its political,
economic, and social conditions; the result was *The Native Problem in Africa*
(New York, 1928). He was research director of the Foreign Policy Association
in New York City from 1927 to 1933 and its president from 1933 to 1939. He
joined the staff of Time, Inc., in 1939, and was foreign affairs adviser to Wendell
L. Wilkie in the presidential campaign of 1940. He also wrote *Liberia: A Century
of Survival* (Philadelphia, 1947). Died February 20, 1946, in Montreal, Canada.
References: Raymond Leslie Buell Papers, Houghton Library, Harvard University, Cambridge, Mass.; *CB* 1946; *NCAB* 34:156; *NYT*, February 21, 1946; and
WWWA.

BURGESS, ANDREW (SEVERANCE) (1897-   ). Missionary, born September 29, 1897, at Herscher, Illinois. Burgess graduated from St. Olaf College
and Luther Seminary, and was ordained in 1924. He served in the army during
World War I and then taught and did relief work in Kikungshan, China, from
1919 to 1921. He was field secretary of the Foreign Mission Department of the
Evangelical Lutheran Church* from 1924 to 1926, visitor of the mission field
in South Africa and Madagascar in 1926–1927, and missionary in Ft. Dauphin,
Madagascar, from 1927 to 1932. He was field representative of the Foreign
Mission Department of the Evangelical Lutheran Church from 1932 to 1947,
director of the Missionary Education Department from 1944 to 1948, and pro-
fessor of missions at Luther Seminary from 1947 until his retirement in 1968.
He wrote *Zanahary in South Madagascar* (Minneapolis, 1932), *Ra-ha-la-hi-ko.
My Brother in Madagascar* (Minneapolis, 1938), and *Unkulunkulu in Zululand*
(Minneapolis, 1934). *References*: *Biographical Directory of Clergymen of the
American Lutheran Church*, ed. Arnold R. Mickelson (Minneapolis, 1972);
Luther Theological Seminary Review 7 (April 1968): 9–11; and *WWPNL*.

BURGESS, EBENEZER (1790–1870). Clergyman and colonial agent, born
April 1, 1790, in Wareham, Massachusetts. Burgess graduated from Brown
University and Andover Theological Seminary and was ordained in 1821. He
was professor of mathematics and natural philosophy at the University of Vermont from 1815 to 1817. He and Samuel J. Mills, Jr.* went to Africa in 1818,
as agents of the American Colonization Society* to explore the west coast of
Africa and to locate a site that could be purchased for a colony of free Black
Americans. He was later pastor in Dedham, Massachusetts, from 1821 until his
death. Died December 5, 1870, in Dedham, Massachusetts. *References*: *ACAB;*
and *Huberich*.

BURKE, LINDSAY GAINES (1870–1897). Soldier, born November 17, 1870, in New Orleans. Burke enlisted in the service of the Congo Free State in 1896 as deputy commissary. He arrived in the Congo in that year, was involved in military operations against the Batetelas, and was killed January 18, 1897, at Goie Kbamba, Congo Free State. *Reference*: *BCB 2*.

BURNHAM, FREDERICK RUSSELL (1861–1947). Explorer, scout, and soldier of fortune, born May 11, 1861, in Tivoli (near Mankato), Minnesota, and grew up in Los Angeles. Burnham had limited formal education, but spent his early years in the Southwest and Mexico, where he hunted, prospected for gold, served as deputy sheriff, and learned scouting. He went to Matabeleland, Southern Africa, in 1893; served as a scout for the British South Africa Company during the first Matabele War; and served again as a scout for the Bulawayo Field Force in the second Matabele War of 1896–1897. He led several expeditions to explore the area north of the Zambesi River. He prospected for gold in the Klondike, Alaska, from 1897 to 1899, but returned to Africa in 1899, and served as chief scout for the British Army until he was wounded in 1900. He explored the Volta River in West Africa in 1901, and later was a representative of the British East Africa Company in the area around Lake Rudolph. He returned to the United States in 1904, and was involved in exploring and prospecting, particularly in Mexico, and producing oil in California. He wrote *Scouting on Two Continents* (Garden City, N.Y., 1928) and *Taking Chances* (Los Angeles, 1944). Died September 1, 1947, in Santa Barbara, California. *References*: Frederick R. Burnham Papers, Yale University Library, New Haven, Conn.; Frederick R. Burnham Papers, Hoover Institution Archives, Stanford, Calif.; *DAB S4*; *NCAB* 36:101; *NYT*, September 2, 1947; *SESA*; Alistair Tough, "Papers of Frederick R. Burnham (1861–1947) in the Hoover Institution Archives," *History in Africa* 12 (1985): 385–87; *WAMB*; and *WWWA*.

BURNS, FRANCIS (1809–1863). Missionary, born free December 5, 1809, in Albany, New York. Burns was indentured to a farmer in Greene County, New York, when he was four years old, and remained there until he was twenty-one. He was then licensed to preach. He was appointed to the Liberian mission of the Methodist Episcopal Church in 1834, was a teacher at the Monrovia Academy, and edited *Africa's Luminary*. He was ordained in 1844, and was presiding elder and preacher of the Cape Palmas district from 1848 to 1858. He was consecrated a bishop and elected the first missionary bishop of the Methodist Episcopal Church in 1858. He returned to the United States in 1863 because of ill health. Died April 18, 1863, in Baltimore. *References*: *ACAB*; *EWM*; Sylvia M. Jacobs, "Francis Burns, First Missionary Bishop of the Methodist Episcopal Church, North," in *Black Apostles at Home and Abroad: Afro-Americans and the Christian Mission from the Revolution to Reconstruction*, ed. David W. Wills and Richard Newman (Boston, 1982), pp. 255–63; *Leete*; and *NCAB* 13:173.

BUSHNELL, ALBERT (1818–1879). Missionary, born February 9, 1818, in Rome, New York. Bushnell graduated from Lane Theological Seminary (Cincinnati). He was missionary under the American Board of Commissioners for Foreign Missions (ABCFM)* in Gabon from 1844 to 1879. He directed boys' and girls' schools at Baraka and translated parts of the Bible into Mpongwe. Died December 2, 1879, in Sierra Leone. *References*: Graham C. Campbell, *A Consecrated Life. Albert Bushnell, Missionary to Africa* (Auburn, N.Y., 1880); and *LC*.

BUTTERFIELD, KENYON LEECH (1868–1935). Sociologist, born June 11, 1868, in Lapeer, Michigan. Butterfield graduated from Michigan State College of Agriculture and Applied Science. He was president and professor of political economy and rural sociology at the Rhode Island State College of Agriculture and Mechanical Arts from 1903 to 1906, president and head of the division of rural social science at Massachusetts State College from 1906 to 1924, and president of Michigan State College from 1924 to 1928. In 1929 he went to South Africa and took part in the investigations of the Carnegie Commission inquiring into the problems of poor whites in South Africa. Died November 25, 1935, in Amherst, Massachusetts. *References*: *BDAE*; *DAB* S1; *NCAB* 27:138; and *WWWA*.

BUTTERS, CHARLES (1854–1933). Mining engineer and metallurgist, born August 10, 1854, in Haverhill, Massachusetts. Butters graduated from the University of California. He served as metallurgist for several mines in the west. He came to the Transvaal in 1890 at the request of Hermann Eckstein & Company to erect a chlorination plant at the Robinson Mine for the treatment of gold ore, and pioneered the use of the cyanide process for extracting gold. He left Eckstein in 1894 and played a leading role in establishing the Rand Central Ore Reduction Company. He joined the Reform Committee* in 1895, took part in the Jameson Raid, was arrested as an accomplice, and was fined $2,000 for his part. He returned to the United States in 1898, and held various mine holdings. Died November 27, 1933, in Berkeley, California. *References*: Charles and Jessie Butters Memorial Collection, Bancroft Library, University of California, Berkeley, Calif.; *DSAB* 4; T. A. Ricard, *Interviews with Mining Engineers* (San Francisco, 1922), pp. 117–31; and *SADNB*.

BYRD AMENDMENT. Named after Senator Harry F. Byrd (Virginia) and signed on November 17, 1971, by President Richard M. Nixon, the amendment relaxed the embargo on the regime of Ian Smith in Rhodesia by authorizing the importation into the United States of strategic minerals, particularly chrome, from Rhodesia. As a result, it damaged the American sanctions program against Rhodesia. *References*: Anthony Lake, *The "Tar Baby" Option: American Policy toward Southern Rhodesia* (New York, 1976), ch. 6; and Randolph P. Sean, "The Byrd Amendment: A Postmortem," *World Affairs* 14 (1978): 57–70.

C

CALLOWAY, JAMES NATHAN (fl. 1890–1930). Agriculturist. Calloway graduated from Fisk University and studied at Tuskegee Institute. He taught mathematics at Tuskegee Institute from 1890 to 1893, and was business agent there from 1893 to 1897 and manager of the Marshall Farm at Tuskegee from 1897 to 1900. He was in charge of the Tuskegee cotton-raising experimental station in German Togoland in 1900–1901. He was later teacher of agriculture in Tuskegee until at least 1930. *Reference:* Louis R. Harlan, ed., *The Booker T. Washington Papers* 3 (Urbana, Ill., 1974): 105–6.

CAMPBELL, GUY G(IBSON) (1890–1957). Physician, born August 6, 1890, in Petersburg, Pennsylvania. Campbell graduated from Jefferson Medical College (Philadelphia) and served in World War I. He went to British North Borneo in 1916 and there organized and carried out campaigns of nutrition and health. He was in private practice in Indiana from 1932 to 1937, medical director for the Firestone Plantations Company* in Liberia from 1937 to 1943, principal adviser to the Ministry of Health of Ethiopia from 1944 to 1948 and personal physician to Ethiopian Emperor Haile Selassie. He was largely instrumental in the forming of the Ethiopian Medical Society and served as its first president. In 1948 he was member of the staff of the Institute of Inter-American Affairs in La Paz, Bolivia, and later in Bogota, Colombia. He then went into private practice in Hammond and Dyer, Indiana. Died December 2, 1957, in Dyer, Indiana. *References: Journal of the American Medical Association* 166 (February 22, 1958): 954; and *NYT*, December 5, 1957.

CAMPBELL, ROBERT (1829–1884). Colonist, born May 7, 1829, in Kingston, Jamaica. Campbell was a printer's apprentice, worked in a printing shop, attended Jamaican Normal School (Spanish Town, Jamaica), and became a teacher. He went to Nicaragua and Panama in 1852, and came to the United States in 1853. He worked in a printing shop in Brooklyn and was a teacher and assistant principal of the Institute for Colored Youth in Philadelphia from 1855

until 1858. In 1858 he was invited by Martin R. Delany* to become a member
of the Niger Valley Exploring Party,* and went to Nigeria in 1859–1860 to
inspect the area around Abeokuta as a possible site for a settlement of free black
Americans. He returned to the United States in 1860. He wrote *A Few Facts
Relating to Lagos, Abeokuta and Other Sections of Central Africa* (Philadelphia,
1860) and *A Pilgrimage to the Motherland: An Account of a Journey Among
the Egbas and Yorubas of Central Africa, in 1859–60* (New York, 1861; reprinted
in *Search for a Place: Black Separatism and Africa, 1860*, ed. Howard H. Bell,
Ann Arbor, 1971). He went back in Nigeria in 1862, published a newspaper,
Afro-America, in Lagos from 1863 to 1865, was active in the literary and sci-
entific life of Lagos, and after 1865 was involved in various commercial un-
dertakings. Died January 19, 1884, in Lagos, Nigeria. *References*: R.J.M.
Blackett, *Beating against the Barriers: Biographical Essays in Nineteenth Cen-
tury Afro-American History* (Baton Rouge, La., 1986), ch. 3; R.J.M. Blackett,
"Martin R. Delaney and Robert Campbell: Black Americans in Search of an
African Colony," *JNH* 62 (1977): 1–25; and R.J.M. Blackett, "Return to the
Motherland: Robert Campbell, a Jamaican in Early Colonial Lagos," *Phylon* 40
(1979): 375–86.

CAMPBELL, ROBERT ERSKINE (1884–1977). Clergyman, born August
13, 1884, in Florida, New York. Campbell graduated from Columbia University
and General Theological Seminary (New York City) and was ordained in 1909.
He was headmaster of the St. Andrew's School (Tenn.) from 1911 to 1915 and
from 1918 to 1922. He entered the Order of the Holy Cross in 1915. He was
prior of the Holy Cross Liberian Mission,* in Bolahun, Liberia, from 1922 to
1925, was consecrated in 1925, and was Episcopal bishop of Liberia from 1925
to 1936. He retired in 1936 from diocesan duties, and was prior of Saint Andrews
from 1936 to 1948. He was Father Superior of the Order of the Holy Cross at
its monastery in West Park, New York, from 1948 to 1954, returned to Liberia
from 1955 to 1957, and served at Holy Cross's monastery in Santa Barbara,
California, from 1959 to 1977. He wrote *Within the Green Wall: The Story of
the Holy Cross Liberian Mission, 1922–1957* (West Park, N.Y., 1957). Died
August 23, 1977, in Santa Barbara, California. *Reference*: *NYT*, August 26,
1977.

CAMPHOR, ALEXANDER PRIESTLEY (1865–1919). Missionary, born
August 9, 1865, in Soniat, Jefferson County, Louisiana. Camphor attended
Leland University, graduated from New Orleans University and Gammon The-
ological Seminary, and studied at Columbia University and the University of
Chicago. He was professor of mathematics at New Orleans University from 1889
to 1893 and pastor in Philadelphia and in Orange, New Jersey. He was missionary
under the Board of Foreign Missions of the Methodist Episcopal Church* in
Monrovia from 1897 to 1918, and served as president of the College of West
Africa* from 1898 to 1908. He also served as vice consul in Monrovia. He

wrote *Missionary Story Sketches; Folk-lore from Africa* (Cincinnati, 1909). He returned to the United States in 1908 and was president of the Central Alabama Institute (Birmingham, Ala.) until 1916. He was elected bishop for Africa in 1916 and returned to Liberia. Died December 10, 1919, in Orange, New Jersey. *References*: *EWM*; *Leete*; and *NYT*, December 12, 1919.

CANADAY, JOHN (EDWIN). *See* HEAD, MATTHEW

CAREY [CARY], LOTT (ca. 1780–1828). Missionary, born a slave in Charles City County, Virginia. Carey went to Richmond in 1804 to work as a hired slave laborer in a tobacco warehouse. He purchased his freedom in 1813 and then became a Baptist preacher. He went to Sierra Leone in 1821 as missionary under the American Baptist Missionary Union.* He went to Cape Mesurado (now Monrovia, Liberia) in 1822, and was instrumental in the success of the Baptist church established there in 1822. He became vice agent in Liberia in 1826 and acting agent of Liberia in 1828. Died November 10, 1828, at Cape Mesurado. *References*: *DANB*; *Davis*; Miles M. Fisher, "Lott Carey, the Colonizing Missionary," *JNH* 7 (1922): 380–418 (reprinted in *Black Apostles at Home and Abroad: Afro-Americans and the Christian Mission from the Revolution to Reconstruction*, ed. David W. Wills and Richard Newman [Boston, 1982], pp. 211–42); Leroy Fitts, *Lott Carey, First Black Missionary to Africa* (Valley Forge, Pa., 1978); *Huberich*; *NCAB* 9:546; William A. Poe, "Lott Carey: Man of Purchased Freedom," *Church History* 39 (1970): 49–61; and *WWWA*.

CARLSON, PAUL (EARLE) (1928–1964). Medical missionary, born March 31, 1928, in Culver City, California. Carlson graduated from Stanford University and George Washington University School of Medicine. He was medical missionary under the Board of World Missions of the Evangelical Covenant Church of America* in the Congo from 1961 until his death, and was stationed at the Wasolo mission station in the northeastern part of the Ubangi Province, the Republic of Congo. He was seized in the summer of 1964 by Congolese rebels called Simbas (Swahili for "lions"). He was held hostage and killed by them, November 24, 1964, in Stanleyville, the Republic of Congo. *References*: Lois Carlson, *Monganga Paul: The Congo Ministry and Martyrdom of Paul Carlson, M.D.* (New York, 1966); Homer E. Dowdy, *Out of the Jaws of the Lion: Christian Martyrdom in the Congo* (New York, 1965); and *Time*, December 4, 1964.

CARNES, JOSHUA A. (fl. 1815–1852). Sea captain. Carnes accompanied his father, sea captain John Carnes, on a voyage to West Africa in 1815–1816. He later recounted his experiences in *Journal of a Voyage from Boston to the West Coast of Africa; With a Full Description of the Manners of Trading with the Natives on the Coast* (Boston, 1852).

CARPENTER, FRANK GEORGE (1855–1924). Journalist, traveler, and photographer, born May 8, 1855, in Mansfield, Ohio. Carpenter graduated from the University of Wooster. He became legislative correspondent for the *Cleveland Leader* in 1879 and its Washington correspondent in 1882. He traveled to Europe and Egypt in 1881, and in 1888 began traveling around the world, publishing a weekly foreign travel letter for a newspaper syndicate. He traveled in Africa in 1906–1907, going from Morocco to Egypt and from Cairo to the Cape, and wrote *Cairo to Kisumu: Egypt—the Sudan—Kenya Colony* (Garden City, N.Y., 1924) and *Uganda to the Cape* (Garden City, N.Y., 1926). All his books included original photographs. Died June 18, 1924, in Nanking, China. *References*: Photographs of Frank George Carpenter, Prints and Photographs Division, Library of Congress; *DAB*; Milton Kaplan, "Africa through the Eye of a Camera," *The Quarterly Journal of the Library of Congress* 27 (1970): 222–37; *NYT*, June 18, 1924; and *WWWA*.

CARPENTER, GEORGE WAYLAND (1901–1976). Missionary, born January 6, 1901, in Saratoga Springs, New York. Carpenter graduated from Union College, Rochester Theological Seminary (now Colgate-Rochester Divinity School), and Yale University, and was ordained in 1925. He was a missionary under the American Baptist Foreign Mission Society (see American Baptist Missionary Union*) from 1925 until 1953. He was a teacher at the Congo Evangelical Training Institute, Kimpese, Belgian Congo, from 1926 to 1935; educational secretary to the Congo Protestant Council from 1938 to 1948; and managing director of the Protestant Literature Agency and Press in Léopoldville from 1940 until 1953. He was executive secretary of the Africa Committee of the Division of Foreign Missions of the National Council of Churches of Christ in the United States of America from 1953 to 1956, New York secretary of the International Missionary Council from 1956 to 1961, and New York secretary of the Division of Missions and Evangelism of the World Council of Churches from 1961 to 1965. He wrote *Highways for God in Congo; Commemorating Seventy-five Years of Protestant Missions 1878–1953* (Leopoldville, Belgian Congo, 1952) and *The Way in Africa* (New York, 1959). Died May 1, 1976, in Brant Lake, New York. *Reference*: *WWWA*.

CARTER, T(HOMAS) DONALD (1893–1972). Zoologist, born January 28, 1893, in Boonton, New Jersey. After high school, he was assistant keeper at the New York Zoological Garden from 1913 to 1916 and participated in a zoological expedition to Costa Rica. He joined the American Museum of Natural History in 1920, was assistant in the department of Mammalogy from 1920 to 1928, and assistant curator in the department from 1928 to 1960. Between 1928 and 1959, he conducted six expeditions to Africa. He coauthored *The Mammals of Angola, Africa* (New York, 1941). He retired in 1960. Died March 30, 1972, in Denville, New Jersey. *References*: *AMWS*; and *NYT*, April 2, 1972.

CARTWRIGHT, ANDREW (1835–1903). Missionary, born a slave in eastern North Carolina. He escaped to New England before the Civil War, became a preacher, and followed the Union Army to Virginia in 1863. He organized the first African Methodist Episcopal Zion (AMEZ) churches in the South, and served as agent for the American Colonization Society.* He went to Liberia in 1876, organized the first AMEZ Church in Africa in Brewerville, Liberia, in 1878, and served it until his death. Died January 14, 1903, in Brewerville, Liberia.

CATLIN, ROBERT MAYO (1853–1934). Mining engineer, born June 8, 1853, in Burlington, Vermont. Catlin graduated from the University of Vermont. He was surveyor for Elks County, Nevada, from 1875 to 1879; superintendent of the Navajo Mining Company, Tuscarora, Nevada, from 1879 until 1892; and superintendent of the Victorine Gold Mining Company from 1892 to 1895. He was general manager, under John Hays Hammond,* of eight deep-level mines in Johannesburg, South Africa, from 1895 to 1906, and consulting engineer to the Consolidated Gold Fields of South Africa Limited. He was general superintendent of New Jersey Zinc Company from 1906 to 1930. Died November 22, 1934, in Oakland, California. *References*: *Burlington* (Vt.) *Free Press and Times*, November 23, 1934; and *WWWA*.

CHAILLÉ-LONG, CHARLES (1842–1917). Army officer and explorer, born July 2, 1842, in Princess Anne, Somerset County, Maryland. Chaillé-Long served in the Confederate Army during the Civil War. He joined the Egyptian Army in 1869, and in 1874 was chief of staff to General Charles Gordon, governor of Equatoria Province in Southern Sudan, who was suppressing the slave traffic in the region of the White Nile. He was sent by the Khedive of Egypt on a secret mission to King Mutesa of Buganda, and recorded his journey in *Central Africa: Naked Truths of Naked People; an Account of an Expedition to the Lake Victoria Nyanza and the Makrak Niam-Niam, West of the Bahr-el-Abiad (White Nile)* (London, 1876). On this journey he explored the Upper Nile basin. In 1875 he made another trip from Gondokoro, along the Congo-Nile divide region. He returned to the United States in 1877 because of ill health, studied law at Columbia University, and after 1882, practiced international law, first in Alexandria, Egypt, and later in Paris. He was consul general and secretary of legation in Korea from 1887 to 1889. He wrote an autobiography, *My Life in Four Continents* (London, 1912). Died March 24, 1917, in Virginia Beach, Norfolk, Virginia. *References*: Charles Chaillé-Long Papers, Manuscript Division, Library of Congress; Edward A. Alpers, ''Charles Chaillé-Long's Mission to Mutessa of Buganda,'' *Uganda Journal* 29 (1965): 1–11; *DAB*; *NCAB* 10:28; *NYT*, March 26, 1917; *WAMB*; and *WWWA*.

CHAMBERLAIN, GEORGE AGNEW (1879–1966). Consul and author, born March 15, 1879, in São Paulo, Brazil, to American parents. Chamberlain graduated from Princeton University. He entered the consular service in 1904; was deputy consul general in Rio de Janiero from 1904 to 1906; consul at Pernambuco, Brazil, from 1906 to 1909; consul at Lourenço Marques, Mozambique, from 1909 to 1916; and consul general at Mexico City from 1917 to 1919. He resigned in 1919 and wrote popular fiction. He wrote *African Hunting among the Thongas* (New York, 1923) and the novel, *Two on Safari* (Indianapolis, 1935). Died March 4, 1966, in Salem, New Jersey. *References*: *NYT*. March 5, 1966; and *WWWA*.

CHAMPION, GEORGE (1810–1841). Missionary, born June 3, 1810, in Winchester, Connecticut. Champion graduated from Yale University, Dartmouth Medical College, and Andover Theological Seminary, and was ordained in 1834. He served as a missionary under the American Board of Commissioners for Foreign Missions (ABCFM)* in South Africa from 1834 to 1839. He established the first permanent mission in Natal for Zulus at Umlazi in 1836 and opened there the first school sponsored by an American mission in Africa. He later established the first mission station in Zululand and was the first missionary to preach regularly in the Zulu language. He left in 1838 because of a war between the Zulus and the Boers. He returned to the United States in 1839 and was a pastor in Dover, Massachusetts. Died December 17, 1841, in Santa Cruz, West Indies, while on a voyage for his health. His journals were published as *The Journal of an American Missionary in the Cape Colony*, ed. Alan R. Booth (Cape Town, 1968) and *Journal of the Rev. George Champion, American Missionary in Zululand, 1835–1839*, ed. Alan R. Booth (Cape Town, 1967). *References*: Edwards Family Papers, Sterling Memorial Library, Yale University, New Haven, Conn.; *AndoverTS*; Sarah E. Champion, *Rev. George Champion, Pioneer Missionary to the Zulus* (New Haven, Conn., 1896); *DASB* 3; and *SESA*.

CHANLER, WILLIAM ASTOR (1867–1934). Explorer, born June 11, 1867, in Newport, Rhode Island. Chanler attended Harvard University. He traveled and explored the region around Mt. Kilimanjaro in East Africa in 1888–1889. He explored East Africa again from 1892 to 1894, mapped the area, and wrote *Through Jungle and Desert: Travels in Eastern Africa* (London, 1896). He was member of the New York Assembly in 1897, a member of the U.S. House of Representatives from 1899 to 1901, and served in the Spanish-American War. He later had business interests in Mexico and Cuba, served in the Turkish Army in the war against Italy in 1912, and lived in Paris after 1912. He worked for the naval intelligence service in Paris during World War I. Died March 4, 1934, in Menton, France. *References*: William Astor Chanler Papers, New York Historical Society; *BDAC*; *NCAB* 25:279; *NYT*, March 5, 1934; Lately Thomas [pseud.], *Pride of Lions: The Astor Orphans: the Chanler Chronicle* (New York, 1971); and *WWWA*.

CHAPIN, JAMES P(AUL) (1889–1964). Ornithologist, born July 9, 1889, in New York City. Chapin graduated from Columbia University and served during World War I. He joined the American Museum of Natural History in 1905, was assistant on the Congo expedition from 1909 to 1915, assistant in the department of ornithology from 1915 to 1919, assistant curator from 1919 to 1923, associate curator from 1923 until his retirement in 1948, and research associate in African ornithology after 1948. He was a member of the Ruwenzori-Kivu expedition to East Africa and the Belgian Congo in 1926–1927, the expedition to the Congo River in 1930–1931, and the Congo Peacock expedition in 1937. He was a representative of the Office of Strategic Services (OSS) in the Belgian Congo and Asuncion Island in 1942. He made a final expedition to the Belgian Congo from 1953 to 1958 under the auspices of the Institut pour la Recherche Scientifique en Afrique Centrale (IRSAC). He wrote *The Birds of the Belgian Congo* (New York, 1932–1954). Died April 5, 1964, in New York City. *References*: *The Auk* 33 (1966): 247–52; *BCB* 7; *DAB* S7; *NYT*, April 7, 1964; J. K. Terres, "On the Trail of Congo Jim," *Audubon Magazine* 48 (July 1946): 230–38; and *WWWA*.

CHAPMAN, HELEN EMILY. See SPRINGER, HELEN EMILY CHAPMAN

CHASE, ISAAC (1803–1850). Merchant and consul, born November 6, 1803, probably in Rockingham County, New Hampshire. Chase owned a share of his brother's firm, Hezekiah Chase and Company of Boston, and worked there. He was consul in Cape Town from 1835 to 1847, and was involved in the protection of American whalers in Southern Africa and in commercial enterprises in Cape Town. He was agent for American insurance companies and the first large-scale importer of goods from the United States to South Africa. He published an article on the Hottentots and sent geological samples to the National Institution for the Promotion of Science in Washington, D.C. Died December 22, 1850, in New York City. *Reference*: *DASB* 3.

CHATELAIN, HÉLI (1859–1908). Missionary and linguist, born April 29, 1859, in Morat, Switzerland. Chatelain was in the United States from 1883 to 1885, studied theology in Bloomfield, New Jersey, and medicine in New York City, and became a United States citizen in the 1880s. He went to Loanda, Angola, in 1885 and served until 1889 as missionary and linguist for William Taylor's* Methodist mission. He returned to the United States in 1889, but was back in Angola in 1889–1890 as a guide and linguist for the American eclipse expedition, and was consul in Loanda in 1891–1892. He returned to the United States in 1893, organized the Philafrican Liberator's League, edited African terms and names in the *Standard Dictionary* and in the *Century Dictionary of Names*, and wrote *Kimbundu Grammar; Grammatica Elementar do Kimbundu ou Lingua de Angola* (Genebra, 1889) and *Folk-tales of Angola* (Boston, 1894). He was a missionary under the Philafrican League in Angola from 1897 until

44 CHEEK, LANDON N.

1908, and established a mission station in Lincoln in Central Angola. Died July 22, 1908, in Lausanne, Switzerland. *References*: Alida Chatelain and A. Roch, *Héli Chatelain, l'Ami de l'Angola* (Lausanne, 1918); and W. K. McNeil, "The First American Collectors of African Folklore," *Kentucky Folklore Record* 28 (1982): 40–47.

CHEEK, LANDON N. (1871- ?). Missionary, born December 8, 1871, in Canton, Madison County, Mississippi. Cheek attended a college in Jackson, Mississippi, and graduated from Western College (Macon, Miss.). He was missionary under the National Baptist Convention USA, Inc.* in Nyasaland from 1901 until 1906 and helped John Chilembwe establish the Providence Industrial Mission. He returned to the United States in 1906. He published his reminiscences in the September-October 1940 issue of the *Missionary Herald*.

CHESHAM, MARION (CAHER) (DONOGHUE) (EDWARDS) (1903–1973). Government official and philanthropist, born Marion Caher Donoghue in Philadelphia. She married John Compton, 4th Lord Chesham (1894–1952) in 1938. They settled in Tanganyika, but returned to England in 1939 and she served in the Auxiliary Territorial Service (ATS) and the American Red Cross during World War II. The couple went back to live in Tanganyika in 1946 because of Lord Chesham's health. She left Tanganyika after his death in 1952, but returned in 1956 and introduced coffee growing at Mafinga. She was a member of the Legislative Council and the National Assembly of Tanganyika for Iringa and became a citizen of Tanganyika in 1961. She founded the Community Development Trust Fund and was its executive director until 1971. Died September 6, 1973, in London. *Reference*: *Times* (London), September 8, 1973.

***CHESTER*, U.S.S.** Light cruiser. The *Chester* was sent in 1915 to the Liberian coast to rescue American missionaries and Liberian officials and to protect American interests during the Kru rebellion. Its commander, Captain Frank H. Schofield, was successful in mediating the end of the revolt in 1916. *Reference*: *DANFS*.

CHILDS, GLADWYN MURRAY (1896–1975). Missionary and anthropologist, born December 29, 1896, in Endeavor, Wisconsin. Childs graduated from Pomona College, Columbia University Teachers College, and Union Theological Seminary, and was ordained in 1923. He was missionary under the American Board of Commissioners for Foreign Missions (ABCFM)* in Angola. He was stationed at Bailundo, Angola, from 1925 to 1929, and at Sachikela, Angola, from 1929 to 1930. There he established the first college preparatory course for Africans and was religious editor. He was in charge of the station at Sachikela, Angola, after 1932. He wrote *Umbundu Kinship and Character; Being a Description of Social Structure and Individual Development of the Ovimbundu of Angola*

(London, 1949). After retiring from missionary work, he worked for the World Council of Churches in Lisbon, but sought to return to Angola to work on a prehistoric project. Died July 22, 1975, in Seattle, Washington. *References*: Gladwyn Murray Childs Papers, University of Washington Libraries, Seattle, Wash.

CHRISTIAN AND MISSIONARY ALLIANCE: FOREIGN DEPARTMENT. Formed in 1897 by the union of the Christian Alliance and the International Missionary Alliance, both of which were established in 1887. It began missionary work in the Cabinda Enclave in 1884, in Angola in 1907, in Guinea in 1918, in Mali and Upper Volta in 1924, in the Ivory Coast in 1930, and in Gabon in 1934. *References*: Christian and Missionary Alliance Records, A. B. Simpson Memorial Historical Library, Nyack College, Nyack, N. Y.; Robert B. Ekvall et al., *After Fifty Years: A Record of God's Working Through the Christian and Missionary Alliance* (Harrisburg, Pa., 1939); James H. Hunter, *Beside All Waters: The Story of Seventy Five Years of World-wide Ministry of the Christian and Missionary Alliance* (Harrisburg, Pa., 1964); and Grace A. Macaw, *Congo, the First Alliance Mission Field* (Harrisburg, Pa., 1937).

CHRISTIAN CHURCH (DISCIPLES OF CHRIST) IN THE USA AND CANADA: DIVISION OF OVERSEAS MINISTRIES. *See* UNITED CHRISTIAN MISSIONARY SOCIETY

CHRISTIAN REFORMED BOARD OF FOREIGN MISSIONS. Organized in 1888 by the Christian Reformed Church, it began missionary work in Nigeria in 1940, in Liberia in 1975, and in Sierra Leone in 1980. Its name was later changed to the Christian Reformed World Mission. *References*: Christian Reformed Church Archives, Heritage Hall, Calvin College and Seminary, Grand Rapids, Mich.; John C. De Krone, *To Who I Now Send Thee: Mission Work of the Christian Reformed Church in Nigeria* (Grand Rapids, Mich., 1945); and *EMCM*.

CHRISTIE, LANSDELL K(ISNER) (1903–1965). Mining company executive, born November 20, 1903, in Brooklyn, New York. Christie attended the United States Military Academy. He was engaged in the marine transport business in New York City and founded Christie Scow Company and served as its president until 1942. He served in the army during World War II and discovered Liberia's potential iron resources while serving in the United States Army Engineers. He founded the Liberian Mining Company* in 1946, became its president, secured a concession to develop the Bomi Hills region, and began developing the iron ore deposits. (The Republic Steel Company bought an 80 percent interest in the company in 1949.) He organized Monrovia Port Management Company and the National Iron Ore Company, in cooperation with the Liberian government. Died November 16, 1965, in Syosset, Long Island, New York. *References*: *NYT*, November 17, 1965; and *WWWA*.

CHURCH OF THE BRETHREN: FOREIGN MISSION COMMISSION.
Organized in 1908, it began missionary work in Nigeria in 1922. The name was
changed later to the World Ministries Commission. *References*: Church of the
Brethren Archives, Brethren Historical Library and Archives, Elgin, Ill.; *BE*;
and Elgin Moyer, *Missions in the Church of the Brethren; Their Development
and Effect upon the Denomination* (Elgin, Ill., 1931).

**CHURCH OF THE NAZARENE: DEPARTMENT OF FOREIGN MIS-
SIONS.** Organized in 1907 as an outgrowth of previous mission boards elected
by the individual holiness groups that united in 1907–1908 to form the Church
of the Nazarene. It began missionary work in Cape Verde Islands in 1907, in
Swaziland in 1910, in South Africa in 1919, and in Mozambique in 1922. It
later also did missionary work in Nyasaland, Southern and Northern Rhodesia,
and Namibia. The name was later changed to the World Mission Division.
References: Department of Foreign Mission Records, Church of the Nazarene
Archives, Kansas City, Mo.; Mendell Taylor and R. DeLong, *Fifty Years of
Nazarene Missions*, vol. 2 (Kansas City, Mo., 1958).

CLARK, JAMES L(IPPITT) (1883–1969). Naturalist, taxidermist, and animal
sculptor, born November 18, 1883, in Providence, Rhode Island. Clark graduated
from the Rhode Island School of Design. He joined the staff of the American
Museum of Natural History in 1902 as an animal sculptor, but resigned in 1908
to join A. Radclyffe Dugmore* in an expedition to Kenya, and was Carl Ethan
Akeley's* assistant there. He returned to the United States in 1910 and established
the James L. Clark Studios of Taxidermy. He made a second trip to Africa in
1922, and then became assistant to the director in charge of preparation at the
American Museum of Natural History, becoming assistant director in 1925; he
was vice director in charge of preparation and exhibits from 1931 until 1949.
He was also president of James L. Clark Studios, Inc., and of James L. Clark
Industrial Exhibits, Inc., from 1927 until 1940. He was leader of the Carlisle-
Clark African expedition in 1928, the O'Donnell-Clark African expedition in
1931, and the Central African expedition of the American Museum of Natural
History in 1947–1948. He also made expeditions to Southeast Asia, Mongolia,
and North America. He wrote his memoirs, *Good Hunting: Fifty Years of Col-
lecting and Preparing Habitat Groups for the American Museum* (Norman,
Okla., 1966). Died March 16, 1969, in New York City. *References*: *NCAB*
55:432; *NYT*, March 17, 1969; and *WWWA*.

CLARK, REED PAIGE (1878–1958). Consul, born August 19, 1878, in Lon-
donderry, New Hampshire. Clark graduated from Columbian (now George Washington) University and was admitted to the bar. He taught from 1898 to 1901
and was private secretary to Senator Henry Eben Burnham of New Hampshire
and clerk to various senate committees from 1901 to 1911. He was general
receiver of customs and financial adviser to the Liberian government from 1911

to 1916 and agent of a New York commercial house in Accra, the Gold Coast, in 1918–1919. He entered the consular service in 1919; was consul in Loanda, Angola, from 1919 to 1924; in Port Elizabeth, South Africa, in 1924–1925; and in Mexico City in 1925–1926; chargé d'affaires in Monrovia in 1926–1927; consul at Mexico City in 1927–1928; at Guadalajara, Mexico, in 1928–1929; at Santo Domingo in 1929–1930; at Belgrade from 1930 to 1936; first secretary in Vienna in 1936–1937; and consul at Victoria, British Columbia, from 1937 to 1943. Died September 5, 1958. *Reference*: *WWWA*.

CLARK, WALTER HALSEY (1832–1912). Missionary, born July 2, 1832, in Milton-on-the-Hudson, New York. Clark graduated from Williams College, Auburn and Union theological seminaries, and was ordained in 1859. He became a missionary under the American Board of Commissioners for Foreign Missions (ABCFM)* in Gabon in 1860, and joined the Corisco mission of the Board of Foreign Missions of the Presbyterian Church in the U.S.A.* in 1861. He translated portions of the New Testament into Benga. He returned to the United States in 1868, was pastor in Ponca, Elk Valley, and Daily Branch, Nebraska; school teacher in Silver Ridge, Nebraska, from 1878 to 1887; and was secretary and treasurer of Park College (Parkville, Mo.) from 1887 until his death. Died March 21, 1912. *Reference*: *Hewitt*.

CLARK AMENDMENT. An amendment passed overwhelmingly in both houses of Congress in 1976 and named after Senator Dick Clark (Democrat of Iowa), chair of the Senate's Subcommittee on Africa Affairs, which prohibited funding for covert operations in Angola and Zaire. The amendment was repealed in 1985.

CLARKE, GEORGE H(OBSON) (1867–1929) and **CLARKE, MARY LANE** (1872–1970). Missionaries. George Hobson Clarke was born November 20, 1867, in Bradwell-on-the-Sea, Essex, England. He came with his family to the United States in 1873, and grew up in Gerry, Chautauqua County, and Levant, New York. He was missionary under the Department of World Missions of the Wesleyan Methodist Church in Sierra Leone from 1893 until his death and founded the mission among the Limbas. He was founder of the Young Missionary Workers' Band (YMWB). Died January 27, 1929, in Sierra Leone. Mary Lane Clarke was born December 1, 1872, in Lyndon, New York, graduated from Houghton Seminary (Houghton, N.Y.), and was instructor there from 1895 to 1900. The couple was married in 1900. She was a missionary under the Department of World Missions of the Wesleyan Methodist Church of America* in Sierra Leone from 1900 to 1943 and from 1947 to 1951. She was cofounder of the YMWB and was its superintendent. She translated parts of the New Testament into the Limba language and compiled a Limba dictionary. She died May 4, 1970, in Cleveland, Tennessee. The Clarkes wrote *American Wesleyan Methodist*

Missions of Sierra Leone, West Africa (n.p., 1919). *References*: *The Wesleyan Methodist*, February 27, 1929; and *WWAW*.

CLARKE, ROGER (1899–1935). Missionary, born October 3, 1899, in Indianapolis. Clarke was a missionary under the Disciples of Christ in the Belgian Congo from 1927 until his death, served in the Disciples of Christ Congo Mission (DCCM) in Lotumbe, and was teacher at the Institut Chrétien in Bolenge after 1932. He represented his mission in the Protestant Council at Leopoldville in 1935. Died March 14, 1935, in Coquilhatville, Belgian Congo. *Reference*: *BCB* 2.

CLARKE, WILLIAM H(ENRY) (1829–1871). Missionary, born April 13, 1829, in Eatonton, Putnam County, Georgia. Clarke graduated from Mercer University. He was a missionary under the Foreign Missionary Board of the Southern Baptist Convention* in Nigeria from 1854 until 1860. He went to Ijaye, Yorubaland, in 1854, and was field leader of the Yoruba Baptist Mission from 1856 until 1860, when he resigned. He studied Yoruba country and society in detail and wrote *Travels and Explorations in Yorubaland 1854–1858*, ed. J. A. Atanda (Ibadan, Nigeria, 1972). He was later pastor in Dougherty and Baker Counties, Georgia. Died November 12, 1871, in Thomasville, Georgia.

CLAYTON, IDA MAY (1867–1932). Artist, born February 16, 1867, in California. Clayton was trained in the art school in Los Angeles. Her family moved to South Africa in 1885, and settled in Johannesburg in 1888. She concentrated on studies in watercolor, pastels, and crayon drawings, which have some historical significance. Died May 27, 1932, in Nylstroom, Transvaal. *Reference*: *DASB* 2.

CLEVELAND, RICHARD JEFFREY (1773–1860). Sea captain, born December 19, 1773, in Salem, Massachusetts. He went to sea at eighteen as captain's clerk and became a captain in 1797. In 1797–1798 he took a cutter sloop from Le Havre, France, to the Cape of Good Hope, and in 1800 sailed from Balasore Roads, near Calcutta, to Ile de France (Mauritius). He later made other voyages, and described his adventures in his *Narrative of Voyages and Commercial Enterprises* (Cambridge, 1842). He was vice consul in Havana from 1828 until 1833 and then lived in Burlington, New Jersey, and later in Danvers, Massachusetts. Died November 23, 1860, in Danvers, Massachusetts. *References*: *ACAB*; *DAB*; *NCAB* 24:100; Walter M. Teller, ed., *Five Sea Captains . . . : Their Own Accounts of Voyages under Sail* (New York, 1960), pp. 207–99; and *WWWA*.

COAN, JOSEPHUS ROOSEVELT (1902-   ). Clergyman and educator, born November 26, 1902, near Spartansburg, South Carolina. Coan graduated from Howard and Yale universities, Morris Brown College, and Hartford Theological

Seminary, and was ordained in 1932. He was pastor in Rhode Island and Georgia until 1936 and professor of psychology, philosophy, and religious education at Morris Brown College from 1934 to 1938. He was dean of the R. R. Wright School of Religion in Evaton, Transvaal, South Africa, from 1938 to 1947; superintendent of the Wilberforce Institute; and general superintendent of the African Methodist Episcopal Church* mission in South Africa from 1940 to 1947. He returned to the United States in 1947; he was professor at Morris Brown University from 1948 to 1962 and professor at the Interdenominational Theological Center (Atlanta) from 1959 to 1974. *References*: *DAS*; and *Who's Who in Religion* (Chicago, 1977).

COBB, FREEMAN (1830–1878). Coach proprietor, born October 10, 1830, in Brewster, Massachusetts. Cobb drove coaches for Adams & Company during the California gold rush. From 1854 until 1856 he ran a coach service in Australia, between Melbourne and the gold diggings. He returned to the United States in 1856 and was state senator in Massachusetts. He came to South Africa in 1871 and began coach service from Port Elizabeth to the diamond diggings in Kimberley. His venture failed in 1874. Died May 24, 1878, in Port Elizabeth. *References*: *DSAB* 3; and *SADNB*.

COCKERILL, WALTER B(ENJAMIN) (1866–1984). Missionary, born April 12, 1886, near Berlin, Wisconsin. Cockerill attended Milton Academy, was a cowboy in South Dakota, and taught school at Redgranite Junction, Wisconsin. He was a missionary under the Seventh-Day Baptists but at his own expense in Nyasaland in 1914–1915. He was witness to the native uprising of 1915 and later provided much source material for the book *Independent African: John Chilembwe and the Origins, Setting and Significance of the Nyasaland Native Rising in 1915* by George Shepperson and Thomas Price (Edinburgh, 1958). He was deported from Nyasaland by the British authorities in 1915, accused of teaching sedition to the natives. He farmed in Berlin, Wisconsin, from 1917 to 1939, and worked for Burdick Corporation in Milton Junction, Wisconsin, from 1944 until his retirement in 1977. Died May 9, 1984, in Janesville, Wisconsin. *References*: Walter B. Cockerill Papers, Wisconsin State Historical Society, Madison, Wis.; and *Sabbath Recorder* 206 (August 1984): 33.

CODERE, HELEN (FRANCES) (1917-   ). Anthropologist, born September 10, 1917, in Winnipeg, Manitoba, Canada. Codere came to the United States in 1919 and became a naturalized citizen in 1924. She graduated from the University of Minnesota and Columbia University. She was instructor, assistant professor, associate professor, and professor of anthropology at Vassar College from 1946 to 1963; professor of anthropology at Bennington College in 1963–1964; and at Brandeis University after 1964. She conducted field work in Rwanda in 1959–1960, wrote *The Biography of an African Society: Rwanda 1900–1960: Based on Forty-eight Rwandan Autobiographies* (Tervuren, Belgium, 1973), and described her experiences in Rwanda in *Women in the Field: Anthropological Experiences*, ed. Peggy Golde (Chicago, 1970), pp. 141–64. *References*: *AMWS*; *CA*; *WWA*; and *WWAW*.

COKER, DANIEL (1780–1846). Clergyman and colonial agent, born a slave in Baltimore County, Maryland. Coker escaped as a youth to New York. He taught in the African School in Baltimore from 1802 to 1816 and in the African Bethel School there from 1816 to 1820. He was ordained, and in 1816 was elected as the first bishop of the African Methodist Episcopal Church,* but declined the position. He went to Africa in 1820 with the first group of expatriated slaves sent out by the American Colonization Society,* and was agent of the society until 1821. He first settled in Liberia, but then went to Sierra Leone, settled there, and established a church in Freetown. He kept a diary of his experiences published as *The Journal of Daniel Coker, a Descendant of Africa . . . in the Ship Elizabeth, on a Voyage for Sherbro in Africa . . .* (Baltimore, 1820). Died in Freetown, Sierra Leone. *References*: Daniel Coker, "Journal," (1821), MS, Manuscript Division, Library of Congress; *DANB*; *Huberich*; and Matei Markwei, "The Rev. Daniel Coker of Sierra Leone," in *Black Apostles at Home and Abroad: Afro-Americans and the Christian Mission from the Revolution to Reconstruction*, ed. David W. Wills and Richard Newman (Boston, 1982), pp. 203–10.

COLES, JOHN J. (1856–1894). Missionary, from Virginia. Coles graduated from the Richmond Theological Seminary. He was missionary under the Baptist Foreign Mission Convention of the U.S.A. (later National Baptist Convention*) among the Vai in Liberia from 1883 to 1893. He wrote *Africa in Brief* (New York, 1886).

COLES, SAMUEL B(RACEY) ("SAM") (1888–1957). Missionary, born in Tilden, Alabama. Coles graduated from Talladega College (Ala.). He was missionary under the Congregational Christian Churches in Angola from 1923 until 1954, serving in the Galangue mission station, but was loaned to the Booker Washington Institute of Liberia* in 1935–1936. He was ordained in 1946. He returned to Angola in 1955 to build the Pestalozzi Children's Shelter, an agricultural and industrial school for abandoned or parentless children. He wrote *Preacher with a Plow* (Boston, 1957). Died March 9, 1957, in Queens, New York. *References*: Samuel B. Coles Papers, Talladega College Historical Collections, Savery Library, Talladega College, Talladega, Ala.; and *NYT*, March 14, 1957.

COLLEGE OF WEST AFRICA. The oldest school in Liberia. Opened in 1838 by the Methodist mission as the Liberia Conference seminary, it functioned mostly as a primary school. It was later renamed Monrovia Seminary. It was reorganized in 1898 as the College of West Africa and included collegiate, theological, industrial, and normal departments. It was reorganized again in the 1920s as a high school. *Reference*: *EWM*.

COLLEY, WILLIAM W. (1847–1909). Missionary, born February 12, 1847, in Prince Edward County, Virginia. Colley graduated from the Richmond Theological Seminary. He was missionary under the the Foreign Mission Board of the Southern Baptist Convention* in Nigeria from 1875 to 1879. He returned to the United States in 1879, and traveled through the South for the Foreign Mission Board of the Virginia Baptist State Convention to interest black Baptists in the foreign mission enterprise, and was corresponding secretary for the Baptist Foreign Mission Convention in 1881–1882. He went to Liberia in 1883 as one of the first missionaries of the Baptist Foreign Mission Convention of the U.S.A. (later the National Baptist Convention, U.S.A., Inc.*), and headed the mission among the Vai in Liberia from 1883 to 1909. Died December 24, 1909, in Winston-Salem, North Carolina. *Reference*: Lewis G. Jordan, *Negro Baptist History U.S.A. 1750–1930* (Nashville, Tenn., n.d.).

COLLINS, GUY N. (1872–1938). Botanist, born August 9, 1872, in Mertensia, New York. Collins graduated from Syracuse University. He conducted explorations in Liberia for the New York Colonization Society from 1891 to 1897, working on settlement problems for American blacks who were sent to Africa. He served as assistant botanist in the Bureau of Plant Industry of the United States Department of Agriculture from 1901 to 1910, botanist from 1910 to 1920, and botanist in charge of biophysical investigations after 1920. He introduced the avocado to the United States. Died August 14, 1938, in Lanham, Maryland. *References*: *DAB* S2; *NYT*, August 16, 1938; and *WWWA*.

COLSON, ELIZABETH FLORENCE (1917-   ). Anthropologist, born June 15, 1917, in Hewitt, Minnesota. Colson graduated from the University of Minnesota and Radcliffe College. She was a research officer of the Rhodes-Livingstone Institute in Northern Rhodesia in 1946–1947 and its director from 1947 to 1951. She was senior lecturer at Manchester University from 1951 to 1953; associate professor at Goucher College in 1954–1955; research associate at the African Research Program, Boston University, from 1955 to 1959; professor of anthropology at Brandeis University from 1959 to 1963; and at the University of California at Berkeley after 1964. She wrote *The Makah* (Manchester, England, 1953); *Marriage and the Family among the Plateau Tonga* (Manchester, England, 1958), and *Social Organization of the Gwembe Tonga* (Manchester, England, 1960). *References*: *African Social Research* 24 (December 1977): 341–42; *WWA*; and *WWAW*.

COLSON, EVERETT A(NDREW) (1885–1937). Financial adviser, born in Warren, Maine. Colson graduated from Georgetown University College of Law. He entered the consular service in 1904 and served in the Philippines from 1904 to 1909, and in Canton, China, from 1909 to 1911. He was an employee of the Civil Service Commission in Washington, D.C.; returned to the Philippines in 1915 as director of its Civil Service Commission; served as auditor of the War Department in France during World War I; and was financial adviser in Port au Prince, Haiti, from 1920 until 1930. He was financial adviser in Ethiopia, was confidential adviser on financial matters and foreign matters to Emperor Haile Selassie from 1930 to 1936, assisted the emperor during the Italo-Ethiopian War, and wrote his speeches, radio broadcasts, state papers, and the notes to the League of Nations. He remained in Ethiopia until January 1936. Died February 23, 1937, in Washington, D.C. *References*: *NYT*, February 24, 1937; and *Washington Herald*, February 25, 1937.

CONGO COMPANY. Formally the United States and Congo National Emigration Company, chartered in 1886, and in 1894 transported a colony of black Americans to Liberia. *Reference*: Edwin S. Redkey, *Black Exodus: Black Nationalist and Back-to-Africa Movements, 1890–1910* (New Haven, Conn., 1969), ch. 7.

CONGO INLAND MISSION. Founded in 1911 as the United Mennonite Board of Missions by the United Mission Board of the Central Conference of Mennonites and the Defenseless Mennonite Church (later Evangelical Mennonite Church). It established the mission on the Kasai River in the south central Belgian Congo and changed its name to the Congo Inland Mission in 1912. The mission properties and rights were officially transferred to the Zaire church in 1971. The mission was then renamed the Africa Inter-Mennonite Mission and expanded its work to Lesotho in 1973, to Botswana in 1975, to Burkina Faso in 1978, and to the Transkei, South Africa, in 1982. *References*: Congo Inland Mission Records, Mennonite Historical Library, Bluffton College Library, Bluffton, Ohio; *BE*; Melvin J. Loewen, *Three Score* (Elkhurst, Ind., 1972); and William B. Weaver, *Thirty Five Years in the Congo: A History of the Demonstrations of Divine Power in the Congo* (Chicago, 1945).

CONSTRUCTIVE ENGAGEMENT POLICY. United States policy toward South Africa adopted in 1981 by the administration of President Ronald Reagan. To protect the economic and strategic interests of the United States, the policy emphasized the need for stability in the region and was willing to give the South African government time to implement limited change in its policies toward its Black citizens. *References*: Christopher Coker, *The United States and South Africa, 1968–1985: Constructive Engagement and Its Critics* (Durham, N.C., 1986); and Ann Seidman, *The Roots of Crisis in Southern Africa* (Trenton, N.J., 1985).

COOK, ORATOR F(ULLER) (1867–1949). Botanist, born May 28, 1867, in Clyde, New York. Cook graduated from Syracuse University. He was special agent of the New York Colonization Society in Liberia from 1891 to 1898, established an industrial department in Liberia College, and served as its president from 1896 to 1898. He was in charge of seed and plant introduction and of tropical agricultural investigations in the United States Department of Agriculture from 1898 until 1934, and served in the division of plant exploration and introduction from 1934 to 1937. Died April 23, 1949, in Lanham, Maryland. *References*: Orator F. Cook Papers, Joseph Regenstein Library, University of Chicago; *NCAB* 38:369; and *WWWA*.

COOKE, CALEB (1836–1880). Naturalist, born February 5, 1836, in Salem, Massachusetts. Cooke studied under Louis Agassiz at Harvard University. He became curator in the natural history department of the Essex Institute in 1856 and was its cabinet-keeper from 1857 to 1860. He was sent by Agassiz to Para, Brazil, in 1859, and to East Africa in 1860. He studied the natural history of Zanzibar and Madagascar from 1861 to 1865, where he collected natural history specimens for the Museum of Comparative Zoology of Harvard University. He returned to the United States in 1865, and was assistant on the staff of the Peabody Academy of Science in Salem from 1867 until 1875, and curator of mollusca from 1875 until his death. Died June 5, 1880, in Salem, Massachusetts. *References*: Caleb Cooke, Journal, MS, Essex Institute, Salem, Mass.; and Ralph W. Dexter, "Peabody Academy's Caleb Cooke, the Devoted," *The Biologist* 52 (1970): 112–19.

COOLEY, ROBERT ALLEN (1873–1968). Entomologist, born June 27, 1873, in South Deerfield, Massachusetts. Cooley graduated from Massachusetts Agricultural College (later the University of Massachusetts). He was professor of zoology and entomology at Montana State College (later Montana State University) from 1899 until 1931, state entomologist of Montana from 1903 to 1933, and entomologist in the Montana Agricultural Experiment Station (Bozeman). He was senior entomologist at the United States Public Health Service Rocky Mountain Laboratory in Hamilton, Montana, from 1931 until his retirement in 1946, one of the first scientists to study the Rocky Mountain spotted fever tick, and an innovator in the control of agricultural insect pests. He went to the Transvaal and to Orange Free State, South Africa, in 1928–1929, to collect and study the natural enemies of the tick on the veld. Died November 17, 1968, in Hamilton, Montana. *References*: *Journal of Economic Entomology* 62 (August 1969): 972; *NCAB* 54:270; *NYT*, November 20, 1968; and *WWWA*.

COPPIN, LEVI JENKINS (1848–1924). Clergyman and missionary, born free December 24, 1848, in Frederick Town, Maryland. Coppin studied at the Protestant Episcopal Divinity School (West Philadelphia), was ordained in 1877, and was city missionary in Philadelphia, pastor in Philadelphia and Baltimore, and editor of the *A.M.E. Church Review* from 1888 to 1896. He was elected bishop of the African Methodist Episcopal Church* in 1900, and was resident bishop in South Africa, residing in Cape Town from 1900 to 1904. He returned to the United States in 1904 and served as bishop until his death. He wrote *Observations of Persons and Things in South Africa, 1900–1904* (Philadelphia, n.d.) and an autobiography, *Unwritten History* (Philadelphia, 1919). Died June 25, 1924, in Philadelphia. *References*: *DANB*; *EWM*; *NCAB* 3:146; *WWCR*; and *WWWA*.

COTHEAL, ALEXANDER I(SAAC) (1804–1894). Merchant, born November 5, 1804, in New York City. Cotheal was a member of his father's shipping firm from 1836 to 1849, and became interested in East Africa during the visit of *al-Sultanah*, the first Zanzibari vessel to arrive in the United States, which landed in New York in 1840. His father's death in 1849 resulted in the dissolution of the firm, and he spent three years traveling in the East. In the 1850s he tried to establish a trading center on the Juba River in southern Somalia, without success. He was later a founder and president of the American Ethnological Society. He went to Nicaragua in 1852 and was the consul general of Nicaragua in New York City from 1871 until his death. Died February 25, 1894, in New York City. *Reference*: *NCAB* 1:322.

COULTER, CHARLES WELLSLEY (1884–1968). Sociologist, born February 14, 1884, in Lampton, Ontario, Canada. Coulter graduated from the University of Toronto, Victoria College, and Yale University; studied at the University of Chicago, and was ordained in 1909. He served as pastor in Waterbury and Derby, Connecticut; was assistant professor at Western Reserve University 1914 to 1923, and professor of sociology at Ohio Wesleyan University 1923 to 1945. He was in South Africa in 1929–1930 where he took part in the investigations of the Carnegie Commission, and in 1932–1933 he conducted sociological investigations for the National Industrialization Survey of Central Africa. He was head of the department of sociology at the University of New Hampshire from 1935 to 1953, and member of the New Hampshire Prison Board and Board of Parole. Died June 23, 1968, in Sarasota, Florida. *References*: *AMWS*; and *WWWA*.

COWLES, R(AYMOND) B(RIDGMAN) (1896–1975). Naturalist and ecologist, born December 1, 1896, in Natal, South Africa, to American parents. Cowles graduated from Pomona College and Cornell University. He was assistant professor, associate professor, and professor at the University of California at Los Angeles from 1930 until his retirement in 1963. He conducted investigations in South and East Africa from 1925 to 1927 and wrote *Zulu Journal: Field Notes of a Naturalist in South Africa* (Berkeley, Calif., 1959), in which he described the disastrous effects of overgrazing on an African valley. Died December 7, 1975, in Santa Barbara, California. *Desert Journal: Reflections of a Naturalist* (coauthored with Elena S. Bakker) (Berkeley, Calif., 1978), was published posthumously. *References*: *AMWS*; *CA;* and *The Washington Post*, December 12, 1975.

COX, MELVILLE B(EVERIDGE) (1799–1833). Missionary, born November 9, 1799, in Hallowell, Maine. Cox served as Methodist minister in Exeter, New Hampshire, and Raleigh, Virginia; settled in Baltimore in 1827; edited *The Itinerant* from 1827 to 1829; and was again minister in Raleigh, Virginia, in 1831–1832. He came to Liberia in 1833 as the first foreign missionary of the Board of Foreign Missions of the Methodist Episcopal Church.* He made a survey of the religious situation in Monrovia and was superintendent of the Methodist Mission in Liberia. Died July 21, 1833, in Monrovia. *References*: *ACAB*; G. F. Cox, *Remains of Melville B. Cox, Missionary to Liberia with a Memoir* (Boston, 1835); *EWM*; and *LC*.

CRILE, GEORGE (WASHINGTON) (1864–1943). Physician and hunter, born November 11, 1864, near Chili, Ohio. Crile graduated from Northwestern Ohio Normal School (later Ohio Northern University) and the University of Wooster Medical School. He served in the Spanish-American War and World War I, practiced medicine in Cleveland, was clinical professor at the Western Reserve School of Medicine from 1900 to 1911, and professor of surgery there from 1911 to 1924. He was founder of the Cleveland Clinic and was its chief surgeon and president. He went on a safari to East Africa in 1927. He returned to East Africa in 1935, set up a laboratory at Maji Moto, Kenya, and collected and dissected animals to study the comparative anatomy of their neuroendocrine systems. Died January 7, 1943. His wife **GRACE (MCBRIDE) CRILE** (1876–1948), was born January 23, 1876, in Cleveland. She accompanied her husband on the expeditions to Africa and wrote *Skyways to a Jungle Laboratory: An African Adventure* (New York, 1936). She also edited *George Crile: An Autobiography, ed. with Sidelights by Grace Crile* (Philadelphia, 1947). She died August 23, 1948. *References*: *DAB* S3; *DAMB* 1984; *NCAB* 31:10; *NYT*, January 8, 1943; *OAB*; and *WWWA*.

CROSSROADS AFRICA, OPERATION. Private, not-for-profit organization, conceived and founded by James Herman Robinson* in 1957 and put into operation in 1958, to give American and Canadian students the experience of living and working alongside Africans in the independent countries of Africa. *References*: Operation Crossroads Africa Archives, Amistad Research Center, New Orleans, La.; C. H. Hall, "Operation Crossroads Gets to the Heart of Africa," *Reader's Digest* 93 (July 1968): 159–64; Harold R. Isaacs, *Emergent Americans: A Report on "Crossroads Africa"* (New York, 1961); and Ruth R. Plimpton, *Operation Crossroads Africa* (New York, 1962).

CRUM, WILLIAM DEMOS (1859–1912). Government official and diplomat, born near Orangeburg, South Carolina. Crum attended the University of South Carolina and graduated from Howard University Medical School. He practiced medicine in Charleston from 1881 to 1910 and was collector of customs for the port of Charleston from 1904 until 1910. He was minister resident and consul general to Liberia from 1910 to 1912. He sought vigorously to aid Liberia in settling the republic's boundary difficulties and financial crises. In 1909, following the report of Emmett Jay Scott,* the United States decided to establish, in effect, a protectorate over Liberia, and Crum's efforts had little effect. Died November 1912, in Charleston, South Carolina. *References*: *DANB*; Willard B. Gatewood, Jr., "Square Deal for Dr. Crum," in *Theodore Roosevelt and the Art of Controversy: Episodes of the White House Years* (Baton Rouge, 1970), pp. 90–134; *NYT*, December 8, 1912; and *WWWA*.

CRUMMELL, ALEXANDER (1819–1898). Missionary, clergyman, and educator, born free in New York City. Crummell studied theology and was ordained in 1844. He was pastor in New York City and then lived in England from 1848 to 1853 and studied at Queen's College, Cambridge. He went to Liberia in 1853 as missionary under the Domestic and Foreign Missionary Society of the Protestant Episcopal Church in the United States of America* and was a minister in Monrovia. He became master of Mount Vaughn High School at Cape Palmas in 1858, and a member of the faculty of Liberia College, Monrovia, in 1861. He was dismissed in 1866 because of long-standing differences with the school administration, and tried to establish his own school. He returned to the United States in 1872, and was minister in Washington, D.C., from 1873 until his retirement in 1894. Died September 10, 1898, in Red Bank, New Jersey. *References*: Alexander Crummell Papers, Schomburg Center for Research in Black Culture, New York City; M. B. Akpan, "Alexander Crummell and His African 'Racework': An Assessment of His Contributions in Liberia to African 'Redemption,' " *Historical Magazine of the Protestant Episcopal Church* 45 (1976): 177–99 (reprinted in *Black Apostles at Home and Abroad: Afro-Americans and the Christian Mission from the Revolution to Reconstruction*, ed. David W. Wills and Richard Newman [Boston, 1982], pp. 283–310); *DANB*; *DARB*; *Davis*; Luckson B. Ejofodomi, "The Missionary Career of Alexander Crummell in Liberia: 1853 to 1873," Ph.D. diss., Boston University, 1974; Wilson J. Moses, "Civilizing Missionary: A Study of Alexander Crummell," *JNH* 60 (1975): 229–51; Wilson J. Moses, *The Golden Age of Black Nationalism 1850–1925* (Hamden, Conn., 1978), ch. 3; *NCAB* 5:553; Gregory U. Rigby, *Alexander Crummell: Pioneer in Nineteenth-Century Pan-African Thought* (Westport, Conn., 1987); and Kathleen Wahle, "Alexander Crummell: Black Evangelist and Pan-Negro Nationalist," *Phylon* 29 (1968): 388–95.

CUFFE, PAUL (1759–1817). Merchant, shipowner, and leader in the early movement for the settlement of blacks from the United States in Sierra Leone, born on the island of Cuttyhunk, opposite New Bedford, Massachusetts, and grew up in Westport, Massachusetts. Cuffe became involved in whaling, coastal shipping, and foreign trade, and amassed a fortune. He made an exploratory trip to Sierra Leone from 1810 to 1812 and a second trip to Sierra Leone in 1815 during which his ship, the *Traveller*, carried thirty-eight settlers. He wrote *A Brief Account of the Settlement and Present Situation of the Colony of Sierra Leone in Africa* (New York, 1812). Died September 7, 1817, in Westport, Massachusetts. *References*: Paul Cuffe Papers, New Bedford Free Public Library, New Bedford, Mass.; Paul Cuffe Papers, Old Dartmouth Historical Society Whaling Museum, New Bedford, Mass.; *DAB*; *DANB*; ''An American's Impressions of Sierra Leone in 1811,'' ed. Sheldon H. Harris *JNH* 47 (1962): 35–41; *Huberich*; Sally Loomis, ''The Evolution of Paul Cuffe's 'Black Nationalism,' '' in *Black Apostles at Home and Abroad: Afro-Americans and the Christian Mission from the Revolution to Reconstruction*, ed. David W. Wills and Richard Newman (Boston, 1982), pp. 191–202; Floyd J. Miller, *The Search for Black Nationality: Black Emigration and Colonization 1787–1863* (Urbana, Ill., 1975), ch. 2; Henry N. Sherwood, *Paul Cuffe, Black America and the African Return* (New York, 1972); Lamont D. Thomas, *Rose to Be a People: A Biography of Paul Cuffe* (Urbana, Ill., 1986); and *WWWA*.

CURTIS, JOSEPH STORY (1845–1918). Mining geologist, born in Boston. Curtis graduated from Harvard University and studied in Paris and the Freiberg School of Mines in Saxony. He came to Johannesburg in 1887 as geologist for Hermann Eckstein & Company, and made an intensive geological study of the gold-bearing land in the Witwatersrand. He was elected in 1894 to serve on the South African Chamber of Mines. He became a noted racehorse breeder in the Transvaal. He joined the Reform Committee* and was arrested after the Jameson Raid in 1896, but was never tried. He later became managing director of the Transvaal Corporation Limited. He went to England in 1899, where he lost his considerable fortune. He was back in the Transvaal in 1902 and died in poverty. Died July 6, 1918, in Johannesburg. *Reference*: *DASB* 4.

CUSHMAN, MARY FLOYD (1870–1965). Medical missionary, born July 24, 1870, in Boston. Cushman graduated from Eastern State Normal School (Castine, Me.) and Boston University School of Medicine. She practiced medicine in Farmington, Maine, from 1893 until 1922. She was a medical missionary under the American Board of Commissioners for Foreign Missions (ABCFM)* in the Angola mission at Chilesso from 1922 to 1942 and from 1946 to 1953 and established a hospital there. She wrote an autobiography, *Missionary Doctor: The Story of Twenty Years in Africa* (New York, 1944). Died September 25, 1965, in Laconia, New Hampshire. *References*: *Laconia* (N.H.) *Evening Citizen*, September 27, 1965; and *NYT*, October 11, 1965.

CUTTINGTON COLLEGIATE AND DIVINITY SCHOOL. Founded in 1889 in Harper, Maryland County, Liberia, by the Domestic and Foreign Missionary Society of the Protestant Episcopal Church in the United States of America* and operated as a high school and school of theology. It was closed in 1929, but was reopened in 1949 as the Cuttington College and Divinity School in Suakoko, Liberia. The name was changed later to Cuttington University College, and it was administered and financed by the Episcopalian Church. *Reference*: Yorke Allen, *A Seminary Survey* (New York, 1960).

CUYLER, JACOB GLEN (1775–1854). Soldier, landdrost (magistrate), and farmer, born August 20, 1775, in Albany, New York. Cuyler immigrated to Canada in 1781 with his loyalist family and was educated in Canada. He joined the British Army in 1799, came to South Africa in 1806 with the British expedition under the command of Sir David Baird, and took part in the capture and occupation of the cape. In 1806 he became landdrost of the district of Uitenhage and principal magistrate and commandant of Fort Frederick. Died April 14, 1854, in Uitenhage, South Africa. *References*: *DSAB* 1; and *SESA*.

D

DABNEY, JOHN BASS (1766–1826). Merchant and consul, born December 13, 1766, in Boston. Dabney first visited Fayal, Azores, in 1795 and settled there in 1804. He was consul in Fayal from 1806 until his death. Died September 2, 1826, in Fayal. His son, **CHARLES WILLIAM DABNEY** (1794–1871), was born March 19, 1794, in Alexandria, Virginia. He was employed in the counting house of T. B. Wales & Company of Boston from 1810 to 1813 and in his father's counting house in Fayal from 1813 to 1826. On his father's death, Charles William succeeded to his shipping business and to the consulate, and served as consul in Fayal from 1826 to 1870. He built a commercial enterprise in Fayal and during the political trouble of 1830 in Portugal he acted as mediator between the factions in the islands. He was known in the Azores as "father of the poor" because of his benefactions. Died March 12, 1871, in Fayal, Azores. **WILLIAM HENRY DABNEY** (1817–1888), son of John Bass Dabney, was born May 25, 1817, in Fayal, went to school in Waltham, Massachusetts, returned to Fayal in 1832, and was employed in the counting house of his brother. William Henry was vice consul in the island of Terceira from 1844 to 1848 and consul general in Tenerife, the Canary Islands, from 1862 to 1882. He wrote *Sketch of the Dabneys of Virginia, with Some of Their Family Records* (Chicago, 1888). Died February 16, 1888, in Boston. **SAMUEL WYLLYS DABNEY** (1826–1893), son of Charles William Dabney, was born January 6, 1826, in Fayal, and became a clerk in his father's office. Samuel Wyllys was deputy consul and then consul in Fayal from 1872 to 1892. He returned to the United States in 1892. Died December 26, 1893, in San Diego, California. *References*: *ACAB*; Roxana L. Dabney, comp., *Annals of the Dabney Family in Fayal* (Boston, 1899); Alice F. Howland, *The Descendents of John Bass Dabney and Roxana Lewis Dabney 1766–1966* (Milton, Mass., 1966); *NCAB* 4:474; Francis M. Rogers, *Atlantic Islanders of the Azores and Madeiras* (North Quincy, Mass., 1979), ch. 8; and *WWWA*.

DALE, **U.S.S.** Sloop of war. From 1850 to 1859, the *Dale* made three extended cruises along the African coast to suppress the slave trade. Commanded by Commodore William Pearson, in 1851 it bombarded the fort of Sultan Selim of Johanna (Anjouan), one of the Comoro Islands, to secure reparations for the imprisonment of Captain Moores (or Mooers) in Anjouan in 1850. *References*: *DANFS*; Kenneth R. Stevens, "Of Whaling Ships and Kings: The Johanna Bombardment of 1851," *Prologue: Journal of the National Archives* 18 (1986): 241–49.

DANIELSON, ELMER R(EINHOLD) (1903-   ). Missionary, born May 22, 1903, in Meriden, Connecticut. Danielson graduated from Upsala College and Mt. Airy and Augustana seminaries, and was ordained in 1928. He was a missionary under the Board of Foreign Missions of the Augustana Lutheran Church in America* in Tanganyika from 1928 until 1968. He wrote *Stars Over Africa* (Rock Island, Ill., 1953), *Gateway to Sonjo* (Rock Island, Ill., 1959), and *Forty Years with Christ in Tanzania 1928–1968* (New York, 1977). *Reference*: George F. Hall, *The Missionary Spirit in the Augustana Church* (Rock Island, Ill., 1984), ch. 21.

DARLING, SAMUEL TAYLOR (1872–1925). Pathologist and authority on tropical medicine, born April 6, 1872, in Harrison, New Jersey, and grew up in Pawtucket, Rhode Island. Darling was first a pharmacist and then graduated from the College of Physicians and Surgeons (Baltimore). He was chief of laboratories of the Isthmian Canal Commission from 1906 to 1915. He went with Willian Crawford Gorgas* to South Africa and Rhodesia in 1913–1914 to investigate the sanitary conditions of the Rand mines. He was on the staff of the International Health Board from 1915 to 1918, investigating anemia in Fiji, Java, and Malaya; professor of hygiene and director of laboratories of hygiene at the medical school of São Paulo, Brazil, from 1918 to 1921; and director of the field laboratories for research in malaria under the International Health Board of the Rockefeller Foundation in Leesburg, Georgia, from 1922 until his death. Killed May 20, 1925, in a motor accident near Beirut, Lebanon. *References*: *ACAB*; *DAB*; *DAMB*; *NCAB* 19:417; *NYT*, May 23, 1925; and *WWWA*.

DARLINGTON, CHARLES F(RANCIS) (1904–1986). Government official and diplomat, born September 13, 1904, in New York City. Darlington graduated from Harvard University and studied at Oxford University and the University of Geneva. He was a member of the League of Nations secretariat in Geneva from 1929 to 1931, member of the central banking department of the International Bank for Settlements in Basel from 1931 to 1934, assistant chief of the trade agreements division of the U.S. Department of State in Washington from 1935 to 1939, and foreign exchange manager of overseas operations of the General Motors Corporation in New York City in 1940–1941. He served in the navy during World War II. He was employed by Socony Vacuum Oil Company from

1946 to 1961, was chairman of Standard Fuel Oil Company from 1949 to 1953, vice president of Socony Vacuum Overseas Supply Company from 1952 to 1956, and vice president and then president of Near East Development Corporation from 1953 to 1958. He was the first ambassador to Gabon from 1961 to 1964, and coauthored (with his wife) *African Betrayal* (New York, 1968), an eyewitness account of Gabon's political evolution. *References*: *WWA*; and *WWE*.

DAVID, WILLIAM JOSHUA (1850–1919). Missionary, born September 28, 1850, near Meridian, Mississippi. David attended Mississippi College and graduated from Crozier Theological Seminary. He was missionary under the Foreign Mission Board of the Southern Baptist Convention* in Nigeria from 1875 until 1889, the first representative of the board in Africa after the Civil War. He constructed the first Baptist church in Lagos, Nigeria. He was later pastor in Meridian, Mississippi; Pine Bluff, Arkansas; and Bellville and Woodland, Texas. Died June 25, 1919, in Bellville, Texas. *References*: *ESBS*; George W. Sadler, "William Joshua David," in *Builders of a New Africa*, comp. Nan F. Weeks (Nashville, Tenn., 1944), pp. 31–52.

DAVIDSON, H(ANNAH) FRANCES (1860–1935). Missionary, born near Smithville, Ohio. Davidson graduated from Kalamazoo College (Mich.) and the University of Chicago. She taught at McPherson College (Kansas) until 1897, when she went to Africa as a missionary under the Brethren in Christ Foreign Missions* and helped found Matopo mission in Southern Rhodesia. She traveled to Northern Rhodesia with Adda Engle Taylor (see Myron Taylor*) in 1906 and founded the Macha mission, near Choma. She returned to the United States in 1924 and taught at Messiah Bible College (now Messiah College) in Harrisburg, Pennsylvania, until her retirement in 1932. She wrote *South and South Central Africa: A Record of Fifteen Years' Missionary Labors among Primitive Peoples* (Elgin, Ill., 1915). Died December 11, 1935, in Abelene, Kansas. *References*: *BE*; *Engle*; and E. Morris Sider, *Nine Portraits: Brethren in Christ Biographical Sketches* (Nappanee, Ind., 1978), pp. 159–212.

DAVIS, CARL RAYMOND (1874–1956). Mining engineer, born January 12, 1874, in Cleveland, Ohio. Davis graduated from the Colorado School of Mines. He was general superintendent of Centre Star and Star Eagle Mines in Rossland, British Columbia, from 1900 to 1904. He went to South Africa in 1905 and was general manager of the Lancaster Gold Mining Company and the Lancaster West Gold Mining Company in Krugersdorf district, Transvaal, from 1905 to 1911, and general manager of the Brakpan Mines Limited from 1911 to 1918. He served as technical director and consulting engineer to the Anglo-American Corporation of South Africa Limited and its subsidiary companies from 1918 to 1928. He was sent to the Copperbelt in Northern Rhodesia in 1923 and submitted optimistic reports about it. He was director of the Anglo-American Corporation of South Africa and resided in London, from 1928 until 1949. Died January 16,

1956, in Cape Town, South Africa. *References*: *NYT*, January 17, 1956; and *The Times* (London), January 18, 1956.

DAVIS, REES ALFRED (1855–1940). Horticulturist and fruit expert, born in Chepstow, Monmouthshire, England. He came to the United States, worked in California, helped to start the Co-operative Fruit Growers' Association, and became an authority on citrus culture. He went to South Africa in 1898, after being invited to manage orchards belonging to Cecil Rhodes. He became government horticulturist for the Transvaal in 1902. He wrote *Citrus-growing in South Africa: Oranges, Lemons, Naartjes, etc.* (Pretoria, 1919), *Citrus-growing in South Africa* (Cape Town, 1924), and *Fruit-growing in South Africa* (Johannesburg, 1928). *Reference*: *SADNB*.

DAVIS, RICHARD HARDING (1864–1916). Journalist, born April 18, 1864, in Philadelphia. Davis graduated from Lehigh and Johns Hopkins universities. He was a reporter for the *Philadelphia Record* and then the *Philadelphia Press* from 1886 to 1889, the New York *Evening Sun* from 1889 to 1891, and managing editor of the *Harper's Weekly* from 1891 to 1893. He became famous as war correspondent and novelist of adventure-style fiction. He reported on the South African War and wrote *With Both Armies in South Africa* (New York, 1900). In 1907 he made a trip to the Congo Free State to investigate the reported atrocities and wrote *The Congo and Coasts of Africa* (New York, 1907). Died April 12, 1916, in Mount Kisco, New York. *References*: *ACAB*; *DADH*; *DLB*; Fairfax Downey, *Richard Harding Davis: His Day* (New York, 1948); *EAJ*; Gerald Langford, *The Richard Harding Davis Years* (New York, 1961); *NCAB* 8:176; *NYT*, April 13, 1916; Scott C. Osborn and Robert L. Phillips, Jr., *Richard Harding Davis* (Boston, 1978); and *WWWA*.

DAVIS, WILLIAM E(LLSWORTH) (1896–1987). Medical missionary, born December 30, 1896, in Morton, Oregon. Davis attended Lynchburg (Va.) College, College of Mission, and Butler University. He graduated from Whitman College (Walla Walla, Wash.) and Northwestern University Medical School, and studied at the London School of Tropical Medicine and the University of Grenoble. He served as a marine pilot in World War I. He was a missionary under the Foreign Christian Missionary Society (see United Christian Missionary Society*) in the Belgian Congo from 1928 until 1938. He was stationed at Wema, where he built a hospital, and later in Lotumbe. He returned to the United States in 1938, and practiced medicine in North Middletown, Kentucky, until 1958, was public health officer for several central Kentucky counties, and medical director of a health district from 1974 until 1983. He wrote *Ten Years in the Congo* (New York, 1938), *Caring and Curing in the Congo and Kentucky* (North Middletown, Ky., 1984), and *Water under the Bridge* (North Middletown, Ky., 1985?). Died April 2, 1987, near North Middletown, Kentucky. *References*: *CB* 1940; and *Lexington* (Ky.) *Herald-Leader*, April 3, 1987.

DAY, DAVID A(LEXANDER) (1851–1897). Missionary, born February 17, 1851, near Dillsburg, Adams County, Pennsylvania. Day served in the Civil War as a youth, attended Missionary Institute (now Susquehanna University, Selinsgrove, Pa.) and was ordained in 1874. He was a missionary under Foreign Missionary Society of the Lutheran Church and served in the Muhlenberg Mission in Liberia from 1874 to 1897. He organized schools and industrial operations, and had a small steamboat built, the first steam vessel to navigate the St. Paul River. Died December 17, 1897, aboard a ship on his way to the United States. *References*: David A. Day Papers, Abdel Ross Wentz Library, Lutheran Theological Seminary, Gettysburg, Pa.; *DAB*; *LC*; and *WWWA*.

DEAN, WILLIAM HENRY, JR. (1910–1952). Economist, born July 6, 1910, in Lynchburg, Virginia. Dean graduated from Bowdoin College and Harvard University. He was on the faculty of Atlanta University from 1933 to 1942, served in the Office of Price Administration from 1942 to 1944, and was director of Community Relations Project for the Industrial Social Planning from 1944 to 1946. He served the United Nations from 1946 until his death. Concerned with the economic conditions and exploitation of blacks in Africa, he was acting chief of the African Unit of the Division of Economic Stability and Development from 1946 to 1949 and its chief after 1949. He was secretary of the technical assistance mission to Haiti in 1948–1949 and to Libya in 1950. In 1951 he headed a technical assistance mission to Italian Somaliland, an experience that affected him greatly. Died January 9, 1952, in New York City. *References*: *DAB* S5; *DANB*; *JNH* 38 (1953): 134–36; and *NYT*, January 9, 1952.

DEAN(E), HARRY (FOSTER) (1864–1935). Sea captain and colonizationist, born in Philadelphia. Dean went to sea as a youth and became a captain in the 1890s. In 1900 he purchased the ship *Pedro Gorino* and brought it to Cape Town, South Africa. There he opened a shipping concern and a confectioner's shop. He received a land concession in Basutoland and tried unsuccessfully to establish an agricultural colony there. He eventually had to give up his business holdings in South Africa and returned to the United States in 1914. He wrote (with Sterling North) *The Pedro Gorino: The Adventures of a Negro Sea-captain in Africa and on the Seven Seas in His Attempts to Found an Ethiopian Empire, an Autobiographical Narrative* (New York, 1929). Died in Chicago. *References*: Harry Deane Diaries, DuSable Museum of African American History, Chicago; John S. Burger, "Captain Harry Dean: Pan-Negro-Nationalist in South Africa," *IJAHS* 9 (1976): 83–90.

DE CRANO, EDMUND GERARD (? –1895). Mining engineer. De Crano was involved with gold mining in California. He and Hamilton Smith* founded in 1886 the Exploration Company, Limited, one of the forerunners of the British South Africa Company. He played an important part in the final negotiations in

1887 for the establishment of De Beers Consolidated Mines by Cecil Rhodes. *Reference*: *SADNB*.

DELANEY, EMMA B. (? –1922). Missionary, born in Fernandina Beach, Florida. DeLaney graduated from the training department of Spelman College and received nurse's training. She was matron of the Florida Institute in Live Oak, Florida. She was missionary under the Foreign Mission Board of the National Baptist Convention, U.S.A., Inc.,* in Nyasaland from 1902 to 1905. She worked at the Providence Industrial Mission founded by John Chilembwe, an early nationalist leader, and developed programs for women. Later she was a missionary in Liberia from 1912 to 1920 and founded the Seuhn Industrial Mission. Died October 7, 1922, in Fernandina Beach, Florida. *Reference*: Sandy D. Martin, "Spelman's Emma B. DeLaney and the African Mission," *Journal of Religious Thought* 41 (1984): 22–37.

DELANY, MARTIN R(OBINSON) (1812–1885). Editor, black nationalist and colonizationist, born free May 6, 1812, in Charles Town, Virginia, and grew up in Chambersburg, Pennsylvania. Delany moved to Pittsburgh in 1831 and practiced there as cupper, leecher, and bleeder until 1850 when he began to practice medicine. He was publisher of *The Mystery*, the first Negro newspaper west of the Allegheny mountains, from 1843 to 1847, and was coeditor of the *North Star* in 1847–1848. He began advocating black emigration in 1852, and in 1859–1860 went with Robert Campbell* on the Niger Valley Exploring Party* to Liberia and the Niger Valley, to look for territory for the settlement of American blacks, and in Abeokuta signed a treaty that granted him the right to establish a self-governing colony. He wrote the *Official Report of the Niger Valley Exploration Party* (New York, 1861), which was reprinted in *A Search for a Place: Black Separatism and Africa, 1860*, ed. Howard H. Bell (Ann Arbor, Mich., 1971). He traveled in the United States and Canada from 1861 to 1863, trying to sign up settlers. He was assistant commissioner of the Freedmen's Bureau in South Carolina from 1865 to 1868, customs inspector in Charleston in 1873–1874, and trial judge there from 1874 until 1880. Died January 24, 1885, in Xenia, Ohio. *References*: *DAB*; *DAMB* 1984; *DANB*; *DLB*; Cyril E. Griffith, *The African Dream: Martin R. Delany and the Emergence of Pan-African Thought* (University Park, Pa., 1975); Dorothy Sterling, *The Making of an Afro-American: Martin R. Delany, 1812– 1885* (Garden City, N.Y., 1971); Victor Ullman, *Martin R. Delany, the Beginning of Black Nationalism* (Boston, 1971); and *WWWA*.

DE LA RUE, SIDNEY (1888–1975). Government official and financial adviser, born August 22, 1888, in Haddonfield, New Jersey. De La Rue attended the University of Pennsylvania. He served in the United States Military Government in the Dominican Republic as an accountant and supply and purchasing officer from 1918 to 1920. He went to Liberia in 1921, was auditor of the receivership in 1921–1922, and general receiver and financial adviser from 1922 until 1928 (except for 1924 when he was adviser to the Turkish ministry of finance). He wrote *The Land of the Pepper Bird; Liberia* (New York, 1930). He was financial adviser and general receiver of Haiti from 1929 to 1941, president of the Haitian National Bank of Issue from 1935 to 1941, served with the Anglo-American Caribbean Commission during World War II, and was consultant to various government agencies until 1957. Died in Chestertown, Kent County, Maryland. *Reference*: *WWWA*.

DENIS, ARMAND (1896–1971). Television film director, born in Brussels, Belgium. Denis went to England as a refugee during World War I and graduated from Oxford University. He immigrated to the United States and became a United States citizen. He was research fellow in chemistry at California Institute of Technology and became interested in wildlife. He made 105 half-hour television color films dealing mainly with African wildlife, the "Filming in Africa" series, and "Savage Splendor," the first full-length color film to be produced in Africa. He was technical adviser for the film "King Solomon's Mines" (1950). He later settled in Kenya. He wrote an autobiography, *On Safari: The Story of a Life* (New York, 1963). Died April 14, 1971, in Nairobi, Kenya. *Reference*: *NYT*, April 15, 1971.

DEVLIN, LAWRENCE RAYMOND (1922–   ). Government official, born June 18, 1922, in New Hampshire. Devlin graduated from San Diego State College and Harvard University. He served in the army during World War II. He was associate editor for a publishing company from 1950 to 1953 and political affairs analyst for the Department of the Army from 1953 to 1957. He joined the foreign service in 1957 and was political officer in Brussels from 1957 to 1960. He was Central Intelligence Agency (CIA) chief of station in Léopoldville, Republic of the Congo, from 1960 to 1963 and again from 1965 to 1967, and CIA chief of mission in Vientiane, Laos, from 1968 to 1970. He was chief of the African Division of the CIA from 1972 until his retirement in 1974. Due to his connection with Sese Seko Mobutu, President of Zaire, he was Maurice Tempelsman's* resident representative in Zaire from 1974 until 1978 and remained in Zaire until 1979. *References*: *Dirty Work 2*; and *WWG*.

DEVORE, IRVEN (BOYD) (1934–   ). Anthropologist, born October 7, 1934, in Joy, Texas. DeVore graduated from the universities of Texas and Chicago. He was assistant professor of anthropology at the University of California at Berkeley in 1960–1961, lecturer in anthropology at Harvard University from 1963 to 1966, associate professor at Harvard from 1966 to 1969, and professor there after 1969. He made studies of baboon behavior and ecology in Kenya in 1959 and wrote *Primate Behavior: Field Studies of Monkeys and Apes* (New York, 1965) and later *Selections from the Field Notes, Kenya-Baboon Studies 1959, March-August* (Washington, D.C., 1970). He established, with Richard

B. Lee,* the Harvard Kalahari Research Group and conducted research among the Bushmen in Botswana in 1963–1964 and in 1967–1968, and wrote *Kalahari Hunter-gatherers: Studies of the !Kung San and Their Neighbors* (Cambridge, Mass., 1976). *References*: *CA*; Scot Morris, "A Man in the Middle," *Psychology Today* 10 (February 1977): 44–45; and *WWA*.

DEWOLF, JAMES (1764–1837). Slave trader, born March 18, 1764, in Bristol County, Rhode Island. Dewolf became a privateer during the American Revolution. He then made a number of voyages to Africa where he seized Africans and transported them as slaves to the United States. After the War of 1812 he established a cotton mill at Coventry, Rhode Island, was a representative in the Rhode Island legislature and speaker of the house, and served as United States Senator from 1821 to 1825. Died December 21, 1837, in New York City. *References*: James Dewolf Papers, Baker Library, Harvard University, Boston, Mass.; James Dewolf Papers, Bristol Historical Society, Bristol, R.I.; *BDAC*; *DAB*; George Howe, *Mount Hope: A New England Chronicle* (New York, 1959); *NCAB* 8:61; and *WWWA*.

DEYAMPERT, LILLIAN MAY THOMAS (1872–1930). Missionary, born September 14, 1872, in Mobile, Alabama. DeYampert graduated from Talladega (Ala.) College. She was missionary under the Board of Foreign Missions of the Presbyterian Church in the United States* and served in the American Presbyterian Congo Mission (APCM)* in Luebo, Congo Free State, from 1894 to 1915. She was involved in the Pantops Home for Girls, ultimately becoming its superintendent, and was instrumental in starting a day school. She resided in Selma, Alabama, after 1915. Died May 29, 1930. *Reference*: DeYampert collection, Historical Foundation, Montreat, N.C.

DICKINSON, HAROLD THOMAS (1876–1953). Mining engineer, born in Woodstock, Illinois. Dickinson graduated from Columbia University. He came to Kimberley, South Africa, in 1902 to join the staff of the De Beers Consolidated Mines Limited. In 1915 he became superintendent of explosive factories for the British Ministry of Munitions. After World War I, he was manager of the Cape Explosive Works in Somerset West, Cape Province, joined the Anglo-American Corporation and became the manager of the Bwana Mkubwa Copper Mine in Northern Rhodesia in 1924. He was later consulting engineer to De Beers. Died October 5, 1953, in Johannesburg. *References*: *NYT*, October 6, 1953; and *SADNB*.

DICKSON, WILLIAM KENNEDY LAURIE (1860–1935). Motion picture photographer, born August 1860 in Minihic-sur-Rance, Britanny, France, to English parents. Dickson came to the United States in 1879, joined Thomas Alva Edison's laboratory in 1883, and left in 1895. He constructed the first kinematograph (motion picture machine) and in 1895 developed a movie camera and a projector called the biograph. He was cofounder and chief cameraman of the Biograph Company. He went to Europe in 1897, became established in London, and was supplier of European motion picture subjects for the Biograph Company. He was in South Africa in 1899–1900, took motion pictures of the South African War for the Biograph Company, and recounted his adventures in *The Biograph in Battle: Its Story in the South African War* (London, 1901). He settled in Twickenham, England, after 1915. Died September 28, 1935, in Twickenham. *References*: Gordon Hendricks, *The Edison Motion Picture Myth* (Berkeley, Calif., 1961), pp. 143–57; John M. Smith and Tim Cawkwell, eds., *The World Encyclopedia of the Film*, (New York, 1972), pp. 70–71; John Stewart, comp., *Filmrama* (Metuchen, N.J., 1975).

DISCIPLES OF CHRIST. *See* UNITED CHRISTIAN MISSIONARY SOCIETY

DODGE, RALPH E(DWARD) (1907-   ). Missionary, born January 25, 1907 in Terril, Iowa. Dodge graduated from Taylor (Upland, Ia.) and Boston universities, and the Kennedy School of Missions of the Hartford Seminary Foundation. He was missionary under the Board of Missions of the Methodist Episcopal Church in Angola from 1936 until 1941 and from 1945 until 1950, stationed first in Loanda and later in Quessua. He was executive secretary for Africa of the Board of Missions of the Methodist Church in New York City from 1950 until 1956. He was elected bishop of Central Africa in 1956, headquartered in Salisbury, Southern Rhodesia. He was expelled from Southern Rhodesia in 1964. He retired in 1968 and lived in Zambia. He wrote *The Unpopular Missionary* (Westwood, N.J., 1964) and *The Revolutionary Bishop who Saw God at Work in Africa: An Autobiography* (Pasadena, Calif., 1986). *Reference*: EWM.

DRAGON ROUGE. An airborne rescue mission launched by the United States and Belgium in November 1964 to rescue a large number of foreign nationals, including Americans, who were seized in the summer of 1964 by the Simbas (Swahili for "lions"), Congolese rebels, and held as hostages in and around Stanleyville. *Reference*: Fred E. Wagoner, *Dragon Rouge: The Rescue of Hostages in the Congo* (Washington, D.C., 1980).

DRAKE, PHILIP (fl. 1807–1857). Sea captain and slave smuggler, born in England and came to the United States. He made his first voyage to Africa in his teens and continued as a slave smuggler until the 1850s. Died in New York City. He wrote an account of his slave trading, *Revelations of a Slave Smuggler: Being the Autobiography of Capt. Richard [sic] Drake, an African Trader for Fifty Years—from 1807 to 1857; During Which Period He Was Concerned in the Transportation of Half a Million Blacks from African Coasts to America* (New York, 1860; new ed., Northbrook, Ill., 1972), which was published after his death and the authenticity of which is open to question.

DRAYTON, BOSTON J. (1821–1864). Colonist, from Charleston, South Carolina. Drayton immigrated to Liberia in 1845, was lieutenant governor and governor of Maryland in Africa* in 1856–1857 and superintendent of the Baptist Board of Missions in the Cape Palmas area. He was the unsuccessful candidate for the presidency in 1863 and later chief justice of Liberia from 1861 until his death. Died December 12, 1864, in Monrovia. *Reference*: *African Repository* 41 (1865): 124–25.

DU BOIS, SHIRLEY (LOLA) GRAHAM (MCCANNS) (1907–1977). Author, composer and playwright, wife of W.E.B. Du Bois,* born November 11, 1907, in Indianapolis. Shirley Du Bois graduated from Oberlin College and studied at New York University, Yale University Drama School, and the Sorbonne (Paris). She taught music at Morgan College (Baltimore) from 1930 to 1932, was supervisor of the Negro unit of the Chicago Federal Theater from 1936 to 1939, served with the United Service Organizations (USO) during World War II, was field secretary for the National Association for the Advancement of Colored People (NAACP) from 1942 to 1944, and editor of *Freedomways*. She accompanied her husband to Ghana in 1961, became a citizen of Ghana in 1963, and was organizing director of Ghana's television network from 1964 to 1966. She was forced to leave Ghana in 1967 when President Kwame Nkrumah was overthrown and went to live in Egypt and later in China. She wrote a memoir of her husband, *His Day Is Marching On* (Philadelphia, 1971). Died March 27, 1977, in Peking, China. *References*: *CA*; *CB* 1946; *IAB*; *NYT*, April 5, 1977; and Bernard L. Peterson, Jr., "Shirley Graham Du Bois: Composer and Playwright," *Crisis* 84 (1977): 177–79.

DU BOIS, W(ILLIAM) E(DWARD) B(URGHARDT) (1868–1963). Historian, educator, author, and black leader, born February 26, 1868, in Great Barrington, Massachusetts. Du Bois graduated from Fisk and Harvard universities. He was a member of the faculty of Atlanta University from 1895 to 1910, director of publications and research for the National Association for the Advancement of Colored People (NAACP), and editor of its official publication, *Crisis*, from 1910 to 1934. He attended several of the Pan-African congresses between 1900 and 1945, and went to Africa in 1923. He was head of the sociology department at Atlanta University from 1934 until 1942, when he rejoined the NAACP as director of special research, but was fired from the NAACP in 1948. He immigrated to Ghana in 1961 to work on *Encyclopedia Africana* and became a citizen of Ghana in 1963. Died August 27, 1963, in Accra, Ghana. *The Autobiography of W. E. B. DuBois* (New York, 1968) appeared posthumously. *References*: W.E.B. DuBois Papers, University of Massachusetts Library, Amherst, Mass.; Herbert Aptheker, ed., *The Correspondence of W.E.B. DuBois*, (Amherst, Mass., 1973–1978); Herbert Aptheker, "W.E.B. DuBois and Africa," *Political Affairs* 60 (1981): 19–29; Herbert Aptheker, "W.E.B. Du Bois and Africa," in *Pan-African Biography*, ed. Robert A. Hill (Los Angeles, 1987), pp. 97–117; Clarence G. Contee, "W.E.B. DuBois and African Nationalism," Ph.D. diss., American University, 1969; Clarence G. Contee, "The Emergence of DuBois as an African Nationalist," *JNH* 54 (1969): 48–63; Clarence G. Contee, "A Crucial Friendship Begins: DuBois and Nkrumah, 1935–1945," *Crisis* 78 (1971): 181–85; Clarence G. Contee, "W.E.B. DuBois and African Nationalism: Notes on Primary Sources," *CBAA* 3 (February 1970): 21–26; *DAB*; *DANB*; Jack B. Moore, *W.E.B. Du Bois* (Boston, 1981); *NYT*, August 28, 1963; and *WWWA*.

DU CHAILLU, PAUL BELLONI (1835–1903). Explorer, born July 31, 1835, in Paris. Du Chaillu joined his father, who was operating a trading post in Gabon in 1848 and remained there until 1852. He came to the United States in 1852, studied natural history in Philadelphia, and became a United States citizen. He returned to Gabon in 1855 and explored and collected plant and animal specimens for Philadelphia museums, first in north Gabon, and, after 1857, in the area south of the Ogowe River. He made a second exploring expedition to Gabon from 1863 to 1865 and again collected animal specimens. He wrote *Explorations and Adventures in Equatorial Africa; with Accounts of the Manners and Customs of the People, and of the Chase of the Gorilla, the Crocodile, Leopard, Elephant, Hippopotamus, and Other Animals* (New York, 1861); *A Journey to Ashango-Land; and Further Penetration into Equatorial Africa* (New York 1867); *Adventures in the Great Forest of Equatorial Africa and the Country of the Dwarfs* (New York, 1871); *My Mpingi Kingdom; with Life in the Great Sahara* (New York, 1871); *King Mombo* (New York, 1902); and *In African Forest and Jungle* (New York, 1903). In 1871 he went to Sweden and Norway and in 1901 to Russia. Died April 30, 1903, in St. Petersburg, Russia. *References*: *ACAB*; *DAB*; K. David Patterson, "Paul B. Du Chaillu and the Exploration of Gabon, 1855–1865," *IJAHS* 7 (1974): 647–67; Michel Vaucaire, *Paul de Chaillu: Gorilla Hunter* (New York, 1930); and *WWWA*.

DUDLEY, EDWARD RICHARD (1911-). Jurist and diplomat, born March 11, 1911, in South Boston, Virginia. Dudley graduated from Johnson C. Smith University (Charlotte, N.C.), Howard University, and St. Johns University Law School (Brooklyn, N.Y.), and was admitted to the bar. He was assistant attorney general for New York State in 1942, member of the legal defense staff of the National Association for the Advancement of Colored People (NAACP) from 1943 to 1945, and legal counsel to the governor of the Virgin Islands from 1945 to 1947. He was ambassador to Liberia from 1948 to 1953 and started the Point 4 program in Africa. He later resumed his affiliation with the NAACP and was in charge of the Freedom Fund from 1953 to 1955. He was justice in the domestic relations court of New York City from 1955 to 1961, president of the Borough of Manhattan from 1961 to 1965, administrative judge of the criminal court of New York City from 1967 to 1971, and administrative judge of the New York Supreme Court after 1971. *References*: Edward Richard Dudley Papers, Amistad

Research Center, New Orleans; *Christmas*; *Ebony* 1; *NYT*, May 12, 1970; *WWA*; *WWBA*; and *WWE*.

DUFF, CLARENCE W(ALKER) (1899–1982). Missionary, born June 1, 1899, in Mount Jackson, Pennsylvania. Duff graduated from Westminster College (Pa.) and Princeton Theological Seminary, and was ordained in 1927. He was a missionary under the Sudan Interior Mission (SIM)* in Southern Ethiopia from 1927 to 1938 and later under the Committee on Foreign Missions of the Orthodox Presbyterian Church in Asmara, Eritrea, from 1944 until his retirement in 1970. He wrote *God's Higher Ways: The Birth of a Church* (Nutley, N.J., 1977) and *Cords of Love: A Testimony to God's Grace in Pre-Italian Ethiopia as Recorded in Memorabilia of One of the Sudan Interior Mission's "C.O.D. Boys"* (Phillipsburg, N.J., 1980). Died December 13, 1982, in Ocoee, Florida. *Reference*: Clarence W. Duff, "Ordinary People, Used of God: Memoirs of Clarence Walker Duff with Selected Chronicles of the Duff and Walker Clans," Westminster Theological Seminary Library (Glenside, Pa., 1984).

DUGGAN, WILLIAM R(EDMAN) (1915–1977). Diplomat, born February 11, 1915, in Durango, Colorado. Duggan attended Western State College (Gunnison, Colo.), graduated from the University of Notre Dame, and studied at Boston University. He was field office manager for the Social Security Board from 1940 to 1944 and entered the foreign service in 1944. He was vice consul in Durban, South Africa, and Vancouver; second secretary and consul in Copenhagen; officer in charge of West African affairs in the State Department in 1957–1958; consul general in Dar-es-Salaam from 1958 to 1962; member of the Policy Planning Council in the Department of State from 1962 to 1967; and consul general in Durban from 1967 until his retirement in 1971. He was professor of political science at Willamette University (Salem, Ore.) from 1972 to 1979. He wrote *A Socioeconomic Profile of South Africa* (New York, 1973) and co-authored *Tanzania and Nyerere* (Maryknoll, N.Y., 1976). Died July 11, 1977, in Salem, Oregon. *References*: *CA*; *Capital Journal* (Salem, Ore.), July 12, 1977; *Newsweek*, December 24, 1962; and *WWWA*.

DUGMORE, A(RTHUR) RADCLYFFE (1870–1955). Artist and photographer, born December 25, 1870, in Wales. Dugmore studied painting in Naples and Rome in 1887–1888, and came to the United States in 1889. He traveled in North and South America, in Southern Europe, and in Asia Minor, in pursuit of his studies of bird and animal life, and wrote articles for *Collier's* magazine. He invented the technique of photographing wildlife at night using a trip wire. He went with James L. Clark* on an expedition to East Africa in 1909, and wrote *Camera Adventures in the African Wilds: Being an Account of a Four Months' Expedition in British East Africa* (New York, 1910). He returned to England in 1914 and served in the British Army during World War I. He wrote *The Vast Sudan* (London, 1924); *The Wonderland of Big Game, Being an Account* *of Two Trips Through Tanganyika and Kenya* (London, 1928); *African Jungle Life* (London, 1928); and *The Autobiography of a Wanderer* (London, 1930). Died March 21, 1955, in Christchurch, Hampshire, England. *References*: Lowell J. Thomas, *Rolling Stone: The Life and Adventures of Arthur Radclyffe Dugmore* (Garden City, N.Y., 1931); Grant M. Waters, *Dictionary of British Artists, Working 1900–1950* (Eastbourne, Eng., 1975); and *WWWA*.

DUNAWAY, JOHN ALLDER (1886–1965). Economist, born October 10, 1886, in Stockton, Missouri. Dunaway graduated from Park College (Parkville, Mo.) and studied at the Wharton School of Economics of the University of Pennsylvania. He was treasurer of Near East Relief in Syria in 1919, assistant chief and later chief of the research division of the Bureau of Foreign and Domestic Commerce in the U.S. Department of Commerce in Washington in 1921–1922, statistician and provincial director of finances in Persia from 1922 to 1928, and economist and later senior marketing specialist in the dairy section of the Agricultural Adjustment Administration from 1933 to 1935. He was supervisor of revenue of the Republic of Liberia from 1935 to 1939 and became its financial adviser in 1938. He served as delegate of Liberia to the United Nations Conference on International Trade in Havana in 1947–1948. He was acting director of the Technical Co-operation Administration (TCA) in Saudi Arabia and chief of its public administration division until his retirement in 1953. Died June 20, 1969, in Phoenix, Arizona. *Reference*: *WWWA*.

DURNING, DENNIS VINCENT (1923-   ). Clergyman, born May 18, 1923, in Philadelphia. Durning attended Holy Ghost College, graduated from St. Mary's Seminary, and was ordained in 1949. He became a missionary in Tanganyika in 1950 and served at Mashati from 1950 to 1956 and at Loliondo, Arusha, from 1957 to 1962. He was consecrated bishop in 1963 and became the first bishop of Arusha. *References*: *ACWW*; and *WWA*.

DYE, ROYAL J. (1874–1966). Medical missionary, born October 23, 1874. Dye practiced medicine in New York City. He was missionary under the Foreign Christian Missionary Society (Disciples of Christ; see United Christian Missionary Society*) in the Congo Free State from 1899 to 1911, stationed in Bolenge. He returned to the United States in 1911 and served as field representative of the United Christian Missionary Society until his retirement in 1942. Died April 1, 1966, in San Gabriel, California. His wife, **EVA (NICHOLS) DYE** (1877–1951), wrote *Bolenge, the Story of the Gospel Triumphs on the Congo* (Cincinnati, 1909). *Reference*: *TWTA*.

DYRNES, JOHANNES OLSEN (1867–1943). Medical missionary, born May 5, 1867, at Edø, Ytre Nordmøre, Norway, and came to the United States in 1883. Dyrnes graduated from Augsburg College and Seminary and Hamline College of Physicians and Surgeons, and studied at Paris University (France).

He practiced medicine at Hanley Falls, Minnesota, from 1897 to 1899. He was a missionary under the Board of Missions of the Lutheran Free Church in Madagascar from 1900 until his death. He was stationed in Manasoa from 1900 to 1910, at Tongobory, Yulear, from 1912 to 1917, and again at Manasoa from 1917 to 1919 and from 1921 until 1943. Died December 7, 1943, in Manasoa, Madagascar. *Reference*: *WWPNL*.

E

EASTERN MENNONITE BOARD OF MISSIONS AND CHARITIES. Established in 1914 as the mission board of the Lancaster Conference of the Mennonite Church, it established a mission in Tanganyika in 1934, and later in Ethiopia and the Somali Republic. In 1960 it handed over the Tanganyika mission to the Tanganyika (later Tanzania) Mennonite Church. *References*: Eastern Mennonite Board of Missions and Charities Records, Church Headquarters, Eastern Mennonite Board of Missions, Salunga, Pa.; George R. Anchak, "An Experience in the Paradox of Indigenous Church Building: A History of the Eastern Mennonite Mission in Tanganyika, 1934–1961," Ph.D. diss., Michigan State University, 1975; *EMCM*; Mahlon M. Hess, *The Pilgrimage of Faith of Tanzania Mennonite Church, 1934–83* (Salunga, Pa., 1985); Paul N. Kraybill, ed., *Called to Be Sent: Essays in Honor of the Fiftieth Anniversary of the Founding of the Eastern Mennonite Board of Missions and Charities 1914–1964* (Scottsdale, Pa., 1964).

EDEL, MAY (MANDELBAUM) (1909–1964). Anthropologist, born December 1, 1909, in Brooklyn, New York. Edel was graduated from Barnard College and Columbia University. She was an instructor at Brooklyn College from 1934 to 1941 and at the New School for Social Research after 1956. The first woman anthropologist to do fieldwork among an African tribe, she did fieldwork in Uganda in 1932–1933, and wrote *The Customs of the Baganda* (New York, 1934) and *The Chiga of Western Uganda* (New York, 1957). Died May 23, 1964, in Queens, New York. *References*: *AA* 68 (1966): 986–89; *AMWS*; *NYT*, May 24, 1964; and *WWAW*.

EDMISTON, ALTHEA BROWN (1874–1937). Missionary, born December 17, 1874, in Russelville, DeKalb County, Alabama. Edmiston graduated from Fisk University. She was a missionary under the Board of Foreign Missions of the Presbyterian Church in the United States* in the Belgian Congo from 1902 to 1937. She was stationed in Ibanche station, in the Bulape station at Mushenge

74 EDWARDS, MARY KELLY

in the Bakuba Kingdom, and in Mutoto. She assisted in school work and compiled a grammar and dictionary of the Bakuba language, which was printed in Luebo in 1932. Died June 9, 1937, in Mutoto Station, Belgian Congo. *References*: Althea Brown Edmiston Papers, Talladega College Historical Collections, Savery Library, Talladega College, Talladega, Ala.; Robert D. Bedinger, "Althea Brown Edmiston," in *Glorious Living: Informal Sketches of Seven Women Missionaries of the Presbyterian Church, U.S.*, ed. H. P. Winsborough and S.L.V. Timmons (Atlanta, 1937), pp. 261–86; Julia L. Kellersberger, *A Life for the Congo: The Story of Althea Brown Edmiston* (New York, 1947); and *WWCR*.

EDWARDS, MARY KELLY (1829–1927). Missionary, born July 8, 1829, in Ohio. She was the first woman appointed by the Woman's Board of Missions in America. She came to the mission station in Inanda in 1869 and began a school for African girls (which became the Inanda Seminary for Girls) in Zululand in 1869. She turned over the administration in 1895, but remained in Inanda. Died September 23, 1927, in Inanda, Natal, South Africa. *Reference*: *SESA*.

EHNES, MORRIS W(ELLINGTON) (1873–1945). Missionary, born March 3, 1873, in Dashwood, Ontario, Canada. Ehnes came to the United States in 1891, graduated from Ohio Wesleyan University and studied at Columbia University. He was a missionary under the Board of Foreign Missions of the Methodist Episcopal Church*, and was the first Methodist missionary in Southern Rhodesia, where he established the Old Umtali mission at Umtali. He served there from 1898 to 1901. He returned to the United States because of ill health, was assistant general secretary of the Student Volunteer Movement for Foreign Missions in 1904–1905, editorial secretary for the Missionary Education Movement, editor of missionary textbooks from 1905 to 1916, and executive secretary of the Ohio Wesleyan University from 1916 to 1919. He was treasurer of the Board of Foreign Missions of the Methodist Episcopal Church from 1924 until his retirement in 1943. Died July 3, 1945, in Englewood, New Jersey. *References*: *NYT*, July 5, 1945; and *WWWA*.

ELDRED, R(OBERT) RAY (1872–1913). Missionary, born September 24, 1872, near Quincy, Michigan. Eldred attended Eureka College, graduated from the College of the Bible of Kentucky University (later Transylvania College), and was ordained in 1902. He was a missionary under the Foreign Christian Missionary Society (see United Christian Missionary Society*) of the Christian Church (Disciples of Christ) to Bolenge, Congo Free State, from 1902 until his death. He operated a missionary station at Longa, on the Congo River, after 1909. Died September 3, 1913, near Eyengo, on the Lokolo River, Belgian Congo. *References*: Andrew F. Hensey, *A Master Builder on the Congo: A Memorial to the Service and Devotion of Robert Day Eldred and Lillian Byers Eldred* (New York, 1916); and *TWTA*.

ELISOFON, ELIOT (1911–1973). Photographer, born April 17, 1911, in New York City. Elisofon graduated from Fordham University. He became a professional photographer in 1935, was free-lance magazine photographer from 1938 to 1942, chiefly for *Life* Magazine, and correspondent for *Life* during World War II. After 1943, he traveled all over the world and produced photographic essays for *Life*. He photographed the Nile Valley in 1947 and traveled in the Mountains of the Moon in the Belgian Congo in 1951. He visited most countries of Africa in 1967 and was chief cameraman on an assignment for the American Broadcasting Corporation (ABC) to prepare a comprehensive documentary on Africa, resulting in the four one-hour programs entitled "Africa," which he edited and which were presented on ABC-TV in 1967. He was again in Africa in 1970–1971 to make four films on African culture, and again in 1972 for the *National Geographic Magazine*. He was coauthor of *The Sculpture of Africa* (New York, 1958), and *Africa's Animals* (New York, 1967), and wrote *The Nile* (New York, 1964), *A Week in Joseph's World: Zaire* (New York, 1973), and *Africa and Its Art* (New York, 1974). Died April 7, 1973, in New York City. *References*: CB 1972; *EAJ*; *MBEP*; *NYT*, April 8, 1973; and *Tribute to Africa: The Photography and the Collection of Eliot Elisofon* (Washington, D.C., 1974); George Walsh, Colin Naylor, and Michael Held, eds., *Contemporary Photographers* (New York, 1982).

ELIZABETH. First vessel to carry immigrants from the United States to Africa. Chartered and outfitted by the United States government, the *Elizabeth* was accompanied by the U.S.S. *Cyane*. It arrived in Sierra Leone in 1820 with eighty-eight black Americans who attempted to settle at Sherbro Island, off Sierra Leone. The attempt proved abortive. In 1822, Lieutenant Robert Stockton* rescued the survivors at Sherbro, and carried them and a new group of settlers from the United States to the Grain Coast, landing at Cape Mesurado (near present day Monrovia).

ELLIOT, DANIEL GIROUD (1835–1915). Zoologist, born March 7, 1835, in New York City. Elliot did not study in college but traveled extensively. He lived in London from 1869 to 1879 and was one of the founders of the American Ornithologists' Union and its second president. He traveled in Europe, Africa, Palestine, and Asia Minor from 1856 to 1878, and later visited the greater part of the United States, Canada, Alaska, and South America. He was curator of zoology at the Field Museum of Natural History from 1894 to 1906. He led an expedition into the interior of East Africa in 1896. Died December 22, 1915, in New York City. *References*: *DAB*; C. Franklin, "American Gould: Daniel Giroud Elliot (1835–1915)," *Country Life* 157 (April 3, 1975): 834–35; *NCAB* 16:196; *NYT*, December 23, 1915; and *WWWA*.

ELLIOTT, ARTHUR (1870–1938). Photographer, born in Boston. Elliott was taken to England as a baby. He came to South Africa in the 1880s with a theatrical company, engaged in various road shows. He helped to introduce the gramophone into South Africa and recorded President Paul Kruger's voice. He took up photography in 1900 and practiced in Pretoria until 1905 and later in Cape Town. He photographed historic buildings, preserved pictures of historical importance, and documented historical events. Died November 11, 1938, in Cape Town. *References*: *Architectural Beauty of the Old Cape as Seen by Arthur Elliott*, selected, annotated, and introduced by Hans Fransen (Cape Town, 1969); *DSAB* 2; *MBEP*; and *SADNB*.

ELLIS, GEORGE WASHINGTON (1875–1919). Sociologist and author, born May 4, 1875, in Weston, Missouri. Ellis graduated from the University of Kansas, and studied at Howard University and Gunton Institute of Economics and Sociology (N.Y.C.). He was clerk in the U.S. Census Department in Washington, D.C., from 1900 to 1902. He was secretary of the legation in Liberia from 1902 to 1910. He undertook several expeditions into Liberia's hinterland, the rural area not included in the coastal counties, and investigated and reported on the various tribes of the interior. He conducted ethnological, linguistic, sociological, and economic studies, and wrote *Negro Culture in West Africa: A Social Study of the Negro Group of Val-speaking People* (New York, 1914), and a novel, *The Leopard's Claw: A Thrilling Story of Love and Adventure from a European Castle Through the West African Jungle* (New York, 1917). He also made an extensive collection of ethnological specimens which was given to the National Museum in Washington, D.C. He later practiced law in Chicago and was assistant corporation counsel of Chicago from 1917 until his death. Died November 26, 1919, in Chicago. *References*: *DAB*; *DANB*; *NCAB* 17:400; and *WWWA*.

ELLIS, WILLIAM HENRY (1864– ?). Businessman, born near Victoria, Texas. Ellis worked as a cowboy on ranches in Texas and Mexico, attended a college in Tennessee, and was involved in the wool and cotton industry. He opened a hide and wool exchange in San Antonio, Texas, in 1886. In 1889 he launched a scheme to establish colonies for Afro-Americans in Mexico and in 1894–1895 established a colony near the Mexican village of Mapimi, a project that failed. He moved to New York City in 1897 and became a Wall Street stockbroker. In 1903 he went to Addis Ababa, Abyssinia, with plans for developing commercial enterprises in Abyssinia and establishing a refuge there for American blacks. He assisted Robert P. Skinner* in negotiating the commercial treaty of 1903 with Abyssinia. He made a second trip to Abyssinia in 1904 to bring back the signed copy of the treaty and obtained concessions for land for cotton growing. *References*: Richard Pankhurst, "William H. Ellis—Guillaume Enriques Ellesion: The First Black American Ethiopianist?" *Ethiopia Observer* 15 (1972): 89–121; and William R. Scott, "A Study of Afro-American and

Ethiopian Relations: 1896–1941,'' Ph.D. diss., Princeton University, 1971, pp. 51–66.

ENGELHARD, CHARLES W(ILLIAM), JR. (1917–1971). Businessman, born February 15, 1917, in New York City. Engelhard graduated from Princeton University, and served as a bomber pilot in World War II. He took over as president of Engelhard Minerals and Chemicals Corporation, the world's largest refiner and fabricator of precious metals, on the death of his father in 1950. He was chairman of Engelhard Hanovia, a finance holding company, and of the American-South African Investment Company of Johannesburg. He settled in Johannesburg in the 1950s, bought himself into the chairmanship of Rand Mines, became chairman of American–South African Investment Company, Limited, which he organized in 1958, and was the leading individual United States investor in South Africa. He was also a prime mover of the South Africa Foundation and President Lyndon Johnson's representative to Zambia's independence celebrations. Died March 2, 1971, in Boca Grande, Florida. *References*: *Forbes*, August 1, 1965; Paul Jacobs, "Our Man in South Africa: Charles Engelhard," *Ramparts* 5 (November 1966): 23–28; *NYT*, March 3, 1971; *Time*, January 27, 1961; and *WWWA*.

ENGLE, JESSE M. (1838–1900). Missionary, born July 19, 1838, in Bainbridge, Pennsylvania. Engle was ordained in 1850, elected bishop in 1874, and served the Brethren in Christ Church in Pennsylvania and Kansas. He became secretary of the Foreign Mission Board in 1895 and leader of the Brethren in Christ* mission in Africa in 1897. He established a mission station in Matopo Hills, Southern Rhodesia, in 1898. Died April 3, 1900 in Matopo Hills. *Reference*: *Engle*.

ENNIS, MERLIN W(ALTER) (1874–1964). Medical missionary, born June 29, 1874, in Douglass Center, Wisconsin. Ennis graduated from Beloit College and Yale University Divinity School, studied at Andover Theological Seminary, and was ordained in 1903. He was missionary under the American Board of Commissioners for Foreign Missions (ABCFM)* from 1903 until 1944. He founded Elende Station in Angola in 1906, translated the Bible into Umbundu, and wrote *Umbundu Folk Tales from Angola* (Boston, 1902). He returned to the United States in 1944 and lived in Lexington, Massachusetts. Died August 20, 1964, in Marblehead, Massachusetts. *Reference*: *NYT*, August 22, 1964.

EVANGELICAL ALLIANCE MISSION, THE (TEAM). Founded in 1890 as the Scandinavian Alliance Mission of North America, it began missionary work in South Africa and Swaziland in 1892, in Southern Rhodesia in 1942, and in Chad in 1969. *References*: Thomas J. Bach, *Pioneer Missionaries for Christ and His Church* (Wheaton, Ill., 1955); *EMCM*; and J. W. Swanson, comp. and ed., *Three Score Years . . . and Then: Sixty Years of Worldwide Missionary Advance* (Chicago, 1951?).

EVANGELICAL BAPTIST MISSIONS, INC. Founded as the Africa Christian Mission. The name was later changed to Christian Missions, Inc., and still later to the Evangelical Baptist Missions, Inc. It began missionary work in Niger in 1929, in Mali in 1951, in Benin in 1966, and in the Ivory Coast in 1979. *Reference*: *EMCM*.

EVANGELICAL COVENANT CHURCH OF AMERICA: BOARD OF MISSIONS. Founded in 1885, it began missionary work in the Belgian Congo in 1934. In 1937 it assumed the responsibility for half the field that was served by the Evangelical Free Church of America in Northwest Congo, and the two churches in the Congo were united in 1949 to become the Church of Christ in the Ubangi. The name was changed to the Department of World Missions. *References*: L. Arden Almquist, *Covenant Missions in Congo* (Chicago, 1958); and *EMCM*.

EVANGELICAL FREE CHURCH OF AMERICA: BOARD OF OVERSEAS MISSION. Founded in 1888, it began missionary work in the Belgian Congo in 1922. *References*: Evangelical Free Church of America Archives, Rolfing Memorial Library, Trinity Evangelical Divinity School, Deerfield, Ill.; and *EMCM*.

EVANGELICAL LUTHERAN CHURCH. Formed in 1917 and known until 1946 as the Norwegian Lutheran Church of America. It began missionary work in Madagascar in 1888, in Cameroon in 1923, and in the Central African Republic in 1930. In 1927 it assumed control of the mission began by the Norwegian Lutheran Church in South Africa in 1844. In 1960 it merged with the American Lutheran Church and the United Evangelical Lutheran Church to become the American Lutheran Church, Division of World Missions. *References*: Archives of the American Lutheran Church, Luther Northwestern Seminary Library, St. Paul, Minn.; and Ruth Christiansen, *For the Heart of Africa* (Minneapolis, 1956).

F

FALLERS, LLOYD A(SHTON) (1925–1974). Anthropologist, born August 29, 1925, in Nebraska City, Nebraska. Fallers attended the University of Utah and Deep Springs College, graduated from the University of Chicago, and studied at the London School of Economics and Political Science. He was research fellow at the East African Institute of Social Research in Kampala, Uganda, from 1950 to 1952 and in 1954–1955, and was director of the institute in 1956–1957. He studied the Basoga, a tribe on the northern shore of Lake Victoria, and wrote *Bantu Bureaucracy: A Study of Integration and Conflict in the Political Institutions of an East African People* (Cambridge, Eng., 1956; republished as *Bantu Bureaucracy: A Century of Political Evolution among the Basoga of Uganda* [Chicago, 1965]) and *Law without Precedent: Legal Ideas in Action in the Courts of Colonial Basoga* (Chicago, 1969). He was assistant professor and associate professor of anthropology at the University of California (Berkeley) from 1957 to 1960, and associate professor and professor of anthropology at the University of Chicago from 1960 until his death. He edited *The King's Men: Leadership and Status in Buganda on the Eve of Independence* (London, 1964). Died July 4, 1974, in Chicago. *References*: *AMWS*; *CA*; (London) *Times*, July 8, 1974; and *WWWA*.

FARINI, GILARMI (GUILLERMO) ANTONIO (1839–1929). Showman and traveler, real name William Leonard Hunt, born in Lockport, New York. He was part owner of cattle ranches, a cowboy, and a tight-rope walker who performed under the name "Farini the Great" and crossed the Niagara Falls on a tight-rope in 1864. He then staged various shows in New York and London, and brought over a group of Bushmen. He went on an expedition to the Kalahari Desert in 1885. He collected insects, butterflies, and flowers (which were later given to Kew Gardens), and investigated the possibilities of establishing cattle ranches there. He also claimed to have discovered the ruins of an old city in the desert, known later as "the lost city of the Kalahari," and wrote *Through the Kalahari Desert: A Narrative of a Journey with Gun, Camera, and Note-book* *to Lake N' Gami and Back* (London, 1886). Died January 17, 1929, in Port Hope, Ontario, Canada. *References*: *DASB* 3; and *SESA*.

FARIS, ELLSWORTH (1874–1953). Missionary and sociologist, born September 30, 1874, in Salem, Franklin County, Tennessee. Faris graduated from Texas Christian University (Fort Worth) and the University of Chicago. He was missionary under the Foreign Christian Missionary Society* and went with Harry N. Biddle* to Congo Free State in 1897. He founded the Bolenge mission and served there until 1904. He returned to the United States in 1904 because of ill health, was professor of philosophy and psychology at Texas Christian University from 1906 to 1911, and professor of sociology at the University of Chicago from 1917 until his retirement in 1939. He went to the Belgian Congo and the Sudan in 1932–1933 to study the effect of civilization on the native peoples, and returned to the Belgian Congo and Uganda in 1949. Died December 19, 1953, in Lake Forest, Illinois. *References*: *American Journal of Sociology* 59 (1954): 470–71; *NYT*, December 20, 1953; *Social Forces* 33 (1954): 101–3; *TWTA*; and *WWWA*.

FARRELL LINES, INC. Founded in 1925 by James Augustine Farrell (1862–1943), president of U.S. Steel Corporation. Farrell Lines established the first regular steamship service under the U.S. flag from the east coast and the Great Lakes of the United States to Africa south of the Sahara. It also introduced American diesel-electric locomotives on South African railways. *Reference*: Robert G. Albion, *Seaports South of the Sahara; the Achievements of an American Steamship Service* (New York, 1959).

FARSON, (JAMES) NEGLEY (1890–1960). Journalist, born May 14, 1890, in Plainfield, New Jersey. Farson attended the University of Pennsylvania, served in the Royal Flying Corps, was wounded when his plane crashed near Cairo and spent two years recuperating. He was foreign correspondent for the *Chicago Daily News* from 1924 to 1935 and free-lance foreign correspondent after 1935. He wrote perceptive and widely circulated reports about his travels in Africa, including *Behind God's Back* (New York, 1941) and *Last Chance in Africa* (New York, 1950). He wrote two autobiographies, *The Way of a Transgressor* (New York, 1936) and *Mirror for Narcissus* (New York, 1957). Died December 12, 1960, near Georgeham, North Devon, England. *References*: *CA*; *DAB* S6; *EAJ*; *NYT*, December 14, 1960; and *WWWA*.

FEARING, MARIA (1838–1937). Missionary, born near Gainesville, Alabama. Fearing attended Talladega College. She taught at a rural school in Anniston, Alabama, and returned to Talladega as assistant matron in the boarding department. She was missionary under the Board of Foreign Missions of the Presbyterian Church in the United States* serving in the American Presbyterian Congo Mission (APCM)* in Luebo, Kasai district, Congo Free State, from 1894 to 1915, and opened a school there. *Reference*: Althea B. Edmiston, "Maria Fearing: A Mother to African Girls," in *Glorious Living: Informal Sketches of Seven Missionaries of the Presbyterian Church, U.S.*, ed. by Sarah Lee Thomas (Atlanta, 1937), pp. 288–318.

FEELING, THOMAS ("TOM") (1933-   ). Artist and illustrator, born May 19, 1933, in Brooklyn, New York. Feeling served in the United States Air Force. He was illustrator for the *African Review* and free-lance illustrator for Ghana television programs and for various businesses in Ghana from 1964 to 1966. He was a teacher of illustration for the Ministry of Education in Guyana after 1971. He wrote and illustrated several children's books about Africa, including an illustrated autobiography, *Black Pilgrimage* (New York, 1972). *References*: *CA*; Ernest Dunbar, ed., *Black Expatriates, A Study of American Negroes in Exile* (New York, 1968), pp. 39–50; *WWBA*; and *WWE*.

FERGUSON, ABBIE PARK (1837–1919). Educator, sister of George Reid Ferguson,* born April 4, 1837, at Whately, Massachusetts. Ferguson graduated from Mount Holyoke Seminary and studied in Geneva and Hamburg. She taught in Niles, Michigan, and New Haven, Connecticut, and did missionary work in New Haven. With Anna Elvira Bliss* she went to the Cape, South Africa, in 1873 to teach in a girls' seminary. They established the Huguenot Seminary* in 1874 and Ferguson was principal of the high school. She established the Huguenot College in 1896 and was the first president of the college from 1899 until her retirement in 1910. Died March 25, 1919, at Wellington, Cape, South Africa. *References*: *DSAB* 2; *NAW*; and *SADNB*.

FERGUSON, GEORGE R(EID) (1829–1896). Missionary, brother of Abbie Park Ferguson,* born March 19, 1829, in Attleborough, Massachusetts. Ferguson was a civil engineer in New Orleans, Mexico, and Ohio from 1849 to 1857; attended Andover Theological Seminary; and was ordained in 1860. He was a pastor in North East and Torringford, Connecticut, and a teacher in Lakeville, Connecticut from 1859 to 1877. He went to South Africa in 1877 as a missionary under the Dutch Reformed Church of South Africa, and was principal of a missionary and teachers training institute in Wellington, Cape, which he put on a firm foundation. He served until his death. Died June 19, 1896, in Wellington, Cape, South Africa. *References*: *AndoverTS*; and *DASB* 3.

FERGUSON, MILTON J(AMES) (1879–1954). Librarian, born April 11, 1879, in Hubbardstown, West Virginia. Ferguson graduated from the University of Oklahoma and studied at the New York State Library School. He was librarian at the University of Oklahoma from 1902 to 1907, assistant librarian at the California State Library from 1908 to 1917, and librarian there from 1917 to 1930. He conducted a library survey of the Union of South Africa, Rhodesia, and Kenya for the Carnegie Corporation of New York in 1928–1929, and prepared a *Report . . . on the Libraries in the Union of South Africa, Rhodesia and Kenya Colony* (New York, 1929). He was chief librarian of the Brooklyn Public Library from 1930 until his retirement in 1949. Died October 23, 1954, in Brooklyn, New York. *References*: *Dictionary of American Library Biography*, ed. Bohdan S. Wynor (Littleton, Colo., 1978); *NCAB* 40:387; *NYT*, October 24, 1954; and *WWWA*.

FERGUSON, SAMUEL DAVID (1842–1916). Missionary, born January 1, 1842, in Charleston, South Carolina. Ferguson immigrated with his parents to Liberia in 1848. He was a missionary under the Domestic and Foreign Missionary Society of the Protestant Episcopal Church in the United States of America* in Cape Palmas, Liberia, from 1865 until 1916. He also served there as agent for the American Colonization Society.* He was consecrated in 1885 as the first black bishop in the Protestant Episcopal Church and served as its first missionary bishop from 1885 until 1916. Died August 3, 1916, in Monrovia, Liberia. *References*: Samuel David Ferguson Papers, Liberia Papers, Church Historical Society, Austin, Texas; *ACAB*; *Davis*; *LC*; *NCAB* 13:544; *NYT*, August 4, 1916; *WWCR*; and *WWWA*.

FERGUSSON, C(LARENCE) CLYDE, JR. (1924–1983). Educator and diplomat, born November 4, 1924, in Wilmington, North Carolina. Fergusson graduated from Ohio State and Harvard universities and was admitted to the bar. He served in the army during World War II. He practiced law in New York City from 1951 to 1954, was assistant United States attorney for the southern district of New York in 1954–1955, professor of law at Rutgers University Law School from 1955 to 1963, professor of law and dean of Howard University Law School from 1964 to 1969, and professor of law at Harvard Law School from 1977 until his death. He was chief coordinator of the United States relief assistance to the civilian victims of the Nigerian Civil War in 1969–1970, and coordinated relief to the victims of the war between Nigeria and Biafra. He was ambassador to Uganda from 1970 to 1972, deputy assistant secretary of state for African affairs in 1972–1973, and served as United States Representative to the United Nations Economic and Social Council from 1973 to 1975. Died December 10, 1983, in Boston. *References*: *CA*; *NYT*, December 22, 1983; *WWAP*; and *WWWA*.

FINLEY, JOSIAH F. C. (fl. 1837–1838). Clergyman. Finley was the leader of Mississippi in Africa* and its governor in 1837–1838. Murdered in 1838 near Bassa Cove on his way to Monrovia, Liberia.

FIRESTONE PLANTATIONS COMPANY. Harvey Samuel Firestone (1868–1938), president of Firestone Tire and Rubber Company, acquired in 1924 a plantation in Liberia as a source for an American-controlled supply of crude rubber. By 1926 he had obtained a ninety-nine year lease of one million acres, sixty thousand of which had been planted by 1936. At the same time, Firestone made a loan to the Liberian government to get rid of non-American influence in Liberia. The company improved Monrovia harbor and developed living quarters for its workers, and it also held a dominant position in Liberia's affairs. *References*: Frank Chalk, ''The Anatomy of an Investment: Firestone's 1927 Loan to Liberia,'' *Canadian Journal of African Studies* 1 (1967): 12–32; and Wayne C. Talbot, *The Firestone Operation in Liberia* (Washington, 1956).

FLEMING, LULU CECILIA (1862–1899). Medical missionary, born January 28, 1862, in Hibernia, Clay County, Florida. Fleming graduated from Shaw University (Raleigh, N.C.) and the Woman's Medical College of Pennsylvania. She was missionary under the American Baptist Foreign Mission Society (see American Baptist Missionary Union*) in the Congo Free State, and served at Mpalabala from 1886 to 1891, and at Irebu from 1895 until 1899, when she contracted sleeping sickness and returned to the United States. Died June 20, 1899, in Philadelphia. *Reference*: Lawson A. Scruggs, *Women of Distinction: Remarkable in Works and Invincible in Character* (Raleigh, 1893), pp. 197–203.

FLICKINGER, DANIEL K(RUMBLER) (1824–1911). Clergyman, born May 25, 1824, in Sevenmile, Butler County, Ohio. He became a preacher for the United Brethren in Christ Church in 1850, and was ordained in 1853. He preached and traveled in the west and was city missionary in Cincinnati from 1851 to 1855. He was in Africa in 1855–1856 for the Home, Frontier and Foreign Missionary Society (later Board of Missions) of the United Brethren in Christ* to select a mission site and returned to Africa again in 1857. He was secretary of the missionary society from 1857 until 1885, missionary bishop from 1885 to 1889, and missionary secretary of the radical wing of the United Brethren in Christ from 1897 to 1905. He traveled to Africa twelve more times, and wrote *Sketches in Africa* (Dayton, 1857); *Offhand Sketches of Men and Things in Africa* (Dayton, 1857); *Ethiopia: or, Twenty Years of Missionary Life in Western Africa* (Dayton, Ohio, 1877); *History of the Origin, Development and Condition of Missions Among the Sherbro and Mendi Tribes in Western Africa* (Dayton, 1885); and his autobiography, *Fifty-five Years of Active Ministerial Life* (Dayton, 1907). Died August 29, 1911, in Columbus, Ohio. *References*: *ACAB*; *DAB; EWM*; *OAB*; *NCAB* 19:177; and *WWWA*.

FOOTE, ANDREW H(ULL) (1806–1863). Naval officer, born September 12, 1806, in New Haven, Connecticut, and grew up in Cheshire, Connecticut, in 1822. He was appointed acting midshipman in the navy and served in the Mediterranean and on a cruise around the globe. He was commander of the U.S. brig *Perry* on the African coast from 1849 to 1851. He wrote *Africa and the American Flag* (New York, 1854). He later served in the Far East and in the Union Navy during the Civil War. Died June 26, 1863, in New York City.

References: Andrew H. Foote Papers, Manuscript Division, Library of Congress; *ACAB*; *CWD*; *DAB*; *DAMB*; Allan Keller, *Andrew Hull Foote, Gunboat Commodore (1806–1863)* (Hartford, Conn., 1964); John D. Milligan, "Andrew Foote: Zealous Reformer, Administrator, Warrior," in *Captains of the Old Steam Navy: Makers of the American Naval Tradition, 1840–1880*, ed. James C. Bradford (Annapolis, 1986), pp. 115–41; *NCAB* 5:10; *WAMB*; and *WWWA*.

FORD, ARNOLD J(OSIAH) (ca. 1875–1935). Black rabbi, born in Barbados, British West Indies. Ford came to New York City and settled in Harlem after World War I and became an influential force in the Ethiopian Hebrew movement (the black Jews) of Harlem. He wrote the anthem for the Universal Negro Improvement Association (UNIA), entitled "Ethiopia, Thou Land of Our Fathers"; was musical director of the UNIA from 1920 to 1922; and in 1925 established a black Jewish congregation of Beth B'nai Abraham in Harlem. He left for Ethiopa in 1930 to represent his congregation at the coronation of Haile Selassie I and to explore the possibilities for black settlement in Ethiopia. He proposed to lay the foundation for an Afro-American settlement near Lake Tana. He settled in Addis Ababa and emerged as the unofficial leader of an Afro-American colony there. Died September 16, 1935, in Addis Ababa. *References*: K. J. King, "Some Notes on Arnold J. Ford and New World Black Attitudes to Ethiopia," *Journal of Ethiopian Studies* 10 (1972): 81–88 (reprinted in *Black Apostles: Afro-American Clergy Confront the Twentieth Century*, eds. Randall K. Burkett and Richard Newman [Boston, 1978)], pp. 49–55); J. Gordon Melton, *Biographical Dictionary of American Cult and Sect Leaders* (New York, 1986), pp. 90–92; William R. Scott, "Rabbi Arnold Ford's Back-to-Ethiopia Movement: A Study of Black Emigration 1930–1935," *Pan-African Journal* 8 (1975): 191–202; and William R. Scott, *Going to the Promised Land—Afro-American Immigrants in Ethiopia 1930–1935* (Atlanta, 1975).

FORD, HENRY A(LEXANDER) (1818–1858). Medical missionary, born May 4, 1818, in Lisle, New York. Ford graduated from Williams College, taught in Hudson, New York, and studied medicine in New York City. He became a missionary under the American Board of Commissioners for Foreign Missions (ABCFM)* in 1850, was stationed as a physician at Baraka in Gabon, and was superintendent of a boarding school for boys. He wrote *Observations on the Fevers of the West Coast of Africa* (New York, 1856). Died February 2, 1858, at Baraka, Gabon. *Reference*: Hewitt.

FOREIGN CHRISTIAN MISSIONARY SOCIETY. *See* UNITED CHRISTIAN MISSIONARY SOCIETY

FORSBERG, MALCOLM (1908–   ). Missionary, born December 14, 1908, in Tacoma, Washington. Forsberg graduated from Wheaton (Ill.) College. He was missionary under the Sudan Interior Mission (SIM)* in Ethiopia from 1933

to 1937 and in the Sudan from 1938 to 1964. He returned to the United States in 1964 and was candidate secretary for personnel for SIM from 1964 to 1974. He wrote two autobiographies, *Land Beyond the Nile* (New York, 1958) and *Last Days on the Nile* (New York, 1966), and coauthored *In Famine He Shall Redeem Thee: Famine Relief and Rehabilitation in Ethiopia* (Summer Hill, Australia, 1975). *Reference*: *CA*.

FOSSEY, DIAN (1932–1985). Primatologist, born January 16, 1932, in San Francisco. Fossey graduated from San Jose State College (later University) and Cambridge University. She was an occupational therapist in Kentucky from 1955 to 1966, and first came to Africa on a safari in 1963. She returned to Africa in 1967 under the auspices of the National Geographic Society, established the Karisoke Research Center in Ruhengeri, Rwanda, and was its scientific director from 1967 to 1980, project coordinator from 1980 to 1983, and again scientific director from 1983 until her death. She studied Rwanda's mountain gorillas in the Virunga Mountains and wrote *Gorillas in the Mist* (Boston, 1983). Killed December 26, 1985, at her forest camp in Rwanda. *References*: *CA*; *CB* 1985; Farley Mowat, *Woman in the Mists: The Story of Dian Fossey and the Mountain Gorillas of Africa* (New York, 1987); and *NYT*, December 30, 1985.

FRASER, MELVIN (1858–1936). Missionary, born March 7, 1858, in Lyndon, New York. Fraser attended Lake Forest (Ill.) College, graduated from Lafayette College and McCormick Theological Seminary, and was ordained in 1885. He was pastor at Iron Mountain and Mt. Pleasant, Michigan, until 1894. He was a missionary under the Board of Foreign Missions of the Presbyterian Church in the U.S.A.* in Cameroon from 1894 to 1924. He compiled and cotranslated a hymn book in the Bulu language. He was later pastor in Elgin, Illinois. Died December 15, 1936. *Reference*: *WWWA*.

FREDERICK, JOHN RICHARD (fl. 1886–1897). Missionary, from Rhode Island. Frederick was the first African Methodist Episcopal Church* missionary to West Africa. He was missionary to the Creoles and the Mende under the African Methodist Episcopal Church in Sierra Leone from 1886 to 1897. He then withdrew from that church and joined the Wesleyan Methodist Church, taking the mission property and members with him.

FREEMAN, MARTIN HENRY (1826–1889). Educator, born May 11, 1826, in Rutland, Vermont. Freeman graduated from Middlebury College (Vt.). He was principal of the Avery Institution (Pittsburgh, Pa.) from 1851 to 1862. He was professor of mathematics and natural philosophy at Liberia College, Monrovia, from 1863 to 1868, and its president in 1868. Died May 26, 1889, in Monrovia, Liberia. *Reference*: *Middlebury College, General Catalogue: Sesquicentennial Edition* (Middlebury, Vt., 1950).

**FREE METHODIST CHURCH OF NORTH AMERICA: GENERAL MIS-
SIONARY BOARD.** Organized in 1885, it began missionary work in Moz-
ambique in 1885, in South Africa in 1891, in Ruanda-Burundi in 1935, in
Southern Rhodesia in 1938, and in the Republic of Congo in 1963. *References*:
Free Methodist Church of North America Papers, Marston Memorial Historical
Center, Winona Lake, Ind.; Carrie T. Burritt, *The Story of Fifty Years* (Winona
Lake, Ind., n.d.); Byron S. Lamson, *Lights in the World: Free Methodist Mis-
sions at Work* (Winona Lake, Ind., 1951); Byron S. Lamson, *Venture: The
Frontiers of Free Methodism* (Winona Lake, Ind., 1960); and Victor W. Macy
and Lela De Mille, *Discovery under the Southern Cross: Below the Equator—
Missions Adventures in Mozambique and South Africa* (Winona Lake, Ind.,
1984).

FRENCH-SHELDON, MAY (1847–1936). Author, lecturer, and explorer,
born May French, May 10, 1847, in Beaver, Pennsylvania, but spent most of
her adult life in England and France. She was the proprietor of the publishing
house Saxon and Company of New York and London. She organized and led
an independent expedition to explore the region of Mount Kilimanjaro in East
Africa in 1891 and wrote *Sultan to Sultan: Adventures Among the Masai and
Other Tribes of East Africa* (Boston, 1892). She traveled in the Congo Free
State in 1894, returned there in 1903–1904, and traveled in Liberia in 1905.
Died February 10, 1936, in West Kensington, London. *References*: May French-
Sheldon Papers, Manuscript Division, Library of Congress; François Bontinck,
*Aux Origines de l'État Indépendant du Congo: Documents Tirés d'Archives
Américaines* (Louvain, 1966), pp. 450–58; Dorothy Middleton, *Victorian Lady
Travellers* (New York, 1965), pp. 90–103; Jeanne M. Moore, "Bebe Bwana,"
American History Illustrated 21 (October 1986): 36–42; and *NYT*, February 11,
1936.

FRICK, CHILDS (1883–1965). Paleontologist and art patron, born March 12,
1883, in Pittsburgh. Frick graduated from Princeton University. He established
the Frick Laboratory of Vertebrate Paleontology at the American Museum of
Natural History and led an expedition to Abyssinia and Kenya in 1912. He was
president of the board of the trustees of the Frick Collection (established by his
father) in New York City from 1921 until his death. Died May 9, 1965, in
Roslyn, Long Island, New York. *Reference*: *NYT*, May 10, 1965.

FRIEDMANN, HERBERT (1900–   ). Ornithologist, born April 22, 1900, in
New York City. Friedmann graduated from City College of New York and
Cornell University, and studied at Harvard University. He was curator of ornithology at the National Museum of the Smithsonian Institution from 1929 to
1958, head curator of zoology from 1958 to 1961, director of the Los Angeles
County Museum of Natural History from 1961 to 1970, and professor of zoology
at the University of California at Los Angeles from 1963 to 1967. He did research

in Africa in 1924–1925 and studied parasitic birds in South Africa in 1950. He wrote *Birds Collected by the Childs Frick Expedition to Ethiopia and the Kenya Colony* (Washington, D.C., 1930–1937); coauthored (with Arthur Loveridge*) *Notes on the Ornithology of Tropical East Africa* (Cambridge, Mass., 1937), and wrote *The Parasitic Cuckoos of Africa* (Washington, 1948). *References*: *AMWS*; *CA*; *McGraw-Hill Modern Scientists and Engineers* (New York, 1980); and *WWA*.

FRIENDS AFRICA INDUSTRIAL MISSION BOARD. Organized in 1902, it established the Friends Africa Industrial Mission in British East Africa in 1902. It transferred the mission in 1911 to the American Friends Board of Foreign Missions (organized in 1894), which was united in 1927 with the Board of Home Missions to form the American Friends Board of Missions. In 1963 the ownership of the mission passed to the East Africa Yearly Meeting in Kenya (which was established in 1946). *References*: *Among Friends in Kenya, Africa* (Richmond, Ind., 1959); and *EMCM*.

FUERTES, LOUIS AGASSIZ (1874–1927). Artist-naturalist, born February 7, 1874, in Ithaca, New York. Fuertes graduated from Cornell University. He began a series of expeditions in which he studied and painted birds in countries including Alaska, the Bahamas, Canada, Mexico, and Colombia. He made an expedition to Abyssinia with Wilfred H. Osgood* for the Field Museum of Natural History and the *Chicago Daily News* in 1926–1927 and wrote (with Osgood) *Artist and Naturalist in Ethiopia* (Garden City, N.Y., 1936). Died August 22, 1927, in Ithaca, New York. The *Album of Abyssinian Birds and Mammals from Paintings by Louis Agassiz Fuertes* (Chicago, 1930) was published posthumously. *References*: Louis Agassiz Fuertes Papers, Olin Library, Cornell University, Ithaca, N.Y.; Robert M. Back, *A Celebration of Birds: The Life and Art of Louis Agassiz Fuertes* (New York, 1982); Mary F. Boynton, *Louis Agassiz Fuertes* (New York, 1956); *DAB*; and Frederick G. Marcham, *Louis Agassiz Fuertes and the Singular Beauty of Birds* (New York, 1971).

FURBAY, JOHN HARVEY (1903-   ). Educator, born September 23, 1903, in Mt. Gilead, Ohio. Furbay attended Otterbein College and Ohio State University, and graduated from Asbury College (Wilmore) and New York and Yale universities. He was professor of biology and education at Taylor University (Upland, Ind.) from 1927 to 1933 and at the College of Emporia (Kans.) from 1933 to 1935. He was president of the College of West Africa,* Monrovia, Liberia, from 1935 to 1939. He was professor of education at Mills College from 1939 to 1944 and director of cultural and educational service of Trans World Airlines, Inc., from 1945 until 1980. He was United States delegate to UNESCO from 1947 to 1950 and conducted an educational mission to Ethiopia and Kenya in 1956 and a tourism and trade mission to Liberia in 1983. His wife, **ELIZABETH JANE (DEARMIN) FURBAY** (? - 1946), accompanied her husband to Liberia, and wrote her observations in *Top Hats and Tom-toms* (Chicago, 1943). *References*: *IAB*; *OAB*; and *WWA*.

G

GARNER, RICHARD LYNCH (1848–1920). Naturalist and author, born February 19, 1848, in Abington, Virginia. Garner served in the Confederate Army during the Civil War. He taught school and was involved in real estate and other business until 1890. An early pioneer of primate field studies, he began to investigate the habits of gorillas and chimpanzees. He first went to Africa in 1892, going up the Ogowe River in Gabon, made four more expeditions to Africa, and spent twenty-five years of his life in Africa, particularly in the Belgian Congo, exploring and studying animals, especially apes. He wrote *Gorillas and Chimpanzees* (London, 1896). Died January 22, 1920, in Chattanooga, Tennessee. *References*: *NCAB* 13:314; *NYT*, January 24, 1920; and *WWWA*.

GARNET, HENRY HIGHLAND (1815–1882). Clergyman and diplomat, born a slave December 23, 1815, at New Market, Kent County, Maryland, and grew up on Long Island, New York. Garnet studied at Oneida Institute. He was pastor in Troy, New York, from 1842 to 1848 and became publisher of the *United States Clarion* in Troy in 1843. He was pastor in Jamaica from 1853 until 1856, and then in New York City and Washington, D.C. He was the founder and president of the American Civilization Society in 1858. He was minister resident and consul general in Liberia in 1881–1882. Died February 12, 1882, in Monrovia, Liberia. *References*: *ACAB*; *DAB*; *DANB*; Richard K. MacMaster, "Henry Highland Garnet and the African Civilization Society," *Journal of Presbyterian History* 48 (1970): 95–112 (reprinted in *Black Apostles at Home and Abroad: Afro-Americans and the Christian Mission from the Revolution to Reconstruction*, ed. David W. Wills and Richard Newmann [Boston, 1982], pp. 265–82); *NCAB* 2:414; *NYT*, March 11, 1882; Earl Ofari, *"Let Your Motto Be Resistance": The Life and Thought of Henry Highland Garnet* (Boston, 1972); Joel Schor, *Henry Highland Garnet: A Voice of Black Radicalism in the Nineteenth Century* (Westport, Conn., 1977); William Seraile, "The Brief Diplomatic Career of Henry Highland Garnet," *Phylon* 46 (1985): 71–81; Hanes Walton et al., "Henry

Highland Garnet Revisited via His Diplomatic Correspondence: The Correction of Misconceptions and Errors,'' *JNH* 68 (1983): 80–92; and *WWWA*.

GEBAUER, PAUL (1900–1977). Missionary and authority on African art, born October 17, 1900, in southeastern Germany. Gebauer served in the German Army in World War I, came to the United States in 1925, and became a United States citizen in 1931. He graduated from Southern Baptist Seminary (Louisville, Ky.) and Northwestern University. He was a missionary under the General Missionary Society of the North American Baptist General Conference* in Cameroon from 1931 to 1961, formed the Cameroon Baptist Mission, and was superintendent of the Cameroon Baptist Mission U.S.A. from 1946 until his retirement. He served as a chaplain during World War II. He taught at Linfield College (McMinnville, Ore.) after 1961 and was chair of its language department. For thirty years he collected Cameroonian art (now in the Portland Art Museum and the Metropolitan Museum of Art). He wrote *Spider Divination in the Cameroons* (Milwaukee, 1964) and *Art of Cameroon* (Portland, Ore., 1979). Died June 22, 1977, in Ely, Nevada. *References*: *African Arts* 11 (October 1977): 6; *Linfield College Bulletin*, October 1977.

GEIL, WILLIAM EDGAR (1865–1925). Explorer and author, born near Doylestown, Pennsylvania. Geil graduated from Lafayette College (Easton, Pa.). He made a four-year trip around the world and was best known for his exploration of the Great Wall of China. He traveled into the interior of the Congo Free State to study the pygmies and wrote *A Yankee in Pigmyland* (London, 1905) and *Adventures in the African Jungle Hunting Pigmies* (New York, 1917). He lectured all over the United States and later became an evangelist. Died April 12, 1925, in Venice, Italy, on his way back from Jerusalem. *References*: *ACAB*; *NYT*, April 14, 1925; and *WWWA*.

GEORGE, DAVID (ca. 1742–1810). Clergyman, born a slave in Essex County, Virginia. On reaching maturity, George escaped. He later worked among the Natchez Indians and on an estate at Silver Bluff, near Augusta, Georgia, and became pastor to the Silver Bluff Negroes. He was forced in 1779 to take refuge behind the British lines, and when the British evacuated Charleston in 1782, he and his family were among the Loyalists who went to Nova Scotia. He went to Sierra Leone in 1792 and established a Baptist church there. Died in Sierra Leone. *References*: *DANB*; and *Dictionary of Canadian Biography* (Toronto, 1983), 5:340–42.

GEORGE, ELIZA DAVIS (1879–1979). Missionary, born January 20, 1879, in Bastrop County, Texas. George attended Guadelupe College and Central Texas College, and taught at Central Texas College from 1908 to 1913. She was a missionary in Liberia from 1913 to 1953, first as an independent missionary and later under the American Baptist Foreign Mission Society (see American

Baptist Missionary Union*). She served in Forstville, Grand Bassa County, and there established the Bible Industrial Academy. She was stationed in Sinoe County after 1918. Died March 8, 1979, in Austin, Texas. *Reference*: Lorry Lutz, *Born to Lose, Bound to Win: The Amazing Journey of Mother Eliza George* (Irvine, Calif., 1980).

GIBBS, MIFFLIN W(ISTAR) (1823–1915). Businessman, lawyer, politician, and consul, born in Philadelphia. Gibbs became a carpenter's apprentice and later a journeyman contractor and was active in the abolitionist movement. He became a partner in a clothing store in San Francisco in 1850 and went to Victoria, British Columbia, in 1858 and set up a store there. He returned to the United States in 1869, was trained in law in Oberlin, Ohio, and began to practice law in Little Rock, Arkansas, in 1871. He was elected municipal judge of Little Rock in 1873 and served as receiver of the United States Land Office for the Little Rock district of Arkansas from 1877 until 1889. He was consul at Tamatave, Madagascar, from 1898 to 1901, when he resigned for reasons of ill health. He wrote *Shadow and Light: An Autobiography with Reminiscences of the Last and Present Century* (Washington, D.C., 1902; reprinted 1969). Died July 11, 1915, in Little Rock, Arkansas. *References*: *DANB*; *NCAB* 10:114; and *WWCR*.

GILSON, HANNAH JULIETTE (1845–1924). Educator, born January 11, 1845, in Brookline, New Hampshire. Gilson graduated from Mount Holyoke Seminary and attended Hartford Theological Seminary. She was a teacher in Du-Quoin, Illinois, and Milford, New Hampshire, from 1868 to 1874. She was the founder and principal of the Bloemhof Seminary, a high school for girls, in Stellenbosch, Cape Colony, South Africa, from 1874 until 1883, and a missionary teacher under the Woman's Board of Missions in Rhodesia from 1896 to 1914, teaching at Umzumbe, and later in charge of a girls' school in Mount Silinda, Rhodesia. She returned to the United States in 1914. Died April 25, 1924, in Nashua, New Hampshire. *Reference*: *One Hundred Year Biographical Directory of Mount Holyoke College 1837–1937* (South Hadley, Mass., 1937).

GIROUARD, PAUL JOSEPH (1898–1964). Missionary, born December 27, 1964, in Hamilton, Rhode Island. Girouard graduated from La Salette Seminary (Hartford, Conn.) and the Gregorian University (Rome) and was ordained in 1927. He was missionary in Madagascar from 1928 until his death. He was appointed prefect apostolic of Morondava, Madagascar, in 1955 and was the first bishop of the diocese of Morondava. Died February 1964 in Morondava, Madagascar. *Reference*: *DACB*.

GLASSFORD, WILLIAM ALEXANDER, 2ND (1886–1958). Naval officer, born June 6, 1886, in San Francisco. Glassford graduated from the United States Naval Academy in 1906 and was commissioned ensign in the United States

Navy. He served as gunnery officer on destroyers and destroyer tenders in World War I and was commander of the *Shaw*. He later commanded the destroyers *Chauncey* and *Bradford*, served as officer in charge of the hydrographic office in San Francisco, commander of the destroyer *Tracy* and of Destroyer Division 38, and executive officer of the *California*. He served on the staff of the Naval War College, on duty with the Argentine Navy Department in Buenos Aires from 1935 to 1937, and as commander of the Yangtze Naval Patrol in China from 1939 to 1941. He served as commander of the United States Naval Forces, Southwest Pacific, in 1942. He was deputy commander-in-chief of the Allied Expeditionary Forces in French West Africa and deputy commander of the United States Naval Forces in the Northwest African waters. He was also made head of the United States mission in Dakar, Senegal, French West Africa, to develop the Dakar harbor and the Wakan airport, and President Franklin D. Roosevelt's personal representative at Dakar, French West Africa, in 1943. He retired in 1947 with the rank of vice admiral. Died July 30, 1958, in San Diego, California. *References*: NCAB 47:32; *NYT*, July 31, 1958; and *WWWA*.

GODLEY, G(EORGE) MCMURTIE (1917-   ). Diplomat, born August 23, 1917, in New York City. Godley graduated from Yale University and studied at the University of Chicago; he served in the navy and the marines during World War II. He entered the foreign service in 1941, served in Marseilles, Bern, and Brussels, was first secretary in Paris from 1952 to 1955, and counselor of embassy in Cambodia from 1955 to 1957 and in the Congo (Léopoldville) in 1961–1962. He was director of Central African affairs at the U.S. State Department from 1962 to 1964 and ambassador to the Democratic Republic of the Congo from 1964 to 1966, during a period in which the U.S. role was crucial. He coordinated American military air transport with Belgium in suppressing the Simba rebellion of 1964. He was deputy assistant secretary of state for East Asian and Pacific affairs in 1968–1969, ambassador to Laos from 1969 to 1973, and ambassador to Lebanon from 1974 to 1976. *References*: *NYT*, July 12, 1973; *WWA*; and *WWG*.

GOLDSCHMIDT, WALTER R(OCHS) (1913-   ). Anthropologist, born February 23, 1913, in San Antonio, Texas. Goldschmidt graduated from the universities of Texas and California at Berkeley. He was a social scientist with the U.S. Bureau of Agricultural Economics from 1940 to 1946, member of the faculty of the University of California in Los Angeles after 1946, and professor of anthropology there from 1956 until 1983. He conducted fieldwork in East Africa in 1954 and in 1961–1962; wrote *Sebei Law* (Berkeley, Calif., 1967); *Kambuya's Cattle, the Legacy of an African Herdsman* (Berkeley, Calif., 1969); and *Culture and Behavior of the Sebei: A Study of Continuity and Adaptation* (Berkeley, Calif., 1976); and edited *The United States and Africa*, rev. ed. (New York, 1963). *References*: AMWS; CA; WWA; and WWW.

GOMER, JOSEPH (1834–1892). Missionary, born July 20, 1834, in Ann Arbor, Michigan. Gomer was employed in a home furnishing store in Chicago, served as a cook during the Civil War, and was later an upholsterer and foreman in a department store in Dayton, Ohio. He was ordained in 1876. He was missionary under the United Brethren in Christ* in Mende, Sierra Leone, from 1871 until 1892, and superintendent of the mission during part of that period. Died September 5, 1892, in Freetown, Sierra Leone. *References*: Joseph Gomer Papers, Evangelical United Brethren Division of the United Methodist Commission on Archives and History, Dayton, Ohio; *EWM*; Marcella H. Miller, "Joseph and Mary Gomer, Missionaries," *NHB* 26 (February 1963): 163–64.

GOOD, ADOLPHUS CLEMENS (1856–1894). Missionary and naturalist, born December 19, 1856, at West Mahooning, Pennsylvania, and grew up at Glade Run, Pennsylvania. Good graduated from Washington and Jefferson College and Western Theological Seminary and was ordained in 1882. In 1882 he became a missionary under the Board of Foreign Missions of the Presbyterian Church in the U.S.A.,* stationed in Baraka on the Gabon River in the French Congo. When the mission was closed by the French authorities, who required that all religious and educational work be conducted in French, he opened a mission station at Kangwe on the Ogowe River in 1885, traveling constantly into the interior, and began work in Efulen in the Bulu country in German Cameroon in 1892. He prepared a Bulu primer, revised the translation of the New Testament into Mpongwe and translated the Gospels into Bulu. He collected natural history specimens, including many species previously unknown to science. Died December 13, 1894, in Efulen, German Cameroon. *References*: *DAB*; *NCAB* 23:62; W. Reginald Wheeler, *The Words of God in an African Forest: The Story of an American Mission in West Africa* (New York, 1931), ch. 6; and *WWWA*.

GOODENOUGH, HERBERT D(ELOS) (1852–1927). Missionary, born May 22, 1852, in Barton, Wisconsin. Goodenough graduated from Oberlin College, attended Oberlin and Andover Theological seminaries, and was ordained in 1881. He was a missionary under the American Board of Commissioners for Foreign Missions (ABCFM)* in South Africa from 1881 until 1913. He served in Durban from 1881 to 1888; was principal of the Amanzimtoti Seminary from 1882 to 1888; served in the Zulu Mission at Umvoti, Natal, from 1890 until 1894; in Johannesburg from 1894 until 1908; and again in Durban from 1908 until his retirement in 1913. He was also secretary of the Zulu Mission for many years. Died August 24, 1927, in Rochester, Massachusetts. *Reference*: *AndoverTS*.

GORDON, NORA ANTONIA (1866–1901). Teacher and missionary, born in Columbus, Georgia, and grew up in La Grange, Georgia. Gordon graduated from Spelman Seminary and studied in London. She founded the African Missionary Movement at Spelman Seminary and later taught in Atlanta public

schools. She was a missionary under the Society of the West in Palabala, Congo
Free State, from 1889 to 1893 and from 1896 to 1900, teaching in an elementary
school. She returned to the United States in 1900. Died in Atlanta, Georgia.
References: Benjamin G. Brawley, *Women of Achievement* (Chicago, 1919);
Hallie Q. Brown, *Homespun Heroines and Other Women of Distinction* (Xenia,
Ohio, 1926); Sylvia G. L. Dannett, *Profiles of Negro Womanhood 1619–1900*
(New York, 1964), pp. 258–59; and Lawson A. Scruggs, *Women of Distinction:
Remarkable in Works and Invincible in Character* (Raleigh, N.C., 1893), pp.
217–22.

GORGAS, WILLIAM CRAWFORD (1854–1920). Army officer and physician, born October 3, 1854, in Mobile, Alabama. Gorgas graduated from the
University of the South and Bellevue Medical College (N.Y.C.). He was appointed a surgeon in the United States Army in 1880, became head of sanitation
in Cuba in 1898, chief sanitary officer for the Panama Canal Zone in 1904, and
surgeon general of the United States Army in 1914. He visited South Africa in
1913–1914 as a consultant to the Transvaal Chamber of Mines to advise on
measures for improving the health of the African miners and to reform the health
organization of the Witwatersrand gold fields. He supervised the army medical
service during World War I and retired in 1918 with the rank of major general.
Died July 3, 1920, in London. *References*: William Crawford Gorgas Papers,
University of Alabama Library, University, Ala.; William Crawford Gorgas
Papers, Manuscript Division, Library of Congress; *ACAB*; *DAB*; *DAMB*; *NCAB*
32:4; *NYT*, July 6, 1920; and *WWWA*.

GORHAM, SARAH J. (1832–1894). Missionary, born December 25, 1832,
in Fredericksburg, Virginia. Gorham was the first woman missionary of the
African Methodist Episcopal Church* to be appointed to a foreign field, and
served as missionary to the Creoles and Mende in Sierra Leone from 1890 to
1894. Died August 10, 1894, in Freetown, Sierra Leone.

GREENVILLE. *See* MISSISSIPPI IN AFRICA

GREGORY, WILLIAM KING (1876–1970). Paleontologist, born May 19,
1876, in New York City. Gregory attended Columbia School of Mines and
graduated from Columbia University. He joined the American Museum of Natural History in 1899, was research assistant from 1899 to 1913, assistant curator
in the department of vertebrate paleontology from 1911 to 1914, associate in
paleontology from 1914 to 1926, curator of comparative anatomy from 1921 to
1944, curator of the department of ichthyology from 1925 to 1944, and professor
of vertebrate paleontology at Columbia University until his retirement in 1944.
He was a member of an expedition to Australia in 1921–1922 and of the *Arcturus*
expedition to the Sargasso Sea in 1925. With Henry Cushier Raven,* he explored
Africa in 1929–1930 studying gorillas and was coauthor of *In Quest of Gorillas*

(New Bedford, Mass., 1937). He went to South Africa in 1938 to study the Australopithecines. Died December 29, 1970, in Woodstock, New York. *References*: *American Journal of Physical Anthropology* 56 (1981): 393–95; *AMWS*; *BMNAS* 46 (1975): 91–133; *NCAB* A:105; *NYT*, December 30, 1970; and *WWWA*.

GRIBBLE, JAMES S. (1883–1923). Missionary, born February 25, 1883, in Mechanicsburg, Pennsylvania. Gribble was missionary under the Africa Inland Mission* in British East Africa from 1909 to 1914. He led the pioneer mission of the Foreign Missionary Society of the Brethren Church* to Oubangui-Chari, French Equatorial Africa, in 1918, and established the first mission station at Bassai in 1921. Died June 4, 1923, at Basai, Oubangui-Chari. His wife, **FLORENCE ALMA (NEWBERRY) GRIBBLE** (1879–1942), a medical missionary, was born December 3, 1879, in Louisville, Nebraska. She graduated from Hahnemann Medical College and studied at Moody Bible Institute. She was a missionary under the Africa Inland Mission in British East Africa from 1908 to 1912, in the Belgian Congo from 1912 to 1914, and in Oubangui-Chari from 1918 until 1942. Died March 3, 1942, at Bellevue station, Oubangui-Chari. She wrote *Undaunted Hope: Life of James Gribble* (Ashland, Ohio, 1932) and her autobiography, *Stranger Than Fiction* (Winona Lake, Ind., 1949), which appeared after her death. *Reference*: *BE*.

GROUT, ALDIN (1803–1894). Missionary, born September 2, 1803, in Pelham, Massachusetts. Grout graduated from Amherst College and Andover Theological Seminary and was ordained in 1834. He was missionary under the American Board of Commissioners for Foreign Missions (ABCFM)* in South Africa from 1835 until 1870. He set up a mission station in Zululand in 1840, but was forced to leave in 1842 and returned to Natal. He then established missions on the Umgeni River near Durban and at Umvoti (now Groutville), Natal, which he served from 1843 until 1870. He returned to the United States in 1870 and resided in Springfield, Massachusetts. Died February 12, 1894, in Springfield. *References*: *Amherst*; *AndoverTS*; *DASB* 3; *SADNB*; *SESA*; and *Tabler/Natal*.

GROUT, LEWIS (1815–1905). Missionary, born January 28, 1815, at Newfane, Vermont. Grout graduated from Yale University, attended Yale Divinity School, graduated from Andover Theological Seminary, and was ordained in 1846. He was missionary under the American Board of Commissioners for Foreign Missions (ABCFM)* to the Zulus from 1846 to 1862. He was stationed at Msunduzi in 1847 and opened a school there. He became a Zulu linguist, and wrote *The Isizulu: A Grammar of the Zulu Language* (London, 1859) and *Zululand; or, Life Among the Zulu-kafirs of Natal and Zulu-land, South Africa* (Philadelphia, 1864), and translated parts of the Bible into Zulu. He returned to the United States in 1862, was pastor at Saxton's River and Sudbury, Vermont, and

Feeding Hills and Agawam, Massachusetts, and was an agent of the American Missionary Association* for New Hampshire and Vermont from 1865 to 1884; he lived in Brattleboro, Vermont, after 1888. His *Autobiography of the Rev. Lewis Grout* (Brattleboro, Vt., 1905) was published posthumously. Died March 12, 1905, at West Brattleboro, Vermont. *References*: *AndoverTS*; *DSAB* 1; W. K. McNeil, "The First American Collectors of African Folklore," *Kentucky Folklore Record* 28 (1982): 40–47; *SADNB*; *SESA*; and *WWWA*.

GULLION, EDMUND A(SBURY) (1913-   ). Diplomat, born March 2, 1913, in Lexington, Kentucky. Gullion graduated from Princeton University and the National War College. He entered the foreign service in 1937, served in Marseilles, Salonika (Greece), and London, was chargé d'affaires in Helsinki in 1943, second secretary in Stockholm in 1944, counselor of legation in Saigon, Vietnam, in 1950, and deputy director of the U.S. Disarmament Administration in 1960. He was ambassador to the Congo from 1961 to 1964. Almost single-handedly he wrought an agreement ending the Katanga secession. He was dean of the Fletcher School of Law and Diplomacy of Tufts University after 1964. *References*: W. A. Nielen, "Our Envoy Searches for Peace in the Congo," *NYT Magazine*, April 15, 1962; and *WWA*.

GUNDERSON, ADOLPHUS EUGENE (1878–1951). Missionary. Gunderson was a missionary under the Sudan Interior Mission* from 1912 to 1916, working at Miango, Northern Nigeria. He returned to the United States in 1916, but was back in Africa in 1923, under the Evangelical Lutheran Church.* He established the Sudan Mission at Mboula, French Cameroon, and was its director. He returned to the United States in 1935. Died April 25, 1951, in Minneapolis. *Reference*: Ruth Christiansen, *For the Heart of Africa* (Minneapolis, 1956).

GUNTHER, JOHN (1901–1970). Journalist, born August 30, 1901, in Chicago. Gunther graduated from the University of Chicago. He was correspondent for the *Chicago Daily News* in Europe until 1936, when he became a free-lance journalist, and published the first book in his "Inside" series. He was special consultant to the U.S. war department from 1942 to 1944. He traveled in Africa in 1953–1954, interviewing and collecting data for *Inside Africa* (New York, 1955), an activity he described in *A Fragment of Autobiography: The Fun of Writing the Inside Books* (New York, 1961). Died May 29, 1970, in New York City. *References*: *CB* 1941, 1961; *DADH*; *EAJ*; *NCAB* J:468; *NYT*, May 30, 1970; and *WWWA*.

GURLEY, RALPH RANDOLPH (1797–1872). Clergyman, born May 26, 1797, in Lebanon, Connecticut. Gurley graduated from Yale University. He became general agent of the American Colonization Society (ACS)* in 1822, corresponding secretary in 1838, and vice president in 1854. He was founder of the *African Repository* and edited it for twenty-five years, and also founded and edited the *Colonial Journal*. He went first to Liberia in 1824 for the ACS and the United States government to investigate charges against Jehudi Ashmun* who was unofficially acting as governor and to straighten out existing difficulties in the colony. He was sent again by the United States government in 1849 and in 1867 as special agent to Liberia to examine the stability of the government with a view to U.S. recognition of Liberian independence. In 1835 he published a biography of Ashmun. Died July 30, 1872, Washington, D.C. *References*: *African Repository* 49 (1873): 99–105; *DAB*; *Huberich*; *NCAB* 2:252; and *WWWA*.

GURNEY, SAMUEL (1860–1924). Medical missionary, born September 3, 1860, in Long Branch, New Jersey. Gurney attended New York Missionary Training School, graduated from Drew Theological Seminary and Yale University Medical School, and was ordained in 1891. He was a pastor in Long Island, New York, and Connecticut. He was a missionary under the Foreign Missionary Society of the Methodist Episcopal Church* in Southern Rhodesia from 1903 until his death. He was stationed first at Old Umtali, and later at Mrewa, Mtoko, and Nyadiri. He built and equipped two hospitals, one at Old Umtali and the other at Mtoko. Died August 3, 1924, in Salisbury, Southern Rhodesia. *References*: *EWM*; and *NYT*, August 14, 1924.

H

HAAS, WILLIAM CLARENCE (1873–1924). Missionary, born January 4, 1873, in Mendon, Michigan. Haas was ordained in 1894 and was a pastor in Union City, Michigan, and Caldwell and Columbus, Ohio. He was a missionary under the Africa Inland Mission* from 1912 to 1916, stationed in Rafai, British East Africa. In 1920 he founded the General Council of Cooperating Baptist Missions of North America, Inc. (later renamed Baptist Mid-Missions*) in Oubangui-Chari, French Equatorial Africa. Died May 28, 1924, in Bangassou, on the bank of the Bomu River, French Equatorial Africa.

HAIGH, L(AWRENCE) B(ENJAMIN) (1882–1963). Missionary, born January 15, 1882, in Eaton Bradford, Yorkshire, England, and brought to the United States in 1885. Haigh graduated from the Moody Bible Institute, and was ordained in 1910. He was missionary under the Africa Inland Mission* in Kijabe, British East Africa, from 1906 to 1909. He returned to Africa in 1911 as the first missionary under the United Mennonite Board of Missions and began the Congo Inland Mission*. He established a mission station at Djoko Punda (later Charlesville) in the Kasai District and later a second mission at Kalamba. He was also the legal representative and business manager for the mission. He returned to the United States in 1920, was pastor in Danvers, Illinois, and then farmed in Roseboro, North Carolina, until 1949. In 1952 he settled in Salisbury, North Carolina. Died December 4, 1963, in Salisbury.

HALL, GEORGE (fl. 1871–1888). Miner and trader. Hall came to South Africa in the early 1870s, and was employed by Cobb & Company (see Freeman Cobb*), which operated a coach line between Port Elizabeth and Kimberley. He was a trader at Bulawayo, Rhodesia, from 1876 to 1886, and mined at Tati, Matabelaland, in 1888. *Reference: Tabler/Rhodesia*.

HALL, HENRY USHER (1876?–1944). Anthropologist. Hall studied at Oxford University. He was assistant curator of the section of general ethnology at the

University Museum of the University of Pennsylvania from 1916 to 1924, and curator there from 1924 to 1937; he then became curator of ethnology in the museum's section of general ethnology and anthropology from 1931 to 1935. He conducted research in Sierra Leone in 1936–1937, and wrote *The Sherbro of Sierra Leone* (Philadelphia, 1938). Died November 2, 1944, in Philadelphia. *Reference: NYT*, November 4, 1944.

HALL, JAMES (1802–1889). Physician and colonial agent. Hall graduated from the Medical School of Maine. He went to Liberia in 1831 to serve as colonial physician for the American Colonization Society.* He returned to the United States in 1833 because of ill health, but was back in Africa the same year to lead the Maryland expedition. He served as colonial physician and first governor of Maryland in Africa* and purchased Cape Palmas by treaty in 1834. He resigned as governor and returned to the United States in 1836. He then entered the shipping business on the Liberian coast and served at the same time as general agent for the Maryland State Colonization Society. He was later business manager of the Maryland State Colonization Society and editor of the *Maryland Colonization Journal*. Died August 31, 1889, near Elkridge Landing, Howard County, Maryland. *Reference: African Repository* 65 (1889): 117–19.

HAMBLY, WILFRID D(YSON) (1886–1962). Anthropologist, born in Clayton, Yorkshire, England. Hambly graduated from Hartley University College and Oxford University. He was archaeological assistant in the Wellcome expedition to the Anglo-Egyptian Sudan in 1913, served in the British Navy during World War I, was lecturer in biology at Eastham Technical College and investigator for the British Industrial Research Board from 1919 to 1923, and lecturer in biology at the Essex Museum of Natural History from 1923 to 1926. He came to the United States in 1926 and was the first full-time curator of African ethnology at the Field Museum of Natural History from 1926 until 1952. He headed the Frederick H. Rawson–Field Museum ethnological expedition to West Africa in 1929–1930, which explored Nigeria and Angola, and wrote *With a Motor Truck in West Africa* (New York, 1931); *Serpent Worship in Africa* (Chicago, 1931); *The Ovimbundu of Angola* (Chicago, 1934); *Culture Areas of Nigeria* (Chicago, 1935); *Anthropometry of the Ovimbundu, Angola* (Chicago, 1938); and *Desert Boy* (Chicago, 1957). He compiled *Source Book for African Anthropology* (Chicago, 1937) and *Bibliography of African Anthropology, 1937–49* (Chicago, 1952). Died July 18, 1962, in Chicago. *References: AMWS; Chicago Natural History Museum Bulletin* 33 (September 1962): 4.

HAMMOND, JOHN HAYS (1855–1936). Mining engineer, born March 31, 1855, in San Francisco. Hammond graduated from Sheffield Scientific School of Yale University and from the Royal School of Mines in Freiberg, Saxony. He was employed in various mining jobs in California from 1879 to 1881, became a consulting engineer in 1881, and was consulting engineer to the mining department of the Union Iron Works in San Francisco from 1884 to 1891, when he and a group of associates bought the Bunker Hill and Sullivan Mine in the Coeur d'Alene district of Idaho and he became its president. He went to South Africa in 1893 as manager of the properties of Barney Barnato on the Rand in the Transvaal, but left after six months and was hired by Cecil Rhodes as chief consulting engineer of the Consolidated Gold Fields of South Africa and the British South African Company. He was in the forefront of the Reform Committee* and after the Jameson Raid of 1896 was convicted of treason and sentenced to death. He was ultimately released after five months in jail and the payment of a fine. He was a consulting engineer in London from 1896 to 1899, returned to the United States in 1899 and became a consulting engineer in New York City. He was also a consulting engineer and general manager of the Guggenheim Exploring Company until 1907. He participated actively in the peace movement and in the National Civic Federation. He wrote *The Autobiography of John Hays Hammond* (New York, 1935; reprinted, 1974). Died June 8, 1936, in Gloucester, Massachusetts. *References*: John Hays Hammond Papers, Sterling Memorial Library, Yale University, New Haven, Conn.; *DAB* S2; *DSAB* 2; *NCAB* 26:45; *NYT*, June 9, 1936; and *WWWA*.

HAMMOND, PETER B(OYD) (1928-). Anthropologist, born August 7, 1928, in Glendale, California. Hammond attended the University of Puerto Rico, graduated from the University of the Americas, studied at the University of Paris, and graduated from Northwestern University. He conducted research in Upper Volta and Mali, French West Africa, from 1954 to 1956, and wrote *Yatenga: Technology in the Culture of a West African Kingdom* (New York, 1966). He was assistant professor of anthropology at the University of Pittsburgh from 1957 to 1962; associate professor at Indiana University from 1962 to 1965; lecturer in psychiatry at Children's Hospital, Washington, D.C., from 1968 to 1972; and an independent researcher and writer after 1973. *References*: AMWS; CA.

HANCE, WILLIAM ADAMS (1916-). Geographer, born December 29, 1916, in New York City. Hance graduated from Columbia University. He served in the navy during World War II. He became a member of the faculty of Columbia University in 1942 and was professor of economic geography from 1959 until his retirement in 1982. He did fieldwork in Africa in 1951, 1952, 1956, 1962–1963, 1965, 1969, 1970, and 1974. He wrote *African Economic Development* (New York, 1958; rev. ed. New York, 1967), *The Geography of Modern Africa* (New York, 1964; rev. ed. New York, 1975), and *Black Africa Develops* (Waltham, Mass., 1977), and edited *Southern Africa and the United States* (New York, 1968). He became president of the American Geographical Society in 1972. *References*: AMWS; *Geographical Review* 62 (July 1972): 307–08; and *WWA*.

HANSON, ABRAHAM (1818?–1866). Clergyman and consul. Hanson was minister of the Methodist Episcopal Church in the Northwest. He was the first commissioner and consul general in Liberia from 1864 to 1866. Died July 20, 1866, in Monrovia, Liberia.

HANSON, HERBERT M(ARTIN) (1894–1966). Missionary, born in Chokio, Minnesota. Hanson graduated from Hutchinson Theological Seminary. He went to Norway in 1921, established a Seventh-Day Adventist academy in Onsrud, Jessheim, Norway, and served as its principal until 1934. He came to Ethiopia in 1934 and was principal of the mission school that he opened at Addis Alem. He established the Akaki school in Addis Ababa in 1943 and served as its principal. Died October 27, 1966, in Addis Ababa. His wife, **DELLA HANSON** (1897–1981), was born October 9, 1897. She was housekeeper to Emperor Haile Selassie from 1941 until 1974, when she returned to the United States. They wrote *For God and Emperor* (Mountain View, Calif., 1958). She died November 17, 1981, at Riverside, California. *Reference*: *SDAE*.

HARLEY, GEORGE W(AY) (1894–1966). Medical missionary, born August 8, 1894, in Asheville, North Carolina. Harley graduated from Duke University and Yale University Medical School and studied at the London School of Tropical Medicine and the Hartford Seminary Foundation. He was a missionary under the Board of Foreign Missions of the Methodist Episcopal Church.* He came to Ganta, Liberia, in 1926 and established a medical mission there. He also built the first sawmill in Liberia, as well as a blacksmith shop and a tile-and-brick factory. He wrote *Native African Medicine with Special Reference to Its Practice in the Mano Tribes of Liberia* (Cambridge, Mass., 1941), *Notes on the Poro in Liberia* (Cambridge, Mass., 1941), *Masks as Agents of Social Control in Northeast Liberia* (Cambridge, Mass., 1950), and edited and added material to George Schwab's* *Tribes of the Liberian Hinterland* (Cambridge, Mass., 1947). Died November 7, 1966, in Ganta, Liberia. His wife **WINIFRED FRANCES J(EWELL) HARLEY** (1895–   ) wrote *Handbook of Liberian Ferns* (Wakefield, Mass., 1957) and *A Third of a Century with George Way Harley in Liberia* (Newark, Del., 1973). *References*: George W. Harley Papers, Duke University Library, Durham, N.C.; *AMWS*; *EWM*; Edward H. Hume, *Doctors Courageous* (New York, 1950), ch. 5; *Newsweek*, August 21, 1950; L. T. Wells, "Harley Masks of Northeast Liberia," *African Arts* 10 (January 1977): 22–27.

HARPER. *See* MARYLAND IN AFRICA

HARRINGTON, EDWARD (fl. 1840). Sea captain, from Salem, Massachusetts. Harrington was in the employ of the Salem merchants Robert Brookhouse and William Hunt, and made several trips to West Africa to trade tobacco, rum, lumber, shingles, flour, beef, pork, dried fish, and cotton goods for peanuts, hides, gold dust, palm oil, ivory, and gum copal. *References*: Edward Harrington,

"Letter Book," Essex Institute, Salem, Mass.; George F. Brooks, Jr., "The Letter Book of Captain Edward Harrington," *Transactions of the Historical Society of Ghana* 6 (1962): 71–77; George F. Brooks, "A Salem Merchant at Cape Palmas, Liberia in 1840," *EIHC* 98 (1962): 161–74.

HARRIS, BRAVID WASHINGTON (1896–1965). Clergyman and missionary, born January 6, 1896, in Warrenton, North Carolina. Harris graduated from St. Augustine's College (Raleigh, N.C.) and Bishop Payne Divinity School, and was ordained in 1922. He served in the U.S. army during World War I. He was a priest in Warrenton, North Carolina, and Norfolk, Virginia, from 1922 to 1944, and archdeacon of Negro work in the Diocese of Southern Virginia from 1937 to 1943. He was consecrated bishop in 1945 and was missionary bishop of the Protestant Episcopal Church in Liberia from 1945 until his retirement in 1964. He rebuilt and reopened Cuttington Collegiate and Divinity School.* Died October 21, 1965, near Fredericksburg, Virginia. *References*: *NCAB* 43:89; *NYT*, October 23, 1965; and *WWWA*.

HARRIS, SION (ca. 1811–1854). Colonist, possibly freeborn, from Knox County, Kansas. Harris immigrated to Liberia in 1830 and was a carpenter and farmer. Almost single-handedly he repulsed an attack by natives on the mission station at Heddington in March 1840, and killed their chief. He was later a member of the Liberian House of Representatives. Killed by lightning, April 25, 1854, in Caldwell, Liberia. *Reference*: *African Repository* 30 (1954): 228–29; Bell I. Wiley, ed., *Slaves No More: Letters from Liberia 1833– 1869* (Lexington, Ky., 1980).

HARTZELL, JOSEPH CRANE (1842–1928). Clergyman, born June 1, 1842, near Moline, Illinois. Hartzell graduated from Illinois Wesleyan University and Garrett Biblical Institute, and was ordained in 1868. He was a pastor in Pekin, Illinois, and New Orleans until 1882. He was assistant corresponding secretary and then corresponding secretary of the Freedmen's Aid and Southern Education Society at Cincinnati from 1882 until 1896. He was consecrated missionary bishop for Africa in 1896 and served until his retirement in 1916. Residing at Funchal, Madeira, he made thirteen tours of Africa and established missions in Rhodesia, North Africa, Angola and Mozambique. In 1898 he acted as special representative for Liberia to request Great Britain and the United States to establish a joint protectorate over Liberia. He wrote *The Africa Mission of the Methodist Episcopal Church* (New York, 1909). Died September 6, 1928, at Blue Ash, Ohio. *References*: Joseph Crane Hartzell Papers, Methodist Publishing House Library, Nashville, Tenn.; *ACAB*; *DAB*; *EWM*; *Leete*; *NCAB* 13:128; and *WWWA*.

HARVARD AFRICAN EXPEDITION (1926–1927). The expedition, led by Richard P. Strong,* made a biological and medical survey of Liberia, then crossed the continent from the west to the east coast traveling through the Belgian Congo, and made comparative studies of these regions. It published its findings in *The African Republic of Liberia and the Belgian Congo, Based on Observations Made and Material Collected During the Harvard African Expedition, 1926– 1927*, ed. Richard P. Strong (Cambridge, Mass., 1930).

HASSELL'S SCOUTS. A body of American volunteers under Captain John Arthur Hassell, from New Jersey, who was given full citizenship by the Transvaal Volksraad in recognition for his services during the Jameson Raid. Hassell's Scouts fought with the Boers during the South African War, took part in operations in Natal, saw action near Brandfort in May 1900, and in a number of small battles and skirmishes. On June 14, 1900, it attacked a party of British engineers working on a bridge across the Zand River, and among those killed was Louis Irving Seymour.* Hassell was wounded at Estcourt. With Alan Richard Illeigh Hiley, he wrote *The Mobile Boer. Being the Record of Observations of Two Burgher Officers* (New York, 1902). *Reference*: SESA.

HATFIELD, WILLIS CHARLES ("LUKE") (1898–1970). Geologist, born November 23, 1898, in Ipswich, Massachusetts. Hatfield graduated from Wesleyan University (Middletown, Conn.) and Columbia University. He conducted mineral exploration work in Northern Rhodesia for the Rhodesia Congo Border Concessions, Limited, from 1928 to 1932, and wrote *The Geology of the Solwezi District, Northern Rhodesia* (London, 1937). He was instructor in geology at Hunter College from 1935 to 1937, and then geologist and chief geologist of the Texas Petroleum Company in Colombia, from 1937 until his retirement in 1957. Died March 10, 1970, in Freedom, New Hampshire. *References*: *American Association of Petroleum Geologists Bulletin* 54 (1970): 1951–1953; and *Geological Society of America Memorials* 2 (1973): 52–53.

HATHORNE, WILLIAM H(OLLINGSWORTH) (? –1886). Sea captain and consul, from Salem, Massachusetts. Hathorne served in the Union Navy during the Civil War. After 1865, he commanded ships for John Bertram in the Western Indian Ocean trade. He was resident agent for the firms of John Bertram of Salem and Arnold Hines and Company of New York in Zanzibar from 1875 to 1880. He was also consul in Zanzibar from 1876 to 1880, when he returned to the United States. Died in Salem. *References*: William H. Hathorne Letters, Peabody Museum of Salem, Mass.; Norman R. Bennett, "William H. Hathorne: Merchant and Consul in Zanzibar," *EIHC* 99 (1963): 117–46.

HAVEN, JESSE (1814–1905). Missionary, born March 28, 1814, in Holliston, Middlesex County, Massachusetts. He was ordained an elder in the Church of Jesus Christ of Latter-day Saints in 1839. He moved to Nauvoo, Illinois, filled several missions for the church in the eastern states, and then moved to the Salt Lake Valley, Utah, in 1850. He came to South Africa in 1853, established the South African Mission, and served as its president from 1853 to 1855. He wrote and published in Cape Town several Mormon tracts. He was a missionary in Scotland in 1855–1856 and returned to the United States in 1856. Died December 13, 1905, at Peterson, Morgan County, Utah. *References*: Jesse Haven Journals and papers, Historical Department, The Church of Jesus Christ of Latter-day Saints, Salt Lake City, Utah; Andrew Jensen, *Latter-day Saint Biographical Encyclopedia* (Salt Lake City, 1936): 4:378–79; and David J. Whittaker, "Early Mormon Imprints in South Africa," *Brigham Young University Studies* 20 (1986): 404–16.

HAY, ADELBERT S(TONE) (1876–1901). Consul, born in Cleveland, son of John Hay, who was secretary of state. Hay graduated from Yale University. He was consul in Pretoria, South African Republic, from 1899 to 1900. He rendered personal services to the sick and wounded of the belligerents and was a neutral representative of the British prisoners of war in the Transvaal during the South African War. He was appointed assistant private secretary to President William McKinley in 1901, but died June 23, 1901, in New Haven, Connecticut. *References*: *NCAB* 11:14; and *NYT*, June 24, 1901.

HEAD, MATTHEW (1907–1985). Pseudonym for John (Edwin) Canaday, author and art critic, born February 1, 1907, in Fort Scott, Kansas. Canaday graduated from the University of Texas at Austin and Yale University. He taught art history at the University of Virginia (Charlottesville) from 1938 to 1950. He spent a year in the Belgian Congo in 1942 on a mission for the U.S. Bureau of Economic Warfare. He wrote several mysteries based on his experiences and impressions: *The Devil in the Bush* (New York, 1945), described as the first modern view in fiction of emerging Africa, *The Cabinda Affair* (New York, 1949) and *The Congo Venus* (New York, 1950). He then served with the marines during World War II. He was head of the School of Art of Tulane University (New Orleans) from 1950 to 1952, chief of the division of education of the Philadelphia Museum of Art from 1952 to 1959, and art critic of the New York Times from 1959 to 1977. Died July 19, 1985, in New York City. *References*: John Canaday Papers, Manuscript Collection, Alderman Library, University of Virginia, Charlottesville, Va.; *CA*; *CB* 1962; *NYT*, July 21, 1985; John M. Reilly, ed. *Twentieth Century Crime and Mystery Writers* (New York, 1985), pp. 434–35; and *WWWA*.

HEANY, MAURICE (1856–1927). Soldier and pioneer, born in Virginia. Heany served in the United States Army. He came to South Africa in the 1870s, took part in the occupation of Bechuanaland in 1884–1885 as part of the Warren expedition, joined the Bechuanaland Border Police, and was a member of the Pioneer Column which occupied Mashonaland in 1890. He founded and was general manager of the Bechuanaland Trading Company. He was later an aide of Cecil Rhodes and took part in the Matabele War. In 1895 he participated in the Jameson Raid but escaped. Died June 25, 1927, in Bulawayo, Southern Rhodesia. *References*: A. S. Hickman, *Men Who Made Rhodesia: A Register of Those Who Served in the British South Africa Company's Police* (Salisbury, Southern Rhodesia, 1960), pp. 30–31; *SADNB*; and *SESA*.

HEARD, WILLIAM HENRY (1850–1937). Clergyman and diplomat, born a slave June 25, 1850, in Elberton, Elbert County, Georgia. Heard attended the University of South Carolina, Atlanta, Clark (Atlanta) and Allen (Columbia, S.C.) universities, and the Reformed Episcopal Divinity School (Philadelphia), and was ordained in 1881. He was a member of the South Carolina House of Representatives in 1876. He was pastor in Aiken and Charleston, South Carolina; Philadelphia and Harrisburg, Pennsylvania; and Wilmington, Delaware. He was minister and consul general to Liberia from 1895 to 1898, and wrote *The Bright Side of African Life* (Philadelphia, 1898). He was elected bishop of the African Methodist Episcopal Church* for West Africa in 1908 and served there until 1912. He then served as bishop in various districts in the United States until his death. He wrote *From Slavery to the Bishopric in the A.M.E. Church, an Autobiography* (Philadelphia, 1924). Died September 13, 1937, in Philadelphia. *References*: *Christmas*; *NCAB* 12:212; *NYT*, September 13, 1937; *WWCR*; and *WWWA*.

HELLER, EDMUND (1875–1939). Naturalist, born May 21, 1875, in Freeport, Illinois. Heller graduated from Stanford University. He participated in the Stanford Zoology expedition to the Galapagos Islands in 1898–1899 and was assistant naturalist in the United States Biological Survey in Alaska in 1900. He was naturalist in the Field Museum of Natural History from 1901 to 1907 and accompanied Carl Ethan Akeley* on his expedition to East Africa. He was curator of mammals in the University of California Museum of Natural History in 1907–1908, and member of the Paul J. Rainey* East African expedition in 1911–1912. He accompanied Theodore Roosevelt on his expedition to East Africa in 1909–1910 and was joint author of *Life Histories of African Game Animals* (New York, 1914). He was a member of the Peruvian expedition in 1915 under the auspices of Yale University and the National Geographic Society, the expedition to southwest China of the American Museum of Natural History in 1916–1917, and served on the photographic staff of the Czechoslovak Army with Paul Rainey in Siberia in 1918. He participated in the Cape to Cairo African expedition of the Smithsonian Institution in 1919–1920, the expedition across Peru and down the Amazon River in 1922–1923, and the expedition to the Central African Mountains of the Moon from 1924 to 1926. He was assistant curator of the Field Museum of Natural History, director of the Milwaukee Zoological Gardens from 1928 to 1935, and director of the Fleishhacker Zoo in San Francisco after 1935. Died July 18, 1939, in San Francisco. *References*: Edmund Heller Papers, Smithsonian Institution Archives, Washington, D.C.; *AMWS*; *NCAB* 34:196; *NYT*, July 20, 1939; and *WWWA*.

HELSER, ALBERT DAVID (1897–1969). Missionary, born July 10, 1897, in Thornville, Perry County, Ohio. Helser graduated from Manchester College (Ind.) and Columbia University, and studied at Columbia University Teachers College, the University of London, and Livingstone College (London); he was ordained in 1922. He was a missionary under the Foreign Mission Commission of the Church of the Brethren (see Brethren Church*). With H. Stover Kulp,* he founded the mission at Garkida in Bornu Province in the northeastern part of Nigeria in 1923, and served there until 1936. In 1936 he left the mission because of differences of opinion, joined the Sudan Interior Mission (SIM),* and served at Kano, Nigeria, until 1957. He was general director of SIM from 1958 until 1962. He wrote *In Sunny Nigeria; Experiences among a Primitive People in the Interior of North Central Africa* (New York, 1926); *Education of a Primitive People; a Presentation of the Folklore of the Bura Animists* (New York, 1934); *The Glory of the Impossible; Demonstrations of Divine Power in the Sudan* (New York, 1940); *African Stories* (New York, 1934); and *The Hand of God in the Sudan; More Demonstrations of Divine Power in the Sudan* (New York, 1946). He cotranslated parts of the New Testament into Bura. Died December 20, 1969. *References*: *BE*; *OAB*; and *WWWA*.

HEMINGWAY, ERNEST (MILLER) (1899–1961). Author, born July 21, 1899, in Oak Park, Illinois. Hemingway became a reporter for the *Kansas City Star*, served with a volunteer ambulance unit in Italy during World War I, and then settled in Paris. He became European correspondent for the *Toronto Star* and began to publish short stories and novels. He went on a safari to East Africa in 1933–1934, wrote letters from Tanganyika to *Esquire* in 1934, and later wrote *The Green Hills of Africa* (New York, 1935) and the stories "The Short and Happy Life of Francis Macomber" and "The Snows of Kilimanjaro." He made a second safari to East Africa in 1953. Died July 2, 1961, in Ketchum, Idaho. *References*: Carlos Baker, *Ernest Hemingway: A Life Story* (New York, 1969); Carlos Baker, "The Slopes of Kilimanjaro," *American Heritage* 19 (August 1968): 40–43, 90–91; *DAB S7*; John M. Howell, comp., *Hemingway's African Stories; The Stories, Their Sources, Their Critics* (New York, 1969); Jeffrey Meyers, *Hemingway: A Biography* (New York, 1985); *NCAB* 57:288; *NYT*, July 3, 1961; and *WWWA*.

HENSEY, ANDREW F(ITCH) (1880–1951). Missionary, born June 1, 1880, in Bedford, Cuyahoga County, Ohio. Hensey attended Hiram College, graduated from the University of Kentucky, and studied at the University of Chicago. He was a missionary under the Foreign Christian Missionary Society (Disciples of Christ, see United Christian Missionary Society*) in the Belgian Congo from 1905 to 1927. He helped reduce Lomkundo to a written language, acted as legal adviser for the mission, and was a member of the Royal Commission for Protection of the Natives. He returned to the United States in 1931, was professor of African languages and customs at the College of Missions (Indianapolis), and later headed the Africa department of the Kennedy School of Missions (Hartford, Conn.) until his retirement in 1935. He wrote a biography of Robert Ray and Lillian Byers Eldred,* *Opals from Africa* (Cincinnati, 1910), and *My Children of the Forest* (New York, 1924). Died April 21, 1951, in Lexington, Kentucky. *References*: Andrew F. Hensey Papers, Bosworth Memorial Library, Lexington Theological Seminary, Lexington, Ky.; *OAB*; and *TWTA*.

HENZE, PAUL B(ERNARD) (1924-   ). Government official, born August 29, 1924, in Redwood Falls, Minnesota. Henze graduated from St. Olaf College and Harvard University and studied at the University of Nebraska. He was foreign affairs officer in the U.S. Department of Defense in 1950–1951; policy adviser to Radio Free Europe, Munich, from 1952 to 1958; communications adviser in Turkey in 1958–1959; member of the senior research staff of the Operations Research Office of Johns Hopkins University in 1960–1961; and executive of the Department of Defense from 1961 to 1968. He was Central Intelligence Agency (CIA) chief of mission in Addis Ababa from 1969 to 1972. He traveled in Ethiopia, and wrote *Ethiopian Journeys: Travels in Ethiopia 1969–1972* (London, 1977). He was CIA chief of mission in Turkey from 1974 to 1977, member of the staff of the National Security Council from 1977 to 1980, and resident consultant of the RAND Corporation after 1982. *References*: *Dirty War 2*; *WWA*; and *WWG*.

HERSKOVITS, MELVILLE J(EAN) (1895–1963). Anthropologist, born September 10, 1895, in Bellefontaine, Ohio, and grew up in El Paso, Texas, and Erie, Pennsylvania. Herskovits attended Hebrew Union College and the University of Cincinnati, served in the army during World War I, and graduated from the University of Chicago and Columbia University. He became assistant professor of anthropology at Northwestern University in 1927 and professor in 1935. In 1961 he was appointed to the first chair of African studies in the United States. He did fieldwork in Surinam (Dutch Guiana) in 1928–1929 and in Dahomey in 1931. He wrote *Dahomey: An Ancient West African Kingdom* (New York, 1938) and *The Human Factor in Changing Africa* (New York, 1962). Died February 25, 1963. His wife, **FRANCES (SHAPIRO) HERSKOVITS** (1897–1972) worked with her husband on African cultural anthropology, and taught at Northwestern University. Died May 2, 1972, in Evanston, Illinois. Together they wrote *An Outline of Dahomean Religious Belief* (Menasha, Wis., 1933) and *Dahomean Narrative: A Cross-Cultural Analysis* (Evanston, Ill., 1958). *References*: Melville J. Herskovits Papers, Northwestern University Library, Evanston, Ill.; *AA* 66 (1964): 83–109; *American Sociological Review* 29 (1964): 278–79; *BMNAS* 42 (1971): 65–93; *CA*; *CB* 1948; *NYT*, February 27, 1963; *NYT*, May 8, 1972; *OAB*; and *WWWA*.

HICKLING, THOMAS (1745–1834). Merchant and diplomat, born February 21, 1745, in Boston. In 1769 Hickling came to Ponta Delgada, Azores. He became a prosperous merchant, cultivating and exporting oranges to England and Russia, and was vice consul on St. Michael, Azores, from 1776 until his death. Died August 31, 1834, at Ponta Delgada. *Reference*: Joao H. Anglin, "Thomas Hickling," *Insulana* (Ponta Delgada) 5 (1949): 108–115.

HILLEGAS, HOWARD C(LEMENS) (1872–1918). Journalist, born December 30, 1872, in Pennsburg, Pennsylvania. Hillegas graduated from Franklin and Marshall College (Pa.). He was on the staff of *New York World* from 1895 to 1898, was war correspondent in South Africa in 1899–1900, and wrote *Oom Paul's People: A Narrative of the British-Boers Troubles in South Africa* (New York, 1899), and *The Boers at War: The Story of the British-Boer War of 1899–1900, as Seen from the Boer Side, with a Description of the Men and Methods of the Republican Armies* (New York, 1900). He published and edited *The Saratoga Sun* and was on the staff of *The World* and the *Evening World*. He was on the staff of the *New York Herald* after 1906, successively as night city editor, day city editor, city editor, and editorial writer. Died January 29, 1918, in New Brighton, Staten Island, New York. *References*: *NYT*, January 30, 1918; and *WWWA*.

HODGES, SAMUEL (1792–1827). Merchant and consul, born January 27, 1792, in Taunton, Massachusetts. Hodges was engaged in business with his father in Easton, Massachusetts. He served in the War of 1812 and was then involved in cotton and wool yarns manufacturing in Stoughton, Massachusetts. He was the first consul at Porto Praia on Sao Tiago, the Cape Verde Islands from 1818 to 1827, although he was not recognized by the Portuguese until 1823. He was active in commission trade, exporting goat skins, hides, and salt from Cape Verde. He prepared a Crioulo-English dictionary. Died October 26, 1827, in Praia, Cape Verde Islands. *References*: Samuel Hodges Papers, American Antiquarian Society, Worcester, Mass.; Peabody Museum, Salem, Mass.; and *Genealogical Record of the Hodges Family in New England* (Boston, 1853).

HOEFLER, PAUL L(OUIS) (1893–1982). Journalist and explorer, born September 6, 1893, in Spokane, Washington. Hoefler attended the University of California at Berkeley. He was leader of the expedition to the Kalahari Desert in 1925–1926 and the Colorado African expedition to Central Africa in 1928–1929, during which he made a sound movie of African wildlife and wrote an account of it in *Africa Speaks: A Story of Adventure* (Chicago, 1931). He became president of Paul Hoefler Productions, La Jolla, California, in 1939, made several additional trips to Africa, and produced more than 100 educational films. Died September 24, 1982, in San Diego, California. *References*: *San Diego Union*, September 28, 1982; and *WWW*.

HOFFMAN, JOHN WESLEY (1870- ?). Agriculturist, born August 11, 1870, in Charleston, South Carolina. Hoffman graduated from Michigan Agricultural College (Lansing) and the University of Cincinnati. He was professor of agricultural biology at Tuskegee Institute from 1894 to 1896, and later professor of agricultural biology at the State Agricultural and Mechanical College of Orangeburg, S.C., and at the Florida State Industrial College. He was director of the department of agriculture in the Colony of Lagos, Southern Nigeria, from 1902 to 1907. He traveled extensively through Nigeria, and served as an expert on the cultivation of cotton. He was a teacher of science and agricultural work at Tougaloo University (Miss.) after 1912, and later professor of agriculture at Lincoln Institute (later University) in Jefferson City, Mo. References: *WWCR*; and *WWWA*.

HOGSTAD, JOHN [JOHAN] PETER (1858–1911). Missionary, born December 2, 1858, in Inderen, Indhened, Norway. Hogstad came to the United States in 1866, graduated from Augsburg Seminary, and was ordained in 1887. He was the first missionary sent by the Norwegian Lutheran Church in the U.S., and served under the Norwegian Mission Society (and later the United Norwegian Lutheran Church). He was the first resident protestant missionary in Southern Madagascar. He established the American mission in Ft. Dauphin, Madagascar, and served there from 1887 to 1894 and in Manantenina, Madagascar, from 1896 to 1911. Died October 24, 1911, in Manantenina, Madagascar. *Reference*: *WWPNL*.

HOLLIS, GEORGE F(EARING) (1838–1903). Consul, born in Cambridge, Massachusetts, and grew up in Chelsea, Massachusetts. He was engaged in newspaper publishing in Chelsea, Massachusetts, served in the army and navy during the Civil War, and was then engaged in business in Boston. He was consul in Cape Town from 1888 to 1891. In 1888 he toured American consular agencies and prepared a detailed report on South Africa. Fervently pro-Boer, he attempted to shift America to his position. He also had an unauthorized meeting with Paul Kruger, president of the Transvaal. Fired in 1891, he remained in South Africa and was head of the consulate in Lourenço Marques, Mozambique, during the South African War. After his return to the United States, he served in the Boston customs house until his death. Died August 6, 1903, in Melrose, Massachusetts. *References*: *Arlington* [Mass.] *Advocate*, August 15, 1903; and *NYT*, August 7, 1903.

HOLLIS, W(ILLIAM) STANLEY (1866–1930). Consul, born April 4, 1866, in Chelsea, Massachusetts. Hollis attended the United States Naval Academy but left because of an injury. He was consular clerk in Cape Town from 1890 to 1891, consular agent in Durban from 1891 to 1892, consul in Mozambique from 1892 to 1898, and at Lourenço Marques from 1898 to 1909. He was later consul in Dundee, Scotland; consul general in Beirut, Syria; in London; and in

Lisbon until 1928. He served in the U.S. Department of State after 1928. Died June 8, 1930. *Reference*: *WWWA*.

HOLMES, GIDEON SKULL (1811–1880). Shipmaster, merchant, and diplomat, born February 10, 1811, in New Jersey. Holmes was a seaman and later a sea captain. He began regular trading voyages from Boston to the Cape and other ports on the east coast of Africa in 1834. He settled in Cape Town in the late 1840s as a merchant, and established there G. S. Holmes and Company, the first American business firm in Cape Town. He was consul in Cape Town from 1851 to 1855 and from 1856 to 1860. Died February 29, 1880, in Boston Highlands, Massachusetts. *Reference*: *DASB* 3.

HOLTON, CALVIN (1797–1826). Missionary, born March 10, 1797, in Gill, Massachusetts. Holton graduated from Colby College (Waterville, Me.). He was the first white missionary sent to Africa by the American Baptist Missionary Union*. He served in Monrovia, Liberia, in 1826. Died July 23, 1826, in Monrovia. *Reference*: *Centennial Catalogue of Officers, Graduates and Former Students of Colby College* (Waterville, Me., 1920).

HOLY CROSS LIBERIAN MISSION. Founded by the Order of the Holy Cross of the Episcopal Church in Bolahun, Liberia, in 1922. *References*: *ECMC*; and Robert B. Campbell, *Within the Green Wall: The Story of Holy Cross Liberian Mission 1922–1957* (West Park, N.Y., 1957).

HONNOLD, WILLIAM LINCOLN (1866–1950). Mining engineer and company director, born April 16, 1866, in Oconee, Illinois. Honnold graduated from Knox College (Galesburg, Ill.), the University of Michigan, and the Michigan School of Mines. He served as foreman, superintendent, manager, and consulting engineer in mines in Minnesota and California from 1895 to 1902. He came to the Transvaal in 1902 and was consulting engineer to the Consolidated Mines Selection Co. Limited; he was managing director of that company from 1912 to 1915. He was also chairman of the Transvaal Coal Trust, Brakpan Mines, Springs Mines, and the New Era Company, and member of the Witwatersrand Council of Education from 1909 to 1915. He was involved with relief work in Belgium during World War I. In 1917 he was cofounder, with Sir Ernest Oppenheimer, of the Anglo-American Corporation of South Africa, Limited. He was the permanent director of the corporation in the United States and represented its interests in the United States from 1917 until his death. Died May 6, 1950, in Los Angeles. *References*: *ACAB*; *NYT*, May 7, 1950; *SESA*; and *WWWA*.

HOOD, SOLOMON PORTER (1853–1943). Educator and diplomat, born July 30, 1853, in Lancaster, Pennsylvania, and grew up in Oxford, Pennsylvania. Hood graduated from Lincoln University and Lincoln University Seminary and studied at Union Theological Seminary and New York University. He was assistant to Henry Highland Garnet* in New York from 1880 to 1884 and school principal in Beauford, South Carolina. He was missionary under the African Methodist Episcopal Church* in Haiti from 1888 until 1893. He was then pastor in Pennsylvania and New Jersey and presiding elder of the African Methodist Episcopal Church in Trenton, New Jersey. He was minister to Liberia from 1922 to 1926. He helped to arrange the contract between the Liberian government and Firestone Rubber Company of America (see Firestone Plantations Company*) for the leasing of Liberian land for growing rubber. He was president of Campbell College (Jackson, Miss.) from 1927 to 1930, and later dean of theology at Paul Quinn College (Waco, Texas). Died October 12, 1943, in Atlantic Highlands, New Jersey. *References*: David McBride, "Solomon Porter Hood, 1853–1943: Black Missionary, Educator and Minister to Liberia," *Journal of the Lancaster County Historical Society* 84 (1980): 2–9; *NCAB* 36:499; and *NYT*, October 14, 1943.

HOPKINS, MOSES AARON (1846–1886). Clergyman and diplomat, born a slave, December 25, 1846, in Montgomery County, Virginia. Hopkins attended Avery College (Allegheny City, Pa.), and graduated from Lincoln University and Auburn Theological Seminary; he was ordained in 1877. He was pastor and teacher in Baltimore in 1877 and in Franklinton, North Carolina, from 1877 to 1885. He was minister resident and consul general to Liberia in 1885–1886. Died August 3, 1886, in Monrovia, Liberia. *References*: *ACAB*; *Christmas*; and *NCAB* 12:112.

HORNER, PRESTON K(ING) (1885–1964). Mining engineer, born October 17, 1885, in St. Louis, Missouri. Horner graduated from the Missouri School of Mines and Metallurgy (now the University of Missouri at Rolla). He worked for a mining company in Nevada. He went to the Belgian Congo in 1909 as construction engineer for the Union Minière du Haut-Katanga, and was its African director general from 1912 until 1918. He was forced to resign in 1918 when the company insisted that only Belgian nationals should hold the top jobs. He moved to London in 1921 and was consulting engineer for British mining companies. He took an active interest in Northern Rhodesia's copper and became a consulting engineer to Minerals Separation, Limited, to the Bwana Mkubwa Copper Mining Company, the Rhodesian Congo Border Concessions, the Southern Rhodesia Base Metals, and to other African companies. He became managing director of British American Tin Mines in 1940 and was a consulting engineer after 1947. Died December 4, 1964, in Clayton, Missouri. *Reference*: *St. Louis Post-Dispatch*, December 5, 1964.

HOTCHKISS, WILLIS R(AY) (1873–1948). Missionary, born October 11, 1873, in Doylestown, Wayne County, Ohio, and grew up in Cleveland. Hotchkiss graduated from the Friends' Bible Institute (Cleveland). He began missionary work in Africa in 1895 and founded the Friends' Africa Industrial Mission* in

1900 and the Lumbua Industrial Mission in 1905. He converted several Bantu languages to writing. He wrote *Sketches from the Dark Continent* (Cleveland, 1901), *Then and Now in Kenya Colony*, and *Forty Adventurous Years in East Africa* (New York, 1937). Died June 25, 1948. *References: OAB*; and *WWWA*.

HOWLAND, FREDERICK HOPPIN (1871–1916). War correspondent, born in New Bedford, Massachusetts. Howland graduated from the Massachusetts Institute of Technology. He joined the staff of the *Providence Journal* in 1893 and later became its Washington and New York correspondent. He went to South Africa in 1902 as war correspondent for the *London Daily Mail*, the *London Evening News*, and the *Providence Journal* during the South African War. He wrote *The Chase of De Wet, and Later Phases of the Boer War as Seen by an American Correspondent* (Providence, 1901). Later he was again Washington correspondent for the *Providence Journal*, editor and part owner of the *Providence Tribune* in 1906–1907, in charge of the publicity department of the Boston Chamber of Commerce in 1909–1910, on the staff of the *Philadelphia Press* from 1910 to 1915, and publicity manager for the Philadelphia Chamber of Commerce. Died June 5, 1916, in Philadelphia. *References: NYT*, June 7, 1916; and *WWWA*.

HUBBARD, MARGARET (CARSON) (1897-   ). Journalist, filmmaker, author, and diplomat; wife of Wynant Davis Hubbard,* born July 27, 1897, in Clinton, Iowa. Hubbard graduated from Vassar College. She was copywriter for John Wanamaker, New York City, from 1919 to 1921, and for R. H. Macy & Company from 1925 to 1927, 1929 to 1930 and 1936 to 1937. She accompanied her husband to Africa and was codirector with him of "Adventures in Africa" for Warner Brothers in 1931–1932. She wrote *No One to Blame: An African Adventure* (New York, 1934), *African Gamble* (New York, 1937), and *Boss Chombale* (New York, 1957). She was analyst for the U.S. War Department during World War II, vice consul in South Africa in 1946, journalist in South Africa in 1952, and head resident of Radcliffe College from 1955 to 1957. *References*: Margaret Hubbard Papers, Special Collections, University of New Hampshire, Durham, N.H.; and *WWAW*.

HUBBARD, WYNANT D(AVIS) (1900–1961). Author, big-game hunter, film producer, and expert on Africa, born August 28, 1900, in Kansas City, Missouri. Hubbard attended Harvard University. He was a prospector for asbestos mines in Quebec in 1921–1922, and went to Africa in 1922 as a consulting engineer for a mining consortium in British Central Africa. He remained in Africa as a professional hunter and collector of animals for zoos. In 1925–1926 he led an expedition for the National Pictures Company to produce films on wild animals and produced the films "Adventures in Africa" (1931) and "Untamed Africa" (1931). He established a research station at Ibamba, and, with his wife, Margaret Carson Hubbard,* attempted to corner the African animal market, first from

Rhodesia and later from Mozambique, an endeavour that failed when the financial backer withdrew. He wrote *Wild Animals: A White Man's Conquest of Jungle Beasts* (New York, 1926), and *Bong'kwe* (Garden City, N.Y., 1930). He was war correspondent in the Italo-Ethiopian War in 1935–1936 and wrote *Fiasco in Ethiopia: The Story of the So-called War by a Reporter on the Ground* (New York, 1936). From 1925 to 1945 he was an adviser to Franklin Delano Roosevelt on the economic and political developments in Africa. He was president of the Africa Company, an export firm, in 1938–1939, served in military intelligence during World War II, and was chief of the United Nations Relief and Rehabilitation Agency (UNRRA) in Ethiopia in 1945. He wrote *Wild Animal Hunter* (New York, 1958) and *Ibamba* (Greenwich, Conn., 1962). Died December 9, 1961, in Miami, Florida. *References*: *DAB* S7; *NYT*, December 10, 1961; and *WWWA*.

HUCKINS, DANIEL MONTGOMERY (c. 1814–1862). Merchant and consul, born in Sedgwick, Hancock County, Maine. Huckins resided in Boston until 1855 and was involved in the trade of hides and skins with South Africa. He was consul in Cape Colony from 1855 until his death and played a part in the early American-South African trade. Died February 18, 1862, in Cape Town, South Africa. *Reference*: *DASB* 3.

HUGUENOT SEMINARY. Founded in 1874 in Wellington, Cape Province, South Africa, as a girls' school by Andrew Murray, Dutch Reformed Church minister in Cape Province, and modeled after Mount Holyoke Seminary (South Hadley, Mass.). Murray obtained Anna Bliss* and Abbie Ferguson* of Mount Holyoke as the nucleus of its staff. It was recognized as a college in 1907 and was given the status of a university college by the Cape Parliament in 1907. In 1918 it became a constituent college of the University of South Africa and was renamed Huguenot University College. It was closed in 1950 on the recommendation of a government commission and became a college for training social workers. *References*: George P. Ferguson, *The Builders of Huguenot (Being the History of the Huguenot Institution at Wellington, from the Intimate Papers of the Builders)* (Cape Town, 1927); and *SESA*.

HULT, RALPH D. (1888–1943). Missionary, born July 9, 1888, in Kearney, Nebraska, and grew up near Axtell, Nebraska. Hult graduated from Augustana College, studied at Chicago Lutheran Theological Seminary and Kennedy School of Missions, and was ordained in 1917. He was a missionary under the Board of Foreign Missions of the Augustana Lutheran Church,* was sent as a missionary to the French Sudan in 1920, and explored the Chari-Chad country. In 1922 he was ordered to Tanganyika, was stationed at Iramba, and was president of the Augustana mission in Tanganyika. He returned to the United States in 1927 and his services as missionary were discontinued in 1929. He served later in home mission fields and settled near Springfield, Missouri. He returned to Tanganyika in 1942 and was superintendent of the Isaramo district of the Lutheran mission in Dar-es-Salaam. Died March 18, 1943, in Dar-es-Salaam, Tanganyika. *References*: George F. Hall, *The Missionary Spirit in the Augustana Church* (Rock Island, Ill., 1984), ch. 7; Ingrid Hult-Trobisch, *On Our Way Rejoicing* (New York, 1964); and Swan H. Swanson, *Three Missionary Pioneers and Some Who Have Followed Them* (Rock Island, Ill., 1945), pp. 105–43.

HUNT, WILLIAM HENRY (1869–1951). Consul, born June 29, 1869, in Hunts' Station, Tennessee, and grew up in Nashville. Hunt attended Williams College. He became secretary to Mifflin W. Gibbs,* consul in Tamatave, Madagascar, in 1899; was vice consul in 1899; and consul in Tamatave from 1901 to 1906. He published a number of articles about Madagascar in the *Bulletin of the American Geographical Society*. He was later consul in Saint-Étienne, France; Guadeloupe, West Indies; and St. Michael, Azores. He was consul and second secretary in Liberia in 1931–1932. He retired in 1933. Died December 19, 1951, in Washington, D.C. *References*: William Henry Hunt Papers, Moorland-Spingarn Research Center, Howard University, Washington, D.C.; *Christmas*; and *DANB*.

HURLBURT, CHARLES E(RWIN) (1860–1936). Missionary, born June 11, 1860, in Fort Atkinson, Iowa, and grew up in Oberlin, Ohio. Hurlburt attended Oberlin College and was ordained in 1896. He was secretary of the Young Men's Christian Association (YMCA) in Cleveland and Watertown, New York; assistant state secretary for Kansas in 1888–1889; and state secretary for Pennsylvania from 1889 to 1893. He was missionary under the Africa Inland Mission* from 1898 to 1908, and general director of the Africa Inland Mission at Kijabe, British East Africa, from 1898 until 1925. Died January 28, 1936, in Los Angeles.

HURLBURT, ELIZABETH (MORSE) (1884–1923). Medical missionary, born November 26, 1884, in New York City. Hurlburt graduated from Mount Holyoke College and studied medicine in Philadelphia and London. She came to Africa in 1913, established a hospital at Kijabe in British East Africa, and served there until 1916. She returned to Africa under the Africa Inland Mission,* was stationed in Aba, the Belgian Congo, and established a hospital there. She was also the director of the leprosarium in Aba. Died February 26, 1923, in Aba, Belgian Congo. *Reference*: *BCB* 5.

I

INTERNATIONAL MIGRATION SOCIETY. Organized in 1894, it transported two groups of American blacks to Liberia in 1895 and 1896. *Reference*: Edwin S. Redkey, *Black Exodus: Black Nationalist and Back-to-Africa Movements, 1890–1910* (New Haven, Conn., 1969), chs. 9–10.

IRELAND, WILLIAM (1821–1888). Missionary, born December 20, 1821, near Ostwestry, Shropshire, England, and came to the United States at an early age. Ireland graduated from Illinois College and Andover Theological Seminary and was ordained in 1848. He was missionary under the American Board of Commissioners for Foreign Missions (ABCFM)* in South Africa from 1849 to 1888. He took over the Imfume station from 1850 to 1862, became involved in the establishment of the Bantu boys' seminary at Amanzimtoti in 1862, and became its principal in 1865. He was also the treasurer of the ABCFM mission in Natal, and wrote *Historical Sketch of the Zulu Mission in South Africa* (Boston, 1864). Died October 12, 1888, in Boston. *References*: *AndoverTS*; and *SESA*.

IRWIN, DAVID D(URYEA) (1887–1971). Businessman and mining executive, born May 4, 1887, in Chicago. Irwin graduated from Yale Engineering School. He held various positions with various mines in Arizona and New Mexico from 1911 to 1917, and was general superintendent of the Phelps Dodge Corporation in Arizona and New Mexico from 1918 to 1928. He was general manager of the Roan Antelope Copper Mines in Northern Rhodesia from 1928 to 1933. He was later president of Pure Oil Pipe Line Company from 1934 until his retirement. Died September 26, 1971, in Evanston, Illinois. His wife's cousin **LUCY (POPE) CULLEN** worked as his secretary in Northern Rhodesia and recorded her experiences there in *Beyond the Smoke That Thunders* (New York, 1940). *Reference*: *WWWA*.

J

JAMES, BENJAMIN VAN RENSSELAER (1814–1849). Printer, born April 21, 1814, in Elizabethtown, New York. James was employed as a printer in New York. He served under the American Board of Commissioners for Foreign Missions (ABCFM)* in Cape Palmas, Liberia, from 1836 to 1844, and at Baraka, Gabon, from 1844 to 1846. He was the first printer in Gabon, and helped to print the first works in Mpongwe. He later settled in Liberia and taught English. Died January 9, 1849, in Monrovia, Liberia.

JENNINGS, (JAMES) HENNEN (1854–1920). Mining engineer, born May 6, 1854, in Hawesville, Kentucky. Jennings graduated from the Lawrence Scientific School of Harvard University. He was employed by various mining enterprises in California from 1877 until 1887 and was manager of El Callao mines in Venezuela from 1887 to 1889. He came to South Africa in 1889 and was consulting engineer to Hermann Eckstein & Company and to Wernher, Beit & Company from 1889 to 1898. He was also consulting engineer to other Transvaal gold mining companies. He went back to the Witwatersrand in 1902–1903 to advise on the reorganization of the mines after the South African War. He returned to the United States in 1905, settled in Washington, D.C., and was consulting engineer to the Conrey Place Mining Company in Montana. Died March 5, 1920, in Washington, D.C. *References*: *DASB* 3; *NCAB* 18:89; and *WWWA*.

JERSTAD, JAKOB BERNTSEN (1865–1911). Missionary, born September 18, 1865, in Kvinesdal, Flekkefjord, Norway, and came to the United States in 1887. Jerstad graduated from Augsburg Seminary and was ordained in 1898. He was a missionary under the Norwegian Lutheran Church in the U.S. in Madagascar from 1898 to 1911, serving in Manasoa in 1898–1899, Vohimari in 1899–1900, Mahafali from 1900 to 1908, St. Augustine in 1909, and again in Manasoa in 1910–1911. Died May 27, 1911, in Manasoa, Madagascar. *Reference*: *WWPNL*.

120   JOBSON, ORVILLE D(EVILLE)

JOBSON, ORVILLE D(EVILLE) (1900–1974). Missionary, born July 11, 1900, in Alcolu, South Carolina. Jobson attended Bible school in Philadelphia and studied in Paris. He was missionary under the Missionary Society of the Brethren Church* (and later the Foreign Missionary Society of the Grace Brethren Church) and served in the Oubangui-Chari mission in French Equatorial Africa from 1921 until 1961. He was stationed in Bassai, Bozoum, and Bangui, and was field superintendent from 1938 until his retirement in 1961. He wrote *Conquering Oubangui-Chari for Christ* (Winona Lake, Ind., 1957), and *Twenty-five Years in Oubangui-Chari 1921–1946* (Long Beach, Calif., 1947). Died October 12, 1974, in Englewood, Ohio. *References*: *BE*; and *Brethren Missionary Herald*, December 14, 1974.

JOHANSON, DONALD C(ARL) (1943-   ). Anthropologist, born June 28, 1943, in Chicago. Johanson graduated from the universities of Illinois and Chicago. He was associate curator of anthropology at the Cleveland Museum of Natural History from 1972 to 1974, curator of physical anthropology at the museum from 1972 to 1981, and director of scientific research and director of the laboratory of physical anthropology there from 1976 to 1981. In 1981 he founded the Institute of Human Origins in Berkeley, California, and became its director. He was a member of the Omo Research Expedition to Ethiopia from 1970 to 1972, a member of the Joint International Afar Research Expedition in Ethiopia from 1972 to 1976, and did fieldwork in Ethiopia again in 1980. There he made discoveries of human fossils and wrote *Lucy: The Beginning of Humankind* (New York, 1981). *References*: *CA*; Roger Lewin, *Bones of Contention: Controversies in the Search for Human Origins* (New York, 1987), chs. 11–12; *Newsweek*, February 16, 1981; and *WWA*.

JOHNSON, AMANDUS (1877–1974). Historian and anthropologist, born October 27, 1877, in Smaland, Sweden, and came to the United States in 1879. Johnson graduated from Gustavus Adolphus College (Minn.) and the universities of Colorado and Pennsylvania. He was instructor of Germanic languages and assistant professor of Scandinavian languages at the University of Pennsylvania from 1910 to 1922. He was director of the university's Educational West African Expedition from 1922 to 1924, carried on research among the Kumbundu in Angola, collected ethnological data, and wrote a Kimbundu-English-Portuguese dictionary. He was a pioneer in historical research on Swedish history in the United States and founded the Swedish Colonial Society and the American Swedish Historical Foundation in Philadelphia. Died June 30, 1974, in Staten Island, New York. *References*: Amandus Johnson Papers, University Museum Archives, Philadelphia; and *NYT*, July 3, 1974.

JOHNSON, CHARLES S(PURGEON) (1893–1956). Sociologist and educator, born July 24, 1893, in Bristol, Virginia. Johnson graduated from Virginia Union University (Richmond) and the University of Chicago, and served in the army during World War I. He became national research director for the Union League in New York in 1921 and founded and edited *Opportunity*; he became professor of sociology and director of the social sciences department at Fisk University in 1928. He was a member of the League of Nations Commission on Forced Labor in Liberia in 1930 which investigated forced labor in Liberia, and wrote "Bitter Canaan," a report of his investigation. It was published posthumously as *Bitter Canaan: The Story of the Negro Republic*, with an introductory essay by John Stanfield (New Brunswick, N.J., 1987). He was president of Fisk University after 1946. Died October 27, 1956, in Louisville, Kentucky. *References*: Charles S. Johnson Papers, Fisk University Library and Media Center, Nashville, Tenn.; *CB* 1946; *DAB* S5; *DANB*; Patrick J. Gilpin, "Charles S. Johnson: An Intellectual Biography," Ph.D. diss., Vanderbilt University, 1973; Patrick J. Gilpin, "Charles S. Johnson: Scholar and Educator," *NHB* 39 (1976): 544–48; *NCAB* 48:179; *NYT*, October 28, 1956; and *WWWA*.

JOHNSON, EBEN SAMUEL (1866–1939). Clergyman, born February 8, 1866, in Warwickshire, England. Johnson attended a teachers' training course in England and was engaged in newspaper work in London. He came to the United States, graduated from Morningside College (Sioux City, Ia.) and was ordained in 1889. He was a pastor of the Methodist Episcopal Church in Danbury, Wall Lake, and Mapleton, Iowa, and served as a chaplain in the Spanish-American War and on the Mexican border. He was a pastor in Sac City, Webster City, Rock Rapids, Sioux City, and Storm Lake, Iowa, and district superintendent of the Sioux City District in 1915. He was elected missionary bishop of Africa in 1916, and resided at Umtali, Rhodesia, from 1916 to 1920, and in Cape Town from 1920 until his retirement in 1936. He made extensive missionary travels in Africa. Died December 9, 1939, in Portland, Oregon. *References*: *EWM*; *Leete*; and *WWWA*.

JOHNSON, ELIJAH (ca. 1787–1849). Colonist, born probably in New Jersey. Johnson served in the War of 1812 and studied for the Methodist ministry. He was one of the emigrants who went to Africa on the ship *Elizabeth** in 1820, arriving at Sherbro Island in Sierra Leone. Along with Daniel Coker,* Johnson was in charge of the colony until 1821. He settled at Cape Mesurado in 1822 and was placed in charge of the colony there. He later became commissary of stores for the colony of Liberia, organized the defense of the settlement, and led the colonial troops in defending it against attacks from the natives. He was a delegate to the Constitutional Convention of Liberia of 1847 and one of the signers of its Declaration of Independence. Died March 23, 1849, in White Plains, a Methodist Episcopal mission station in Liberia. *References*: *DAB*; *Davis*; and *Huberich*.

JOHNSON, JOSEPH L(OWERY) (1874–1945). Diplomat, born February 14, 1874, in Darke County, Ohio. Johnson graduated from Ohio Northern University and Howard University Medical School. He was a special investigator for the United States Pension Bureau until 1910 and practiced medicine in Rendville and Columbus, Ohio, from 1910 to 1918. He was minister to Liberia from 1918 until 1922 and represented Liberia at the Versailles Peace Conference. Died July 18, 1945, in Columbus, Ohio. *References*: *Christmas*; *NYT*, July 20, 1945; and *WWWA*.

JOHNSON, MARTIN (ELMER) (1884–1937) and **JOHNSON, OSA (HELEN) (LEIGHY)** (1894–1953). Explorers and photographers. Martin was born October 9, 1884, in Rockford, Illinois, and grew up in Independence, Kansas. In 1907 he joined Jack London in the cruise of the *Snark*. Osa was born March 14, 1894, in Chanute, Kansas. They were married in 1910, and worked in vaudeville circuits until 1912. They made a trip to the South Pacific in 1912 and produced their first motion picture in 1914. They first went to Africa in 1921–1922 and returned to the United States with much documentary film and a feature film released under the title "Trailing African Wild Animals." They went back to Africa in 1923 for the American Museum of Natural History and for their own company, Martin Johnson African Expedition Corporation, and remained in Africa until 1927. Martin directed the camera work and Osa maintained supplies and camp security. They produced several commercially successful films: "Simba, the King of the Beasts" (1928), "Congorilla" (1932), and "Baboona" (1932). Osa wrote *Camera Trails in Africa* (New York, 1924); *Safari: A Saga of the African Blue* (New York, 1928); *Lion: African Adventure with the King of Beasts* (New York, 1929); *Congorilla: Adventures with Pygmies and Gorillas in Africa* (New York, 1931); and *Over African Jungles; the Record of a Glorious Adventure over the Big Game Country of Africa 60,000 Miles by Airplanes* (New York, 1935). Martin returned to Africa in 1928 and was there again from 1929 to 1931. They made an aerial expedition through Africa in 1933–1934 and an expedition to Borneo in 1935–1936. Martin died in Los Angeles January 13, 1937, from injuries received in a plane crash. Osa led the largest motion picture expedition ever undertaken through East Africa in 1937 to provide footage for the movie "Stanley and Livingstone" (1939). She also wrote *I Married Adventures: The Lives and Adventures of Martin and Osa Johnson* (Philadelphia, 1940) and *Four Years in Paradise* (Philadelphia, 1941), and produced several motion pictures, including "Jungles Calling" (1937), "I Married Adventure" (1940), and "African Paradise" (1941). Osa died January 7, 1953, in New York City. *References*: Martin and Osa Johnson Papers, Dickinson College Library, Carlisle, Pa.; Martin and Osa Johnson Photograph collection and archives, Martin and Osa Johnson Safari Museum, Chanute, Kans.; *BCB* 5; *CB* 1940; *DAB* S5; D. Houston, "The Boy and Girl Next Door Made Movies Far Away," *Smithsonian* 17 (November 1986): 144–48, 150, 152–55;

NCAB 26:65; *NCAB* 39:39; *NYT*, January 8, 1953; Kenhelm W. Stott, Jr., *Exploring with Martin and Osa Johnson* (Chanute, Kans., 1978); and *WWWA*.

JOHNSON, SILAS FRANKLIN (1865–1936). Medical missionary, born December 22, 1865, near Deep River, Iowa, and grew up in Axtell, Kansas. Johnson graduated from the College of Medicine of the University of Southern California, Los Angeles. He was medical missionary under the Board of Missions of the Presbyterian Church in the U.S.A.* in the Cameroon from 1894 until 1934. He was stationed first at Efulan and later at Metet, and became permanent secretary of the mission in 1913. He returned to the United States in 1934. Died April 19, 1936, in Los Angeles, California. *Reference*: Silas Franklin Johnson Papers, Presbyterian Historical Society, Philadelphia; Louis J. McNeill, *Great Ngee: The Story of a Jungle Doctor* (n.p., 1959).

JOHNSON, TITUS M. (1897–1974). Physician and medical missionary, born September 22, 1897, in Väster Färnebo, Västmanland, Sweden, and came to the United States in 1915. Johnson graduated from Moody Bible Institute. He was missionary under the Africa Inland Mission* at Blukwa, the Belgian Congo, in 1921–1922, and then under the Board of Overseas Mission of the Evangelical Free Church of America* in the Belgian Congo from 1922 to 1926. He returned to the United States in 1926, graduated from Wheaton College, Northwestern University, and Rush Medical School of the University of Chicago, and became a United States citizen. He was on the medical staff of the Swedish Covenant Hospital in Chicago after 1936. He returned several times to the Belgian Congo: to Karawa in 1947, to Tandala in 1953, and to Nkingha in 1964. Died January 16, 1974, in Kristianstad, Sweden. *References*: *Chicago Tribune*, January 18, 1974; and Sigurd E. Westberg and Frances J. Mason, *Deep Tracks in Africa: The Life and Work of Titus M. Johnson* (Chicago, 1976).

JOHNSON, V(ICTOR) EUGENE (1895–1982). Missionary, born September 17, 1895, in Minneapolis. Johnson graduated from Minnesota College, Lutheran Bible Institute, and Augustana Theological Seminary, and attended the University of Minnesota and Luther Seminary. He served as a missionary in Tanganyika from 1929 to 1953 and wrote *Pioneering for Christ in East Africa* (Rock Island, Ill., 1948). He later held pastorates in Benton Crooks, South Dakota, and Lake Lillian, Minnesota. Died July 2, 1982.

JOLLY, ALISON (BISHOP) (1937-   ). Zoologist, born May 9, 1937, in Ithaca, New York. Jolly graduated from Cornell and Yale universities. She was research associate in zoology at the New York Zoological Society from 1962 to 1964, research associate in the School of Biological Sciences, University of Sussex in Falmer, Sussex, England, from 1968 to 1981, and guest investigator at Rockefeller University, New York City, after 1982. She conducted intensive field studies in Madagascar, and wrote *Lemur Behavior: A Madagascar Field Study* (Chicago, 1966) and *A World Like Our Own: Man and Nature in Mad-*

agascar (New Haven, Conn., 1980), and coedited *Madagascar* (Oxford, 1984). *References*: *AMWS*; and *CA*.

JONES, CHARLES JESSE ("BUFFALO") (1844–1919). Cowboy and big-game hunter, born in Tazewell County, and grew up in McLean County, Illinois. Jones attended Wesleyan University. He homesteaded in Osborne County, Kansas, and then founded Garden City, Kansas. During the 1860s he was a buffalo hunter, but later became concerned with the preservation of the buffalo, crossed cattle with buffalo, and established a new breed named "cattalo." He was game warden of Yellowstone National Park from 1902 until 1905. He led the Buffalo Jones Expedition to British East Africa in 1910 to lasso big game, and an expedition to the Congo in 1914 to capture live gorillas. Died October 1, 1919, in Topeka, Kansas. *References*: Buffalo Jones Journals, memoirs, and correspondence, in private hands; Robert Easton and Mackenzie Brown, *Lord of Beasts; the Saga of Buffalo Jones* (Tucson, Ariz., 1961); Ralph T. Kersey, *Buffalo Jones; a True Biography* (Garden City, N.Y., 1958); and *NYT*, October 2, 1919.

JONES, EDWARD (1808?–1864). Missionary, born free in Charleston, South Carolina. Jones was the first black to graduate from Amherst College. He also studied at Andover Theological Seminary and at the African Mission School (Hartford, Conn.), and was ordained in 1830. He came to Sierra Leone in 1831, served as a schoolmaster in Kent and then in the Banana Islands. Suspended because of alleged negligence, he worked under the colonial chaplain in Freetown until he was reinstated as a schoolmaster in 1838. He became principal of Fourah Bay Christian Institution in 1841 and became a British subject in 1845. In 1853 he participated in an expedition that sought in vain to establish a mission among the Ibos. He was a pastor in Freetown after 1858 and was editor of the *Sierra Leone Weekly Times and West African* in 1861. He went to England for his health in 1864. Died in Chatham, Kent, England. *References*: *Amherst*; *AndoverTS*; *DANB*; and Hugh Hawkins, "Edward Jones, Marginal Man," in *Black Apostles at Home and Abroad: Afro-Americans and the Christian Mission from the Revolution to Reconstruction*, ed. David W. Wills and Richard Newman (Boston, 1982), pp. 243–53.

JONES, ROBERT LLEWELLYN (1903–1940). Missionary, born June 1903, in Altoona, Kansas. Jones attended Pacific Union and Walla Walla colleges and graduated from Washington Missionary College and the University of Southern California and was ordained in 1934. He was missionary under the Seventh-day Adventists in Cameroon, French Equatorial Africa, in 1928–1929, and in the Belgian Congo from 1929 until his death. He was in charge of the Songa, Kirundu, and Gitwe missions, and directed the Gitwe Training School. Mauled by a wild buffalo, he died November 10, 1940, at the Bikobo Hill mission, Belgian Congo. *References*: *Review and Herald*, March 27, 1941; and *SDAE*.

JONES, THOMAS JESSE (1873–1950). Sociologist, born August 4, 1873, in Llanfacthraeth, Wales, and came to the United States in 1884. Jones attended Washington and Lee University (Lexington, Va.), and graduated from Marietta College (Ohio), Columbia University, and Union Theological Seminary. He was director of the research department at Hampton Institute from 1902 to 1909, statistician with the U.S. Bureau of the Census from 1909 to 1912, and a specialist in education at the U.S. Bureau of Education from 1912 to 1919. He became education director for the Phelps-Stokes Fund in 1913, for which he conducted, from 1914 to 1916, a study of Negro education in the United States, and was director of the fund from 1917 until 1946. He was chair of the Phelps-Stokes Fund's African Education Commission (see African Education Commission*) to West, South, and Equatorial Africa to study the conditions of Africans in 1920, and prepared its report, *Education in Africa: A Study of West, South and Equatorial Africa, by the African Education Commission* (New York, 1922). He was also the chair of the African Education Commission to East Africa in 1924, and prepared its report, *Education in East Africa: A Study of East, Central and South Africa by the Second African Education Commission under the Auspices of the Phelps-Stokes Fund, in Cooperation with the International Education Board* (London, 1925). Died January 5, 1950, in New York City. *References*: *BDAE*; J.W.C. Dougall, "Thomas Jesse Jones, Crusader for Africa," *International Review of Missions* 39 (July 1950): 311–17; *JNH* 35 (1950): 107–9; *NYT*, January 6, 1950; and *WWWA*.

JULIAN, HUBERT FAUNTLEROY (1897-   ). Adventurer and aviator, born in Port-of-Spain, Trinidad. Julian came to the United States in 1921, became an officer in Marcus Garvey's semimilitary unit, the African Legion, in 1922, and developed an interest in flying. He performed flying exhibits and parachute jumps in Harlem, and became known as the "Black Eagle of Harlem." He went to Ethiopia in 1930 but was forced to leave when he crashed the emperor's plane. He returned to Ethiopia in 1935 when the war with Italy erupted, was granted Ethiopian citizenship, was commissioned a colonel in the Ethiopian Army, and became commander of the Ethiopian Air Force; he was replaced after a short time by John Robinson* and returned to the United States. He wrote his memoirs (as told to John Bulloch), *Black Eagle: Colonel Hubert Julian* (London, 1964). *References*: John P. Nugent, *The Black Eagle* (New York, 1971); *NYT*, July 6, 1974; William Scott, "A Study of Afro-American and Ethiopian Relations: 1896–1941," Ph.D. diss., Princeton University, 1971, ch. 7; and William Scott, "Herbert F. Julian and the Italo-Ethiopian War: A Dark Episode in Pan-African Relations," *Umoja: A Scholarly Journal of Black Studies* 2 (1978): 77–93.

K

KAGNEW COMMUNICATIONS STATION. An Italian facility on the outskirts of Asmara, Ethiopia. It was taken over by the United States Army Signal Corps in 1942 and functioned as a relay station. In 1953 the United States negotiated a military assistance agreement with the Ethiopian government which gave the United States a twenty-five year lease on the facilities. In return, the United States undertook the training and equipping of the Ethiopian armed forces. The facilities were used later for tracking satellites and monitoring Soviet missile tests. Operations were curtailed in the early 1970s, and the facilities were closed down in 1977.

KELLERSBERGER, JULIA (LAKE) (SKINNER) (1897-   ). Missionary, born November 23, 1897, in Linden, Alabama. Kellersberger graduated from Agnes Scott College and studied at the Biblical Seminary (N.Y.C.). She was a teacher in Augusta, Georgia, in 1919–1920; religious educational director of the Presbyterian Church in Tennessee, North Carolina, and Florida from 1920 to 1928; and secretary for students of the Christian Education Committee of the Presbyterian Church in the United States. She was a missionary under the Board of Foreign Missions of the Presbyterian Church in the United States* in the Belgian Congo from 1930 to 1941. She was later the promotional secretary of the American Leprosy Missions from 1941 to 1953 and a lecturer. She wrote *Congo Crosses: A Study of Congo Womanhood* (Boston, 1936), *God's Ravens* (New York, 1941), and biographies of Althea Brown Edmiston* and Lucy Gantt Sheppard (see William Henry Sheppard*). *Reference*: WWAW.

KELLY, JOHN (1802–1866). Missionary, born March 27, 1802, in Trillick, County Tyrone, Ireland. Kelly came to the United States in 1825, graduated from Mount St. Mary's, Emmitsburg, and was ordained in 1833. He was a pastor in Albany, New York. With Edward Barron,* he served as a missionary in the Catholic mission in Cape Palmas, Liberia, from 1842 to 1844. He was later a pastor in Jersey City, New Jersey, until his death. Died April 28, 1866,

128   KELLY, LORENA

in Jersey City. *References*: John Kelly Papers and journal, Georgetown University Library, Washington, D.C.; John Kelly, "The Mission to Liberia: Diary of the Rev. John Kelly," *United States Catholic Historical Society Historical Records and Studies* 14 (1920): 120–53; Henry A. Brann, "The Rev. John Kelly," *United States Catholic Historical Society Records and Studies* 5 (1907): 348–53.

KELLY, LORENA (1903-   ). Missionary, born May 17, 1903, at Mt. Mourne, North Carolina. Kelly graduated from the Woman's College of the University of North Carolina and Scarritt College (Nashville, Tenn.). She was a missionary under the Board of Foreign Missions of the Methodist Episcopal Church* in the Belgian Congo from 1936 until 1969. She was stationed at Wembo Nyama, Tunda, Luboni, and Lodja mission stations, and did educational work. She was forced to evacuate Lodja during the Civil War in the Congo from 1960 to 1965. She was director of the home economics department of the Congo Polytechnique Institute at Lodja from 1965 to 1969. She wrote a textbook of the Otetela language. *Reference*: Lorena Kelly Papers, East Carolina Manuscript Collection, East Carolina University, Greenville, N.C.

KEMMERER, EDWIN WALTER (1875–1945). Economist, born June 29, 1875, in Scranton, Pennsylvania. Kemmerer graduated from Wesleyan and Cornell universities. He served as a financial adviser to the United States Philippine Commission in 1903, was chief of the Division of Currency of the Philippines from 1904 to 1906. He was professor of economics and finance at Cornell University from 1906 to 1912 and at Princeton University from 1912 until 1928, and professor of international finance at Princeton from 1928 until his retirement in 1943. He was a financial adviser to foreign governments, served on commissions as adviser for financial matters, and in 1924–1925, with Gerard Vissering, president of the Nederlandsche Bank, was a member of the Kemmerer-Vissering Gold Standard Committee of Inquiry of the Union of South Africa and coauthor of *Report . . . on the Resumption of Gold Payments by the Union of South Africa* (Pretoria, 1925), which recommended that the Union of South Africa return to the gold standard independently of Great Britain. Died December 12, 1945, in Princeton, New Jersey. *References*: Edwin Walter Kemmerer Papers, Princeton University Library, Princeton, N.J.; *American Economic Review* 36 (1946): 219–22; *DAB* S3; *DSAB* 4; *NCAB* E:406; *NYT*, December 17, 1945; *SESA*; and *WWWA*.

KERSEY, RUTH MAY (1889–1958). Missionary nurse, born March 21, 1889, in Hanover County, Virginia. Kersey attended Woman's College (Richmond, Va.), graduated from the Woman's Missionary Union Training School (Louisville, Ky.) and received nurses' training in the Retreat for the Sick (Richmond, Va.). She served as missionary under the Foreign Mission Board of the Southern Baptist Convention* in Nigeria from 1921 until 1955, serving at the Ogbomosho hospital in Ogbomosho, Nigeria. She founded in 1925 and directed the Home for Motherless Children Orphanage (known later as the Kersey Children's Home), and worked at the Baptist Academy in Lagos. She retired in 1955. Died November 8, 1958, in Richmond, Virginia. *Reference: ESB.*

KEYS, PLINY W(HITTIER) (1900?–1942). Missionary, born in Howard, Elk County, Kansas. Keys graduated from Kansas State Agricultural College and Baker University. He was a missionary under the Board of Foreign Missions of the Methodist Episcopal Church* in Mozambique from 1929 until his death. He was director of education, pastor of the Morrumbere Circuit, and superintendent of the Limpopo district and the Transvaal district at Johannesburg. He was later founder and principal of the Bodine (later Central) Training School at Kambini, Mozambique, and superintendent of the Inhambane District. Died September 18, 1942, at Kambini, Mozambique. His wife **CLARA EVANS KEYS** (1884–) wrote *We Pioneered in Portuguese East Africa: A Methodist Missionary's Memoirs of Planning Christian Civilization in Mozambique* (New York, 1959). *Reference: NYT,* October 8, 1942.

KIRKLAND, CAROLINE (1865–1930). Writer, born March 20, 1865, in Syracuse, New York, and grew up in Chicago. She made an extensive trip throughout Eastern and Southern Africa in 1906–1907 and wrote *Some African Highways: A Journey of Two American Women to Uganda and the Transvaal* (Boston, 1908). Under the pen name Madame X, she conducted a column of society news for the *Chicago Tribune* from 1909 until her death. Died August 10, 1930, in Lake Forest, Illinois. *References: Chicago Tribune,* August 11, 1930; and *WWAW.*

KLEIN, ALFRED J. (1883?–1944). Big-game hunter, born in Germany, brought to the United States as an infant, and grew up in Orangeburg, Rockland County, New York. Klein joined the staff of the American Museum of Natural History as a taxidermist, went to Africa in 1910, and remained there for the rest of his life. He first settled in Nairobi and opened a taxidermist shop there, but gradually became an expert hunter and an organizer and director of hunting expeditions; he served as a guide for many famous expeditions. Died May 20, 1944, in Nairobi, Kenya. *Reference: NYT,* May 21, 1944.

KRUG, ADOLPH NICHOLAS (1873–1942). Missionary, born October 4, 1873, in Homberg, Hessen Cassel, Germany; came to the United States as a child and grew up in Massachusetts. Krug graduated from Amherst College. He became a missionary under the Board of Foreign Missions of the Presbyterian Church of the U.S.A.* in West Africa in 1903. He served in the Cameroon from 1903 until 1916, and in Benito, Rio Muni district, Spanish Guinea, from 1918 to 1920, and was in charge of the mission from 1920 to 1923. He was later a teacher of Bible and pedagogy at the Normal School, Foulassi, Cameroon, and was in charge of village schools in the area. Died May 23, 1942, in Miami, Florida. *References*: *Amherst*; and *NYT*, May 28, 1942.

KULP, HAROLD STOVER (1894–1964). Missionary, born September 24, 1894, near Pottstown, Pennsylvania. Kulp graduated from the West Chester State Normal School, Juniata College, and the University of Pennsylvania, and studied at the University of London and Hartford Seminary Foundation. He was a missionary under the Foreign Mission Commission of the Church of the Brethren (see Brethren Church*) in Nigeria from 1922 until his retirement in 1963. Cofounder of the mission, he opened mission stations and served at Garkida, Lassa, Maram, and Mubi in the Adamawa, Bornu, and Sardauna provinces of Nigeria, and was general manager of the mission schools. He created a written system for the Bura and Marghi languages and translated parts of the Bible into these languages. He was the first president of the Nigerian Council of Churches. Died October 12, 1964, in Harrisburg, Pennsylvania. *References*: *BE*; F. H. Fenner, "Pioneers of the Nigerian Church," in *Brethren Trail Blazers* (Elgin, Ill., 1960), pp. 164–69; and Mary A. M. Kulp, *No Longer Strangers (A Biography of H. Stover Kulp)* (Elgin, Ill., 1968).

L

LABRAM, GEORGE (1862–1900). Mechanical engineer, born in Detroit. Labram was mining engineer in Michigan and Mexico and designed and sold machinery in Chicago. He came to South Africa in 1894 to supervise the installation of machinery at the Kimberley diamond fields for De Beers Consolidated Mines and became chief mechanical engineer for De Beers in 1896. He was one of the defenders of Kimberley during its siege by the Boers in the South African War, helped to lay out the military fortifications for the town, and built in the workshops of De Beers a cannon, popularly called "Long Cecil," which fired 29-pound shells. Killed September 2, 1900, in Kimberley, by a Boer shell. *References: DASB* 3; *SESA*; and Richard F. Snow, "George Labram," *American Heritage* 32 (April/May 1981): 48–49.

LACY, LESLIE ALEXANDER (1937-). Author, lecturer, and expatriate, born August 8, 1937, in Franklin, Louisiana. Lacy graduated from the University of Southern California. He went to Ghana in 1963, studied and taught at the University of Ghana at Legon until 1967, and described his experiences in *The Rise and Fall of a Proper Negro: An Autobiography* (New York, 1970). He was a lecturer at Howard and New York universities from 1968 to 1970 and at the New School of Social Research in 1969–1970. *References: CA*; and *WWBA*.

LAKE, JOHN GRAHAM (1870–1935). Evangelist, born March 18, 1870, in Ontario, Canada, and grew up in Michigan. Lake moved to Chicago in 1891, was ordained in 1891, but went into the insurance business and founded a newspaper. He became an independent evangelical preacher and a pentacostal missionary in 1907, and went to South Africa in 1908. He founded the Apostolic Faith Mission in South Africa in 1910, was its first secretary and later its president, and became pastor of the Apostolic Tabernacle of Johannesburg. He was a member of an expedition to the Kalahari Desert in 1912. He returned to the United States in 1912 and founded the Apostolic Church in Spokane, Washington, in 1914. Died September 16, 1935, in Spokane, Washington. *References:*

DASB 4; Gordon Lindsay, *John G. Lake—Apostle to Africa* (Dallas, 1972); Gordon Lindsay, *Sketches from the Life and Ministry of John G. Lake* (Shreveport, La., 1952); and J. Gordon Melton, *Biographical Dictionary of American Cult and Sect Leaders* (New York, 1986), pp. 146–48.

LAMBERT, JONATHAN (1772–1813). Sea captain, born February 11, 1772, in Salem, Massachusetts. Lambert went early to sea and in 1795 became master of the schooner *Ruth*. He went to Tristan da Cunha with two companions in 1811 with the idea of cultivating the main island's fertile soil and making Tristan da Cunha the "Islands of Refreshments," providing food and water for whalers and sailing ships. On February 11, 1811, he proclaimed his possession of the islands. Drowned October 10, 1813, between Tristan and Nightingale islands. *References*: Herbert M. Bratter, "Jonathan Lambert of Salem, the Yankee Who Would be King," *EIHC* 88 (1952): 150–62; and Edwin B. Hewes, "Jonathan Lambert of Salem, King of Tristan d'Acunha," *EIHC* 71 (1935): 1–6.

LAMBIE, THOMAS A(LEXANDER) (1885–1954). Medical missionary, born February 8, 1885, in Pittsburgh, Pennsylvania. Lambie graduated from the University of Pennsylvania and Western Pennsylvania Medical College. He was a medical missionary under the Board of Foreign Missions of the United Presbyterian Church in the United States* in the Sudan from 1907 to 1919. He served in Ethiopia from 1919 to 1936, first as a missionary in Wälläga from 1919 to 1926, and in 1927 as director of the Abyssinian Frontiers Mission, later absorbed in the Sudan Interior Mission (SIM).* He was responsible for the construction of two hospitals in Addis Ababa, including the George Memorial Hospital, of which he was the director. He became an Ethiopian citizen and was executive director of the Ethiopian National Red Cross Society during the Italian invasion of Ethiopia. He left Ethiopia in 1936. He served under the Independent Board of the Presbyterian Foreign Missions in Palestine from 1946 until his death and built a tuberculosis sanatorium there. He wrote *A Doctor Without a Country* (New York, 1939), *A Doctor Carries On* (New York, 1942), *Boot and Saddle in Africa* (New York, 1943), *A Bruised Reed* (New York, 1952), and *A Doctor's Great Commission* (Wheaton, Ill., 1954), which was published posthumously. Died April 14, 1954, in Ain Arrub, Jordan. *References*: F. P. Cotterell, "Dr. T. A. Lambie: Some Biographical Notes," *Journal of Ethiopian Studies* 10 (1972): 43–53; Dorothy C. Haskin, *Medical Missionaries You Would Like to Know* (Grand Rapids, Mich., 1957), pp. 66–71; and *NYT*, April 17, 1954.

LANG, HERBERT (OTTO HENRY) (1879–1957). Naturalist, born March 24, 1879, in Oehringen, Wurttemberg, Germany. Lang attended the University of Zurich, the Sorbonne, and Columbia University. He was a taxidermist at the University of Zurich from 1896 to 1900 and at Maison Fasse, Paris, from 1900 to 1903. He came to the United States in 1903 and joined the taxidermy staff of the American Museum of Natural History. He participated in the Tjader East

African expedition in 1906–1907 and was in charge of the zoological expedition to Belgian Congo from 1909 to 1915. He was assistant in the department of mammalogy from 1915 to 1919, assistant curator from 1919 to 1923, and associate curator after 1924. He was general manager of the Vernay Angola expedition in 1925. He settled in South Africa in 1926, worked with the Transvaal Museum, led the Vernay-Lang Kalahari expedition in 1930, and became a wildlife photographer. He went into the hotel business in the 1930s in Pretoria until his retirement in 1955. Died May 1957 near Pretoria, South Africa. *References*: *Bulletin of the Transvaal Museum*, January 1961; and *WWWA*.

LANIER, RAPHAEL O'HARA (1900–1962). Educator and diplomat, born April 28, 1900, in Winston-Salem, North Carolina. Lanier graduated from Lincoln, Stanford, and New York universities. He taught at Tuskegee Institute from 1923 to 1925 and at Talahassee Institute from 1925 to 1933, was dean of Houston College (Texas) from 1933 to 1938, director of the Division of Negro Affairs at the National Youth Administration in Washington, D.C., from 1938 to 1940, and dean of instruction at Hampton Institute from 1940 to 1945. He was minister to Liberia from 1946 to 1948. He was president of Texas Southern University from 1948 to 1955, consultant on education in Africa from 1946 to 1948, and project director for the Phelps-Stokes Fund project aimed at the identification and placement of Negro talent from 1957 to 1962. Died December 17, 1962, in New York City. *References*: *Christmas*; *NYT*, December 20, 1962; and *WWWA*.

LAPSLEY, SAMUEL NORVELL (1866–1892). Missionary, born April 14, 1866, in Selma, Alabama. Lapsley graduated from the University of Alabama and Union Theological Seminary (Va.), studied at McCormick Seminary (Chicago), and was ordained in 1889. He was missionary under the Board of Foreign Missions of the Presbyterian Church in the United States,* and with William H. Sheppard,* opened the American Presbyterian Congo Mission (APCM)* in Kasai, Congo Free State, in 1890. Died March 26, 1892, near Matadi, Congo Free State. *Reference*: James W. Lapsley, ed., *Life and Letters of Samuel Norvell Lapsley: Missionary to the Congo Valley, West Africa: 1866–1892*, (Richmond, Va., 1893).

LAWLIN, RICHARD E. (? –1861). Sea captain and trader. Lawlin traded in Gabon from 1830 to 1861. He purchased ivory and rubber and was the representative of various American firms. In 1854 he received the island of Adjanga from the Nkomi chief and established a factory there named "Brooklyn." He also established a plantation and tried to develop commercial agriculture among the Nkomi.

LEE, RICHARD BORSHAY [BARRY] (1937-   ). Anthropologist, born September 20, 1937, in New York City. Lee graduated from the universities of Toronto and California at Berkeley. He was associate professor of anthropology at Livingston College from 1970 to 1972 and became associate professor of anthropology at the University of Toronto in 1972. He became a Canadian citizen. He did baboon field study in Kenya in 1963, and organized with Irven DeVore* the Harvard Bushman [San] Research Project in 1963. He carried on fieldwork in Bechuanaland in 1963–1964, 1967 to 1969, and 1973, and wrote *The !Kung San: Men, Women, and Work in a Foreign Society* (Cambridge, Eng., 1979) and *The Dobe !Kung* (New York, 1984). He also coedited *Kalahari Hunter-Gatherers: Studies of the !Kung San and Their Neighbors* (Cambridge, Mass., 1976). *References*: *AMWS*; and *CA*.

LEIGH, WILLIAM ROBINSON (1866–1955). Artist, born September 23, 1866, near Falling Waters, West Virginia. Leigh studied art at the Maryland Institute (Baltimore) and in Munich, Germany. He returned to the United States in 1896 and set up a studio in New York City, devoting himself to painting western scenes and making many trips to the west and southwest. He accompanied Carl Ethan Akeley* in 1926 as an artist on the American Museum of Natural History expedition to Africa and made sketches of animals, landscapes, and natives for the museum's African Hall. He returned to Africa in 1928 with the Carlisle-Clarke expedition. In *Frontiers of Enchantment* (New York, 1938), he detailed his African experiences. From 1932 to 1935, he was in charge of a group of artists painting the background murals for the African Hall exhibits at the museum. Died March 11, 1955, in New York City. *References*: William Robinson Leigh Papers, Thomas Gilcrease Institute of American History and Art Library, Tulsa, Okla.; *DAB* S5; D. Duane Cummings, *William Robinson Leigh: Western Artist* (Norman, Okla., 1980); *NCAB* 41:98; *NYT*, March 13, 1955; and *WWWA*.

LIBERIA COLLEGE. Established in 1851 by an act of the legislature of Liberia, but founded and financed by the Trustees of Donations for Education in Liberia in Boston and the New York Colonization Society. It was the first American degree-granting college to be established abroad. It began operations in 1862. In the 1950s it became the University of Liberia. *References*: Gardner W. Allen, *The Trustees of Donations for Education in Liberia: The Story of Philanthropic Endeavor 1850–1923* (Boston, 1923); Avertus A. Hoff, *A Short History of Liberia College and the University of Liberia* (Monrovia, 1962); and Thomas W. Livingston, "The Exportation of American Higher Education to West Africa: Liberia College, 1850–1900," *Journal of Negro Education* 45 (1976): 246–62.

LIBERIAN FRONTIER FORCE (LFF). Liberia's first professional military organization, formed in 1908 under British direction to patrol the border and to pacify the Hinterland, the rural area of Liberia not included in the coastal counties, and to uphold Liberia's claim to sovereignty along its interior border and forestall possible intervention by the European colonial powers. From 1912 to 1922 the LFF was commanded by United States Army officers who served at the request of the Liberian government. In 1962 it was redesignated the Liberian National Guard. *Reference*: Harrison Akingbade, "Afro-American Officers and the Organization of the Liberian Frontier Force," *NHB* 42 (1979): 74–79.

LIBERIAN MINING COMPANY. An iron mining company, owned by American interests which in 1946 received an eighty-year concession to exploit the iron ore deposit at Bomi Hills, northwest of Monrovia. The Republic Steel Corporation became the major shareholder. In 1951 it constructed the first railroad in Liberia, extending from the mining site at Bomi Hills to the port of Monrovia and began production in 1951. In the 1970s the ores were exhausted and operation costs mounted; the mine was closed in 1977.

LIGHT, RICHARD U(PJOHN) (1902-). Surgeon, geographer, and aviator, born March 29, 1902, in Kalamazoo, Michigan. Light graduated from Yale University and University of Michigan Medical School. He taught surgery at Yale University and the University of Rochester from 1933 to 1936 and practiced neurological surgery in Kalamazoo after 1936. He became a qualified pilot in 1929 and in 1937–1938 flew over the whole length of Africa for the American Geographical Society. He was accompanied by his wife **MARY LIGHT** as wireless operator and photographer, who made the aerial photographs that accompanied his book *Focus on Africa* (New York, 1941). *References*: *AMWS*; *Geographical Review* 37 (1947): 175–76; *Geographical Review* 47 (1957): 309–10; *NCAB* E:41; and Charles E. Planck, *Women with Wings* (New York, 1942), pp. 240–41.

LINDLEY, DANIEL (1801–1880). Missionary, born August 24, 1801, at Ten Creek Mile, Washington County, Pennsylvania. Lindley graduated from Ohio University, studied at the Seminary in Hampden Sydney, Virginia, and was ordained in 1832. He was missionary under the American Board of Commissioners for Foreign Missions (ABCFM)* in South Africa from 1835 until 1873. He first established a mission station at Mosega among the Matabele under Chief Mzilikazi, which was soon abandoned; he then returned to Port Natal. He served as the first ordained minister to the Voortrekkers, the Dutch emigrants in Pietermauritzburg, Natal, from 1841 to 1847. He made long journeys in Natal, Orange Free State, and Transvaal. He established the Zulu mission at Inanda in 1847, and founded there the Inanda Seminary for Zulu girls. He returned to the United States in 1877. Died September 3, 1880, in Morristown, New Jersey. *References*: *DAB* S1; *DSAB* 2; *SESA*; Edwin W. Smith, *The Life and Times of*

Daniel Lindley (1801–1880), Missionary to the Zulus, Pastor of the Voortrekkers Ubebe Umhlope (London, 1949); *Tabler/Natal*; and *WWWA*.

LINTON, RALPH (1893–1953). Anthropologist, born February 27, 1893, in Philadelphia. Linton graduated from Swarthmore College and the University of Pennsylvania, studied at Columbia University, and graduated from Harvard University. He served in the army during World War I. In 1920 and 1922 he conducted fieldwork in the Marquesas Islands, and in 1922 he became assistant curator in North American ethnology at the Field Museum of Natural History. He was a member of the Marshall Field expedition of the Field Museum of Natural History to Madagascar from 1925 to 1927, wrote a series of articles in the *Atlantic Monthly* in 1927–1928, and also wrote *The Tanala, a Hill Tribe of Madagascar* (Chicago, 1933). He was assistant professor and professor of anthropology at the University of Wisconsin from 1928 until 1937, professor of anthropology at Columbia University from 1937 to 1946, and professor of anthropology at Yale University from 1946 until his death. Died December 24, 1953, in New Haven, Connecticut. *References*: *American Antiquity* 19 (1954): 382–83; *BMNAS* 55 (1958): 236–53; *DAB* S5; *Journal of American Folklore* 67 (1954): 309–11; *NCAB* H:232; and *NYT*, December 25, 1953.

LOCKER, JESSE DWIGHT (1891–1955). Lawyer and diplomat, born May 31, 1891, in Cincinnati. Locker graduated from Howard University School of Law and was admitted to the bar. He practiced law in Cincinnati from 1919 until 1953; he was a member of the Cincinnati City Council from 1941 to 1953 and president pro tempore of the city council in 1953. He was ambassador to Liberia from 1953 to 1955 and was largely responsible for the work done under the 1950 general treaty for technical cooperation. Died April 10, 1955, in Monrovia, Liberia. *References*: *CB* 1955; *Christmas*; *NCAB* 44:370; and *NYT*, April 11, 1955.

LOCKETT, BASIL LEE (1879–1933). Medical missionary, born October 6, 1879, in Hartsville, Tennessee. Lockett graduated from Baylor University. He was a missionary to Nigeria under the Foreign Mission Board of the Southern Baptist Convention.* He served in Abeokuta, Oyo, and Ogbomosho, establishing mission schools, clinics, hospitals, and a leper colony. Died November 13, 1933, in Oklahoma City, Oklahoma. *References*: *ESB*; and Elkin L. Lockett, *Basil Lee Lockett. A Beloved Physician* (Richmond, Va., 1936).

LOEB, EDWIN MEYER (1894–1966). Anthropologist, born March 15, 1894, in New York City. Loeb graduated from Yale University. He was on the faculty of the University of California at Berkeley from 1922 to 1961, teaching anthropology and geography. He conducted fieldwork in New Zealand and the island of Niue in 1923 and in Indonesia in 1926–1927. He was a specialist on Southeast Asia for the Office of Strategic Services (OSS) during World War II. He was a member of the University of California Africa Expedition in 1946–1947, studied the Kuanyama Ambo peoples in Southwest Africa, and wrote *In Feudal Africa* (Bloomington, Ind., 1962). He returned again to Indonesia in 1955. Died August 16, 1966, in Santa Monica, California. *References*: *AA* 69 (1967): 200–203; and *NCAB* J:168.

LONG, TEX (1858–1941). Soldier and pioneer, real name Ernest Long, born in Texas. Long worked as a cowboy before he settled as a farmer at Fort Victoria, Rhodesia; he later became a prospector. He served as a scout in the Matabele War of 1893 and participated in the Shangani battle of that year. *Reference*: *SADNB*.

LOOMIS, EBEN JENKS (1828–1912). Mathematician and astronomer, born November 11, 1828, in Oppenheim, New York. Loomis attended Lawrence Scientific School (later part of Harvard University). In 1850 he joined the office of the *American Nautical Almanac*, which was founded by his father, and served as senior assistant in the office of the almanac (which subsequently became the *American Ephemeris and Nautical Almanac*) until his retirement in 1900. He was a member of the expedition sent by the United States Navy in 1899 to the west coast of Africa to observe the total eclipse of the sun, and he described the trip in *An Eclipse Party in Africa* (Boston, 1896). Died December 2, 1912, in Amherst, Massachusetts. *References*: *NCAB* 40:446; *NYT*, December 3, 1912; and *WWWA*.

LOOMIS, JOHN (1875–1956). Financial adviser, born March 29, 1875, in Cleveland, Ohio. Loomis served with the Bureau of Supplies of the Philippine Civil Service from 1905 to 1915, and was chief of the Division of Supplies from 1911 to 1915. He was director general of internal revenue, auditor general, and treasurer general of the Republic of Santo Domingo from 1916 to 1922, and was employed by the General Sugar Company of Havana from 1923 to 1925. He was a member of the American financial mission to Persia and director general of finances of East Persia from 1925 to 1928. He was a financial adviser to the Republic of Liberia from 1928 to 1932 and in 1934–1935. Died May 18, 1956, in Washington, D.C. *Reference*: *WWWA*.

LORING, J(OHN) ALDEN (1871–1947). Zoologist, born March 6, 1871, in Cleveland. Loring was a field naturalist with the United States Biological Survey from 1892 to 1897 and curator of animals at the New York Zoological Park from 1897 to 1901. Later he was a field naturalist for the United States National Museum and was commissioned to collect specimens of birds and mammals in Europe. He accompanied Theodore Roosevelt on his expedition to East Africa in 1909–1910 and wrote *African Adventure Stories* (New York, 1914). He went to South Africa in 1916–1917 to purchase animals for the zoological parks of New York, Philadelphia, and Washington. He served in the U.S. Army during

World War I. Died May 8, 1947, in Owego, Tioga County, New York. *References*: *The Auk* 64 (1947): 504–5; *NYT*, May 9, 1947; *OAB*; and *WWWA*.

LOTT CAREY BAPTIST FOREIGN MISSION CONVENTION. Established in 1897 and took its name from Lott Carey.* The first black organization devoted exclusively to foreign mission work, it began missionary work in Liberia and the Congo Free State in 1900 and later in Nigeria. *Reference*: Leroy Fitts, *Lott Carey: First Black Missionary to Africa* (Valley Forge, Pa., 1978).

LOUNSBURY, CHARLES P(UGSLEY) (1872–1955). Entomologist, born September 20, 1872, in Brooklyn, New York. Lounsbury graduated from the Massachusetts Agricultural College (Amherst) and Boston University. He came to South Africa in 1895 as the first government entomologist in the Cape. In 1898 he began to study the spread of animal diseases by ticks and imported various types of natural enemies to combat plague insects. He was head of the entomological section of the Department of Agriculture of the Union of South Africa in Pretoria from 1911 until his retirement in 1927. He published his reminiscences in 1940 in the *Journal of the Entomological Society of Southern Africa*. Died June 7, 1955, in Pretoria, South Africa. *References*: *DASB* 3; *Journal of Economic Entomology* 43 (1950): 532; and *SADNB*.

LOVERIDGE, ARTHUR (1891–1980). Herpetologist, born May 28, 1891, in Penrath, Glanmorgan, Wales. Loveridge attended the University of South Wales. He was on the staff of the Manchester University Museum, deputy zoologist at the National Museum of Wales from 1911 to 1914, curator at the Natural History Museum of Nairobi from 1914 to 1920, and assistant game warden in Tanganyika from 1921 to 1923. He served in the East African Mounted Rifles during World War I. He came to the United States in 1924, was assistant curator of herpetology at the Museum of Comparative Zoology at Harvard University from 1924 to 1932, associate curator from 1932 to 1934, and curator of herpetology from 1935 until his retirement in 1957. He conducted collecting expeditions to East Africa in 1926–1927, 1928–1929, 1933–1934, 1938–1939, and 1948–1949. He wrote accounts of his African experiences in *Many Happy Days I've Squandered* (New York, 1944), *Tomorrow's a Holiday* (New York, 1947), *I Drank the Zambesi* (New York, 1953) and *Forest Safari* (London, 1956). Died February 16, 1980, on the island of St. Helena in the South Atlantic. *References*: Arthur Loveridge Papers, Museum of Comparative Zoology Library, Cambridge, Mass.; *AMWS*; *Boston Globe*, July 21, 1957; and Ernest Williams, "Arthur Loveridge— a Life in Retrospect," *Breviora* (Museum of Comparative Zoology), 471 (June 30, 1982).

LUGENBEEL, JAMES WASHINGTON (1819–1857). Physician and diplomat, born in Virginia. Lugenbeel went to Liberia in 1843 as colonial physician for the American Colonization Society* and as a United States Government agent for recaptured Africans. He came back to the United States in 1846 but returned to Africa in 1848 as consular agent in Liberia. He returned to the United States in 1849 and was recording secretary of the American Colonization Society until his death. He wrote articles about his residence in Liberia which were published in the *African Repository* and *Sketches of Liberia, Comprising a Brief Account of the Geography, Climate, Productions, and Diseases of the Republic of Liberia* (Washington, D.C., 1850; 2d ed. rev., Washington, D.C., 1853). Died September 22, 1857, in Alexandria, Virginia. *References*: *African Repository* 33 (1857): 351; *Alexandria* (Va.) *Gazette*, September 24, 1857; and *Huberich*.

LUTHER, ERNEST W. (1924–   ). Economist, born February 6, 1924, in Cedarhurst, New York. Luther graduated from Swarthmore College and New York University. He was economic analyst at the Econometric Institute, Inc., from 1946 to 1950, and statistician at the State Bank in Ethiopia from 1950 to 1956. He wrote *Ethiopia Today* (Stanford, 1958). He was later an economist with the Mercantile & Agricultural Bank of Venezuela in 1957, an adviser on monetary statistics to Bank Melli in Iran in 1958–1959, and an economist with the Investors Diversified Services, Inc., after 1959. *Reference*: *AMWS*.

LUTHERAN CHURCH IN AMERICA: BOARD OF WORLD MISSIONS. *See* AUGUSTANA LUTHERAN CHURCH: BOARD OF FOREIGN MISSIONS and UNITED LUTHERAN CHURCH IN AMERICA: BOARD OF FOREIGN MISSIONS

LYNCH, FRANKLIN PIERCE (1859–1948). Medical missionary, born in Philadelphia. Lynch graduated from Bucknell University, Yale University Divinity School, and New York University Medical School, and was ordained. He was a missionary under the American Baptist Foreign Mission (see American Baptist Missionary Union*) from 1893 to 1919, serving in the Belgian Congo and in Mozambique. He established a hospital in Mukimvika, Belgian Congo, and developed a treatment for backwater fever, a tropical disease. Died November 20, 1948, in New York City. *Reference*: *NYT*, November 23, 1948.

LYNCH, WILLIAM FRANCIS (1801–1865). Naval officer, born April 1, 1801, in Norfolk, Virginia. Lynch was appointed a midshipman in the navy in 1819, and served in various stations and in the Mexican War. He headed the expedition to the River Jordan and the Dead Sea in 1848 and wrote *Naval Life; or, Observations Afloat and on Shore* (New York, 1851), which is partly autobiographical. He was assigned in 1853 to the African Squadron, and explored the coast of Liberia for the purpose of recommending points of entry for a large-scale expedition of exploration in that area (which did not take place). His report was published in the *Annual Report of the Secretary of the Navy for 1853* (House Executive Document No. 1, 33rd U.S. Cong., 1st Session). He served in the Confederate Navy during the Civil War. Died October 17, 1865, in Baltimore. *References*: *DAB*; *NCAB* 13:172; and Richard K. MacMaster, "The United States Navy and African Exploration 1851–1860," *Mid-America* 46 (1964): 187–203.

LYON, ERNEST (1860–1938). Clergyman and diplomat, born October 22, 1860, in Belize, British Honduras. Lyon immigrated to the United States, and was naturalized in 1894. He graduated from New Orleans University and University Theological Seminary (N.Y.C.). He was a pastor of the Methodist Episcopal Church in New Orleans, New York City, and Baltimore from 1882 to 1903. He was minister resident and consul general to Liberia from 1903 to 1910 and was consul general of Liberia in Washington and agent for the Board of Education of Liberia from 1911 to 1925. Later he was again a pastor in Baltimore. Died July 17, 1938, in Baltimore. *References*: *Christmas*; *NCAB* 14:421; *NYT*, July 18, 1938; and *WWWA*.

M

MABIE, CATHERINE L(OUISE) (ROE) (1872–1963). Medical missionary, born in Rock Island, Illinois. Mabie graduated from Hahnemann Medical College. She was a missionary under the American Woman's Baptist Foreign Mission Society in the Belgian Congo from 1898 until her retirement in 1942, stationed first at Banza Manteke and after 1911 at Kimpese. She wrote *Congo Cameos* (Philadelphia, 1952). Died June 13, 1963, in Claremont, California. *References*: *Time*, August 5, 1946; *Watchman Examiner* 51 (July 11, 1963): 561.

MCCAULEY, VINCENT J. (1906–1982). Missionary, born March 8, 1906, in Council Bluffs, Iowa. McCauley graduated from Notre Dame University and Holy Cross Foreign Mission Seminary (Washington, D.C.) and was ordained in 1934. He was missionary in India from 1936 to 1944, rector of the Holy Cross Foreign Mission Seminary from 1944 to 1952, and worked in the Holy Cross Foreign Mission Society until 1958. He was missionary under the Holy Cross Foreign Mission Society in Uganda from 1958 until 1972, establishing the Fort Portal mission, and was the first bishop of Fort Portal from 1961 until his retirement in 1972. He was then executive secretary of the Association of Member Episcopal Conferences of Eastern Africa from 1973 until 1979. He returned to the United States in 1982. Died November 1, 1982, in Rochester, Minnesota. *References*: *ACWW*; and *DACB*.

MCCORD, JAMES B(ENNETT) (1870–1950). Medical missionary, born April 5, 1870, in Toulon, Illinois. McCord graduated from Oberlin College and Northwestern University. He practiced medicine in Lake City, Iowa, from 1895 to 1899. He was a missionary under the American Board of Commissioners for Foreign Missions (ABCFM)* in South Africa from 1899 to 1940. He served at Adams Mission at Amanzimtoti from 1899 to 1904 and in 1900 opened the first hospital for blacks in Natal. He moved to Durban in 1904, established a dispensary, and built a hospital for Africans in Durban in 1909. It later grew to become one of the largest mission hospitals in Africa and was renamed McCord Hospital in 1935. He established a training school for black nurses and later a school for midwives and a training program for black medical aides, and tried to establish a medical school for Africans. He retired in 1940, returned to the United States, and wrote (with John S. Douglas) *My Patients Were Zulus* (London, 1951). Died October 5, 1950, in Oakham, Massachusetts. *References*: *DAB* S4; *DASB* 4; *NYT*, February 12, 1952; and *SESA*.

MACCREAGH, GORDON (1886–1953). Traveler, explorer, and author, born August 8, 1886, in Perth, Indiana, and grew up in Scotland and later in France, Germany, and England. MacCreagh attended Hanover College and the universities of Heidelberg and Göttingen. He was a writer for *Adventure* magazine and a contributor to other magazines. He explored Borneo, South America and Africa after 1905, and was a navy flier during World War I. He made two explorations to Abyssinia from 1927 to 1929 and wrote *White Waters and Black* (New York, 1926) and *The Last of Free Africa: The Account of an Expedition into Abyssinia, with Observations on the Manners, Customs and Traditions of the Ethiopians* (New York, 1928). He tried, unsuccessfully, to obtain a mining concession from the Ethiopian government in 1929. He lived in Huntington, Long Island, and later in St. Petersburg, Florida, in Mexico, and again in St. Petersburg. Died August 31, 1953, in St. Petersburg, Florida. *References*: *IAB*; *St. Petersburg Times*, September 1, 1953; and *WWWA*.

MCCUTCHEON, JOHN TINNEY (1870–1949). Cartoonist, born May 6, 1870, near South Raub, Tippecanoe County, Indiana, and grew up in Lafayette, Indiana. McCutcheon graduated from Purdue University. He joined the staff of the *Chicago Morning News* in 1889, was employed by the *Chicago Record* and the *Chicago Record-Herald* until 1903, and was a cartoonist with the *Chicago Tribune* from 1903 until 1946. He was a war correspondent in the Philippines from 1898 to 1900 and in the South African War in 1900–1901. He made a trip to Africa with Carl Ethan Akeley* in 1909–1910, hunting big game, which he described in *In Africa: Hunting Adventures in the Big Game Country* (Indianapolis, 1910). He also participated in Theodore Roosevelt's* expedition to Africa. He was later a war correspondent in Mexico and during World War I. He wrote *Drawn from Memory; Autobiography Containing Many of the Author's Famous Cartoons and Sketches* (Indianapolis, 1950). Died June 10, 1949, in Lake Forest, Illinois. *References: IAB; NCAB* G:162; *NYT*, June 11, 1949; and *WWWA*.

MCDOWELL, HENRY CURTIS (1894–   ). Missionary, born February 7, 1894, in Epes, Sumpter County, Alabama, and grew up in Meridian, Mississippi. McDowell graduated from Talladega College (Ala.) and its theological seminary, and served as a pastor in Chattanooga, Tennessee. He was the first missionary representing the Congregational Churches of the South and served in Galangue,

Angola, from 1919 until 1958. *References*: Henry Curtis McDowell Papers, Talladega College Historical Collections, Savery Library, Talladega, Ala.; Lillie M. Johnson, "Black American Missionaries in Colonial Africa, 1900–1940: A Study of Missionary-Government Relations," Ph.D. diss., University of Chicago, 1981, ch. 6.

MCGEOUGH, JOSEPH F. (1903–1970). Clergyman, born in New York City. McGeough attended Cathedral College and St. Joseph's Seminary (Yonkers, N.Y.), studied at the North American College and the Pontifical Lateran University in Rome, and was ordained in 1930. He taught in New York and was a parish priest in the Bronx. He became an official of the Congregation for the Eastern Church in Rome in 1938 and joined the Vatican Secretariat of State in 1943. He was consecrated a titular archbishop of Hemesa in 1960, was the first apostolic internuncio to Ethiopia from 1957 to 1960, and an apostolic delegate in South Africa from 1960 to 1967. He was an apostolic nuncio to Ireland from 1967 to 1969. Died October 12, 1970, in New York City. *References*: *ACWW*; and *NYT*, October 13, 1970.

MCGILL, GEORGE R. (ca. 1787-?). School teacher, born free. McGill came to Liberia on the brig *Doris* in 1827. He was elected vice-agent in 1833 and took over the administration of the colony from the time Joseph Mechlin, Jr.,* departed until John B. Pinney* arrived in 1834. He left Liberia in 1837 and settled in Cape Palmas, Liberia. His son, **SAMUEL F. MCGILL**, (1815-?), immigrated to Liberia with his father and accompanied him to Cape Palmas in 1837. He became an assistant agent and, after Governor John Brown Russwurm's death in 1851, was governor of the Maryland in Africa* colony until 1854. *Reference: Huberich.*

MCGREGOR, JAMES HOWARD (1872–1954). Zoologist, born July 23, 1872, in Bellaire, Ohio. McGregor graduated from Ohio State and Columbia universities. He joined the faculty of Columbia University in 1897 and was professor of zoology from 1924 until 1942. He was on the staff of the Marine Biological Laboratory at Woods Hole, Massachusetts, from 1899 to 1906, and on the staff of the American Museum of Natural History, where he became an associate in human anatomy in 1916. He was a member of the African Anatomical Expedition sponsored by Columbia University and the American Museum of Natural History in 1929, which brought back five adult gorillas. Died November 14, 1954, in New York City. *References*: *NYT*, November 15, 1954; and *WWWA*.

MACKENZIE, JEAN KENYON (1874–1936). Missionary and author, born January 6, 1874, in Elgin, Illinois. MacKenzie studied at the Sorbonne and the University of California. She was a missionary under the Board of Foreign Missions of the Presbyterian Church in the U.S.A.* She served in German

Cameroon from 1904 to 1918. Because of an accident she returned to the United States and devoted the rest of her life to writing about Africa. She wrote *Black Sheep: Adventures in West Africa* (New York, 1916), *African Adventures: Missionary Education Movement* (New York, 1922), *An African Trail* (West Medford, Mass., 1917), *African Clearings* (New York, 1923), and *Friends of Africa* (Cambridge, Mass., 1928). Died September 2, 1936, in New York City. *References*: *NAW*; *NCAB* 28:280; *NYT*, September 3, 1936; and *WWWA*.

MCKIERNAN, GERALD (1844–1892). Trader and hunter, born May 1, 1844, at Indiana Forge, Westmoreland County, Pennsylvania, and grew up near Lawrence, Kansas. He served in the Civil War and was a superintendent of railroad construction in Texas, Arkansas, Nebraska, Colorado, Wyoming, and Michigan until 1873. He came to South Africa in 1874; he went on a trading venture in Southwest Africa and traveled into the interior from Walvis Bay. He hunted and traded in Damaraland and Ovampoland in 1875–1876 and went on expeditions to Lake Ngami in 1877–1878 and to Okavango River in 1878–1879. He returned to the United States in 1879 and lived in New York City and Altoona, Pennsylvania. Died June 3, 1892, in Altoona, Pennsylvania. His journal was published later as *The Narrative and Journal of Gerald McKiernan in South West Africa 1874–1879*, ed. P. Serton (Cape Town, 1954). *References*: *SADNB*; and *Tabler/South West Africa*.

MCMILLAN, AARON MANASSES (1895–1980). Medical missionary, born in Cotton Plant, Arkansas. McMillan graduated from Bishop College (Marshall, Tex.) and Meharry Medical College (Nashville, Tenn.). He practiced medicine in Omaha, Nebraska, and served in the Nebraska Legislature in 1928–1929. He was a medical missionary under the American Board of Commissioners for Foreign Missions (ABCFM)* from 1929 to 1946, supervising a hospital in the Galangue mission at Bundja, Angola. He wrote a personal narrative, *Majestic Heads* (New York, 1978). Died June 1, 1980, in Los Angeles. *References*: Aaron Manasses McMillan Papers, Talladega College Historical Collections, Savery Library, Talladega, Ala.; *Lincoln* (Neb.) *Journal*, June 4, 1980; Linton Wells, "Jungle Doctor," *Reader's Digest* 40 (May 1942): 103–6.

MCMILLAN, WILLIAM NORTHRUP (1872–1925). Settler, born October 19, 1872, in St. Louis, Missouri. McMillan went to Europe in 1898 as a representative of the American Car and Foundry Company. Becoming a multimillionaire on the death of his father in 1901, he went on a safari in British East Africa, traveled down the White Nile in 1902 by steamer, camel, and on foot to Nairobi, and conducted an expedition to Southern Abyssinia in 1904. He settled in British East Africa in 1904 and owned land at Juja, near Nairobi, Saba Saba, and Ondiri. He was a big-game hunter, but also studied game and experimented with game farming. He served in the British Army in East Africa during World War I and maintained and staffed two convalescent homes for troops at his own expense. He was knighted in 1918. Died March 22, 1925, in Nice, France. *Reference*: *St. Louis Post-Dispatch*, March 24, 1925.

MCMURDO, EDWARD or EDWIN (ca. 1845–1889). Soldier and financier. McMurdo fought in the Civil War, rising to the rank of colonel. In 1883 he received a concession from the Portuguese government to build a railroad from the port of Lourenço Marques in Mozambique to the Transvaal border. He floated the South African Improvement Company Limited in London in 1887, which established the Lebombo Railway Company. Little progress was made before his death, when the Portuguese government seized the concession. Representations made by his widow led to arbitrations that were concluded in 1896. *Reference*: *SADNB*.

MACVEAGH, LINCOLN (1890–1972). Diplomat, born October 1, 1890, in Narragansett Pier, Rhode Island. MacVeagh graduated from Harvard University and studied at the Sorbonne and served in the army during World War I. He founded the Dial Press, a book publishing company, in 1923. He was minister to Greece from 1933 to 1941, first minister to Iceland in 1941–1942, and minister to the Union of South Africa in 1942–1943. He helped to arrange the procurement of vital resources for the United States from South Africa and successfully coordinated the American wartime agencies there. He was later ambassador to the Greek and Yugoslav governments in exile in Cairo, ambassador to Greece from 1944 to 1948, ambassador to Portugal from 1948 to 1952, and ambassador to Spain in 1952–1953. Died January 15, 1972, in Adelphi, Maryland. *References*: Lincoln MacVeagh, "Dear Franklin . . . : Letters to President Roosevelt from Lincoln MacVeagh, United States Minister to South Africa, 1942–1943," *Munger Africana Library Notes*, March 1972; *CB* 1952; and *NYT*, January 17, 1972.

MAHONEY, WILLIAM PATRICK, JR. (1916-   ). Lawyer and diplomat, born November 27, 1916, in Prescott, Arizona. Mahoney graduated from the University of Notre Dame and served in the navy during World War II. He was assistant attorney general of Arizona from 1946 to 1948 and district attorney of Maricopa County, Arizona, from 1953 to 1957. He was ambassador to Ghana from 1962 to 1965 and succeeded in improving the relations between the United States and Ghana. He was the federal aid coordinator for Maricopa County from 1966 to 1968. *References*: *WWA*; and *WWAP*.

MALLY, CHARLES WILLIAM (1872–1953). Economic entomologist, born September 23, 1872, in Des Moines, Iowa. Mally graduated from Iowa State College of Agriculture and Mechanic Arts. He came to Cape Town in 1900 and became an assistant entomologist in the Department of Agriculture of the Cape Colony; he was entomologist for the Eastern Province at Grahamstown from 1903 to 1905. He returned to the United States in 1905, but came back to Grahamstown in 1907 and developed a method of combating fruit flies by means of a poison bait. He became a government entomologist for the Cape Province in 1911 and senior entomologist in 1919. He was also a senior lecturer at the Elsenburg Agricultural College of the University of Stellenbosch from 1926 until his retirement in 1932. Died March 31, 1953, in Stellenbosch, South Africa. *References*: *DASB* 3; and *SESA*.

MANN, WILLIAM M. (1886–1960). Entomologist and zoologist, born July 1, 1886, in Helena, Montana. Mann attended Washington State College and graduated from Stanford and Harvard universities. He joined the United States Department of Agriculture as a tropical explorer in 1916 and later was an entomologist with the Bureau of Entomology. He was director of the National Zoological Park in Washington, D.C., from 1925 until his retirement in 1956. He participated in many expeditions to all parts of the world. He was director of the Smithsonian-Chrysler East African Expedition for the National Zoological Park in 1926, and director of the Smithsonian-Firestone Expedition to Liberia in 1940. He wrote *Wild Animals in and out of the Zoo* (New York, 1930) and his reminiscences, *Ant Hill Odyssey* (Boston, 1948). Died October 10, 1960, in Washington, D.C. *References*: Arnold Mallis, *American Entomologists* (New Brunswick, N.J., 1971), pp. 377–78; *Nature* 178 (November 17, 1956): 1095; *NCAB* 47:412; *NYT*, October 11, 1960; and *WWWA*.

MARBUT, C(URTIS) F(LETCHER) (1863–1935). Soil scientist, born July 19, 1863, in the Ozark Mountain region of Missouri. Marburt graduated from the University of Missouri and Howard University. He was on the staff of the Missouri Geological Survey from 1890 to 1893. He was an instructor, assistant professor, and professor at the University of Missouri from 1895 to 1910, director of the Soil Survey of Missouri from 1905 to 1910, and a special agent of the United States Bureau of Soils in 1909–1910. He became chief of the Division of Soil Survey in the United States Department of Agriculture in 1910, and in 1918 took part in the Inquiry, an organization established by the U.S. government in 1917 to study the problems of peacemaking at the close of World War I. He helped to assemble technical knowledge to be used by the American Commission to Negotiate Peace. In this connection he made, with Homer L. Shantz,* an extensive journey through Africa, and they wrote *Vegetation and Soils of Africa* (New York, 1923). In 1923–1924 he was a member of a Department of Commerce expedition to study the soil of the Amazon River. Died August 25, 1935, in Harbin, Manchukuo, on his way to make an examination of soils in China. *References*: *GSA Proceedings* 1936, pp. 221–24; H. H. Krusekop, ed., *Life and Work of C. F. Marbut, Soil Scientist* (Columbia, Mo., 1930); and Homer L. Shantz, "A Memoir of Curtis Fletcher Marbut," *Annals of the Association of American Geographers* 26 (1936): 113–23.

MARSHALL, LAURENCE K(ENNEDY) (1889–1980). Electronics manufacturer and anthropologist, born May 18, 1889, in Medford, Massachusetts. Marshall graduated from Tufts College and served in World War I. In 1922 he founded the Raytheon Manufacturing Company, a radio tube manufacturer, in Cambridge, Massachusetts. It became an international diversified electronics concern, and he was its president until his retirement in 1950. His wife, **LORNA J(EAN) (MCLEAN) MARSHALL** (1898-   ), was born in Arizona, studied at the University of California at Berkeley, and graduated from Radcliffe College. She taught English at Mount Holyoke College. The family made eight expeditions to the Kalahari Desert of Namibia during the 1950s and 1960s to conduct Bushmen studies. They undertook a study of the !Kung Bushmen mostly in the Nyae Nyae area of Northeast Namibia. They participated in the Peabody Museum of Archaeology and Ethnology Kalahari Expeditions in 1950, 1951, and 1952–1953, and the Peabody-Harvard Smithsonian Kalahari Expeditions, also referred to as the "Marshall Expeditions," in 1955, 1956, 1957–1958, 1959, and 1961. Laurence produced several films of the !Kung Bushmen, and Lorna wrote *The !Kung of Nyae Nyae* (Cambridge, Mass., 1976). Laurence died November 6, 1980, in Cambridge, Massachusetts. Their daughter, **ELIZABETH MARSHALL THOMAS** (1931-   ), was born September 13, 1931, in Boston, Massachusetts. Elizabeth attended Smith College and graduated from Radcliffe College. She participated in the expeditions of 1951, 1952–1953, and 1955, and wrote *The Harmless People* (New York, 1959) and *Warrior Herdsmen* (New York, 1965). *References*: *CA*; *NYT*, November 8, 1980; and *WWWA*.

MARTIN, MOTTE (1879–1946). Missionary, born January 1, 1879, in Marlin, Texas. Martin graduated from Austin College (Sherman, Texas) and Union Theological Seminary (Richmond, Va.) and was ordained in 1903. He was a missionary under the Board of Foreign Missions of the Presbyterian Church in the United States* at Luebo, Kasai district, Congo Free State (and later Belgian Congo), from 1903 to 1941. He was active in stopping native rebellion during World War I, was escort to King Albert and Queen Elizabeth of Belgium at the official opening of the Congo branch of the Cape-to-Cairo railway in 1928, and was president of the Congo Protestant Council in 1938–1939. Died September 14, 1946, in Luebo, Belgian Congo. *Reference*: John Morrison, *Mpande Nashila, 'The Splitter of Paths': The Story of Motte Martin of Africa* (Nashville, Tenn., n.d.); and *WWWA*.

MARYLAND IN AFRICA. In 1827, the Maryland State Colonization Society established a colony called Harper in Cape Palmas. Harper became an independent republic in 1854 and was renamed Maryland in Africa. It was admitted to the Republic of Liberia in 1857 as Maryland County. *References*: Maryland State Colonization Society Papers, Maryland Historical Society, Baltimore; Penelope Campbell, *Maryland in Africa: The Maryland State Colonization Society, 1831–1857* (Urbana, Ill., 1971); Ernest Eastman, *A History of the State of Maryland* *in Liberia* (Monrovia, 1956); William D. Hoyt, "The Papers of the Maryland State Colonization Society," *Maryland Historical Magazine* 22 (1937): 247–71; and John H. B. Latrobe, *Maryland in Liberia: A History of the Colony Planted by the Maryland State Colonization Society . . . at Cape Palmas on the South-West Coast of Africa 1833–1853* (Baltimore, 1885).

MASURY, SAMUEL RICHARD (1821–1858). Merchant, born June 9, 1821, in Salem. Masury arrived in Zanzibar in 1844 to set up business as a resident merchant, and remained for several years. He aided Richard F. Burton in preparing the Burton-Speke expedition of 1857–1858. He also collected the first considerable list of Swahili words and phrases for publication, and prepared *A Vocabulary of the Soahili Language* (Cambridge, 1845). Lost on board the steamer *Austria*, September 13, 1858, on a trip between Southampton and New York City. *Reference*: *Proceedings of the Essex Institute* 2 (1856–1859): 370.

MATTHEWS, THOMAS (TOM) (ca. 1866–1915). Labor leader, born in Newlyn, Cornwall, England. Matthews worked as a miner, immigrated to the United States in 1882, worked in various mines in the west, was shift boss, and opened his own mines. He became an active unionist in Montana, was elected president of the Butte section of the Western Mines' Federation, and was the only labor representative elected in 1892 to the Montana House of Representatives. He became its speaker in 1892 and was commissioner of mines for Montana from 1892 to 1894. He returned to Cornwall in 1894 and studied at the Cambroen School of Mines. He went to the Transvaal in 1897, worked in the gold fields, and helped found the International Independent Labour Party. He was later vice president of the Transvaal Miners' Association and was prominent in the first important miners' strike in 1907. Later he was general secretary of the white miners' union until his death, and played a leading role in the miners' strikes of 1913 and 1914. Died March 10, 1915, in Johannesburg. *References*: *DASB* 2; and *SADNB*.

MAYFIELD, JULIAN (1928–1984). Author and expatriate, born June 6, 1928, in Greer, South Carolina. Mayfield attended Lincoln University. He was editor and theater reviewer for the *Puerto Rico World Journal*. He was communications aide and speech-writer for President Kwame Nkrumah of Ghana and editor of *African Review* in Accra, Ghana, from 1962 to 1966. He was then adviser to Prime Minister Forbes Burnham of Guyana, visiting professor at the University of Maryland from 1975 to 1978, and writer in residence at Howard University from 1978 until his death. Died October 20, 1984, in Tacoma Park, Washington. *References*: *CA*; *DLB*; *NYT*, October 23, 1984; James Vinson, ed., *Contemporary Novelists* (New York, 1982); and *WWA*.

MEARNS, EDGAR A(LEXANDER) (1856–1916). Army surgeon and naturalist, born September 11, 1856, in Highland Falls, Orange County, New York. Mearns graduated from the College of Physicians and Surgeons (New York City). He was commissioned assistant surgeon in the United States Army in 1883 and served in Fort Verde, Arizona, and Fort Snelling, Minnesota; he was a medical officer on the Mexican-United States International Boundary Commission from 1891 to 1894 and served in Fort Clark, Texas, and Fort Adams, Rhode Island, collecting animals and plants. He served in the Philippines in 1903–1904 and from 1905 to 1907. He retired in 1909 due to physical disability with the rank of lieutenant colonel. He was a naturalist in the African expedition of Theodore Roosevelt* in 1909–1910 and made a second trip to Africa with the Childs Frick* expedition in 1911–1912. Died November 1, 1916, in Washington, D.C. *References*: Edgar A. Mearns Papers, Manuscript Division, Library of Congress; *DAB*; *DAMB*; *NCAB* 25:124; *NYT*, November 4, 1916; and *WWWA*.

MECHLIN, JOSEPH, JR. (fl. 1827–1833). Physician, from the District of Columbia. Mechlin graduated from the University of Pennsylvania Medical School. He was assistant agent and physician in Liberia in 1828 and agent of the American Colonization Society* and United States government for recaptured Africans in Liberia from 1829 to 1833.

MEIN, THOMAS ("POPPA") (? –1900). Mining engineer. Mein came to the Witwatersrand, South Africa, and was manager of the Robinson Mine. He tried unsuccessfully to mediate during the Jameson Raid. He returned to the United States at the outbreak of the South African War and later became interested in opening the Alaska gold mines. *Reference*: *SADNB*.

MEIN, WILLIAM W(ALLACE) (1873–1964). Mining engineer and financier, born July 19, 1873, in Nevada City, California. Mein graduated from the University of California at Berkeley. He came to South Africa in 1892 to join the staff of De Beers Consolidated Mines and was involved in gold and nickel mining in South Africa until 1919. He was manager of the Robinson Chlorination Works in Johannesburg from 1894 to 1896, was consulting engineer to the central administration of Hermann Eckstein & Company, and president of the Mine Managers' Association in 1897–1898. He was later associated with the International Nickel Company in developing its properties in Canada. He was director of fertilizer control for the United States in World War I and head mining consultant to the U.S. Office of Industry Operations in World War II. He was founder and president of the Bishop Oil Company and the Calaveras Cement Company. Died May 5, 1964, in San Francisco. *References*: *ACAB*; *Mining Engineering* 16 (January 1964): 44–45; *NYT*, May 7, 1964; *SADNB*; and *WWWA*.

MELADY, THOMAS PATRICK (1927-). Educator and diplomat, born March 4, 1927, in Norwich, Connecticut. Melady graduated from Duquesne University (Pittsburgh) and Catholic University of America. He was foreign trade and investment adviser to the Ethiopian government from 1954 to 1956, director of development and founder of the Institute of African Affairs at Duquesne University from 1956 to 1959, president of Consultants for Overseas Relations and Africa Service Institute in New York City from 1959 to 1967, and professor of Afro-Asian affairs at Seton Hall University (South Orange, N.J.) from 1967 to 1969. He was ambassador to Burundi from 1969 to 1972 and ambassador to Uganda in 1972–1973. He wrote *Burundi: The Tragic Years* (Maryknoll, N.Y., 1974) and coauthored *Idi Amin Dada: Hitler in Africa* (New York, 1978). He was executive vice president of St. Joseph's University (Philadelphia) from 1974 to 1976 and president of Sacred Heart University (Bridgeport, Conn.) after 1976. *References*: *ACWW*; *CA*; and *WWA*.

MELEN, NELS (1864–1897). Soldier, born January 29, 1864, in Lee County, Iowa. Melen served in the United States Army and then as a pilot on the Great Lakes. He enlisted in 1896 as sergeant-major in the Force Publique (the combined frontier guard and police force) of the Congo Free State, rising to the rank of lieutenant. He participated in an expedition to Haut-Ituri in 1897. Killed February 15, 1897, at Mongwa, Congo Free State, in military action against the Batetela. *Reference*: *BCB* 2.

MENDE MISSION. In 1842 the survivors of the slave ship *Amistad*, who revolted in 1837, accompanied by William Raymond,* were brought to the Sherbro district (today in Sierra Leone). Raymond began the Mende Mission under the American Missionary Association.* The mission was turned over to the General Board of Missions of the United Brethren in Christ* in 1883. *Reference*: Mende Mission Archives, The Amistad Research Center, New Orleans.

MERCENARIES. Involvement of Americans in mercenary operations in Africa has been overstated. The United States government actively discouraged Americans from involvement in the Congo, and only a few free-lance pilots flew in the Biafran conflict of 1967. Substantive activity occurred only in the Angolan War and in the Rhodesian conflict of the 1970s. *References*: Cynthia H. Enloe, "Mercenarization in U.S. Military Involvement in Southern Africa," in *U.S. Military Involvement in Southern Africa*, ed. Western Massachusetts Association of Concerned African Scholars (Boston, 1978), pp. 109–29; Richard Lobban, "American Mercenaries in Rhodesia," *Journal of Southern African Affairs* 3 (July 1978): 319–25; Jay Mallin and Robert K. Brown, *Merc: American Soldiers of Fortune* (New York, 1979); and Gerry S. Thomas, *Mercenary Troops in Modern Africa* (Boulder, Colo., 1984).

MERRIAM, ALAN P(ARKHURST) (1923–1980). Ethnomusicologist, born November 1, 1923, in Missoula, Montana. Merriam served in the Army Air Force in World War II and graduated from Montana State College (now University) and Northwestern University. He was assistant professor and associate professor of anthropology at Northwestern University from 1956 to 1962 and professor of anthropology at Indiana University from 1962 until 1980. He conducted ethnomusicological field research in Zaire and Ruanda-Urundi. He wrote *Congo: Background of Conflict* (Evanston, Ill., 1961); *A Prologue to the Study of the African Arts* (Yellow Springs, Ohio, 1961); *An African World: The Basongye Village of Lupupa Ngye* (Bloomington, Ind., 1974); and *Culture History of the Basongye* (Bloomington, Ind., 1975). Died March 14, 1980, in an air accident, over Warsaw, Poland. *References: CA; Ethnomusicology* 24 (1980): v-vii; *Ethnomusicology* 26 (January 1982): 91–120; and *WWWA*.

METHODIST EPISCOPAL CHURCH: BOARD OF FOREIGN MISSIONS. Founded in 1819, it began missionary work in Liberia in 1833. After 1844, when the Methodist Episcopal Church divided, supervision of the Liberian mission field was assigned to the Methodist Episcopal Church, North. It began missionary work in Angola in 1844, in Southern Rhodesia in 1898, in Mozambique and South Africa in 1903, and in the Congo in 1910. It merged in 1939 with the Methodist Protestant Church and the Methodist Episcopal Church, South* to form the Methodist Church, which merged in 1968 with the Evangelical United Brethren Church to form the United Methodist Church and its Board of Global Ministries. *References*: Wade C. Barclay, *History of Methodist Missions* (New York, 1949–1973); Henry I. James, *Missions in Rhodesia under the Methodist Episcopal Church 1898–1934* (Old Umtali, Rhodesia, 1935); and Thomas B. Neely, *The Methodist Episcopal Church and Its Foreign Missions* (New York, 1923).

METHODIST EPISCOPAL CHURCH, SOUTH. Founded in 1844 when it broke off from the Methodist Episcopal Church, it began missionary work in the Belgian Congo in 1913. It merged in 1939 with the Methodist Episcopal Church* and the Methodist Protestant Church to form the Methodist Church, which merged in 1968 with the Evangelical United Brethren Church to form the United Methodist Church and its Board of Global Ministries. *References*: James Cannon III, *History of Southern Methodist Missions* (Nashville, 1926); and Alexander J. Reid, *Congo Drumbeat: History of the First Half Century in the Establishment of the Methodist Church Among the Atetela of Central Congo* (New York, 1964).

MILLIGAN, ROBERT H(ENRY) (1868–1934). Missionary, born in Ontario, Canada. Milligan graduated from Manitoba College (Winnipeg), attended Princeton Theological Seminary, graduated from McCormick Theological Seminary, and was ordained in 1892. He was a missionary under the Board of Foreign

Missions of the Presbyterian Church in the U.S.A.* in Corisco Island and Cameroon from 1893 until 1904. He wrote *The Jungle Folk of Africa* (New York,
1908) and *The Fetish Folk of West Africa* (New York, 1912). He returned to
the United States in 1904 and served in several pastorates and was secretary of
the Upper Andes agency of the American Bible Society from 1927 to 1931.
*Reference: Biographical Catalogue of Princeton Theological Seminary, 1815–
1954* (Princeton, N.J., 1955).

MILLS, SAMUEL J(OHN), JR. (1783–1818). Missionary, born April 21,
1783, in Torrington, Connecticut. Mills graduated from Williams College, attended Yale University, graduated from Andover Theological Seminary, and
became licensed to preach in 1812. He was one of the founders of the American
Board of Commissioners for Foreign Missions (ABCFM)* and worked as a
missionary in the area west of the Allegheny Mountains. He was chief organizer
of the American Bible Society and the United Foreign Missionary Society and
played an important role in the establishment in 1816 of the African school at
Parsippany, New Jersey, for training black preachers. He went to Africa with
Ebenezer Burgess* in 1817 as an agent of the American Colonization Society*
to explore the west coast of Africa and to locate there a site that could be
purchased for a colony of free black Americans. Died June 16, 1818, at sea on
the return trip. *References: AndoverTS; DAB; Huberich;* and Kenneth S. Latourette, *These Sought a Country* (New York, 1950), pp. 40–61.

MINER, HORACE MITCHELL (1912-   ). Anthropologist, born May 26,
1912, in St. Paul, Minnesota. Miner graduated from the universities of Kentucky
and Chicago and studied at Columbia University. He was an instructor in anthropology and sociology at Wayne State University (Detroit) from 1937 to 1939,
served in the army during World War II, was assistant professor, associate
professor, and professor of anthropology and sociology at the University of
Michigan from 1946 to 1980, and was a research associate at the Museum of
Anthropology at the University of Michigan from 1948 to 1970. He first went
to Africa in 1930, crossed the Sahara both ways in 1940 to study Timbuctu, and
wrote *The Primitive City of Timbuctoo* (Princeton, 1953; rev. ed., Garden City,
N.Y., 1965). He conducted research in a Saharan oasis in 1950 and studied the
Hausa in Northern Nigeria in 1957–1958. He edited *Social Science in Action in
Sub-Saharan Africa* (Ithaca, N.Y., 1966) and *The City in Modern Africa* (New
York, 1967). *References: AMWS;* and *WWA.*

MISSISSIPPI IN AFRICA. In 1838 the Mississippi Colonization Society established a colony named Greenville at the mouth of the Sinoe River. The colony
was admitted to the Commonwealth of Liberia in 1842. *References:* Franklin L.
Riley, "A Contribution to the History of the Colonization Movement in Mississippi," *Publications of the Mississippi Historical Society* 9 (1906): 331–415;

and Jo Mary Sullivan, "Settlers in Sinoe County, Liberia, and Their Relations with the Kru, c. 1835–1920," Ph.D. diss., Boston University, 1978, ch. 4.

MITCHELL, CHARLES EDWARD (1870–1937). Businessman and diplomat, born May 3, 1870, in St. Michaels, Maryland. Mitchell attended Boston Commercial College and Interstate Business University (Detroit) and served in the navy. He was the business manager of West Virginia State College and its business instructor from 1904 to 1931. He was also president of the Mutual Savings and Loan Company of Charleston, West Virginia, from 1920 to 1931. A leader among black Republicans, he was a minister to Liberia from 1930 to 1933. He later moved to Institute, West Virginia, and then to New York City. Died March 29, 1937, in New York City. *References*: *Christmas*; *NYT*, March 30, 1937; and *WWWA*.

MITCHELL, LEBBENS H. (1834- ?). Mining engineer, born in Boston. Mitchell served in the Union Army during the Civil War and was employed as a topographical engineer. He resigned his commission in 1864 and joined the Egyptian General Staff in a scientific capacity. He made a geological survey of the country between the Nile and the Red Sea in 1874 and a geological and mineralogical survey of the country between the Red Sea and the Abyssinian Plateau in 1877 and traveled to Ailet to examine the medicinal qualities of its hot springs. While he was in Ailet in early 1877, the village was raided by an Abyssinian force and he and his party were captured and taken to the interior. He was held captive and was ransomed by a local merchant. He had an audience with Ethiopian Emperor Yohannes, possibly the first American to have an audience with an Ethiopian emperor. He wrote an account of his adventures in *Report on the Seizure by the Abyssinians of the Geological and Mineralogical Reconnaissance Expedition Attached to the Genera; Staff of the Egyptian Army Containing an Account of the Subsequent Treatment of the Prisoners and Final Release of the Commander* (Egypt, 1878). *Reference*: Richard L. Hill, *Biographical Dictionary of the Anglo-Egyptian Sudan*, 2d ed. (London, 1967).

MOE, PETRA MALLENA ("MALLA") (1863–1953). Missionary, born September 12, 1863, in Hafslo, County Sogn of Fjordane, Norway. Moe came to the United States in 1884 and worked in a laundry in Chicago. She became a missionary under the Scandinavian Alliance Mission of North America (later the Evangelical Alliance Mission*) in South Africa in 1892. She established the mission in Swaziland in 1893 and served in the Bethel mission station there from 1896 until her death. Died October 16, 1953, in Bethel Mission, Swaziland. *References*: Thomas J. Bach, *Pioneer Missionaries for Christ and His Church* (Wheaton, Ill., 1955), pp. 101–4; and Maria Nilsen (as told to Paul H. Sheets), *Malla Moe* (Chicago, 1956).

MOHUN, RICHARD DORSEY (LORAINE) (1864–1915). Consul and soldier of fortune, born April 12, 1864, in Washington, D.C. Mohun entered the United States Navy in 1881, becoming a lieutenant in 1889. He was a commerical agent at Boma, the Congo Free State, from 1892 to 1895, and explored the Lualaba River. He was consul in Zanzibar from 1895 to 1897, chief of the Congo Free State telegraph expedition from 1898 to 1901, chief of the Mission de Recherches Minières for the Société Internationale Forestière et Minière in the Congo from 1907 to 1909, and agent of the Rubber Exploration Company of New York, seeking concessions in South Africa, Mozambique, and Madagascar in 1910–1911. Died July 13, 1915, in Royal Oak, Maryland. *References*: Richard Dorsey Mohun Papers, National Archives; *BCB* 2; and *NYT*, July 15, 1915.

MOORE, HENRY CLAY (1852–1930). Prospector and hunter, born near Corinth, McNairy County, Mississippi. He was involved in the grocery business in Corinth and was associated with a mining corporation in Mexico from 1876 to 1884. In 1884 or 1885 he went to the South African gold fields, obtained a concession for mining rights for Mashonaland from Lobengula, king of the Matabele, in 1888, and was granted mining rights in Matabeleland or Mashonaland by Cecil Rhodes on behalf of the British South Africa Company in 1891. He hunted in Mozambique and gave collections of skins, horns, and skulls to the Smithsonian Institution in 1893 and 1895. He returned to Corinth in 1897 and established a museum and a zoological park, but was hunting again in Africa in 1907. Died July 26, 1930, in Chicago. *Reference*: Beulah M. D'Olive Price, "Henry Clay Moore of Corinth, Cecil Rhodes, and the British South Africa Company," *Journal of Mississippi History* 31 (1969): 321–33.

MORDEN, WILLIAM J(AMES) (1886–1958). Explorer and big-game hunter, born January 3, 1886, in Chicago. Morden graduated from Sheffield Scientific School of Yale University. He was involved in the manufacture of railroad supplies from 1908 until 1922 and served in the U.S. army engineers during World War I. He became a member of the scientific staff of the American Museum of Natural History in 1917 and was a field associate in the department of mammals from 1926 to 1940. He was a leader of the Morden-Clark Asiatic expedition to Central Asia in 1926–1927 and the Morden-Graves North Asiatic expedition in 1929–1930. He served in the United States Air Corps during World War II. He led the Morden African expedition to Kenya-Turkana in 1949 and went again to Africa in 1953 and 1956 to collect ethnological specimens. Died January 23, 1958, in Chappaqua, New York. *References*: *NYT*, January 24, 1958; and *WWWA*.

MORRELL, BENJAMIN (1795–1839). Sea captain, born July 5, 1795, in Rye, New York. Morrell ran away to sea, and later became a sea captain. He made voyages along the coast of Southwest Africa, established extensive trading networks with the Southwest Africans during the 1820s, and used Spencer Bay as a base for expeditions through the Southwest African Desert. He discovered guano deposits on the islands off the coasts of Southwest Africa and attempted to interest the United States government in colonizing Namibia. He described his voyages in *A Narrative of Four Voyages* (New York, 1832; reprinted, Upper Saddle River, N.J., 1970). Died in Mozambique. *References*: *ACAB*; *DAB*; *SESA*; and *WWWA*.

MORRISON, WILLIAM MCCUTCHAN (1867–1918). Missionary, born November 10, 1867, near Lexington, Virginia. Morrison graduated from Washington and Lee University (Lexington, Va.) and Presbyterian Theological Seminary (Louisville, Ky.) and was ordained in 1896. He was a missionary under the Board of Foreign Missions of the Presbyterian Church in the United States* and served in the American Presbyterian Congo Mission (APCM)* in the Congo Free State from 1896 until his death. He was stationed in Luebo, Kasai province, from 1896 until 1918, and edited the *Kasai Herald* from 1901 until 1917. He exposed the atrocities of King Leopold of Belgium in the Congo Free State, defended the interests of the natives against the Free State government, and cooperated with the Congo Reform Association. In 1906 he was sued, along with W. H. Sheppard,* by the Kasai Company for allegedly libeling the company, but was acquitted in the trial. He converted the Baluba language to writing and prepared *Grammar and Dictionary of the Buluba-Lulua Language as Spoken in the Upper Kasai and Congo Basin* (New York, 1906) and *A Textbook of the Tshilube Language* (Luebo, Democratic Republic of the Congo, 1965). He also translated the Bible into Baluba. Died March 14, 1918, in Luebo, Belgian Congo. *References*: *BCB* 4; *DAB*; and *DADH*.

MORROW, JOHN HOWARD (1910-   ). Educator and diplomat, born February 10, 1910, in Hackensack, New Jersey. Morrow graduated from Rutgers University and the universities of Pennsylvania and Paris. He taught in a high school in Trenton, New Jersey, from 1931 to 1935, and at Bordentown Institute, New Jersey, from 1935 to 1945. In 1945 he became head of the department of Romance languages and professor of French and Spanish at Talladega College (Ala.) and was later head of the department of Romance languages at North Carolina College. He was a member of the U.S. Commission on Government Security in 1957. He was ambassador to Guinea from 1959 to 1961 and wrote *First American Ambassador to Guinea* (New Brunswick, N.J., 1968). He was the permanent representative to UNESCO in Paris from 1961 to 1963, and served in the Foreign Service Institute after 1963. *References*: *DAS*; and *WWA*.

MOTT, JOHN (RALEIGH) (1865–1955). Ecumenical pioneer and Young Men's Christian Association (YMCA) official, born May 25, 1865, near Purvis (later Livingston Manor), Sullivan County, New York, and grew up in Pottsville, Iowa. Mott attended Upper Iowa University (Fayette, Iowa) and graduated from Cornell University. He became affiliated with the YMCA in 1886, became its senior student secretary in 1890, the national executive for the American YMCA from 1915 to 1928, and president of World YMCA in 1926. He was chairman of the Student Volunteer Movement for Foreign Missions from 1888 to 1920, one of the founders of the World's Student Christian Federation in 1895, its general secretary until 1920, and its chairman from 1920 to 1928. He was chairman of the International Missionary Council from 1921 to 1940, traveling throughout the world. He visited South Africa in 1906 on behalf of the Students' Christian Association and made a second visit in 1934 which led to the founding of the Christian Council in South Africa in 1936. He shared in the Nobel Peace Prize in 1946. Died January 31, 1955, in Orlando, Florida. *References*: John R. Mott Archives, Yale Divinity School Library, New Haven, Conn.; *CB* 1947; *DAB* S5; *DASB* 3; C. Howard Hopkins, *John R. Mott, 1865–1955: A Biography* (Grand Rapids, Mich., 1979); *NCAB* 44:346; *NYT*, February 1, 1955; and *WWWA*.

MOTT-SMITH, MAY (1879–1952). Artist and explorer. Mott-Smith spent her early life in Hawaii, studied art in Paris, and was a jewelry and medal designer. She was later an explorer and made an expedition to Africa, which she described in *Africa from Port to Port* (New York, 1930). She served in the Office of Strategic Services (OSS) during World War II. Died June 5, 1952, in New York City. *Reference*: *NYT*, June 7, 1952.

MOUNT BRUKKAROS SOLAR RADIATION OBSERVATION STA-TION. Field station of the Smithsonian Astrophysical Observatory established at Mount Brukkaros, Southwest Africa, in 1926 and which remained in operation until 1931. *Reference*: Bessie Z. Jones, *Lighthouse of the Skies: The Smithsonian Astrophysical Observatory: Background and History 1846–1955* (Washington, D.C., 1965), ch. 9.

MUNROE, HAROLD S(IMONDS) (1883–1948). Mining engineer, born September 27, 1883, in Joliet, Illinois. Munroe attended Cornell University and the Colorado School of Mines. He was employed in Argentina from 1905 to 1907 and with the Sierra Madre Mining Company in Chihuahua, Mexico, from 1907 to 1914. He became general manager of the Consolidated Copper Company's mines in Kimberley, Nevada, in 1914; was vice president and general manager of the Granby Consolidated Mining & Smelting Company in Anyox, British Columbia, from 1918 to 1922; was employed by American Metals Company from 1922 to 1926, and by Newmont Mining Corporation after 1926. He was sent in 1928 to survey the possibilities of developing copper mines in Africa, became consulting manager of the Rhokana Corporation in Northern Rhodesia in 1929, and developed the N'Kana mines and brought them into production. They became one of the largest copper mines in the world. He was consulting engineer and director of Ventures, Limited, of Toronto, Canada, from 1935 until his retirement in 1940. Died October 14, 1948, in Miami Beach, Florida. *References*: *NCAB* 37:391; and *NYT*, October 21, 1948.

MYERS, ESTELLA C(ATHERINE) (1884–1956). Missionary, born August 9, 1884, in Williamsburg, Iowa. She was a missionary under the Foreign Missionary Society of the Brethren Church* in Oubangui-Chari, French Equatorial Africa, from 1921 to 1956. She translated the New Testament into the Karre language (published in 1947), and began a translation into the Pana language. Died November 1, 1956, in Bekoro, French Equatorial Africa. *References*: *BE*; and *The Brethren Missionary Herald* 18 (December 1, 1956): 734–35.

N

NASSAU, ROBERT HAMILL (1835–1921). Medical missionary, born October 11, 1835, in Montgomery Square, near Norristown, Pennsylvania. Nassau attended Lafayette College, graduated from Princeton University, Princeton Theological Seminary, and the University of Pennsylvania Medical School, and was ordained in 1861. He became a missionary under the Board of Foreign Missions of the Presbyterian Church in the U.S.A.* in the West Africa mission in 1861, serving at Corisco Island, and later took charge of the mission station at Benito. He went into the interior in 1874, ascended the Ogowe River, and served there until 1891. He served at Libreville and at Batanga from 1893 until his retirement in 1906. He sent large ethnological collections to the University of Pennsylvania and to Princeton University, including the first carcass of a gorilla sent to the United States and the only perfect gorilla brains examined by anatomists prior to 1891. He wrote *Crowned in Palm-land: A Story of African Mission Life* (Philadelphia, 1874); *Mawedo: The Palm-land Maiden* (New York, 1881), a book of fiction; and *Fetishism in West Africa: Forty Years' Observation of Native Customs and Superstitions* (Philadelphia, 1904); he also prepared a grammar of the Benga language and translated the Bible into that language. He recorded African folktales in *Where Animals Talk: West African Folk Lore Tales* (Boston, 1912), *In an Elephant Corral and Other Tales of West African Experience* (New York, 1912), and *Tales Out of School* (Philadelphia, 1911). He also wrote his memoirs, *Corisco Days: the First Thirty Years of the West African Mission* (Philadelphia, 1892) and *My Ogowe: Being a Narrative of Daily Incidents During Sixteen Years in Equatorial West Africa* (New York, 1914). Died May 6, 1921, in Ambler, Florida. *References*: Robert Hamill Nassau Papers, Langston Hughes Memorial Library, Lincoln University, Lincoln, Penn.; *DAB*; W. Reginald Wheeler, *The Words of God in an African Forest: The Story of an American Mission in West Africa* (New York, 1931); and *WWWA*.

NATIONAL BAPTIST CONVENTION, USA, INC.: FOREIGN MISSION BOARD. The Baptist Foreign Mission Convention was founded in 1880. It began missionary work in Liberia in 1883, in Nigeria in 1887, and in South Africa and Nyasaland in 1895. In 1895 it was succeeded by the Foreign Mission Board of the National Baptist Convention. *References*: C. C. Adams and Marshall A. Talley, *Negro Baptist and Foreign Missions* (Philadelphia, 1944); *EMCM*; Edward A. Freeman, *The Epoch of Negro Baptists and the Foreign Mission Board* (Kansas City, 1933); and Sandy D. Martin, "The Baptist Foreign Mission Convention, 1880–1894," *Baptist History and Heritage* 16, no. 4 (1981): 13–25.

NATIONAL SECURITY STUDY MEMORANDUM (NSSM) 39. A review of United States policy regarding Southern Africa was ordered in the spring of 1969 by Henry A. Kissinger, special assistant to the president for national security affairs, in NSSM 39. The administration of President Richard M. Nixon adopted "Option Two" of the review (dubbed "Tar Baby"* by State Department critics), a position based on the premise that the whites in Southern Africa were there to stay, that the only way that constructive change could come about was through them, and that there was no hope for the blacks to gain the political rights they sought through violence, which would lead to chaos and increased opportunities for communism. "Option Two" urged selected relaxation of the U.S. stance against the white regimes of Southern Africa, easing of the arms embargoes on South Africa and Portugal, weakening of the sanctions against Rhodesia, and increased economic and political contacts with the government of South Africa. The Nixon administration implemented this option from 1970 to 1974. *References*: Mohamed A. El-Khawas and Barry Cohen, eds., *The Kissinger Study of Southern Africa: National Security Study Memorandum 39* (Westport, Conn., 1976); and E. Lockwood, "National Security Study Memorandum 39 and the Future of United States Policy Toward Southern Africa," *Issue, a Quarterly Journal of Africanist Opinion* 4 (Fall 1974): 63–70.

NAU, HENRY (1881–1956). Educator and missionary, born September 21, 1881, in Beltershausen, Marburg, Germany. Nau came to the United States in 1902. He attended the University of Marburg, graduated from Concordia Seminary (St. Louis) and the University of Halle-Wittenberg, and was ordained in 1905. He served as missionary in India from 1905 to 1914, hospital chaplain in Germany during World War I, professor at Luther College (New Orleans, La.) from 1921 to 1925, and president of Immanuel Luther College (Greensboro, N.C.) from 1925 to 1930 and from 1938 to 1949. He was missionary in the Calabar Province of Nigeria under the Evangelical Lutheran Synodical Conference of North America in 1936–1937, exploring mission possibilities among the Ibibos, and wrote *We Move Into Africa: The Story of the Planting of the Lutheran Church in Southeastern Nigeria* (Saint Louis, Mo., 1945). He was again missionary in India from 1951 to 1954. Died May 17, 1956, in Greensboro, North

Carolina. *Reference*: Henry Nau, "Day by Day in Africa," Ms. Journal, Concordia Historical Institute, St. Louis, Mo.

NEWPORT, MATILDA (ca. 1795–1837). Colonist, born possibly in Philadelphia. Newport came to Africa on the *Elizabeth*,* settled first at Sherbro Island, and moved to Cape Mesurado in 1821. According to tradition, she was responsible for the successful defense of the settlement. Died in Monrovia. In 1916 the Liberian Legislature declared December 1 a national holiday in her honor; this was abolished in 1980.

NIGER VALLEY EXPLORING PARTY. An expedition in 1860 by Martin Robinson Delany* and including Robert Campbell,* as commissioners of the party, to inspect the area around Abeokuta, Nigeria, as a possible site on which to establish a colony for free black Americans, and to make a topographical, geological, and geographical examination of the Niger Valley. They negotiated a treaty with the Egba people for the right to establish a colony of Black Americans on Egbaland. *References*: Howard H. Bell, ed., *Search for a Place: Black Separatism and Africa,1860* (Ann Arbor, Mich., 1970); R.J.M. Blackett, *Building an Antislavery Wall: Black Americans in the Atlantic Abolitionist Movement, 1830–1860* (Baton Rouge, La., 1983), ch. 5; A.A.H. Kirk-Greene, "America in the Niger Valley: A Colonization Centenary," *Phylon* 23 (1962): 225–39; and Floyd J. Miller, *The Search for Black Nationality: Black Emigration and Colonization 1787–1863* (Urbana, Ill., 1975), ch. 6.

NISSEN, HENRY W(IEGHORST) (1901–1958). Psychologist, born February 5, 1901, in Chicago. Nissen graduated from the University of Illinois and Columbia University. He was a research associate at Yale University from 1929 to 1933, an associate professor of psychobiology at Yale University from 1933 to 1944, a research associate from 1944 to 1956, assistant director of the Yale (later Yerkes) Laboratory of Primate Biology (Orange Park, Fla.) from 1939 to 1952, associate director there from 1952 to 1955, and director of the lab after 1955. He was professor of psychobiology at Emory University after 1956. He conducted the first field study on chimpanzees in West Africa in 1930 under the sponsorship of Yale University and wrote *A Field Study of Chimpanzees: Observations of Chimpanzee Behavior and Environment in Western French Guinea* (Baltimore, 1931). Died April 27, 1958, in Orange Park, Florida. *References*: *BMNAS* 38 (1965): 205–221; *NYT*, April 30, 1958; and *WWWA*.

NOBLE, ROBERT ERNEST (1870–1956). Army surgeon, born November 5, 1870, in Rome, Georgia. Noble graduated from Alabama Polytechnic Institute, Columbia University, and the Army Medical School. He was commissioned assistant surgeon in 1901. He served in the Philippines from 1900 to 1903, and with the department of sanitation of the Isthmus Canal Commission from 1907 to 1914. He helped to stamp out yellow fever in the Canal Zone, was in charge of the antimosquito campaign in the Philippines in 1911–1912, and was a member of a sanitary commission to Guayaquil, Ecuador, to study yellow fever in 1912–1913. He was a member of a commission to the Rand mines in the Transvaal, South Africa, to study the cause of pneumonia in 1913–1914. He served in Washington during World War I and later in France, and was assistant surgeon general after 1919. He was a member, and later the director of the Rockefeller Foundation Yellow Fever Commission to West Africa in 1920. He retired with the rank of major general in 1925. Died September 18, 1956, in Fort McClellan, near Anniston, Alabama. *References*: Robert Ernest Noble Papers, Alabama Department of Archives and History, Montgomery, Ala.; Robert Ernest Noble Papers, National Library of Medicine, Bethesda, Md.; *AMA Journal* 162 (December 8, 1956): 1408; *NYT*, September 20, 1956; and *WWWA*.

NOGUCHI, HIDEYO (1876–1928). Microbiologist, born Seisaku Noguchi, November 24, 1876, in Sanjogata, Okinashima-mura, Fukushima, Honshu, Japan. Noguchi graduated from medical schools in Tokyo. He came to the United States in 1900, was an assistant, and later a member of the Rockefeller Institute for Medical Research (later Rockefeller University). He made studies of infectious diseases, snake venoms, and techniques of the cultivation of spirochetes. He mistakenly announced that yellow fever was caused by a spirochete and in 1927 went to the Gold Coast to prove his theory. Died of yellow fever, May 21, 1928, in Accra, the Gold Coast. *References*: *DAB*; *DAMB* 1984; C. E. Dolman, "Hideyo Noguchi (1876–1928): His Final Effort," *Clio Medica* 12 (1977): 131–45; *DSB*; *NYT*, May 22, 1928; Isabel R. Plesset, *Noguchi and His Patrons* (Rutherford, N.J., 1980); and *WWWA*.

NORTH AMERICAN BAPTIST MISSIONARY SOCIETY. Organized in 1883 as the General Missionary Society of the German Baptist Churches of North America, it began missionary work in the Cameroon in 1891 and in Nigeria in 1961. *References*: North American Baptist Missionary Society Correspondence, Society headquarters, Oakbrook Terrace, Ill.; and Frank H. Woyke, *Heritage and Ministry of the North American Baptist Conference* (Oakbrook Terrace, Ill., 1979).

NOSER, ADOLPH ALEXANDER (1900–   ). Clergyman, born July 4, 1900, in Belleville, Illinois. Noser graduated from Quincy College (Ill.), St. Mary's Seminary and Collegium Angelicum (Rome). He joined the Society of the Divine Word and was ordained in 1925. He was a teacher and then the rector at the Divine Word Seminary until 1939. He served in the Gold Coast from 1939 until 1953 and became prefect apostolic of Accra in 1945 and vicar apostolic in 1947. He was consecrated in 1947 and raised to bishop in 1950. He was transferred to the Vicarate of Madang, New Guinea, in 1953; he became the first archbishop of Madang in 1966 and retired in 1976. *Reference*: *ACWW*.

O

OFFICER, MORRIS (1823–1874). Missionary, born July 21, 1823, in Holmes County, Ohio. Officer graduated from Wittenberg College and Theological Seminary (Springfield, Ohio), and was ordained in 1851. He was a missionary under the American Missionary Society* in Sierra Leone in 1852–1853. He returned to the United States, but was back in Africa in 1860 as a missionary in Liberia under the Lutheran Missionary Society of the American Lutheran Church in 1860–1861. He established the Muhlenberg Mission on the St. Paul River, explored portions of Liberia, and followed the St. Paul River from Monrovia into the interior. He returned to the United States in 1861, was engaged in home mission work for the American Lutheran Church in Lancaster, Pennsylvania, and Mansfield, York, and Fredericksburg, Ohio, and was superintendent of home missions until 1871. He wrote *Western Africa, a Mission Field; or, the Moral and Physical Condition of Western Africa Considered with Reference to the Founding of Mission Settlements of Colored People* (Pittsburgh, 1856) and *African Bible Pictures; or, Scripture Scenes and Customs in Africa* (Philadelphia, 1859). Died November 1, 1874, in Topeka, Kansas. *References*: Morris Officer, "Diaries," MS, Abdel Ross Wentz Library, Lutheran Theological Seminary, Gettysburg, Pa.; *ACAB*; W. W. Griley, "Morris Officer," in *Missionary Heroes of the Lutheran Church*, ed. L. B. Wolf (Philadelphia, 1911), pp. 117–43; A. J. Imhoff, *The Life of Rev. Morris Officer* (Dayton, Ohio, 1876); and *OAB*.

ORENSTEIN, ALEXANDER JEREMIAH (1879–1972). Physician, born September 26, 1879. Orenstein graduated from Jefferson Medical College (Philadelphia) and studied at the Institute for Tropical Medicine (Hamburg) and the St. Thomas and London hospitals. He was one of William Crawford Gorgas's* chief assistants in the attempt to eradicate yellow fever during the construction of the Panama Canal. He investigated methods of controlling malaria and plague in Tanganyika and Zanzibar and was consultant to the German colonial office in Tanganyika in 1913. He became medical consultant to the Rand Mines in

1914 and then chief adviser on sanitation to the Central Mining-Rand Mines group of companies. He served with the South African Medical Corps during World War I. He helped to curb a severe outbreak of Spanish influenza in Kimberley in 1918, made many medical reforms in the gold mines, and improved hospital facilities, diet, and hygiene for the mine workers. He was director of medical services of South Africa during World War II. Died July 7, 1972, in Johannesburg. *Reference*: *SESA*.

OSGOOD, JOHN FELT (1825–1894). Merchant, born December 18, 1825, in Salem, Massachusetts. Osgood was an employee of the Bertram-Shepard concern, supercargo of the bark *Emily Wilder*, and a resident agent in Arabian ports. He later published his diary, *Notes on Travel: or Recollections of Majunga, Zanzibar, Muscat, Aden, Mocha and Other Eastern Ports* (Salem, Mass., 1845). Died in Salem, Massachusetts. *Reference*: John Felt Osgood, Sketches and diary, Essex Institute, Salem, Mass.

OSGOOD, WILFRED HUDSON (1875–1947). Zoologist, born December 8, 1875, in Rochester, New Hampshire. Osgood graduated from Stanford University and the University of Chicago. He was a biologist with the United States Bureau of Biological Survey in the Department of Agriculture from 1897 to 1909, directing the United States biological investigation of Alaska from 1899 to 1909. He joined the Field Museum of Natural History in 1909, was assistant curator of ornithology and mammalogy from 1909 to 1921, curator of zoology from 1921 to 1936, and chief curator of zoology from 1936 until his retirement in 1940. He led the Marshall Field zoological expedition to Chile in 1922–1923. He led the *Chicago Daily News*–Field Museum expedition to the interior of Abyssinia in 1926–1927, and was coauthor (with Louis Agassiz Fuertes*) of *Artist and Naturalist in Ethiopia* (New York, 1936). He later led expeditions to French Indochina in 1937 and the Magellanic expedition to South America in 1939–1940. Died June 20, 1947, in Chicago. *References*: *Auk* 67 (1950): 183–89; *NCAB* 36:544; *NYT*, June 22, 1947; and *WWWA*.

OVERS, WALTER HENRY (1870–1934). Clergyman, born March 26, 1870, in Harbury, England. Overs graduated from Taylor University (Upland, Ind.). He became a missionary under the Wesleyan Methodist Church* to Central West Africa in 1893 and established thirty-five schools and churches. He came to the United States in 1898 due to ill health and served as pastor in several churches in New York State until 1919. He was a missionary bishop of the Protestant Episcopal Church in Liberia from 1919 to 1925. He wrote *Stories of African Life* (New York, 1924). He was general secretary of the field department of the National Council of the Protestant Episcopal Church after 1925. Died June 17, 1934, in Jamestown, New York. *References*: *NYT*, June 18, 1934; and *WWWA*.

P

PARHAM, CATHERINE (1901-). Missionary, born January 3, 1901, in Stinson (now Durand), Georgia. Parham attended Creighton-Shumaker Business College (Atlanta) and Scarritt College (Nasvhille, Tenn.). She did social work in West Virginia's coal region from 1925 to 1931. She was a missionary under the Board of Foreign Missions of the Methodist Episcopal Church* in the Belgian Congo from 1931 to 1958, was stationed at Tunda in the Central Congo, and was in charge of a boarding school for girls, and later boys' and women's schools. She was transferred to Elizabethville in 1945 and was in charge of kindergartens, a teacher-training program, and women's education in general until 1959. *Reference*: Catherine Parham Papers, East Carolina Manuscript Collection, East Carolina University, Greenville, N.C.

PARK, WALTER E. (fl. 1910). Engineer and radio pioneer, born in Boston. Park came to Transvaal in 1896 as manager of the firm of Fraser & Chalmers Limited and served in the Railway Pioneer Regiment during the South African War. He introduced the first wireless telephone in South Africa in 1908, installing it in a Johannesburg mine for communication between the surface and the working face. *Reference*: *SADNB*.

PARKER, RUSSELL J(ONATHAN) (1897–1949). Mining engineer, born August 31, 1897, in Olney Springs, near Denver, Colorado. Parker graduated from the Colorado School of Mines. He joined Forminière, began prospecting for and developing alluvial diamond deposits, and became acting head of the research department and manager of Société Minière du Luabo; he was active in the diamond business in Africa for many years. He joined the London office of Selection Trust in 1925, and undertook the preliminary inspection of the Roan and Rietbok claims, together with thirty or more projects in Northern Rhodesia from 1926 to 1931. He became assistant to the managing director of the Rhodesian Copper Company in London in 1931, was assistant to the president of Kennecott Copper Corporation in 1942, and vice president in 1948. He was also president of the Quebec Iron & Titanium Company. Killed September 9, 1949, when a time bomb exploded in an aircraft in which he was a passenger, causing it to crash near St. Joachim, Quebec, Canada. *References*: *NYT*, September 10, 1949; *Transactions of the Institution of Mining and Metallurgy* 59 (1948): 327–328.

PAULL, GEORGE (1837–1865). Missionary, born February 3, 1837, near Connellsville, Fayette County, Pennsylvania. Paull graduated from Jefferson College (later Washington and Jefferson) and Western Theological Seminary (Allegheny, Pa.) and was ordained in 1863. He was a missionary under the Board of Foreign Missions of the Presbyterian Church in the U.S.A.* in the Gabon mission from 1864 until his death. He was stationed first at Corisco Island and in 1865 established a mission station at the mouth of the Benita River (later Rio Muni). Died May 14, 1865, in Benita. *References*: W. Reginald Wheeler, *The Words of God in an African Forest: The Story of an American Mission in West Africa* (New York, 1931), ch. 4; and Samuel Wilson, *George Paull of Benita, West Africa. A Memoir* (Philadelphia, 1872).

PAYNE, JAMES SPRIGGS (1819–1882). Colonist, born October 15, 1819, in Richmond, Virginia. Payne immigrated with his family to Liberia in 1829. He became a minister in the Methodist Church and was assistant secretary to the colonial agent. He was elected as delegate to the United States to draw up the agreement by which the American Colonization Society* ceded its rights to Liberia. He served as president of Liberia from 1868 to 1870 and from 1876 to 1878. Died January 31, 1882, in Monrovia. *References*: *Davis*; and *Richardson*.

PAYNE, JOHN (1815–1874). Clergyman, born January 19, 1815, in Westmoreland County, Virginia. Payne graduated from William and Mary College and from the theological seminary in Alexandria, Virginia, and was ordained in 1836. He was a missionary under the Domestic and Foreign Missionary Society of the Protestant Episcopal Church in the United States of America* in Cape Palmas, Liberia, from 1836 until 1841. He was consecrated bishop of the Protestant Episcopal Church in West Africa in 1851, and served until 1869, when he returned to the United States because of ill health. Died October 23, 1874, in Oak Grove, Westmoreland County, Virginia. *References*: *African Repository* 50 (1874): 372–73; *EM*; and *NCAB* 5:21.

PEACE CORPS. U.S. government agency, created in 1961, which sent volunteers to many countries, several thousands of whom went to the countries of Africa south of the Sahara. Volunteers have served in Botswana (1966-), Benin (1968-), Cameroon (1962-), Central African Republic (1962-), Chad (1966–1979), Ethiopia (1962–1977), Gabon (1963–1967, 1972-), The Gambia (1967-), Ghana (1961-), Guinea (1964–1967, 1969–1971), Ivory Coast (1962–1981),

Kenya (1965-), Lesotho (1967-), Liberia (1962-), Malawi (1963–1972, 1979-), Mali (1971-), Mauritania (1967–1968, 1972-), Mauritius (1971–1975), Niger (1962-), Nigeria (1961–1971), Rwanda (1975-), Senegal (1962-), Seychelles (1974-), Sierra Leone (1962-), Somali Republic (1962–1970), Swaziland (1969-), Tanzania (1961–1970, 1979-), Togo (1962-), Uganda (1964–1973), Upper Volta (1967-), and Zaire (1970-). *References*: Kevin Lowther and C. Payne Lucas, *Keeping Kennedy's Promise: The Peace Corps* (Boulder, Colo., 1978); Gerard T. Rice, *Twenty Years of Peace Corps* (Washington, D.C., 1981), and Robert B. Textor, ed., *Cultural Frontiers of the Peace Corps* (Cambridge, Mass., 1966).

PEARCE, LOUISE (1885–1959). Medical researcher, born March 5, 1885, in Winchester, Massachusetts, and grew up in California. Pearce graduated from Stanford University, attended Boston University School of Medicine, and graduated from Johns Hopkins University School of Medicine. She joined the Rockefeller Institute for Medical Research (later Rockefeller University) as a fellow in 1913. She headed a team of scientists for the Rockefeller Institute studying sleeping sickness and searching for a drug to combat it. They discovered the compound tryparsamide to be effective in controling the parasite which caused the disease, and Pearce went to Leopoldville, Belgian Congo, in 1920 to test the drug on humans. She recorded her experiences in the December 1, 1921, issue of the *Journal of Experimental Medicine*. She became associate member of the institute in 1923 and continued her investigations of infectious and inherited diseases. Died August 10, 1959, in New York City. *References*: *DAMB* 1984; *NAW*; *NYT*, August 11, 1959; and *WWWA*.

PEARSON, ERNEST B. (1886–1976). Medical missionary, born May 6, 1886, in Flanagan, Michigan. Pearson graduated from Eureka College and the College of Medicine of the University of Illinois and studied tropical medicine in London. He was a missionary under the Christian Woman's Board of Mission in Liberia, serving in the mission station near Schiefflin from 1914 to 1916, when the mission was discontinued. He then served in the Belgian Congo under the United Christian Missionary Society* from 1917 to 1933 and from 1948 to 1952, serving at Monieka, and later in Bolenge, where he was also the legal representative of the mission. He returned to the United States in 1933, and practiced medicine in Eureka, Michigan, but went back to the Congo in 1948 and served until 1952. Died October 8, 1976. *Reference*: *TWTA*.

PENICK, CHARLES CLIFTON (1843–1914). Clergyman, born December 9, 1843, in Charlotte County, Virginia. Penick attended Hampden-Sydney College and graduated from the Theological Seminary of the Protestant Episcopal Church (Alexandria, Va.); he served during the Civil War and was ordained in 1870. He was a pastor in Mount Savage and Baltimore, Maryland. He was consecrated bishop in the Protestant Episcopal Church in 1877 and was a mis-

sionary bishop at Cape Palmas, Liberia, from 1877 until 1883. He reorganized
the missionary district and established St. John's school among the Vai people.
He retired to the United States in 1883 and resigned. He was later a pastor in
Louisville, Kentucky; Richmond, Virginia; Fairmont, West Virginia; and Frank-
fort, Kentucky. Died April 13, 1914, in Baltimore. *References*: *ACAB*; *DAB*;
NCAB 11:474; and *WWWA*.

**PENTECOSTAL HOLINESS CHURCH: DEPARTMENT OF FOREIGN
MISSION.** Established in 1904, it began missionary work in Liberia in 1910,
in South Africa in 1913, in Nyasaland and Northern and Southern Rhodesia in
1950, in Nigeria in 1955, in Botswana in 1972, and in Kenya in 1973. The
name was changed later to World Missions Department of the International
Pentecostal Holiness Church. *References*: Pentecostal Holiness Church, Department of Foreign Mission Archives, Church headquarters, Oklahoma City,
Okla.; Joseph E. Campbell, *The Pentecostal Holiness Church 1898–1948: Its
Background and History* (Raleigh, N.C., 1951); *EMCM*; and Dallas D. Freeman,
Missions on the March: Pentecostal Holiness Church in Southern Africa (Frank-
lin Springs, Ga., 19–).

PERRY, MATTHEW (CALBRAITH) (1794–1858). Naval officer, born April
10, 1794, in South Kingstown, Rhode Island. Perry joined the navy in 1809 as
a midshipman, took part in the War of 1812, and was commissioned lieutenant
in 1813. He was first lieutenant on the *Cyane* in its cruise of the African coast
in 1820, and in command of the *Shark* in 1821–1822; he helped to establish the
colony at Cape Mesurado (later Monrovia, Liberia). He was commander of the
U.S. African Squadron* from 1843 until 1845 in its effort to suppress the slave
trade. He may be considered the first prominent American collector of African
art. He served in the Mexican War, and commanded the expedition to Japan
from 1852 to 1854. He died March 4, 1858, in New York City. *References*:
Matthew C. Perry Papers, Manuscript Division, Library of Congress; *ACAB*;
DAB; *DAMB*; Samuel Eliot Morison, *"Old Bruin": Commodore Matthew C.
Perry, 1794–1858, the American Naval Officer Who Helped Found Liberia . . .*
(Boston, 1967); *NCAB* 4:42; Donald R. Wright, "Matthew Perry and the African
Squadron," in *America Spreads Her Sails: U.S. Seapower in the 19th Century*,
ed. Clayton R. Barrow (Annapolis, Md., 1973), pp. 80–99; *WAMB*; and *WWWA*.

PERRY, MAY (1890–   ). Missionary educator, born August 12, 1890, in Tate,
Pickens County, Georgia. Perry graduated from the Georgia Normal and In-
dustrial College for Women (now Woman's College of Georgia) in Milledgeville,
Georgia, and attended the Woman's Missionary Union Training School (Louis-
ville, Ky.). She taught school in Georgia and Tennessee from 1912 to 1917.
She was a missionary under the Woman's Missionary Union in Nigeria from
1921 until 1960. There she was a teacher, and after 1928, principal of the Baptist
Girls' School, the largest boarding primary school for girls in Abeokuta, Nigeria.

She retired in 1960 and returned to the United States. *Reference*: Minnie S. Anderson, *May Perry of Africa* (Nashville, Tenn., 1966).

PHELPS-STOKES FUND'S EDUCATION COMMISSIONS. *See* AFRICAN EDUCATION COMMISSIONS

PHILIP, (HERMAN) HOFFMAN (1872–1951). Diplomat, born July 13, 1872, in Washington, D.C. Philip graduated from Cambridge University and Columbia Law School (Washington, D.C.). He served in the Rough Riders during the Spanish-American War and was a close friend of Theodore Roosevelt. He entered the foreign service in 1901 and served in Tangier from 1901 to 1908. He was the first minister to Abyssinia from 1908 to 1910 and recorded his memories of Abyssinia in the December 1943 issue of *Yale Review*. He was later secretary of the embassy in Rio de Janiero from 1910 to 1912, secretary of the embassy in Constantinople from 1912 to 1917, minister to Colombia from 1917 to 1921, ambassador to Uruguay from 1922 to 1925, minister to Persia from 1925 to 1928, minister to Norway from 1930 to 1935, and ambassador to Chile from 1935 until his retirement in 1937. Died October 31, 1951, in Santa Barbara, California. *References*: Hoffman Philip Papers, Van Ness-Philip Family Papers, New York Historical Society, New York City; *DADH*; *NCAB* 44:410; and *NYT*, November 1, 1951.

PHILLIPS, RAY E(DMUND) (1889–1967). Missionary, born September 3, 1889, in Hawthorne, Wisconsin. Phillips graduated from Carleton College, Yale University School of Religion, and Yale University. He was a missionary under the American Board of Commissioners for Foreign Missions (ABCFM)* in Johannesburg, South Africa, from 1918 to 1958. He founded the Bantu Men's Social Center and helped found the Helping Hand for Native Girls in the early 1920s. He founded the Jan H. Hofmeyr School of Social Work in Johannesburg in 1940 and served as its director until 1957. He was a founder of the African Institute of Race Relations and a leader in the struggle for the rights of black Africans. He wrote *The Bantu Are Coming: Phases of South Africa's Race Problem* (New York, 1931) and *The Bantu in the City; a Study of Cultural Adjustment on the Witwatersrand* (Lovedale, South Africa, 1938). He returned to the United States in 1957, was pastor in St. Louis from 1958 to 1961, and moderator of the General Council of the Congregational Christian Churches from 1958 to 1961. Died March 8, 1967, in Morgantown, West Virginia. *References*: *NYT*, March 10, 1967; and *WWWA*.

PIKE, NICHOLAS (1818–1905). Naturalist and diplomat, born January 26, 1818, in Newburyport, Massachusetts. Pike entered the mercantile business in Boston, moved to New York in 1839, became involved in scientific activities, and collected natural history specimens. He was consul general in Portugal from 1852 to 1859, served in the Union Army during the Civil War, and did notable work in adopting photography for military purposes. He was consul in Mauritius from 1866 to 1873. He made the first complete collection of the marine botany of Mauritius, and an extensive collection of the fishes of the Indian Ocean (now in the Museum of Comparative Zoology of Harvard University), as well as hundreds of water-color paintings of these fishes (now in the Morgan Library, New York City). He wrote *Sub-tropical Rambles in the Land of Aphanaptoryx* (New York, 1873). Died April 12, 1905, in New York City. *References*: *NCAB* 24:100; and *NYT*, April 13, 1905.

PINNEY, JOHN B. (1806–1882). Missionary, born November 25, 1806, in Baltimore. Pinney graduated from the University of Georgia (Athens), read law, and was admitted to the bar. He studied at Princeton Theological Seminary and was ordained in 1832. He was a missionary under the Board of Foreign Missions of the Presbyterian Church in the U.S.A.* in Monrovia in 1833 as the first missionary of this church, but soon returned to the United States for health reasons. He came back to Africa in 1834 as a missionary under the Western Foreign Missionary Society and as a temporary colonial agent for the American Colonization Society.* He retired in 1839 and returned to the United States. He was later an agent for the American Colonization Society for New England states, corresponding secretary of the Pennsylvania Colonization Society and later of the New York Colonization Society, and editor of the *New York Colonization Journal* from 1850 to 1858. He went to Liberia four more times. In 1860 he was appointed consul general for Liberia in the United States. Died December 25, 1882, near Ocala, Florida. *Reference*: *Huberich*.

PIXLEY, STEPHEN CLAPP (1829–1914). Missionary, born June 23, 1829, in Plainfield, Massachusetts. Pixley graduated from Williams College and East Windsor Theological Seminary and was ordained in 1855. He was a missionary under the American Board of Commissioners for Foreign Missions (ABCFM)* from 1855 until his death and served in the American Zulu Mission.* He was stationed in Amahlongwa, Amanzimtoti, and Inanda, where he was in charge of the station and outstations. He translated the Old Testament into Zulu and revised the translation of the whole Bible. Died February 21, 1914, in Durban, Natal, South Africa. *Reference*: *Hewitt*.

POINDEXTER, HINDRUS AUGUSTUS (1901-   ). Bacteriologist, born May 10, 1901, in Memphis, Tennessee. Poindexter graduated from Lincoln University, Dartmouth College Medical School, and Harvard Medical School. He was assistant professor and professor of bacteriology, public health, and preventive medicine at Howard University from 1931 to 1946. He was commissioned an officer in the United States Public Health Service in 1947, was chief of laboratory and medical research in West Africa from 1947 to 1952, and chief of health and sanitation of the Point Four unit in Liberia from 1948 to 1952. He was chief of Health and Sanitation of the United States operation mission in French Indochina from 1953 to 1956, in Surinam from 1956 to 1958, in Iraq in 1958–1959, and in Libya from 1959 to 1961. He was a professor of community health practice at Howard University after 1965. He wrote *My World of Reality: Autobiography* (Detroit, 1973). *References: Journal of the National Medical Association* 65 (1973): 243–47; and *WWA*.

POOLE, MARK (KELLER) (1909-   ). Medical missionary, born March 3, 1909, in Bay City, Texas. Poole graduated from the University of Texas and Johns Hopkins Medical School, and studied at the London School for Tropical Diseases. He was a missionary under the Board of Foreign Missions of the Presbyterian Church in the United States* in the American Presbyterian Congo Mission (APCM)* from 1937 until 1962 and was stationed at the Lapsley Memorial Hospital in Bulape. He was the first physician to use the airplane in reaching the sick in the Congo. He also developed a new treatment for the African sleeping sickness disease. He returned to the United States in 1962 and practiced medicine at Bay City until his retirement in 1972. *References: Historic Matagorda County* 2 (Houston, Texas, 1986), p. 410; and George Kent, "20 Years of Eventful Days in the Congo," *Reader's Digest* 69 (July 1956): 177–78.

POWELL, E(DWARD) ALEXANDER (1879–1957). Traveler and author, born August 16, 1879, in Syracuse, New York. Powell graduated from Syracuse University and Oberlin College. He was a correspondent for British and American publications. He attempted to join the British Army in South Africa, and was later a consular official in Beirut and Alexandria. He was special correspondent for *Everybody's Magazine*, traveled in East Africa from 1909 to 1911, and wrote *The Last Frontier: The White Man's War for Civilization in Africa* (New York, 1912). He later returned to Africa and wrote *Beyond the Utmost Purple Rim: Abyssinia, Somaliland, Kenya Colony, Zanzibar, the Comoros, Madagascar* (New York, 1925) and *The Map That is Half Unrolled: Equatorial Africa from the Indian Ocean to the Atlantic* (New York, 1925). He served in the army during World War I and served in the Office of Naval Intelligence and the Office of Censorship during World War II. He wrote an autobiography, *Adventure Road* (Garden City, N.Y., 1954). Died November 13, 1957, in Falls Village, near Camden, Connecticut. *References: NCAB* 46:308; *NYT*, November 14, 1957; and *WWWA*.

PRESBYTERIAN CHURCH IN THE UNITED STATES: BOARD OF FOREIGN MISSIONS. Established in 1861, it began missionary work in Congo Free State in 1890, establishing the American Presbyterian Congo Mission (APCM).* In the 1970s it began missionary work in Lesotho, Nigeria, and Rwanda. It was later renamed the Division of International Mission. *References:* Presbyterian Church in the United States, Board of Foreign Missions Archives, Historical Foundation of the Presbyterian and Reformed Churches, Inc., Montreat, N.C.; *Our Church Faces Foreign Missions* (Nashville, Tenn., 1931).

PRESBYTERIAN CHURCH IN THE U.S.A.: BOARD OF FOREIGN MISSIONS. Organized in 1837, it absorbed the mission that was begun in Liberia in 1833 by the Western Missionary Society. It began missionary work in Rio Muni in 1865 and took over the American Board of Commissioners for Foreign Missions (ABCFM)* missions in Gabon in 1870 and in Cameroon in 1875. It merged in 1958 with the United Presbyterian Church of North America to form the United Presbyterian Church in the USA, which merged in 1983 with the Presbyterian Church in the United States to create the Presbyterian Church (USA). *References*: Presbyterian Church in the U.S.A., Board of Foreign Mission Papers, Presbyterian Historical Society, Philadelphia; Arthur J. Brown, *One Hundred Years: A History of the Foreign Missionary Work of the Presbyterian Church in the U.S.A.* (New York, 1929); Eva Naomi Hodgson, "The Presbyterian Mission to Liberia, 1832–1900." Ph.D. diss., Columbia University, 1980; W. Reginald Wheeler, ed., *The Crisis Decade: A History of the Foreign Missionary Work of the Presbyterian Church in the U.S.A. 1937–1947* (New York, 1951); and W. Reginald Wheeler, *The Words of God in an African Forest: The Story of an American Mission in West Africa* (New York, 1931).

PRESTON, IRA MILLS (1818–1901). Missionary, born April 21, 1818, in Danvers, Connecticut. Preston graduated from Marietta College (Ohio) and Lane Theological Seminary (Cincinnati) and was ordained in 1848. He was a missionary under the American Board of Commissioners for Foreign Missions (ABCFM)* in Gabon from 1848 to 1867. In 1854 he made an exploration trip with William Walker* up the Ogowe River to the site of present day Lambarene. He converted the language of the Bakele people to writing and translated portions of the Bible into that language. He also studied the Fang language and translated the Bible into the Mipongone dialect. He was vice commercial agent in Gabon in 1864–1865. He returned to the United States in 1867, resided in Marietta, Ohio, and was instructor and acting principal of the Marietta Academy from 1876 to 1879. Died February 7, 1901, in Marietta, Ohio. *Reference*: *Marietta* (Ohio) *Register*, February 7, 1901.

PRIEST, JAMES M. (? –1883). Missionary. Priest was a missionary under the Board of Foreign Missions of the Presbyterian Church in the U.S.A.* in Liberia from 1843 until 1883 and was pastor of the Presbyterian Church at Sinoe. He was vice president of Liberia and president of the Liberian Senate from 1864 to 1868 and associate justice of the Liberia Supreme Court. Died May 16, 1883. *Reference*: *African Repository* 60 (1884): 119.

PRINGLE, BENJAMIN (1807–1887). Lawyer, born November 9, 1807, in Richfield Springs, Otsego County, New York. Pringle studied law and was admitted to the bar. He practiced law, was judge of the Genesee County Court from 1841 to 1846, and served in the U.S. House of Representatives from 1853 to 1857. In 1863 he was appointed by President Abraham Lincoln as judge of the mixed (Anglo-American) court of arbitration in Cape Town under the 1862 treaty with Great Britain for the suppression of the slave trade and served until 1866. Died June 7, 1887, in Hastings, Dakota County, Minnesota. *References*: *BDAC*; and *WWWA*.

PROTESTANT EPISCOPAL CHURCH IN THE UNITED STATES OF AMERICA: DOMESTIC AND FOREIGN MISSIONARY SOCIETY. Organized in 1835, it began missionary work in Liberia in 1850, although its first missionary arrived there in 1836. *References*: Protestant Episcopal Church in the United States of America, Domestic and Foreign Missionary Society Archives: Church Historical Society, Austin, Texas; V. Nelle Bellamy, "Library and Archives of the Church Historical Society: Domestic and Foreign Missionary Society, Liberian Papers, 1822–c.1911," *Historical Magazine of the Protestant Episcopal Church* 37 (1968): 77–82; George D. Browne, "History of the Protestant Episcopal Mission in Liberia to 1838," *Historical Magazine of the Protestant Episcopal Church* 39 (1970): 17–27; Julia C. Emery, *A Century of Endeavor 1821–1921: A Record of the First One Hundred Years of the Domestic and Foreign Missionary Society of the Protestant Episcopal Church in the United States of America* (New York, 1921); and Delores C. Haywood and Patricia L. Davis, "The Liberia Papers, 1822–1939," *Historical Magazine of the Protestant Episcopal Church* 39 (1970): 91–94.

PROVIDENCE AFRICAN SOCIETY. *See* SIERRA LEONE EMIGRATION SCHEME (1794–1795)

PROVIDENCE EXPLORING AND TRADING COMPANY. Founded in 1832 by a group of Rhode Islanders, it undertook a voyage to West Africa in 1832–1833 to explore the Niger River, carry on trade with the Africans living along the river and its tributaries, and collect animals and zoological specimens. The expedition was a failure. *Reference*: George E. Brooks and Frances K. Talbot, "The Providence Exploring and Trading Company's Expedition to the Niger River in 1832–1833," *American Neptune* 35 (1975): 77–96.

PUTNAM, HORACE B. (1825–1888). Sea captain, born November 5, 1825, in Danvers, Massachusetts. Putnam attended Pembroke Academy, shipped from Boston as a common sailor in 1845, and received command of a ship in 1852. Employed by John Bertram & Company of Salem, he served in the East African trade until 1859. He was engaged in the grocery trade in Manchester, New Hampshire, from 1859 to 1876, served on the board of aldermen in 1868–1869, was commissioner for Hillsborough County, New Hampshire, from 1876 to 1880, and was mayor of Manchester from 1880 until 1884. Died April 20, 1888, in Manchester, New Hampshire. *Reference*: *Manchester* (N.H.) *Mirror and American*, April 20, 1888.

PUTNAM, PATRICK TRACY LOWELL (1904–1953). Anthropologist and naturalist, born September 15, 1904, in New York City. Putnam graduated from Harvard University. He was member of an expedition to the East Indies in 1926 and went to the Congo as a member of the Harvard African Expedition in 1928. He returned to the Belgian Congo in 1930 and operated a hospital and laboratory in the pygmy village of Putnam (named after him by the Belgian government), in the Ituri Forest on the bank of the Epulu River. He lived among the MaButi people for over twenty years. He also built there a large guest house. Died December 13, 1953, in Mambasa, Belgian Congo. His wife, **ANNE (EISNER) PUTNAM** (1911?–1967), was born in Newark, New Jersey, and studied at the Art Students League. She ran the guest house at Putnam, the Belgian Congo, and created a private zoo there. She returned to the United States in 1956, bringing with her a collection of African art (now in the American Museum of Natural History), and devoted her writings and paintings to capture the life of the pygmies in the Belgian Congo. She wrote (with Allen Keller) *Madami: My Eight Years of Adventure with the Congo Pigmies* (New York, 1954). Died January 28, 1967, in New York City. *References: BCB* 7; Jerome Beatty, *Americans All Over* (New York, 1940), pp. 247–61; *NYT*, December 29, 1953; and *NYT*, January 30, 1967.

Q

QUINAN, WILLIAM RUSSELL (1848–1910) and **QUINAN, KENNETH BINGHAM** (1878–1948). Explosives experts. William Russell was born May 17, 1848, in Calvert County, Maryland. He graduated from the United States Military Academy in 1870 and was commissioned in the artillery, specializing in high explosives. He resigned his commission in 1881 and was manager of the California Powder Company Works in Pinole, California. He came to Cape Town in 1899 and was engaged by Cecil Rhodes to build an explosives works. He established the De Beers Explosives Works (later Cape Explosives Works) at Somerset West, Cape Province, which began manufacturing explosives in 1903, and was its general manager until 1905. Died August 15, 1910, in Sydney, New South Wales, Australia. Kenneth Bingham, nephew of William Russell, was born July 3, 1878, in East Orange, New Jersey. He worked at the California Powder Company explosives factory in Pinole, California. He came to South Africa in 1901 as an assistant to his uncle, was general manager of the explosive works from 1905 to 1915, and was consultant for development at the factory from 1919 until his retirement in 1924. He was in Britain during World War I, building high-explosives factories. He became naturalized in South Africa in 1939. He retired in 1924. Died January 26, 1948, in Somerset West, Cape Province. *References*: *DASB* 4; and *SADNB*.

R

RAINBOW. The first American ship to take slaves directly from the coast of Africa to America in 1654. *Reference*: James M. Bellarosa, "James Smith and the *Rainbow*: America's First African Slaver," *New England Galaxy* 19 (1977): 32–37.

RAINEY, PAUL J(AMES) (1877–1923). Big-game hunter, explorer, and motion picture photographer, born September 18, 1877, in Cleveland. Rainey attended the University of Chicago. He was engaged in the management of his family fortune and made an expedition to the Arctic in 1910. Beginning in 1911 he went on a series of hunting and photography expeditions to Central and British East Africa and made several motion pictures. He served as official photographer for the American Red Cross during World War I. He later established a ranch near Nairobi, Kenya. Died September 18, 1923, during a voyage from Southhampton to Cape Town. *References*: George Fortiss, "Paul Rainey, Sportsman," *Outdoor Magazine* 58 (1911): 746–49; *NCAB* 19:411; and *NYT*, September 20, 1923.

RAINSFORD, WILLIAM STEPHEN (1850–1933). Clergyman and big-game hunter, born October 30, 1850, near Dublin, Ireland. Rainsford graduated from Cambridge University and was ordained in 1874. He was a curate in Norwich, England, a mission preacher in New York City from 1876 to 1878, an assistant rector in Toronto from 1878 to 1882, and a rector in New York from 1882 until 1904. He made an expedition to East Africa in 1908, which he described in *The Land of the Lion* (London, 1909). He left the priesthood in 1912 and led an expedition to East Africa for the American Museum of Natural History in 1912–1913. He wrote *The Story of a Varied Life: An Autobiography* (Garden City, N.Y., 1922). Died December 17, 1933, in New York City. *References*: *DAB* S1; *NCAB* 42:26; *NYT*, December 18, 1933; and *WWWA*.

RALPH, JULIAN (1853–1903). Journalist, born May 27, 1853, in New York City. Ralph left school and went into journalism, was a reporter for the *New York Daily Graphic* from 1873 to 1875, reporter and special correspondent for the *New York Sun* from 1875 to 1895, and for the *New York Journal* from 1895 to 1898. He also wrote for *Harper's Monthly* and *Harper's Weekly*. He went to South Africa in 1899 to cover the South African War and accompanied the forces under Field Marshal Frederick Roberts. With other newspapermen, he edited a daily newspaper titled *The Friend* for these forces in 1900. He returned to the United States in 1902, wrote *Towards Pretoria: A Record of the War Between Briton and Boer, to the Relief of Kimberley* (New York, 1900); *An American with Lord Roberts* (New York, 1901); and *War's Brighter Side: The Story of "The Friend" Newspaper Edited by the Correspondents with Lord Robert's Forces, March-April 1900* (New York, 1901). He also wrote *The Making of a Journalist* (New York, 1903). Died January 20, 1903, in New York City. *References*: *DAB*; *DLB*; *EAJ*; *NCAB* 1:149; and *NYT*, January 21, 1903.

RAMSAY, WILLIAM J. (? –1889). Miner, from North Carolina. Ramsay was employed from 1885 to 1889 by an English company which tried to work the gold mines in Axim in the Gold Coast. Died in the Gold Coast. *Reference*: William J. Ramsay Letters, in James Graham Ramsay Papers, Southern Historical Collection, University of North Carolina, Chapel Hill, N.C.

RAND, AUSTIN L(OOMER) (1905–1982). Explorer and zoologist, born December 16, 1905, in Kentville, Nova Scotia, Canada. Rand graduated from Acadia (Nova Scotia) and Cornell universities. He was on the staff of the American Museum of Natural History from 1929 to 1942 and was research associate at the Archbold Biological Station in Lake Placid, Florida. He was ornithologist on an expedition to Madagascar in 1929 and head of the collection team for the Archbold expedition of the American Museum of Natural History into New Guinea in the 1930s. He wrote *Distribution and Habits of Madagascar Birds* (New York, 1936) and *Birds from Liberia* (Chicago, 1951). He was on the staff of the National Museum of Canada from 1942 to 1947, then curator of birds at the Field Museum of Natural History from 1947 to 1955, and chief curator there from 1955 until his retirement. Died November 6, 1982, in Avon Park, Florida. *References*: *AMWS*; *CA*; *NYT*, November 8, 1982; and *WWWA*.

RANDALL, RICHARD (1796–1829). Physician and colonial agent, born in Annapolis, Maryland. Randall graduated from St. John's College (Annapolis) and the University of Pennsylvania Medical School. He was commissioned a surgeon's mate in the United States Navy in 1818 and was surgeon until 1825, when he resigned his commission, and practiced medicine in Washington, D.C. He became professor of chemistry in the medical department of Columbia University in 1827. He was a member of the board of managers of the American Colonization Society* and was colonial agent of the society in Liberia in 1828–

1829. Died April 19, 1829. *References*: *African Repository* 5 (1829): 125–28; *Huberich*.

RAVEN, HENRY CUSHIER (1889–1944). Zoologist, born April 16, 1889, in Brooklyn, New York. Raven made an expedition to the Netherland East Indies from 1912 to 1918. He joined the American Museum of Natural History in 1921 as a field representative, became assistant curator in 1926, curator of comparative anatomy in 1944, and was lecturer in zoology at Columbia University after 1926. In 1929 he led the Columbia University–American Museum of Natural History expedition to West Africa, and wrote (with William K. Gregory*) *In Quest of Gorillas* (New Bedford, Mass., 1937). He became interested in the study of gorillas and chimpanzees, and his research was published posthumously in *The Henry Cushier Raven Memorial Volume: The Anatomy of the Gorilla, the Studies of Henry Cushier Raven*, ed. William K. Gregory (New York, 1950). Died April 5, 1944, in Sebring, Florida. *References*: *Anatomical Record* 92 (1945): 315–16; William K. Gregory, "Henry Cushier Raven (1889–1944)," in *The Anatomy of the Gorilla*, pp. 1–9; and *NYT*, April 6, 1944.

RAYMOND, WILLIAM (1815–1847). Missionary, born in Ashby, Massachusetts. Raymond attended Amherst College and graduated from Oberlin Collegiate Institute. He accompanied the African slaves who mutinied on the Spanish schooner *Amistad* back to Sierra Leone in 1842 and established the Mende Mission* in Sherbro country. He opened a school there in 1846. The mission was taken over by the American Missionary Association* in 1846. Died November 26, 1847, in Freetown, Sierra Leone. *References*: William Raymond Papers, Amistad Research Center, New Orleans; and *Dictionary of African Biography* 2 (Algonac, Mich., 1979), pp. 135–137.

READING, JOSEPH HANKINSON (1849–1920). Missionary, born in Frenchtown, New Jersey. Reading attended the Military Academy in Allentown, Pennsylvania. He was proprietor of a general store in Frenchtown. He became a missionary under the Board of Foreign Missions of the Presbyterian Church in the U.S.A.* in the Gabon and Corisco missions from 1874 until 1888 and was for a time both secretary and treasurer of the missions. He was also a commercial agent in Central Africa. He wrote *The Ogowe Band, a Narrative of African Travel* (Philadelphia, 1890), which documented his journey along the Ogowe River in Gabon, and *A Voyage Along the Western Coast of Newest Africa* (Philadelphia, 1901). Died July 14, 1920, in Woodstown, New Jersey.

REED, GEORGE CLINTON (1872–1966). Missionary, born in Weeping Water, Nebraska. Reed graduated from Oberlin College. He served as a missionary under the Gospel Missionary Union in Morocco from 1897 to 1916. He made a trip into the French Sudan in 1913 to explore and survey that area for a missionary field. He established a mission station in Bamako, French Sudan,

180   REES, EMORY J.

1919, and served until his retirement in 1951. He was the first Protestant missionary to preach in Timbuctu. He also translated the Bible into Bambara. Died January 21, 1966.

REES, EMORY J. (1870–1947). Missionary, born in Vermilion, Illinois. Rees attended Cleveland Bible College, and taught in county schools in Illinois from 1891 to 1897. He was in South Africa from 1899 to 1903, went to British East Africa in 1903 as a missionary under the American Friends Board of Foreign Missions, and served in the Friends Africa Industrial Mission.* He established a station in Kaimosi and served in Maragoli (later known as Vihiga) after 1906. He converted the Luragoli dialect into a written language and printed the New Testament in that dialect. He returned to the United States in 1926. *Reference*: Elizabeth H. Emerson, *Emory J. Rees Language Pioneer: A Biographical Sketch* (Gowanda, N.Y., 1958).

REFORM COMMITTEE. Organization established in 1895 in Johannesburg by the Uitlander (non-Boer) leaders in Johannesburg aiming at reforms in the Transvaal Republic to protest political and economic restrictions by the Boers, and to obtain a greater role in its government. Of the sixty-six members, eight were Americans. John Hays Hammond* was chairman, dominated the leadership, and drafted most of the protests. The committee planned an uprising in Johannesburg, which was to be supported by Dr. Jameson's expeditionary force. It ceased its activities when the Jameson Raid failed. Almost all the members were arrested and sentenced to death or imprisonment and heavy fines. *References*: Denys Rhoodie, *Conspirators in Conflict: A Study of the Johannesburg Reform Committee and Its Role in the Conspiracy Against the South African Republic* (Cape Town, 1967); and *SESA*.

RENDER(S), ADAM (1822- ?). Hunter and prospector, born in Germany. Renders immigrated to the United States. He then went to Natal, South Africa, in 1842; he settled first in Natal, and in 1848 moved to the Transvaal. He was a hunter in the Transvaal and in what became later Rhodesia. He discovered by chance the ruins of Great Zimbabwe in 1867. He returned there in 1868, married the daughter of a local petty chief and was living in a village near the ruins in 1871. Died after 1872 near Zimbabwe. *References*: *DSAB* 3; *SESA*; and *Tabler/ Rhodesia*.

RICHARDS, ERWIN HART (1851–1928). Missionary, born May 4, 1851, in Orwell, Ohio. Richards graduated from Oberlin College and Andover Theological Seminary and was ordained in 1880. He was a missionary under the American Board of Commissioners for Foreign Missions (ABCFM)* from 1880 to 1889. He served among the Zulus in Natal from 1880 to 1884 and among the Tongas in Inhambane, Mozambique, from 1884 to 1889. When the ABCFM decided to withdraw the mission, Richards was reluctant to leave, and when the mission was taken over by the Methodist Episcopal Church in 1890, he received an appointment from that church. He founded and was superintendent of the East Central African mission. He translated parts of the Bible into Tonga and Sheetswa. He returned to the United States in 1908 and was a speaker on Africa and African missions. He wrote *"Lines and Lights" from Africa; Centenary Celebration of Methodist Missions* (Columbus, 1919). Died January 15, 1928, in Oberlin, Ohio. *References*: Erwin Hart Richards, Diary, MS, Union Theological Seminary Library, New York City; *AndoverTS*; and *WWWA*.

RIDEOUT, CONRAD A. (fl. 1899–1903). Lawyer, born in Ohio. Rideout served a term as a state judge in Arkansas. Forced to flee during the post-Reconstruction period, he settled in Seattle and practiced law. He was in Southern Africa from 1899 to 1903 as an unofficial missionary of the African Methodist Episcopal Church. He lived in 1900 in the royal kraal of Paramount Chief Sigcau of Pondoland and served as his adviser. He then lived in Matsieng, Basutoland, and was Chief Lerotholi's legal adviser and his ambassador to the colonial government. He visited Barotseland in 1902. He raised the ire of the British colonial officials and was forced to leave. *Reference*: Carol Page, "Conrad A. Rideout, Afro-American Adviser to the Chiefs of Lesotho and Pondoland, 1899–1903," in *Pan-African Biography*, ed. Robert A. Hill (Los Angeles, 1987), pp. 1–10.

ROBBINS, ELIJAH (1828–1889). Missionary, born March 12, 1828, in Thompson, Connecticut. Robbins graduated from Yale College and East Windsor Theological Seminary and was ordained in 1859. He was a missionary under the American Board of Commissioners for Foreign Missions (ABCFM)* in the Zulu mission from 1859 until his death. He was stationed first at Umzumbi and later in the mission training school at Amanzimtoti. Died June 30, 1889 at Amanzimtoti. *Reference*: *EM*.

ROBERTS, EDMUND (1784–1836). Merchant and diplomat, born June 29, 1784, in Portsmouth, New Hampshire. In business after 1808, he visited Zanzibar as a trader in 1827 and 1828, returned again to Zanzibar in 1831, and visited parts of India. Dissatisfied with the conditions of trade, he set in motion events that led to the Zanzibar-American Treaty of 1833. In 1832 he was sent on a diplomatic mission to negotiate treaties with Zanzibar, Muscat, Siam, and Cochin China, and signed the first American treaty with the Sultan of Zanzibar in 1833. It was Zanzibar's first treaty with a foreign power. He returned to Zanzibar in 1835 to exchange ratified treaties. Died June 12, 1836, in Macao. His diary was published as *Embassy to the Eastern Courts of Cochin-China, Siam and Muscat; in the U.S. Sloop-of-war Peacock, David Geisinger, Commander, During the Years 1832–3–4* (New York, 1837). *References*: Edmund Roberts Papers, Manuscript Division, Library of Congress; Edmund Roberts Papers, New Hampshire Historical Society, Concord, N.H.; *ACAB*; *DAB*; Frederic A. Greenhut, "Edmund Roberts: Early American Diplomat,'' *Manuscripts* 35 (1983): 273–80; and *WWWA*.

ROBERTS, GEORGE ARTHUR (1882–1973). Agricultural missionary, born April 24, 1882, in Marathon, Iowa. Roberts graduated from Iowa State College (Ames) and was ordained in 1927. He was a missionary under the Board of Foreign Missions of the Methodist Episcopal Church* in Southern Rhodesia from 1907 to 1950, teaching agricultural methods in Old Umtali, Southern Rhodesia. He introduced the plow to Rhodesia and founded the first class of agriculture in Rhodesia in 1909; he then lived on his farm in Mutambara, Southern Rhodesia. He returned to the United States in 1950. He wrote *Let Me Tell You a Story* (Bulwayao, Southern Rhodesia, 1964). Died July 29, 1973, in Penney Farms, Florida.

ROBERTS, JOHN WRIGHT (1812–1875). Missionary, brother of Joseph Jenkins Roberts,* born free September 8, 1812, in Petersburg, Virginia. Roberts immigrated to Liberia with his family in 1829. He was ordained in 1841 and was presiding elder of the Monrovia District of the Methodist Episcopal Church. He was elected the second Episcopal missionary bishop in 1864 and was consecrated bishop in 1866. Died January 30, 1875, in Monrovia. *References*: *EWM*; *Leete*; and *NCAB* 5:506.

ROBERTS, JOSEPH JENKINS (1809–1876). Educator and first president of the Republic of Liberia, born free March 15, 1809, in Petersburg, Virginia. Roberts immigrated to Liberia with his family in 1829 and there established a trading firm that became one of the most prosperous in the colony. He was appointed high sheriff in 1833 and led a military expedition in 1839. He became the first black governor of Liberia in 1841 and held the office until 1847 when he became the first president of the Republic of Liberia. He was reelected president in 1849, 1851, 1853, 1871, and 1873, and served until 1876. He was also president of the College of Liberia after 1856, and professor of jurisprudence and international law from 1861 until his death. Died February 24, 1876, in Monrovia, Liberia. *References*: *DAB*; *Davis*; *EWM*; A. Doris Banks Henries, *The Life of Joseph Jenkins Roberts and His Inaugural Addresses* (London, 1964); *Huberich*; and Pat Mathews, ''Joseph Jenkins Roberts: The Father of Liberia,'' *Virginia Cavalcade* 23 (Autumn 1973): 4–11.

ROBERTS, LEO B(OND) (1887–1954). Engineer, map maker, and explorer, born May 19, 1887, in Osage City, Kansas. Roberts attended the University of Kansas. He served with the United States Geological Survey from 1906 to 1917 and in an army engineering unit during World War I. He was a topographer with the third Asiatic expedition of the American Museum of Natural History from 1924 to 1926. He mapped out the road to Lake Tsana in Ethiopia in 1928, and from 1929 to 1931 led a party sent to Ethiopia by J. G. White Engineering

Corporation to survey the headwaters of the Blue Nile in the interior of Ethiopia in order to establish the feasibility of constructing a dam at the outlet of Lake Tsana. He made a second expedition to the headwaters of the Blue Nile in Ethiopia from 1934 to 1936. He prepared the final reports on the construction of a dam on Lake Tsana and completed the negotiations with the Ethiopian and Egyptian governments. He described his impressions in the September 1935 issue of the *National Geographic Magazine*. He became the director of New York City Emergency Work and Relief Administration in 1932 and was assistant chief engineer in the construction of the New York World's Fair at Flushing Meadows from 1937 to 1939. He served in the U.S. Army Corps of Engineers during World War II as chief of ports in the European theater of war, and after the war was an authority on port, harbor, and dock installations. Died January 17, 1954, in Port Washington, Long Island. *Reference*: *NYT*, January 17, 1954.

ROBERTS FIELD. Liberia's major international airport, developed by the United States military in conjunction with Pan American Airways and Firestone Plantations Company.* It was later renamed Roberts International Airport.

ROBESON, ANTHONY MAURICE (1863–1947). Mechanical engineer, born in Belvedere, Pennsylvania. Robeson worked initially in the steel works in Pennsylvania. He became chief mechanical engineer for De Beers Consolidated Mines, Kimberley, South Africa, in 1890, and assistant general manager in 1897. He was also a consulting mechanical and electrical engineer to the firm of Hermann Eckstein & Company in Johannesburg. He played an important role in the establishment of the Victoria Falls and Transvaal Power Company in 1906. He retired in 1911. Died in South Africa. *Reference*: *SADNB*.

ROBESON, ESLANDA CARDOZO (1896–1965). Anthropologist and author, wife of singer Paul Robeson, born in Washington, D.C., and grew up in New York City. Robeson attended the University of Chicago, graduated from Teachers College of Columbia University, studied at the University of London and London School of Economics and in Leningrad, and graduated from Hartford Seminary Foundation. She married Paul Robeson in 1921 and became his business manager. She traveled in Africa in 1936 and wrote *African Journey* (New York, 1945) based on her diary. She went again to Africa in 1946. Died December 13, 1965, in New York City. *References*: Eslanda Cardozo Robeson Papers, Special Collections, Robert W. Woodruff Library, Atlanta University Center, Atlanta, Ga.; *DANB*; *NAW*; and *NYT*, December 14, 1965.

ROBINS, LORD (ELLIS ROBINS) (1884–1962). Financier and soldier, later Lord Robins of Rhodesia, born October 31, 1884, in Philadelphia. Robins graduated from the University of Pennsylvania and studied at Christ Church, Oxford University, as the first American Rhodes scholar from the state of Pennsylvania. He was assistant editor of *Everybody's Magazine* from 1907 to 1909, when he returned to England, was private secretary to Earl Winterton, M.P., from 1909 to 1914, and became a British citizen. He served with the City of London Yeomanry during World War I, remained in the military until 1921, and was secretary of the Conservative Club from 1921 to 1928. He went to Rhodesia in 1928 as chief representative of the British South Africa Company in Rhodesia. He was later president of the company in London until his death. He served in the Rhodesia Regiment and was quartermaster general of the Southern Rhodesia Forces during World War II. He was knighted in 1954 and created First Baron of Rhodesia and Chelsea in 1958 for his public service in Rhodesia. Died July 21, 1962, in London, England. *References*: *DSAB*; and *Times* (London), July 23, 1962.

ROBINSON, JAMES H(ERMAN) (1907–1972). Clergyman, born in Knoxville, Tennessee. Robinson graduated from Lincoln University and Union Theological Seminary. He was a pastor in New York City from 1938 to 1962. He visited Africa in 1954, and then founded and was executive director of Operation Crossroads Africa (see Crossroads Africa*), taking students from the United States to live and work in Africa. He took the pilot group to West Africa in 1958. He was an adviser on the establishment of the Peace Corps* and a consultant on African affairs to the U.S. State Department. He wrote *Road Without Turning, the Story of Reverend James H. Robinson; an Autobiography* (New York, 1950) and *Africa at the Crossroads* (Philadelphia, 1962). Died November 6, 1972, in New York City. *References*: James H. Robinson Papers, Amistad Research Center, New Orleans, La.; *Crisis* 80 (May 1973): 159–61; Amy Lee, *Throbbing Drums: The Story of James H. Robinson* (New York, 1968); and *NYT*, November 7, 1972.

ROBINSON, JOHN C. (1906–1954). Aviator, born in Florida, and grew up in Gulfport, Mississippi. Robinson graduated from Tuskegee Institute. He opened an auto repair shop in Chicago and later went to work for the Curtiss-Wright Aeronautical School and learned in fly. He went to Ethiopia in 1935, was commissioned colonel in the Ethiopian Army, and was the nominal commander of the Ethiopian Air Force. He flew several missions as a special courier for Emperor Haile Selassie between the capital and the front lines in an unarmed monoplane. He returned to the United States in 1936, served in the Chanute Air Training Center in Chicago, but was back in Ethiopia in 1944, helping to lay the groundwork for the establishment of the modern Ethiopian Air Force. He became a principal instructor in the aviation school of Prince Makonnen Haile Selassie, the Duke of Harrar, in Addis Ababa, and his private pilot. Died March 27, 1954, in Addis Ababa, from injuries received when his plane crashed. *References*: William R. Scott, "Colonel John C. Robinson: The Condor of Ethiopia," *Pan-African Journal* 5 (1972): 59–69; William R. Scott, "A Study of Afro-American and Ethiopian Relations: 1896–1941," Ph.D. diss., Princeton

University, 1971, ch. 6; Thomas E. Simmons, *The Brown Condor: The True Adventures of John C. Robinson* (Silver Spring, Md., 1988).

ROBINSON, WILLIAM W. (1819- ?). Consul, born December 14, 1819, in Fairhaven, Vermont. Robinson attended Norwich Military Academy (Conn.). He was a school teacher in Vermont, New Jersey, and Ohio, and served in the Mexican and Civil wars. He was later engaged in farming in Sparta, Wisconsin, until 1873. He was a consul at Tamatave, Madagscar, from 1875 until 1887. He played a role in preparing a code of law for Madagascar in 1881 and negotiated the Americo-Malagasy Treaty of 1881. He accompanied the Madagascan mission to the United States in 1883, the principal objective of which was to secure American protection for Malagasy independence. *Reference*: *Soldiers and Citizens Album of Biographical Records Containing Personal Sketches of Army Men and Citizens Prominent in Loyalty to the Union* (Chicago, 1890), pp. 553–56.

RO(D)GERS, JAMES W(OOD) (ca. 1860–1911). Ivory poacher. Rogers was a gold miner in the Klondike and there made a fortune which he lost in Monte Carlo. He was forced to flee from South Africa, Rhodesia, and the Belgian Congo because of criminal activities. He was poaching for ivory in the Lado Enclave, the territory on the west bank of the Nile River north of Lake Albert, in 1910–1911. Killed October 7, 1911, by British soldiers in the Lado Enclave, a death that raised questions in Congress. *References*: Robert O. Collins, "Ivory Poaching in the Lado Enclave," *Uganda Journal* 24 (1960): 217–28; and *NYT*, August 21, 1912.

ROGERS, JOEL A(UGUSTUS) (1888–1966). Journalist and author, born in Jamaica, West Indies. He wrote for the *American Mercury* and the *Amsterdam News* and wrote a weekly column for the *Pittsburgh Courier* from 1921 until his death. He was war correspondent for the *Pittsburgh Courier* in Ethiopia and wrote *The Real Facts About Ethiopia* (New York, 1935?). Died March 26, 1966, in New York City. *References*: *NHB* 35 (February 1972): 34–38; *NYT*, March 27, 1966; and W. B. Turner, "J. A. Rogers: Portrait of an Afro-American Historian," *Black Scholar* 10 (May 1975): 22–30.

ROGERS, JOEL C. (1864–1960). Missionary. Rogers graduated from Battle Creek College, and was a teacher at Walla Walla College. He went to Kimberley, South Africa, in 1893, served as pastor of the first Seventh-Day Adventist church in South Africa, was on the staff of the Claremont Union (later Heidelberg) College from 1894 to 1896 and served in the Kolo mission in Basutoland in 1898–1899. He returned to the United States in 1899, but was back in Africa in 1907. He was in charge of the Plainfield (later Malamulo) Mission in Nyasaland from 1907 to 1917, was in South Africa from 1917 to 1919, opened a mission station in Swaziland in 1919, and later did pastoral work among the Indian population in Durban. He returned to the United States in 1952. *Reference*: *SDAE*.

ROGERS, THOMAS (? –1773). Sea captain. Rogers made a career in the slave trade sailing out of Newport, Rhode Island. His maiden voyage was in 1756, and he continued until 1773, making seven voyages to Africa. Died about November 10, 1773, on the coast of Africa. *Reference*: Darold D. Wax, "Thomas Rogers and the Rhode Island Slave Trade," *American Neptune* 35 (1975): 289–301.

ROOD, DAVID (1818–1891). Missionary, born April 25, 1818, in Buckland, Massachusetts, and grew up in Plainfield, Massachusetts. Rood graduated from Williams College and East Windsor Seminary and was ordained in 1847. He was a missionary under the American Board of Commissioners for Foreign Missions (ABCFM)* in South Africa from 1847 until 1888. He served in mission stations in Ifafa, Amanzimtoti, and Umtovi. He established the Amanzimtoti Seminary, a boys' high school in 1853. He wrote a new edition of the New Testament in Zulu. He returned to the United States in 1888. Died April 8, 1891, in Covert, Michigan. *Reference*: *Hewitt*.

ROOSEVELT, THEODORE (1858–1919). President of the United States and big-game hunter, born October 27, 1858, in New York City. Roosevelt graduated from Harvard University. He served in the New York State Assembly, was civil service commissioner from 1889 to 1895, president of New York City's Board of Police Commissioners, assistant secretary of the navy, commander of the "Rough Riders" during the Spanish-American War, and governor of New York. He was elected vice president in 1900 and became president in 1901, serving until 1909. He set out on an extended safari in East Africa in 1909–1910 in which he also collected specimens for the United States National Museum and the American Museum of Natural History. He wrote *African Game Trails: An Account of the African Wanderings of an American Hunter-Naturalist* (London, 1910) and (with Edmund Heller*) *Life Histories of the African Game Animals* (New York, 1914). He was candidate of the Progressive ("Bull Moose") Party in the presidential elections of 1912. Died January 6, 1919, in Sagamore Hill, near Oyster Bay, Long Island, New York. *References*: Theodore Roosevelt Papers, Manuscript Division, Library of Congress; Paul A. Cutright, *Theodore Roosevelt, the Naturalist* (New York, 1956); *DAB*; Joseph L. Gardner, *Departing Glory: Theodore Roosevelt as Ex-president* (New York, 1973); and Kate M. Stewart, "Theodore Roosevelt, Hunter-Naturalist on Safari," *Quarterly Journal of the Library of Congress* 27 (1970): 242–56.

ROPES, EDWARD D(EHONDE), SR. (1838–1902). Consul, born April 3, 1838, in Salem, Massachusetts. Ropes entered a Boston commission house in 1853, became a clerk for Captain John Bertram in 1854, and sailed for Zanzibar.

He was acting consul in Zanzibar in 1859–1860 and consul from 1865 to 1867. He returned to the United States in 1867, remained a member of the Bertram firm until 1882, and then became principal partner in the successor firm of Ropes, Emmerton and Company. Died August 8, 1902, in Salem. *Reference*: Edward D. Ropes, Sr., Papers, Peabody Museum, Salem, Mass.

ROPES, EDWARD D(EHONDE), JR. (1864–1903). Consul, son of Edward D. Ropes, Sr.* born September 4, 1864, and grew up in Salem, Massachusetts. Ropes came to Africa in 1882 as an agent for the John Bertram firm. After a brief stay at Tamatave, Madagascar, he came to Zanzibar. He left Zanzibar in 1885 but returned in 1886 as the firm's chief agent and left again in 1889. He was consul in Zanzibar from 1890 to 1892. He returned to the United States and was employed by Arnold, Cheney & Co. of New York; he was later connected with William E. Hutton & Co., brokers of New York City, until his death. Died October 29, 1903, in Salem, Massachusetts. *References*: Edward D. Ropes, Jr., Papers, Peabody Museum, Salem, Mass.; Norman R. Bennett, ed., *The Zanzibar Letters of Edward D. Ropes, Jr., 1882–1892*; and *NYT*, October 31, 1903.

ROSEBERRY, ROBERT S(HERMAN) (1883–1976). Missionary, born near Tyrone, Pennsylvania. Roseberry graduated from Nyack College. He became a missionary under the Christian and Missionary Alliance* in Sierra Leone in 1909 and served later in French West Africa, establishing mission stations inland and penetrating into the upper part of the Niger Valley. He wrote *The Niger Vision* (Harrisburg, Pa., 1934) and *The Soul of French West Africa* (Harrisburg, Pa., 1947) and coauthored *Among the Cliff Dwellers of French West Africa* (n.p., 1936). Died July 9, 1976, in Altoona, Florida. *References*: "R. S. Roseberry—Autobiography, or Crossing Frontiers with Christ," unfinished MS, A. B. Simpson Memorial Historical Library, Nyack College, Nyack, N.Y.; and *The Alliance Witness* (Nyack, N.Y.), September 8, 1976.

ROSS, EDWARD ALSWORTH (1866–1951). Sociologist, born December 12, 1866, in Virden, Illinois. Ross graduated from Coe College (Cedar Rapids, Iowa) and Johns Hopkins University. He was a professor at Stanford University from 1893 until 1900, at the University of Nebraska from 1901 to 1906, and at the University of Wisconsin from 1906 until his retirement in 1937. He went to Africa in 1924 to investigate the conditions of the natives in Angola and Mozambique. His report, *The Employment of Native Labor in Portuguese Africa* (New York, 1925), was an exposé of the existence of slave labor and the inhuman conditions in the Portuguese colonies. He later wrote *Seventy Years of It: An Autobiography* (New York, 1936). Died July 22, 1951, in Madison, Wisconsin. *References*: *DAB* S5; *NCAB* 18:99; and *WWWA*.

188   ROSS, EMORY

ROSS, EMORY (1887–1973). Missionary, born July 28, 1887, in Kendalville, Indiana. Ross graduated from Eureka College and studied at the universities of Chicago and Wisconsin and the College of Missions (Indianapolis); he was ordained in 1910. He was a missionary under the Christian Woman's Board of Missions of the Disciples of Christ in Liberia from 1912 to 1916 and under the Disciples of Christ Congo Mission (DCCM) in the Belgian Congo from 1917 to 1933, stationed at Lotumbe and later in Bolenge. He was editor of the *Congo Mission News* from 1918 to 1933, general secretary of the Congo Protestant Council in Léopoldville from 1928 to 1933, and member of the Belgian Royal Commission for the Protection of the Natives from 1928 to 1933. He was general secretary of the American Leprosy Missions, Inc., in New York City from 1937 to 1940, vice president of the organization from 1940 to 1948, and chairman in 1948–1949. He was executive secretary of the African Committee on Work in the Congo of the Foreign Missions Conference of North America (later the Africa committee of the National Council of the Churches of Christ in the U.S.A.) from 1935 to 1953, and general secretary of the Foreign Mission Conference of North America from 1940 to 1945. He retired in 1953. He wrote *Out of Africa* (New York, 1936) and *African Heritage* (New York, 1952) and coauthored *Africa Disturbed* (New York, 1959). Died March 16, 1973, in Fairfax, Virginia. *References*: *CA*; *IAB*; *NCAB* 57:565; *NYT*, March 18, 1973; *Survey* 86 (April 1950): 204; *TWTA*; and *WWWA*.

ROYE, EDWARD JAMES (1815–1872). Colonist, merchant, and government official, born February 3, 1815, in Newark, Licking County, Ohio. Roye spent some years in business and came to Liberia in 1846. He became a merchant, exporting African products to England and the United States, and in a few years became the leading merchant and the richest man in Liberia. He owned the first ships to display the Liberian flag in the ports of Liverpool and New York. He was elected speaker of the House of Representatives in 1849, began publishing the *Liberia Sentinel* in 1854 (which suspended publication in 1855), was chief justice from 1865 to 1868, and president of Liberia in 1870–1871. He obtained a loan from Great Britain which was considered a bad loan by Liberians and which caused great resentment against him, and he was deposed. He was summoned to trial but tried to escape and drowned February 12, 1872, in Monrovia harbor. *References*: *DAB*; Svend E. Holsoe, "A Portrait of a Black Midwestern Family During the Early Nineteenth Century: Edward James Roye and His Parents," *Liberian Studies Journal* 3 (1970–1971): 41–52; Christopher T. Minikon, "Edward J. Roye: Traitor or Patriot?" *Liberian Historical Review* 1 (1964): 14–17; *Liberian Historical Review* 2 (1965): 26–36; *Huberich*; and *NHB* 16 (1952): 45.

RUARK, ROBERT CHESTER (1915–1965). Journalist and novelist, born December 29, 1915, in Southport, South Carolina, and grew up in Wilmington, North Carolina. Ruark graduated from the University of North Carolina. He joined the staff of the Washington, D.C., *Daily News* in 1937, becoming assistant city editor in 1942, and then became Washington correspondent for the Newspaper Enterprise Association Service. He served in the navy during World War II. He became Washington correspondent for the Scripps-Howard Newspaper Alliance in 1945 and was a columnist for Scripps-Howard and for United Feature Service from 1946 to 1965. He went to East Africa as a hunter and acted as guide. Two of his books resulted from his experience, *Something of Value* (Garden City, N.Y., 1955) and *Uhuru, a Novel of Africa Today* (New York, 1962). He wrote autobiographies, *Old Man and the Boy* (New York, 1957) and *Old Man's Boy Grows Older* (New York, 1961). Died July 1, 1965, in London. *References*: Robert Chester Ruark Papers, Southern Historical Collection, University of North Carolina at Chapel Hill, N.C.; *DAB* S7; *NYT*, July 1, 1965; and W. Ross, "Rudyard C. Ruark & the White Man's Burden," *Esquire* 15 (March 1961): 109–10.

RUDIN, JOHN JAMES (1916-   ). Clergyman, born November 27, 1916, in Pittsfield, Massachusetts. Rudin graduated from the Maryknoll Seminary and Angelicum University (Rome) and was ordained in 1944. He was a teacher at Venrad College from 1945 to 1947, rector of Maryknoll Junior Seminary from 1949 to 1951, professor at Maryknoll Seminary (N.Y.) from 1951 to 1954, and its vice rector from 1952 to 1954. He was assigned to Shinyanga, Africa, in 1954, became superior of Maryknollers in Africa in 1956, and was the first bishop of Musoma from 1957 until his retirement in 1979. *Reference*: ACWW.

RUSSWURM, JOHN BROWN (1799–1851). Colonist and government official, born October 1, 1799, in Port Antonio, Jamaica, to an American father, and grew up in Portland, Maine. Russwurm graduated from Bowdoin College. He settled in New York City, established *Freedom's Journal*, one of the first black newspapers in the United States, and was its editor from 1827 to 1829. He immigrated to Liberia in 1829, resided in Monrovia, was colonial secretary and editor of the *Liberia Herald* from 1830 to 1835, superintendent of schools for the colony from 1830 to 1836, and colonial agent for the American Colonization Society* from 1834 to 1836. He was governor of the Maryland in Africa* colony at Cape Palmas from 1836 until his death. Russwurm encouraged agriculture and trade, took a census in 1843, and established a court. He collaborated with Joseph Jenkins Roberts,* president of the Republic of Liberia, in foreign affairs, and was instrumental in bringing about the unification of the two colonies. Died June 9, 1851, at Cape Palmas. *References*: *DAB*; *DANB*; *Huberich*; and Mary Sagarin, *John Brown Russwurm; the Story of Freedom's Journal, Freedom's Journey* (New York, 1970).

S

SADLER, GEORGE WASHINGTON (1887–1975). Missionary, born October 10, 1887, in Laneview, Virginia. Sadler graduated from Richmond College, Southern Baptist Theological Seminary (Louisville, Ky.), and Teachers College of Columbia University, and was army chaplain in France during World War I. He was a missionary under the Foreign Mission Board of the Southern Baptist Convention* in Nigeria from 1921 until 1932, and served as principal of the Baptist College and Seminary at Ogbomosho, Nigeria, from 1921 to 1931. He resigned from his mission because of family health problems and returned to the United States in 1932. He was a pastor in Liberty, Missouri, and secretary for Africa, Europe, and the Near East for the Foreign Mission Board from 1939 until 1958. He wrote *A Century in Nigeria* (Nashville, Tenn., 1950). Died July 18, 1975, in Richmond, Virginia. *Reference: ESB.*

SAID, WILLIAM PRESTLEY (1925–1954). Professional hunter, born in Columbus, Ohio. Said became a safari guide and hunter in the Belgian Congo in 1948, specializing in capturing live gorillas for American universities. Died April 11, 1954, in a car accident, in Léopoldville, Belgian Congo. *Reference: BCB* 6.

SANDERS, WILLIAM HENRY (1856–1947). Missionary, born March 2, 1856, in Tellipallai, Jaffna, Ceylon, to American parents, and came to the United States in 1865. Sanders graduated from Williams College and Hartford Theological Seminary and was ordained in 1880. He became a missionary under the American Board of Commissioners for Foreign Missions (ABCFM)* from 1880 to 1930, stationed in Bihé, Angola, one of the first ABCFM missionaries to Angola. He translated the Gospel of John and *Pilgrim's Progress* into Umbundu, and prepared *Vocabulary of the Umbundu Language: Comprising Umbundu-English and English-Umbundu* (Boston, 1885), which he revised and enlarged in 1910. He returned to the United States in 1930. Died May 30, 1947, in Wilmington, Delaware. *References:* William Henry Sanders, "Reminiscences of William H. Sanders'' (1937), MS, American Board Library, Boston; *Hewitt*; and *NYT*, May 31, 1947.

SANFORD EXPLORING EXPEDITION. The first commercial company on the upper Congo, established in 1886 by Henry S. Sanford (1823–1891), who was granted a concession by Leopold II of Belgium. The company founded settlements at Kinshana, Matadi, South Mancagues, Luebo, and Equator to develop trade, and brought the first commercial steamer over the cataracts in Stanley Pool. Emory H. Taunt* was the company's administrator in the Congo. The company failed for lack of capital and became a Belgian company in 1889. *References*: Joseph A. Fry, *Henry S. Sanford: Diplomacy and Business in Nineteenth-century America* (Reno, Nev., 1982); Lysle E. Meyer, "Henry S. Sanford and the Congo: A Reassessment," *African Historical Studies* 4 (1971): 19–39; and James P. White, "The Sanford Exploring Expedition," *JAH* 8 (1967): 291–302.

SAUER, JONATHAN DEININGER (1918-   ). Plant geographer, born July 6, 1918, in Ann Arbor, Michigan. Sauer graduated from the University of California at Berkeley, and Washington University (St. Louis), and served with the air force during World War II. He was a member of the faculty of the University of Wisconsin from 1950 to 1967, professor of geography at the University of California in Los Angeles after 1967, and director of its Botanical Gardens and Herbarium from 1974 to 1981. He conducted research in the Seychelles in 1959 and 1963; he wrote *Coastal Plant Geography of Mauritius* (Baton Rouge, La., 1960) and *Plants and Man on the Seychelles Coast: A Study In Historical Biogeography* (Madison, Wis., 1967). *References*: AMWS; WWA; and WWE.

SAVAGE, THOMAS STAUGHTON (1804–1880). Clergyman, missionary, and naturalist, born June 7, 1804, in Upper Middletown (now Cromwell), Connecticut. Savage graduated from Yale College, Yale Medical School, and the Theological Seminary in Virginia (Alexandria, Va.), and was ordained in 1836. He was the first missionary to Africa under the Domestic and Foreign Missionary Society of the Protestant Episcopal Church in the United States of America.* He arrived in Cape Palmas, Liberia, in 1836, and established a mission on Mount Vaughn. He returned to the United States in 1837 because of ill health, but came back to Cape Palmas in 1839. He traveled along the Slave, Ivory, and Gold coasts in 1840, and reached Accra, the Gold Coast. He was again in the United States in 1843–1844, but returned to Africa in 1844, was transferred to the missionary station at Fishtown, Liberia, in 1845, resigned in 1846, and returned to the United States in 1847. He stopped in the Gabon River in 1847 and obtained skulls and bones of gorillas which he brought back with him and which he first described scientifically in 1847 in the *Proceedings of the Boston Society of Natural History*. He also published articles on chimpanzees and termites. He was later a pastor in Mississippi, Alabama, and Rhinecliff, New York. Died December 29, 1880, in Rhinecliff, New York. *Reference*: *DAB*.

SCHALLER, GEORGE B(EALS) (1933-). Zoologist, born May 26, 1933, in Berlin, Germany, and grew up in Missouri. Schaller graduated from the universities of Alaska and Wisconsin. He was a research associate and assistant professor at Johns Hopkins University from 1963 to 1966, research associate at the New York Zoological Society from 1966 to 1979, and director of its Animal Research and Conservation Center after 1979. In 1959–1960 he studied mountain gorillas at the Virunga volcanoes region of the Albert (now Kivu) National Park in the Belgian Congo and wrote *The Mountain Gorilla: Ecology and Behavior* (Chicago, 1963) and *The Year of the Gorilla* (Chicago, 1964). From 1966 to 1969 he led an expedition to the Serengeti National Park in Tanzania and wrote *The Serengeti Lion: A Study of Predator-Prey Relations* (Chicago, 1972) and *Golden Shadows, Flying Hooves* (New York, 1973). He later conducted expeditions to Pakistan and Nepal to study wild sheep and goats in the Himalayas and to China to study pandas. *References*: *CA*; *CB* 1985; and *WWA*.

SCHLESINGER, ISIDORE WILLIAM (1871–1949). Businessman, born September 15, 1871, in New York City. Schlesinger became a commission and insurance agent. He immigrated to South Africa in 1894 and began his career as commercial traveler, but then joined the American Equitable Insurance Company as an insurance salesman. He launched a property development enterprise and developed new residential areas in Port Elizabeth and Johannesburg, founded his own insurance company, African Life Assurance Society, in Johannesburg in 1904, and was its managing director. He opened his own commercial bank, the Colonial Banking and Trust Company in 1905, and another insurance company, African Guarantee and Indemnity Company in 1911, to handle all forms of insurance. In 1911 he purchased the Empire Theatre in Johannesburg and expanded it into the African Consolidated Theatres; he founded the African Film Productions and its weekly newsreel, ''African Mirror.'' He branched into chain stores, hotels, banking, and commercial pineapple and citrus growing, and pioneered radio broadcasting in South Africa by sponsoring the first chain of radio stations and forming the African Broadcasting Company in 1930. Died March 11, 1949, in Johannesburg. *References*: *DASB* 4; *NYT*, March 12, 1949; and *SESA*.

SCHMELZENBACH, HARMON F. (1882–1929). Missionary, born September 27, 1882, in Northern Ohio. Schmelzenbach attended the Bible school in Peniel, Texas. He was a missionary under the Church of the Nazarene* in South Africa from 1907 to 1910. He established the mission in Swaziland in 1910 in Endingeni and served there until his death. He was the first superintendent of the African work of his church. Died May 22, 1929, in Endingeni, Swaziland. His son **ELMER SCHMELZENBACH** (1910-), was a missionary in Swaziland after 1936, and wrote *Sons of Africa: Stories from the Life of Elmer Schmelzenbach* (as told to Leslie Parrott; Kansas City, 1979). *References: Herald of Holiness*, June 12, 1929; Harmon Schmelzenbach III, *Schmelzenbach of Africa: The Story of Harmon F. Schmelzenbach, Missionary Pioneer to Swaziland, South Africa* (Kansas City, Mo., 1971); Lula Schmelzenbach, *Missionary Prospector: The Life of Harmon Schmelzenbach, Missionary to South Africa* (Kansas City, Mo., 1937).

SCHUYLER, GEORGE S(AMUEL) (1895–1977). Journalist, born February 25, 1895, in Providence, Rhode Island. Schuyler served in the army from 1912 to 1918. He was assistant editor of *The Messenger* from 1923 to 1928, columnist and editor for the *Pittsburgh Courier* from 1924 to 1966, literary editor of the *Manchester Union Leader*, and contributing editor to *Review of the News* and *American Opinion*. He went to Liberia in 1931 on a secret mission to investigate charges of slavery brought against the Liberian government by the League of Nations. He published a series of articles on slavery in Liberia in various newspapers, and the novel *Slaves Today: A Story of Liberia* (New York, 1931; reprinted 1969), the first African novel by a black American. He also wrote *Black and Conservative: The Autobiography of George S. Schuyler* (New Rochelle, N.Y., 1966). Died August 31, 1977, in New York City. *References: DLB; Ebony* 1; *NYT*, September 7, 1977; Michael W. Peplow, *George S. Schuyler* (Boston, 1986); and *WWA*.

SCHWAB, GEORGE (1876–1955). Missionary, born April 25, 1876, in Clinton, Massachusetts. Schwab graduated from Amherst College and Harvard University and studied at the University of Leipzig. He was a missionary under the Board of Foreign Missions of the Presbyterian Church in the U.S.A.* from 1905 until 1941. He served in the West African Mission in Liberia and Cameroon among the Basa and Bulu tribes, and was superintendent of schools and supervisor of education in French and the vernacular. He was a research associate in West African ethnology at Harvard University in 1918–1919, and assisted in preparing a map of African tribes for the U.S. Department of State at the Paris Peace Conference. He studied the hinterland tribes of Liberia in 1928 and the Basa tribe of Cameroon in 1933 for the anthropology department of Harvard University and wrote *Tribes of the Liberian Hinterland* (Cambridge, Mass., 1947). Died October 3, 1955, at Winter Park, Florida. *References*: George Schwab Papers, Presbyterian Historical Society, Philadelphia; *Amherst*.

SCOTT, EMMETT J(AY) (1873–1957). University administrator and government official, born February 13, 1873, in Houston, Texas. Scott attended Wiley University (Marshall, Texas). He was a reporter for the *Houston Post* from 1891 to 1894, and founded the black weekly *Houston Freeman* in Houston in 1894. He was private secretary to Booker T. Washington from 1897 to 1915 as well as his closest confidant and adviser. He was also secretary of the National Bureau

Business League from 1900 to 1922. He was a member of the United States Commission to Liberia in 1909, and wrote a report that strongly influenced the decision to establish, in effect, a United States protectorate over Liberia. He was secretary of the Tuskegee Institute from 1912 to 1917, special assistant to U.S. Secretary of War in charge of Negro affairs during World War I, secretary-treasurer and business manager of Howard University from 1919 to 1932, and its secretary from 1933 until his retirement in 1938. Died December 12, 1957, in Washington, D.C. *References*: Emmett J. Scott Papers, Morris A. Soper Library, Morgan State College, Baltimore; *DAB* S6; *DANB*; *NCAB* 43:194; *NYT*, December 14, 1957; *WWCR*; and *WWWA*.

SCOTT, GEORGE (1706–1740). Slave trader, born May 25, 1706, in Newport, Rhode Island. Scott made several trips to Africa. He was the master of the sloop *Little George* in 1730, carrying slaves from West Africa; the slaves revolted, but he escaped. He operated sugar and still houses, and was commissioned a privateer in the West Indies in 1739. Died October 29, 1740, when his ship was lost at sea. *Reference*: Kenneth Scott, "George Scott, Slave Trader of Newport," *American Neptune* 12 (1952): 222–28.

SCOTT, ISAIAH BENJAMIN (1854–1931). Clergyman, born September 30, 1854, near Midway, Woodford County, Kentucky. Scott attended Clark University (Atlanta) and graduated from Central Tennessee College (later Walden University, Nashville, Tenn.) and New Orleans University and was ordained in 1882. He held pastorates in Nashville, Tennessee, and Houston, Galveston, and Marshall, Texas. He was president of Wiley University from 1893 to 1896, and editor of the *Southwestern Christian Advocate* in New Orleans from 1896 to 1904. He was elected missionary bishop of the Methodist Episcopal Church* for Africa in 1904, with headquarters in Monrovia, Liberia, and served until his retirement in 1916. Died July 4, 1931, in Nashville, Tennessee. *References*: *EWM*; *Leete*; *NCAB* 12:262; and *WWCR*.

SCOTT, PETER CAMERON (1867–1896). Missionary, born March 7, 1867, near Glasgow, Scotland. His family immigrated to the United States in 1879 and settled in Philadelphia. Scott worked in Banana, Congo, under the International Missionary Alliance in 1891, but left the Congo because of ill health and went to London. He founded the Africa Inland Mission* as a nondenominational venture in 1895, went to East Africa with seven companions, and established his mission station at Nzawi, 250 miles inland from Mombasa. He founded three additional mission stations in 1896. Died December 4, 1896. *References*: *LC*; and Catherine S. Miller, *Peter Cameron Scott: The Unlocked Door* (London, 1955).

SCULL, GUY H(AMILTON) (1876–1920). Journalist and adventurer, born November 2, 1876, in Boston. Scull graduated from Harvard University. He joined Theodore Roosevelt's* "Rough Riders" and served in the Spanish-American War. He became a journalist and was a war correspondent in South Africa in 1900, and later in Venezuela, the Balkans, Manchuria, and Russia. He was in charge of the Buffalo Jones (see Charles Jesse Jones*) expedition to Africa in 1910, with the idea of lassoing wildlife and taking motion pictures of them, and wrote *Lassoing Wild Animals in Africa* (New York, 1911). He later served in the U.S. Secret Service on the Mexican border, was head of the police department in Nicaragua, and fifth deputy police commissioner of New York City from 1914 to 1917. He served in the Quartermaster's Corps and later in the U.S. Intelligence Department in Washington, D.C., during World War I. Died October 20, 1920, in New York City. *References*: Henry J. Case, comp., *Guy Hamilton Scull, Soldier, Writer, Explorer and War Correspondent* (New York, 1922); *Harvard University Class of 1898 25th Anniversary Report*; and *NYT*, October 30, 1920.

SEABROOK, WILLIAM B(UEHLER) (1886–1945). Author, born February 22, 1886, in Westminster, Maryland. Seabrook graduated from Newberry College (S.C.). He worked for the *Augusta Chronicle* and the *Augusta Journal* and founded the Lewis-Seabrook Advertising Agency. He served in the American Field Service as an ambulance driver during World War I, moved to New York after the war, and worked for the *New York Times*. He went to the Ivory Coast in 1930 and reported his experience in *Jungle Days* (New York, 1931), a lurid and fanciful account of French West Africa, widely read and widely denounced by scholars. He also traveled to Timbuctu and wrote *The White Monk of Timbuctoo* (New York, 1934). He later became a free-lance writer, living near Rhinebeck, New York, and wrote an autobiography, *No Hiding Place* (Philadelphia, 1942). Died September 20, 1945, in Rhinebeck, New York. *References*: *CB* 1940; *DLB*; *NYT*, September 21, 1945; Marjorie Worthington, *The Strange World of Willie Seabrook* (New York, 1966); and *WWWA*.

SEARS, (PHILIP) MASON (1899–1973). Government official, born December 29, 1899, in Boston. Sears graduated from Harvard University. He served in the army during World War I and in the navy during World War II. He was a representative and a senator in the Massachusetts legislature from 1935 to 1948, United States representative to the Trusteeship Council of the United Nations from 1953 to 1960, and president of the council in 1955–1956. He was a member of the United Nations visiting missions to West Africa and East Africa in 1954, delegate to the silver jubilee of the Emperor of Ethiopia in Addis Ababa in 1955, delegate to the independence celebration of Ghana in 1957, special ambassador to the independence celebration of Cameroon in 1960, and ambassador and chairman of the United Nations mission to the East African trust territories in

1960. Died December 14, 1973, in Boston. His memoirs, *Years of High Purpose: From Trusteeship to Nationhood* (Washington, D.C., 1980) were published posthumously. *References*: *NYT*, December 15, 1973; and *WWWA*.

SELBY, PAUL (1877–1940). Big-game photographer and mining engineer, born August 1, 1877, in San Francisco, and grew up in Los Gatos and Oakland, California. Selby graduated from the School of Mines of the University of California at Berkeley. He came to South Africa in 1902 and held posts in various gold mines on the Witwatersrand. He was general manager of Robinson Gold Mines from 1911 to 1914, and of the G. M. Ferriera Deep Gold Mine, the deepest gold mine in the world, from 1914 until his retirement in 1930. He became prominent for his big-game photography, using cameras that he designed himself, and spent one month each year from 1917 to 1923 photographing big game at the Sabi Game Reserve in Northern Transvaal. His efforts in game protection led to the creation in 1926, by an Act of Parliament, of the Kruger National Park in South Africa. Died October 23, 1940, in Johannesburg, South Africa. *Reference*: *SADNB*.

SEWALL, WILLIAM G(ILMAN) ("BILLY") (1874–1941). Settler, born March 11, 1874, in Boston. Sewall graduated from Harvard University. He went to British East Africa in 1906 and became a big-game hunter. He settled in British East Africa and acquired a rubber plantation and a wheat farm, being the first to attempt the growing of wheat in British East Africa. In 1907 he joined in starting the Boma Trading Company to open up the trade between Abyssinia and British East Africa; he made a reconaissance safari from Djibouti to British East Africa in 1908 and opened up the trade route from Nairobi to the Ethiopian border and beyond. He served as a trooper in the East African Mounted Rifles until 1915 and later in the Ambulance Corps with the French Army; he was commissioned in the British Army during World War I. Died July 14, 1941, in New York City. *Reference*: *Harvard University Class of 1897, 50th Anniversary Report*.

SEYMOUR, LOUIS IRVING (1860–1900). Mechanical engineer, born December 23, 1860, in Whitney Point, New York. Seymour learned his engineering on the job. He came to South Africa in 1889 and was a mechanical engineer for the De Beers Consolidated Mines Limited in Kimberley until 1893. He was then managing director of Fraser & Chalmers works at Firth on the Thames in England from 1893 to 1896. He returned to South Africa as a consulting engineer to the firm of Hermann Eckstein & Company and chief mechanical engineer of the Rand Mines in Johannesburg. At the outbreak of the South African War, he organized the Railway Pioneer Regiment and became its second in command. Killed in action, June 14, 1900, at Sand River Bridge, near Virginia, Orange Free State, South Africa. *References*: *DSAB* 1; and *SESA*.

SEYS, JOHN (1799–1872). Missionary and diplomat, born March 30, 1799, on the island of Saint Croix, West Indies. Seys was ordained and came to the United States in 1829 and was a pastor at Ogdenburg, New York. He went to Liberia in 1834 and was superintendent of the missions of the Methodist Episcopal Church* in West Africa until 1844. He founded and edited the newspaper *Africa's Luminary*. In 1839 he headed a faction that challenged the authority of newly appointed governor Thomas Buchanan. He lost in the rivalry but continued to be active in religious and secular affairs in Liberia. He returned to the United States in 1841; he was a pastor in Wilkes-Barre, Pennsylvania, in 1842–1843, but went back to Liberia in 1843, and became the United States agent for recaptured Africans. He was minister resident and consul general in Liberia from 1866 to 1870, when he returned to the United States. *References*: John Seys Papers, Drew University Library; Yale University Divinity School Library; *African Repository* 48 (1872): 114–16; *Huberich*; and *Minutes of the Annual Conferences of the Methodist Church for the Year 1872* (New York, 1872), pp. 107–8.

SHALER, MILLARD KING (1880–1942). Geologist, born July 26, 1880, in Ellsworth, Kansas. Shaler graduated from the University of Kansas. He served with the United States Geological Survey in 1901–1902 and from 1904 to 1907. He was a geologist with the American expedition to the Belgian Congo from 1908 to 1910, joined the Société Internationale Forestière et Minière du Congo, and was later its chief engineer. He was the manager for the company in Brussels, Belgium, from 1912 until his death. During World War I, he was involved in relief work in Belgium and was secretary of the American Commission for Relief in Belgium in London. After the invasion of Belgium in 1940, he established his office in Portugal but moved to the Belgian Congo in 1941. Died December 11, 1942, in Cape Town, South Africa. *References*: *Economic Geology* 38 (1943): 264–65; *GSA Proceedings* 1944, pp. 305–7; *NCAB* 32:293; and *NYT*, December 16, 1942.

SHANTZ, HOMER LEROY (1876–1958). Botanist and agriculturist, born January 24, 1876, in Kent County, Michigan. Shantz graduated from Colorado College (Colorado Springs) and the University of Nebraska. He was a plant physiologist at the United States Department of Agriculture from 1910 to 1926, professor of botany at the University of Illinois from 1926 to 1928, president of the University of Arizona from 1928 to 1936, and chief of the division of wildlife management of the United States Forest Service from 1936 to 1944. He conducted extensive field research in Africa, was an agricultural explorer in the Smithsonian African expedition of 1919–1920, and a member of the African Education Commission* to East Africa in 1923–1924. He was coauthor (with C. F. Marbut*) of *Vegetation and Soils of Africa* (New York, 1923). He was principal investigator of the Arizona African expedition in 1956–1957. Died June 23, 1958, in Rapid City, South Dakota. *References*: Homer Leroy Shantz Papers,

Special Collections Division, University of Arizona Library, Tucson, Ariz.; *Agronomy Journal* 50 (December 1958): 777; *Association of American Geographers Annals* 51 (December 1964): 392–94; *Geographical Journal* 49 (April 1959): 278–80; *NYT*, June 24, 1958; and *WWWA*.

SHELDON, MAY FRENCH. *See* FRENCH-SHELDON, MAY

SHEPPARD, WILLIAM HENRY (1865–1927). Missionary, born March 8, 1865, in Waynesboro, Virginia. Sheppard attended Hampton Institute and Stillman Institute, and was licensed to preach in 1888. He was a pastor in Atlanta from 1888 to 1890. He was a missionary under the Board of Foreign Missions of the Presbyterian Church in the United States* at the American Presbyterian Congo Mission (APCM)* in Luebo, Kasai region, Congo Free State, from 1890 to 1893 and at Ibanj, among the Bakeba, from 1894 to 1910. He defended the interests of the natives and exposed the atrocities of the government of the Congo Free State. Along with William M. Morrison,* he was sued in 1906 by the Kassai Company for allegedly libeling the company, but was acquitted in the trial. He wrote *Presbyterian Pioneers in Congo* (Richmond, Va., 1917), and an autobiography, *Missionary to the Congo* (Nashville, Tenn., 1924). He was a pastor in Louisville, Kentucky, from 1912 to 1926. Died November 25, 1927, in Louisville. His wife, **LUCY GANTT SHEPPARD** (1867–1941), a missionary, was born February 21, 1867, in Tuscaloosa, Alabama. Lucy Gantt graduated from Talladega (Ala.) College. She was a missionary at the American Presbyterian Congo Mission (APCM)* in Luebo, Kasai Province, Congo Free State, from 1894 until 1910. She opened the first school there. She returned to the United States in 1910 and lived in Louisville, Kentucky. *References*: William H. Sheppard Papers, The Historical Foundation of the Presbyterian and Reformed Churches, Inc., Montreat, N.C.; William H. Sheppard Learning Resources Center, Stillman College, Tuscaloosa, Ala.; Harold G. Cureau, "William H. Sheppard: Missionary to the Congo, and Collector of African Art," *JNH* 67 (1982): 340–52; Julia L. Kellersberger, *Lucy Gantt Sheppard, Shepherdess of His Sheep on Two Continents* (Atlanta, 1938?); Larryetta L. Schall, "William H. Sheppard: Fighter for African Rights," in *Stony the Road: Chapters in the History of Hampton Institute*, ed. Keith L. Schall (Charlottesville, Va., 1977); Stanley Shaloff, "William Henry Sheppard: Congo Pioneer," in *Education for Life in a Multicultural Society*, ed. Albert Berrian (Hampton, Va., 1968); Walter L. Williams, "William Henry Sheppard, Afro-American Missionary in the Congo, 1890–1910," in *Black Americans and the Missionary Movement in Africa*, ed. Sylvia M. Jacobs (Westport, Conn., 1982), pp. 135–53; and *WWCR*.

SHERMAN, REGINALD A. (1838–1894). Colonist, soldier, and government official, born in Savannah, Georgia. Sherman immigrated to Liberia in 1853. He became a general of the army and fought in the third and fourth Grebo wars. He was also secretary of the navy and secretary of war and a member of the executive committee that overthrew President Edward James Roye* in 1871. Died August 1894, in Liverpool, England.

SHUFELDT, MASON A(BERCROMBIE) (1852–1892). Naval officer and explorer, son of Robert Wilson Shufeldt,* born November 4, 1852, in Stamford, Connecticut. Shufeldt graduated from the United States Naval Academy in 1873 and was commissioned ensign in the United States Navy in 1874. He served aboard the *Enterprise* in 1883–1884 and was sent on a special mission by the U.S. Navy Department in 1884 to explore Madagascar and to collect information on the political and social status of the people and on the island's natural resources. He explored the interior of Madagascar, was well received by the queen of the island, and later wrote a series of articles for *The United Service* during 1885 and an article in the March 1891 issue of *Cosmopolitan Magazine*. He resigned from the navy in 1890, was employed by the United States National Museum in 1890, and served as special commissioner of the Chicago World Columbian Exposition to South Africa. Died December 2, 1892, in Cape Town, South Africa. *Reference*: Mason A. Shufeldt Papers, in Papers of Robert W. Shufeldt, Manuscript Division, Library of Congress.

SHUFELDT, ROBERT WILSON (1822–1895). Naval officer, born February 21, 1822, in Red Hook, New York. Shufeldt was appointed midshipman in 1839, resigned in 1854, and was captain of a steamship in the merchant service, consul in Cuba from 1861 to 1863, and a special agent to Mexico in 1862. He was recommissioned in the navy in 1862 and served during the Civil War. He went on a combined diplomatic and commercial mission commanding the *Ticonderoga** from 1878 to 1880 and cruised along the coasts of Africa and through the Indian Ocean in 1878–1879. He went to China in 1881 as a naval attaché and negotiated a treaty with China in 1882, was president of the U.S. Naval Advisory Board and superintendent of the Naval Observatory from 1882 until his retirement in 1884 with the rank of rear admiral. Died November 7, 1895, in Washington, D.C. *References*: Robert W. Shufeldt Papers, Manuscript Division, Library of Congress; *ACAB*; *DAB*; *DADH*; Frederick C. Drake, *The Empire of the Seas: A Biography of Admiral Robert Wilson Shufeldt, USN* (Honolulu, 1984); *NCAB* 4:293; Thomas J. Noer, "Commander Robert W. Shufeldt and America's South African Strategy," *American Neptune* 34 (1974): 81–88; *NYT*, November 8, 1895; *WAMB*; and *WWWA*.

SIBLEY, JAMES L(ONGSTREET) (1883–1929). Educator, born June 1883, in Juniper, Georgia. Sibley taught in a public school in Georgia, in the United States government service in the Philippines, and at the State Normal School in Jacksonville, Alabama, and became state agent for Negro rural schools in Alabama in 1913. He was an educational adviser in Liberia from 1925 until his death and a representative of the Advisory Committee on Education in Liberia, an umbrella organization of missionary and philanthropic organizations to re-organize the schools of missionary societies in Liberia. He prepared a system of schoolbooks for Liberian schools and was one of the founders of the Booker Washington Institute of Liberia*. He became director of education to the Liberian government in 1928. He was coauthor (with D. Westermann) of *Liberia—Old and New* (Garden City, N.Y., 1928). Died June 28, 1929, in Monrovia, during a yellow fever outbreak. *Reference*: Charles W. Dabney, *Universal Education in the South* 2 (New York, 1969), 521–26.

SIERRA LEONE EMIGRATION SCHEME (1794–1795). In 1794–1795, the Providence African Society sent James Mackenzie, one of its officers, to negotiate arrangements for the settlement of black Americans in Sierra Leone. The scheme was not successful. *Reference*: George E. Brooks, Jr., ''The Providence African Society's Sierra Leone Emigration Scheme, 1794–1795: Prologue to the African Colonization Movement,'' *IJAHS* 7 (1974): 183–202.

SIMONTON, IDA VERA (1870?–1931). Author, lecturer, and traveler, born in Pittsburgh. Simonton studied in London and Paris. She went alone to West Africa in 1906 and lived among the Africans of the French Congo and other parts of Africa for three years. She also traveled in Africa, and her novel *Hell's Playground* (New York, 1912) was based on her impressions. She was later a staff lecturer on Africa for the Board of Education of New York City and for various colleges and clubs. Died July 5, 1931, in New York City. *References*: *NYT*, July 6, 1931; and *WWWA*.

SIMS, DAVID HENRY (1886–1965). Clergyman, born July 18, 1886, in Alabama. Sims graduated from Georgia State College, Oberlin College, Oberlin Theological Seminary, and the University of Chicago, and was ordained in 1910. He was a pastor in Painsville, Ohio; Narragansett Pier, Rhode Island; he taught at Morris Brown College and was its pastor; he became dean at Allen University in 1917, and was later its president. He was elected a bishop in 1932 and was bishop of the African Methodist Episcopal Church* in South Africa from 1932 to 1936. He was later a bishop in Alabama. He was expelled from the episcopacy in 1946 but was restored in 1956. He became a bishop in West Africa in 1960. *References*: *EWM*; and *Leete*.

SIMSON, LESLIE (1867–1939). Mining engineer and big-game hunter, born October 8, 1867, in San Francisco. Simson graduated from the University of California School of Mines (Berkeley, Calif.). He was an assayer for the Selby Smelting Company. He joined the staff of John Hays Hammond* and came to Johannesburg in 1895. He then joined Deep Mining and became superintendent engineer of the mining interests of the Consolidated Gold Fields Company, Limited. Following his mother's death in 1910, he resigned and returned to the United States. He then returned to Africa and traveled widely, devoting himself to big-game hunting, and collected the animals for display in the African hall of the California Academy of Sciences in San Francisco. He also provided the funding to construct that wing in the museum. Died October 30, 1939, in Berkeley, California. *Reference*: David D. Oliphant, Jr., *Backyard Bandits, including California Raccoons and Other Exciting Patio Visitors* (Healdsburg, Calif., 1968), ch. 7.

SKINNER, ELLIOTT PERCIVAL (1924-   ). Anthropologist and diplomat, born June 20, 1924, in Port of Spain, Trinidad, West Indies. Skinner became a U.S. citizen in 1943 and served in the army during World War II. He graduated from New York and Columbia universities. He was assistant and associate professor of anthropology at New York University from 1959 to 1963, associate professor of anthropology at Columbia University from 1963 to 1966, and professor at Columbia after 1969. He conducted fieldwork in Sierra Leone in 1942 and in West Africa from 1955 to 1957 and in 1964–1965. He wrote *The Mossi of Upper Volta: An Analysis of the Political Development of a Sudanese People* (Stanford, 1964), and *African Urban Life: The Transformation of Ouagadougou* (Princeton, 1974). He was involved in Operation Crossroads Africa (see Crossroads Africa*) from 1958 to 1966 and led a group to the Ivory Coast in 1960. He was ambassador to Upper Volta from 1966 to 1969. He edited *Beyond Constructive Engagement: United States Policy Toward Africa* (New York, 1986). *References*: Elliott Percival Skinner Papers, Lyndon B. Johnson Library, Austin, Texas; *CA*; and *WWBA*.

SKINNER, ROBERT P(EET) (1866–1960). Diplomat, born February 24, 1866, in Massillon, Ohio. Skinner was owner and editor of the *Massillon Evening Independent* and served on the staff of the *New York World*. A friend of President William McKinley, he became consul in Marseilles in 1897 and was consul general from 1901 until 1908. He proposed that a diplomatic mission be sent to Abyssinia and in 1903 was appointed commissioner to negotiate a commercial treaty with Emperor Menelik of Abyssinia. He described his mission in *Abyssinia To-day; an Account of the First Mission Sent by the American Government to the Court of the King of Kings (1903–1904)* (London, 1906). He was consul general in Hamburg from 1908 to 1914; consul general in Berlin in 1914; consul in London from 1914 to 1924; consul in Paris from 1924 to 1926; minister to Greece from 1926 to 1931; minister to Latvia, Estonia and Lithuania from 1931 to 1933; and ambassador to Turkey from 1933 to 1936. Died July 1, 1960, in Belfast, Maine. *References*: Robert P. Skinner, "Recollections of Life in the Foreign Service of the United States," MS in private hands; Harold G. Marcus, "A Note on the First United States Diplomatic Mission to Ethiopia in 1903," *Ethiopia Observer* 7 (1963): 165–68; Bernard C. Natly, *The Diplomatic Mission to Abyssinia, 1903* (Washington, 1959); *NCAB* B:356; *NYT*, July 3, 1960; *OAB*; Richard Pankhurst, "Robert Skinner's Unpublished Account of the First American Diplomatic Expedition to Ethiopia,'' *Ethiopia Observer* 13 (1970): 31–36; and *WWWA*.

SKIPWITH, PEYTON (1803–1849). Colonist and stone mason, born a slave. He was a slave of General John Hartwell Cocke in Bremo Bluff, Virginia, and was emancipated with his family in 1833 on the condition that they all immigrate to Liberia. He went to Liberia in 1833, was involved in farming and trade, served in the militia, and took part in at least two military campaigns. Died October 14, 1849. His letters were published in *"Dear Master" Letters of a Slave Family*, ed. Randall M. Miller (Ithaca, N.Y., 1978) and *Slaves No More: Letters from Liberia 1833–1869*, ed. Bell I. Wiley (Lexington, Ky., 1980), ch. 2.

SLOCUM, CLARENCE RICE (1868–1912). Consul, born June 22, 1868, in Brooklyn, New York. Slocum attended Williams College. He was consul in Warsaw from 1903 to 1905 and in Weimar, Germany, in 1905–1906. He was consul general in Boma, Congo Free State, in 1906–1907 and was a devastating critic of the Congo Free State government. He was later consul in Zittau, Germany, in 1907–1908 and in Fiume, Austria-Hungary from 1908 until his death. Died February 25, 1912, in Fiume. *Reference*: *WWWA*.

SMITH, ALBERT E. (1875–1958). Businessman and movie photographer, born June 4, 1875, in Faversham, Kent, England. His family immigrated to the United States in 1888 and settled in New York City. Smith became an entertainer and was involved in show business. He was one of the founders of the Vitagraph Company in 1897 and served as its business manager. He filmed the South African War for Vitagraph and wrote of his experiences (with Phil A. Koury) in *Two Reels and a Crank* (Garden City, N.Y., 1952). Died August 1, 1958, in Hollywood, California. *References*: Albert E. Smith Papers, Special Collections, University of California Library, Los Angeles; *NYT*, August 30, 1958; and Anthony Slide, *The Big V: A History of the Vitagraph Company*, rev. ed. (Metuchen, N.J., 1987), ch. 3.

SMITH, AMANDA (BERRY) (1837–1915). Evangelist and missionary, born a slave January 23, 1837, in Long Green, Maryland. She became an evangelist in the African Methodist Episcopal Church* in Philadelphia in 1870 and was a missionary in Monrovia from 1882 to 1890, when she returned to the United States. She wrote *An Autobiography* (Chicago, 1893). Died March 5, 1915, in Seabreeze, Florida. *References*: M. Cadbury, *The Life of Amanda Smith: The African Sybil, the Christian Saint* (Birmingham, Ala., 1916); Sylvia G. L. Dannett, *Profiles of Negro Womanhood 1619–1900* (New York, 1964), pp. 146–49; and *NYT*, March 6, 1915.

SMITH, A(RTHUR) DONALDSON (1864–1939). Physician and explorer, born April 27, 1864, in Andalusia, Pennsylvania. Smith graduated from the University of Pennsylvania and studied at Harvard, Johns Hopkins, and Heidelberg universities. He inherited a fortune in 1892. He went on a big-game hunt in Somaliland and traveled in the country between the Somali coast and Lake Rudolph in 1894–1895 under the auspices of the Royal Geographic Society and with scientific staff provided by the British Museum. He described it in *Through Unknown African Countries: the First Expedition from Somaliland to Lake Lamu* (New York, 1897; reprinted, 1969). He returned to Africa in 1899–1900 and explored the territory between Lake Rudolph and the Nile. Died February 18, 1939, in Philadelphia. *References*: P. J. Imperato, "Arthur Donaldson Smith, MD: Physician, Explorer, Naturalist, and Diplomat," *New York State Journal of Medicine* 87 (1987): 90–105, 161–76, 210–25, 334–51, 436–65; P. J. Imperato, *Arthur Donaldson Smith and the Exploration of Lake Rudolf* (Lake Success, N.Y., 1987); *NCAB* 13:608; *NYT*, February 21, 1939; and *WWWA*.

SMITH, CHARLES EDWIN (1852- ?). Missionary, born July 1, 1852, in Conway, Massachusetts. Smith attended Southern Baptist Theological Seminary. He was a missionary under the Foreign Mission Board of the Southern Baptist Convention* in Africa from 1884 until 1909, serving in Lagos until 1888 and in Ogbomosho until his retirement in 1909 due to ill health. He founded in Ogbomosho a theological seminary in 1901. *Reference*: *ESB*.

SMITH, CHARLES EUGENE (1890-). Missionary, born in Franklin County, Iowa. Smith graduated from Iowa State College (Ames) and Kennedy School of Missions and was ordained in 1922. He was missionary under the American Baptist Foreign Mission Society* in the Belgian Congo from 1923 until 1967, stationed in Léopoldville and at the Kikongo mission station, where he introduced agricultural education. *Reference*: Charles Eugene Smith Papers, University of Oregon Library, Salem, Oregon.

SMITH, CHARLES SPENCER (1852–1923). Clergyman, born March 16, 1852, in Colborne, Ontario, Canada. Smith graduated from Meharry Medical College (Nashville, Tenn.) and was ordained in 1872. He was a member of the Alabama House of Representatives from 1874 to 1876. He visited West and Southwest Africa in 1894 and wrote *Glimpses of Africa, West and SouthWest Coast, Containing the Author's Impressions and Observations During a Voyage of Six Thousand Miles from Sierra Leone, St. Paul de Loanda and Return, Including the Rio del Rey and Cameroons River, and the Congo River, from Its Mouth to Matadi* (Nashville, Tenn., 1895). He was elected bishop of the African Methodist Episcopal Church* in 1900 and was bishop in South Africa from 1904 to 1906. He was later presiding bishop in Michigan, Canada, and the West Indies. Died February 1, 1923, in Detroit, Michigan. *References*: *EWM*; *WWCR*; and *WWWA*.

SMITH, EZEKIEL EZRA (1852–1933). Clergyman and diplomat, born a slave May 23, 1852, in Duplin County, North Carolina. Smith graduated from Shaw University and was ordained in 1879. He was a pastor in Fayetteville, North Carolina, and principal of a school in Goldsboro, North Carolina, from 1879 to 1883; he became principal of the State Colored Normal School in Fayetteville in 1883. He was minister to Liberia from 1888 to 1890. He returned to Liberia in 1892 as an agent of the American Colonization Society.* *References*: *ACAB*; and *Christmas*.

SMITH, HAMILTON (1840–1900). Mining engineer, born July 5, 1840, in Louisville, Kentucky. Smith had little formal education and worked in the Cannelton Coal Mines (Cannelton, Ind.) and in collieries in Kentucky and Indiana until 1869. He then went to the West and was engineer and manager of the Triunfo Gold Mine in California and North Bloomfield Gravel and Milton Gold Mines. He helped found the Vulcan Powder Works. In the late 1870s he moved to New York and became consulting engineer of the El Callo Gold Mines in Venezuela. He moved to London in 1885, was adviser to the Rothschild Group, and in 1886, jointly with Edmund G. de Crano,* established the Exploration Company Limited. He was brought to Kimberley by Alfred Beit in 1892 to advise on the proposed purchase of the French Diamond Mining Company and on the gold prospects in the Eastern Transvaal. His recommendation ultimately made possible the establishment of De Beers Consolidated Mines. He came back to South Africa in 1895 to advise on prospects in the Witwatersrand. He returned to the United States in 1895. Died July 4, 1900, in Durham, New Hampshire. *References*: *DAB*; *DASB 4*; *SADNB*; and *WWWA*.

SMITH, HERBERT (1880–1954). Missionary, born December 3, 1880, in Rochester, Kent, England, and came to the United States in 1903. Smith attended Queen's Bible College and graduated from Bethany (W.Va.) College. He was a missionary under the United Christian Missionary Society* (Disciples of Christ) in the Belgian Congo from 1909 until his retirement in 1946. He established a mission station at Lotumbe on the Momboyo River in 1910, was transferred in 1912, established a mission station at Bolenge, and started the Congo Christian Institute, a training school for evangelists and teachers. He wrote *The Call of the Congo* (Cincinnati, 1924) and *Fifty Years in the Congo: Disciples of Christ at the Equator* (Indianapolis, 1949). Died May 11, 1954, in Bloomington, Indiana. *Reference*: *TWTA*.

SMITH, JAMES SKIVRING (ca. 1825- ?). Physician and colonist, born in Charleston, South Carolina. Smith immigrated to Liberia in 1833. He was educated by James W. Lugenbeel,* came back to the United States, and studied at the Pittsfield Medical Institute (Mass.). He was secretary of state in Liberia from 1856 to 1860, senator in 1868–1869, and vice president in 1870–1871. He became president in 1871, when Edward James Roye* was forced out of office and served until 1872. He was superintendent of Grand Bassa County from 1874 to 1884. Died after 1892. *Reference*: *Huberich*.

SMITHSONIAN AFRICAN EXPEDITION (1919–1920). An expedition to Africa headed by Edmund C. Heller* in conjunction with the Universal Film Manufacturing Company, which filmed the expedition. *Reference*: *Smithsonian Institution Miscellaneous Collections* 72, no. 6 (1921): 21–31.

SMITHSONIAN-CHRYSLER EXPEDITION TO AFRICA (1926). An expedition to East Africa to collect live animals for the National Zoological Park in Washington, D.C. It was financed by Walter P. Chrysler, and headed by William M. Mann.* *Reference*: *Annual Report of the Board of Regents of the Smithsonian Institution . . . 1927* (Washington, D.C., 1928), pp. 7–9.

SMYTH, JOHN HENRY (1844–1908). Lawyer and diplomat, born free, July 14, 1844, near Richmond, Virginia, and grew up in Philadelphia. Smyth attended Pennsylvania Academy of Fine Arts and then resided in England from 1865 to 1869, trying to be an actor. He graduated from Howard University Law School and practiced law in Raleigh, North Carolina, from 1873 to 1877. Active in campaign efforts for the Republican Party, he was appointed minister resident and consul general in Liberia from 1878 until 1881 and from 1882 until 1885. He criticized American-Liberian discrimination against Africans and helped spark a Liberian reform movement in the 1880s. He also supported Liberia's expansionist policies. He later engaged in real estate in Washington, D.C., was editor of the *Reformer* in Richmond, Virginia, and in charge of the Virginia Manual Labor School (Hanover, Va.) from 1899 until his death. Died September 5, 1908, in Hanover, Virginia. *References*: *DAB*; *DADH*; *NCAB* 12:526; Walter L. Williams, "Nineteenth Century Pan-Africanist: John Henry Smyth, United States Minister to Liberia, 1878–1885," *JHN* 63 (1978): 18–25.

SNOW, HENRY A(DELBERT) ("DEL") (1869–1927). Natural history collector and big-game hunter, born December 15, 1869, in Santa Cruz, California. Snow was a laborer in a stove manufacturing company in Newark, California, until 1903 when he became involved in several business ventures. He became a successful contractor and established a real estate business and a Ford automobile agency in Newark. He also managed the Newark (California) Giants. He went to Kenya in 1919 to film "Hunting Big Game in Africa" (released in 1922) and was the first to use a motor vehicle to hunt animals. He acquired specimens for a natural history museum in Oakland, which he proposed to establish, and which was duly opened to house his specimens. Died July 28, 1927, in Oakland, California. *References*: *Oakland Tribune*, July 28, 1927; Keene Sumner, "The Snow Family's Adventures Hunting Wild Animals," *American Magazine* 96 (December 1923): 12–15; and Michael R. Waiczis, *Henry A. Snow and the Snow Museum of Natural History* (Oakland, Calif., 1983).

SNYDER, DEWITT C(LINTON) (1859–1919). Medical missionary, born in New York State. Snyder was a pharmacist in Tampa, Florida. He was a missionary under the Board of Foreign Missions of the Presbyterian Church in the United States* in the American Presbyterian Congo Mission (APCM)* from 1893 to 1902, when he returned to the United States because of his wife's illness. He prepared a Tshikete primer. He was a pastor in Brooklyn, New York; Paterson, New Jersey; and Staten Island, New York. Died December 2, 1919, in New York City. *Reference: Ministerial Directory of the Presbyterian Church U.S. 1861–1941* (Austin, Texas, 1942).

SOUTHARD, ADDISON E. (1884–1970). Consul, born October 18, 1884, in Louisville, Kentucky. Southard graduated from Lebanon University and Santo Tomas University in Manila, Philippines. He was an officer of the Philippine government from 1908 to 1915. He entered the consular service in 1911, and served in Aden, Abyssinia, Somaliland, and Eritrea. He did intelligence work for the United States in Persia in 1918; he was consul in Jerusalem from 1920 to 1922, chief of the consular commercial office from 1922 to 1926, and consul general in Singapore in 1926. He was minister to Abyssinia and consul general in Addis Ababa, Ethiopia, from 1927 to 1934, and described his impressions of Abyssinia in the June 1931 issue of the *National Geographic Magazine*. He was consul general and counselor in Stockholm in 1934–1935 and in Paris in 1936–1937 and consul general in Hong Kong and Macao from 1938 to 1941. He was interned by the Japanese and returned to the United States in 1942. Died February 11, 1970. *Reference: WWWA*.

SOUTHERN BAPTIST CONVENTION: FOREIGN MISSION BOARD. Founded in 1845, it began missionary work in Liberia in 1846, but did not support any missionaries there until 1960. It began missionary work in Nigeria in 1850 and in Sierra Leone from 1857 until 1875. Missionary work in other African countries began after World War II. *References*: Southern Baptist Convention, Foreign Mission Board Archives, Historical Commission of the Southern Baptist Convention, Nashville, Tenn.; Baptist Historical Collection, James P. Boyce Centennial Library, Southern Baptist Theological Seminary, Louisville, Ky.; Baker J. Cauthen, *Advance: A History of Southern Baptist Foreign Missions* (Nashville, Tenn., 1970); Louis M. Duval, *Baptist Missions in Nigeria* (Richmond, Va., 1928); and George W. Sadler, *A Century in Nigeria* (Nashville, Tenn., 1950); Davis L. Saunder, "A History of Baptists in Central and Southern Africa," Ph.D. diss., Southern Baptist Theological Seminary, 1973.

SPARHAWK, AUGUSTUS (fl. 1879–1881). Trader. Sparhawk was an agent for the firm of John Bertram of Salem in Zanzibar. He joined the service of Henry Morton Stanley* in the Congo in 1879 as an agent of the African International Association. He was in charge of constructing trading stations on the lower Congo and became commander of the Vivi station. He left the Congo in December 1881 because of illness. *Reference*: *BCB* 1.

SPENCER, JOHN HATHAWAY (1907-   ). Legal adviser, born September 19, 1907, in Rome, Italy, to American parents. Spencer graduated from Grinnell College, Harvard University, and the University of Paris, and studied at the University of Berlin. He was an adviser on international law to the Ethiopian Ministry of Foreign Affairs, Addis Ababa, in 1936. He was Far Eastern affairs officer in the U.S. Department of State from 1936 to 1938, officer in the U.S. Department of Justice in 1941–1942 and served in the U.S. navy during World War II. He returned to Ethiopia in 1943 as principal adviser to the Ethiopian Ministry of Foreign Affairs and served until 1961; he also assisted in drafting the Ethiopian Constitution of 1951. He was later professor of international law and diplomacy at Fletcher School of Law and Diplomacy in Tufts University (Medford, Mass.) from 1960 to 1971. He wrote *Ethiopia at Bay: A Personal Account of the Haile Selassie Years* (Algonac, Mich., 1984) and *Ethiopia, the Horn of Africa, and U. S. Policy* (Cambridge, Mass., 1977). *Reference*: *CA*.

SPRINGER, HELEN EMILY CHAPMAN (1868–1949). Medical missionary, wife of John McKendree Springer,* born April 21, 1868, in New Sharon, Maine. Springer graduated from the Woman's Medical College (Philadelphia). She was a missionary under the Board of Foreign Missions of the Methodist Episcopal Church* in Rhodesia from 1901 to 1910. She moved with her husband to the Congo Free State, and they walked across Central Africa in 1907 to dramatize the needs of the African peoples. She then resided at Mulungwishi, Belgian Congo, where she helped convert three spoken languages to writing and translated parts of the Bible into several African languages. She wrote *Snap Shots from Sunny Africa* (New York, 1909) and *Camp Fires in the Congo* (Cambridge, Mass., 1928). Died August 23, 1949, in Mulungwishi, Katanga, Belgian Congo. *References*: *BCB* 7; *EWM*; *NYT*, August 26, 1949; and John M. Springer, *I Love the Trail: A Sketch of the Life of Helen Emily Springer* (New York, 1952).

SPRINGER, JOHN MCKENDREE (1873–1963). Missionary, born September 7, 1873, in Cataract, Wisconsin. Springer graduated from Northwestern University and the Garrett Biblical Institute and was ordained in 1901. He was a missionary under the Board of Foreign Missions of the Methodist Episcopal Church* and superintendent of the Umtali industrial mission in Southern Rhodesia from 1901 to 1906. With his wife, Helen Emily Chapman Springer,* he crossed Central Africa on foot from Umtali, Southern Rhodesia, to Malange, Angola, in 1907, to dramatize the needs of the African peoples. He founded the Congo mission in 1910 and was its superintendent from 1910 to 1921 and from 1923 to 1936. He was in charge of the Mutumbara station and superintendent of the Southern Rhodesia district from 1921 to 1923. He was elected missionary bishop for Africa in 1936 and served until his retirement in 1944, then continued his missionary work at the Springer Institute, Mulungwishi, Belgian Congo, until 1959. He wrote *Pioneering in the Congo* (New York, 1916), *The Heart of Central Africa: Mineral Wealth and Missionary Opportunity* (New York, 1909), *Christian Conquests in the Congo* (New York, 1927), and a biography of his wife, *I Love the Trail: A Sketch of the Life of Helen Emily Springer*. Died December 2, 1963, in Penney Farms, Florida. *References*: *EWM*; *Leete*; *NYT*, December 8, 1963; and *WWWA*.

STALLINGS, LAURENCE (TUCKER) (1894–1968). Playwright, journalist, and author, born November 25, 1894, in Macon, Georgia. Stallings graduated from Wake Forest College (N.C.) and Georgetown University. He became a reporter on the *Atlanta Journal* in 1915 and served with the marines during World War I. He worked for the *Washington Times* from 1920 to 1922, and the *New York Herald* from 1922 to 1926; he was editor of a literary column for the *New York World* and literary editor of the *New York Sun*. He collaborated with Maxwell Anderson on the play *What Price Glory?* (produced in 1924). He was editor-in-chief of Fox Movietone System from 1934 to 1936; he led a Fox Movietone News expedition to Ethiopia in 1935–1936, sponsored also by the North American Newspaper Alliance and the *New York Times*. He was later literary editor of *American Mercury* and served in World War II. Died February 28, 1968, in Brentwood, California. *References*: Joan T. Brittain, *Laurence Stallings* (Boston, 1975); *DLB*; *NCAB* 55:123; and *NYT*, February 29, 1968.

STANLEY, HENRY MORTON (1841–1904). Explorer and journalist, born John Rowlands, January 31, 1841, in Denbigh, Wales. Stanley came to the United States in 1858 and was adopted by a New Orleans merchant who gave him his name. He served in the Civil War and later became a newspaper reporter. He began working for the *New York Herald* in 1868. The newspaper sent him on an expedition to Lake Tanganyika in 1871–1872 to find David Livingstone. From 1874 to 1877 he made an expedition from Zanzibar to the Atlantic coast of Africa and was the first white man to explore the Congo River. He made a systematic investigation of the Congo region from 1879 to 1884 while opening the interior of the Congo for King Leopold II of Belgium. He led the Emin Pasha rescue expedition from 1886 to 1889 and made a second crossing of Africa. He wrote *How I Found Livingstone* (New York, 1872); *My Kalulu* (New York, 1874); *Coomassie and Magdala* (New York, 1874); *Through the Dark Continent* (New York, 1878); *The Congo and the Founding of Its Free State* (New York, 1885); *In Darkest Africa* (New York, 1890); *My Dark Companions and Their Strange Stories* (London, 1893); and *Through South Africa* (New York, 1898). He settled in England and became a British subject in 1892. *The Autobiography of Henry Morton Stanley*, ed. Dorothy Stanley (Boston, 1909) was published posthumously. Died May 10, 1904, near Pirbright, Surrey, England. *References*: Norman R. Bennett, ed., *Stanley's Despatches to the New*

York Herald 1871–1872, 1874–1877 (Boston, 1970); *DAB*; Richard Hall, *Stanley: An Adventurer Explored* (Boston, 1975); Marcel Luwel, *Stanley* (Brussels, 1959); Albert Maurice, ed., *H. M. Stanley: Unpublished Letters* (London, 1957); *NCAB* 4:253; *NYT*, May 10, 1904; Richard Stanley and Alan Neame, eds., *The Exploration Diaries of H. M. Stanley* (London, 1961); and *WWWA*.

STARR, FREDERICK (1858–1933). Anthropologist, born September 2, 1858, in Auburn, New York. Starr graduated from Lafayette College (Easton, Pa.). He was professor of biology at Coe College (Cedar Rapids, Iowa) from 1883 to 1887, in charge of ethnology at the American Museum of Natural History from 1889 to 1891, and professor of geology and anthropology at Pomona College (Claremont, Calif.). He was assistant professor of anthropology at the University of Chicago from 1892 to 1895, associate professor there from 1895 to 1923, and curator of anthropology at the Walker Museum of the University of Chicago. He did fieldwork in ethnology and physical anthropology in Mexico, Japan, Korea, and the Philippines. He led an expedition into the Congo Free State in 1905–1906, investigated conditions there, and visited twenty-eight different tribes. He went to Liberia in 1912. He wrote *Congo Natives: An Ethnographic Album* (Chicago, 1912), *The Truth about the Congo* (Chicago, 1907), and *Liberia: Description, History, Problems* (Chicago, 1913). Died August 14, 1933, in Tokyo, Japan. *References*: *DAB*; B. Berkeley Miller, "Anthropology and Institutionalization: Frederick Starr at the University of Chicago, 1892–1923," *The Kroeber Anthropological Society Papers* 51–52 (Spring and Fall 1975): 49–60; *NCAB* 13:115; *NYT*, August 15, 1933; and *WWWA*.

STARR, GEORGE W(ILLIAM) (1862–1940). Mining engineer, born January 30, 1862, in San Francisco, California. Starr attended Episcopal Missionary College of St. Augustine (Benicia, Calif.). He was an assayer and superintendent of the Empire Gold Mine in Grass Valley, California, after 1888. He went to Johannesburg, South Africa, in 1893 at the invitation of John Hays Hammond* and was associated with Barney Barnato in gold mining. He returned to the United States during the South African War and managed the Empire mines until his retirement in 1929. Died January 21, 1940, in San Francisco. *Reference*: *NCAB* 30:567.

STAUFFACHER, JOHN (1878–1944). Missionary, born near Monroe, Wisconsin. Stauffacher graduated from Northcentral College (Naperville, Ill.). He was a missionary in the Africa Inland Mission* from 1903 until 1940. He was stationed first at Kijabe, British East Africa, and then started the mission's outreach to the Masai tribe and established a mission station at Laikipia Masai Reserve. He made an expedition to the Belgian Congo and Uganda from 1912 to 1914. He resumed work with the Masai at Narok in 1918. He compiled a dictionary of the Masai language and completed the translation of the Bible into Masai. He was also corresponding secretary of the mission from 1906 to 1912, field director for East Kenya from 1912 to 1916, and deputy general director from 1921 to 1923. He retired in 1940 and opened a guest house for missionaries at Ruwenzori, Irumu, Belgian Congo. Died November 14, 1944, on his way to Nairobi, Kenya. *References*: John Stauffacher Papers, Billy Graham Center Archives, Wheaton College, Wheaton, Ill.; Gladys Stauffacher, *Faster Beats the Drum* (Pearl River, N.Y., 1977); and Josephine H. Westervelt, *On Safari for God: An Account of the Life and Labors of John Stauffacher, a Pioneer Missionary of the Africa Inland Mission* (Brooklyn, N.Y., 1954).

STAUFFER, ELAM W(EIDMAN) (1889–1981). Clergyman and missionary, born January 20, 1889, in Rapho Township, Pennsylvania. Stauffer attended Millersville Normal School and was ordained in 1933. He was a missionary under the Eastern Mennonite Board of Missions and Charities* in Tanganyika from 1933 to 1938, was ordained bishop in 1938, and served as a missionary bishop in the Eastern Mennonite Mission in Tanganyika from 1938 to 1964. He was bishop of the Lancaster Conference of the Mennonite Church (Pa.) after 1964. Died January 9, 1981, in Lancaster, Pennsylvania. *References*: Elam W. Stauffer Papers, Lancaster Mennonite Historical Society, Lancaster, Pa.; *Missionary Messenger*, October 1981; and *Who's Who in Religion* (Chicago, 1977).

STEIDEL, FLORENCE (1897–1962). Missionary nurse, born January 9, 1897, in Greenfield, Illinois. Steidel attended Benton College of Law (Chicago, Ill.), received nurse's training at the Missouri Baptist Hospital (St. Louis), and attended the Central Bible Institute (Springfield, Mo.). She was a missionary under the Foreign Missions Department of the Assemblies of God* in Liberia from 1935 until her death. She taught at the Newaka Girls School until 1946, when she established the New Hope Town leper colony and mission, one of the largest leper colonies in the world, at Cape Palmas, Liberia. Died April 5, 1962, in New Hope, Liberia. *References*: *NYT*, April 7, 1962; and Inez Spence, *These Are My People: Florence Steidel* (Springfield, Mo., 1961?).

STEVENS, THOMAS (1855- ?). Correspondent and author, born December 24, 1855, in Great Berkhamstead, Hertfordshire, England, and came to the United States. Stevens was an enthusiastic bicyclist and made a tour around the world on bicycle from 1884 to 1886. As reporter-adventurer for the *New York World*, he was its representative during the search for David Livingstone. He was in Zanzibar in 1889 and wrote *Scouting with Stanley in East Africa* (New York, 1890) and *Africa as Seen by Thomas Stevens and the Hawke-Eye* (Boston, 1890). *Reference*: ACAB.

STEWART, MARGARET M(CBRIDE) (1927-   ). Herpetologist, born February 6, 1927, in Greensboro, North Carolina. Stewart graduated from the University of North Carolina and Cornell University. She was assistant professor, associate professor, and professor of vertebrate biology at the State University of New York in Albany after 1956. She investigated amphibians in Nyasaland in 1963 and wrote *Amphibia of Malawi* (Albany, N.Y., 1967). *References*: *AMWS*; Anne LaBastille, *Women and Wilderness* (San Francisco, 1980), pp. 210–23; *WWA*; and *WWAW*.

STEWART, T(HOMAS) MCCANTS (1854–1923). Lawyer and educator, born December 28, 1854, in Charleston, South Carolina. Stewart attended Howard and Princeton universities, graduated from the University of South Carolina, and was admitted to the bar. He practiced in South Carolina from 1875 to 1877 and was professor of mathematics at the State Agricultural College of South Carolina in 1877–1878. He was professor of belles lettres and law at the Liberia College from 1882 to 1885 and was later general agent for industrial education in Liberia. He wrote *Liberia: The Americo-African Republic. Being Impressions of the Climate, Resources, and People, Resulting from Personal Observations and Experiences in West Africa* (New York, 1886). He practiced law again from 1886 to 1898, moved to Honolulu, organized and was counsel to Palolo Land & Improvement Company and took part in organizing the Republican Party of Hawaii. *References*: T. McCants Stewart, Stewart-Flippin Papers, Moorland-Spingran Research Center, Manuscripts Division, Howard University, Washington, D.C.; *ACAB*; and *WWWA*.

STOCKTON, ROBERT F(IELD) (1795–1866). Naval officer, born August 20, 1795, in Princeton, New Jersey. Stockton attended the College of New Jersey (later Princeton University), and joined the United States Navy in 1811 as a midshipman. He served in the War of 1812 and in the war against Algiers in 1815. He conveyed the officials of the American Colonization Society* to Africa in 1821, and together with Eli Ayres,* as agents of the United States government, he purchased Cape Mesurado. He served in the West Indies from 1822 to 1824 and was on inactive status from 1828 to 1838, when he returned to active duty. He assumed command of the Pacific Squadron in 1846–1847, and was involved in the operations bringing California under U.S. sovereignty. He resigned from the navy in 1850, was U.S. Senator from New Jersey from 1851 to 1853 and was president of the Delaware and Raritan Canal Company from 1853 until his death. Died October 7, 1866, in Princeton, New Jersey. *References*: Robert F. Stockton Papers, University Library, Princeton, N.J.; *DAB*; *DADH*; Marvin L. Duke, "Robert F. Stockton: Early U.S. Naval Activities in Africa," *Naval War College Review* 24 (1972): 86–94; and Harold D. Langley, "Robert F. Stockton: Naval Officer and Reformer," in *Command under Sail: Makers of Naval Tradition*, ed. James C. Bradford (Annapolis, Md., 1985), pp. 273–304.

STOCKWELL, JOHN (1932-   ). Government official, born August 27, 1932, in Texas, and grew up in the Belgian Congo with missionary parents. Stockwell graduated from the University of Texas and served with the marines. He served in the U.S. Department of the Army in 1964–1965; was a political officer at Abidjan, the Ivory Coast, in 1966–1967; Central Intelligence Agency (CIA) chief of mission at Lubumbashi, Congo, from 1967 to 1969; and CIA chief of mission in Bujumbura, Burundi, from 1969 to 1972. He was chief of the CIA Kenya-Uganda section in 1972–1973, and officer in charge of the CIA in Tay Ninh province, Vietnam, from 1973 to 1975. He was chief of the CIA Angola Task Force in 1975–1976, serving in Kinshana, Zaire, and in Luanda, Ambriz, and Caxito, Angola. He was chief of the CIA Horn and Central Africa Branch in Langley. He wrote *In Search of Enemies: A CIA Story* (New York, 1978). *Reference*: *Dirty Work 2*; and *Washington Post*, April 10, 1977.

STONE, SETH BRADLEY (1817–1877). Missionary, born April 30, 1817, in Madison, Connecticut. Stone graduated from Yale College and Union Theological Seminary. He was a missionary under the American Board of Commissioners for Foreign Missions (ABCFM)* in South Africa from 1850 to 1875, stationed among the Zulus. He translated portions of the Bible into Zulu and translated and composed hymns in Zulu. He returned to the United States in 1875. Died January 27, 1877, in New York City. *Reference*: *EM*.

STONEMAN, BERTHA (1866–1943). Botanist and educator, born August 18, 1866, in Lakewood, Chautauqua County, New York. Stoneman graduated from Cornell University. She came to South Africa in 1897 as a lecturer in botany and philosophy at Huguenot College, Wellington, Cape Province. She was principal of what by then had become Huguenot University College from 1921 until her retirement in 1933. She played an important role in the South African Association of University Women. She wrote *Plants and Their Ways in South Africa* (London, 1906). Died April 30, 1943, in Bain's Kloof, Wellington, South Africa. *References*: *DASB* 3; *DSANB*; *NAW*; *NYT*, May 1, 1943; and *SESA*.

STORKE, ARTHUR DITCHFIELD (1894–1949). Engineer and mining executive, born May 21, 1894, in Auburn, New York. Storke went to the West at sixteen to work as a gold miner at Cripple Creek, Colorado, and then attended the University of Colorado and Stanford University. He joined Climax Molybdenum Corporation in 1916, served in the army during World War I, and was an independent engineer in Los Angeles from 1918 until 1925. He became general superintendent of American Metal Company, Limited, in South Africa in 1927, and managing director of Roan Antelope and Mufulira mines in Northern Rhodesia. He was managing director of Roan Antelope, Mufulira, and the Rhodesian Selection Trust in London from 1930 to 1943, and minerals adviser of Britain's Ministry of Supply in World War II, traveling extensively through South Africa to expedite wartime mining operations. He became president of Climax Molybdenum Company in 1947 and president of Kennecott Copper Company in 1949. Died September 9, 1949, in an airplane crash near St. Joachim, Quebec, Canada. *References*: *NCAB* 38:291; *NYT*, September 10, 1949; and *WWWA*.

STOUT, BENJAMIN (fl. 1796). Sea captain. Stout was master of the ship *Hercules* from Boston, lost in 1796 at Madagascar Reef, South Africa, on its way from India to England. The crew reached land and traveled overland to Cape Town. Stout later published an account of his adventures, *Narrative of the Loss of the Ship Hercules, Commanded by Captain Benjamin Stout, on the Coast of Caffraria, the 16th of June, 1796; also a Circumstantial Detail of His Travels Through the Southern Desert of Africa and the Colonies to the Cape of Good Hope. With an Introductory Address to the Rt. Hon. John Adams, President of the Continental Congress of America* (London, 1798; reprinted as *The Loss of the Ship Hercules 16th June, 1796*, ed. A. Porter, Port Elizabeth, 1975); the work proposed an American settlement around Cape Town.

STRAUS WEST AFRICAN EXPEDITION (1934). An expedition of the Field Museum of Natural History in Chicago, sponsored by Mrs. Oscar Straus of New York City, and headed by W. Rudyerd Boulton.* The expedition covered most of West Africa in 1934, collecting animal specimens for the museum. *Reference*: *NYT*, September 25, 1934.

STREETER, DANIEL W(ILLARD) (1883–1964). Businessman, big-game hunter, and traveler, born November 22, 1883, in Highland, Illinois. Streeter graduated from Harvard University. He began his business career with the Buffalo Weaving and Belting Company, of which he became president. He was vice president of Niagara Share Corporation of New York from 1930 to 1936 and president of the Credag, Inc. A big-game hunter, he made several trips to the Sudan and Kenya in the 1920s and wrote *Denatured Africa* (New York, 1926). He also served as a hunter on the G. P. Putnam Greenland Expedition. Died July 27, 1964, in Buffalo, New York. *References*: Daniel W. Streeter Papers, Buffalo and Erie County Historical Society, Buffalo, N.Y.; and *WWWA*.

STRICKLAND, PETER (1837–1922). Shipmaster, merchant, and consul, born August 1, 1837, in Montville, Connecticut. Strickland went to sea in his teens, became chief mate at the age of twenty, and master a short time later. He became interested in business with Africa at the close of the Civil War, made more than forty voyages between Boston and the coast of Africa as master and supercargo between 1865 and 1878, and established a business in Africa in 1878. He established the consulate in Gorée, Dakar, Senegal, in 1883, and served as consul until 1906; he was also a manufacturer's agent. He published a grammar of the Joluf language and prepared a report on trading monopolies in West Africa. He returned to the United States in 1905. Died in Dorchester, Massachusetts. *References*: Peter Strickland Papers, G. W. Blunt White Library, Mystic Seaport Museum, Mystic, Conn.; Peter Strickland Papers, University of Delaware Library, Newark, Del.; and *NCAB* 9:502.

STRONG, RICHARD P(EARSON) (1872–1948). Authority on tropical medicine, born March 18, 1872, in Fortress Monroe, Virginia. Strong graduated from the Sheffield Scientific School of Yale University and the medical school of Johns Hopkins University and studied in Berlin. He was assistant surgeon in the army during the Spanish-American War, director of the Army Pathological Laboratory in the Isthmus of Panama, director of the biological laboratories of the Bureau of Science in the Philippines from 1901 to 1913, professor of tropical medicine at the University of the Philippine Islands from 1907 to 1913, and chief of medicine at the Philippine Islands General Hospital from 1910 to 1913. He served on the chief surgeon's staff during World War I. He was professor of tropical medicine at the Harvard University Medical School from 1913 until his retirement in 1938. He led several expeditions to study tropical diseases, including the Harvard African expedition to make a biological and medical survey of Liberia and to investigate the diseases of the Belgian Congo in 1926–1927, and to the Belgian Congo and Northern Rhodesia in 1934; he wrote *The African Republic of Liberia and the Belgian Congo, Harvard African Expedition, 1926–27* (Cambridge, Mass., 1930). Died July 4, 1948, in Boston. *References*: *DAB* S4; W. C. Forbes and E. Bowditch, "Richard Pearson Strong," in *Saturday Club: A Century Completed 1920–1956*, ed. Edward W. Forbes and John H. Finley, Jr. (Boston, 1958), pp. 215–26; *NYT*, July 5, 1948; and *WWWA*.

SUDAN INTERIOR MISSION (SIM). Mission was established in 1893 in Toronto, Canada, and established its first mission in Nigeria in 1893. Intially named the Africa Industrial Mission, it changed its name to the Africa Evangelistic Mission in 1905 and adopted the name Sudan Interior Mission in 1907. It began missionary work in Niger in 1924, in Ethiopia in 1927, in Upper Volta in 1930, in the Sudan in 1936, in Dahomey in 1946, in Liberia in 1952, in Somaliland in 1954, in the Gold Coast in 1956, in Kenya in 1977, and in the Ivory Coast in 1978. One the mission's home offices is in the United States, and many Americans have served as missionaries under this mission. *References*: F. Peter Cotterell, *Born at Midnight* (Chicago, 1973); and *EMCM*.

SULLIVAN PRINCIPLES. In 1977, Reverend Leon H. Sullivan (1922–   ), a black member of General Motors' board of directors, devised a corporate code of conduct for U.S. firms operating in South Africa. The voluntary code called for signatory companies to strive for equal pay for equal work, fair employment practices, more training for blacks, integrated work-site amenities, and greater corporate attention to black workers' nonwork problems such as housing, health care, and transportation. *References*: *Fortune*, July 9, 1984; E. J. Kahn, "Annals of International Trade" *New Yorker* 55 (May 14, 1979): 135–53; and Elizabeth Schmidt, *One Step in the Wrong Direction: An Analysis of the Sullivan Principles* (New York, 1983).

SUTHERLAND, WILLIAM H. ("BILL") (1918-   ). Expatriate, born December 24, 1918, in Orange, New Jersey. Sutherland graduated from Bates College. A pacifist, he served three years in federal prison for opposition to service in World War II. He was involved in various civil rights movements from 1940 to 1953 and was one of the founding members of New York Core. He was personal secretary to Ghana's minister of finance from 1957 to 1960; served on the staff of the secretariat of the first All-African People's Conference in Accra, Ghana; helped to found the World Peace Brigade; and was an adviser on the African program of the Histadrut in Israel in 1961–1962. He moved to Tanzania in 1962 and was assistant secretary in the Tanzanian Ministry of Information and Tourism. He was Southern African representative of the American Friends Service Committee from 1974 to 1981. *Reference*: Ernest Dunbar, ed., *The Black Expatriates: A Study of American Negroes in Exile* (New York, 1966), pp. 157–72.

SWAN, SAMUEL, JR. (1779–1823). Sea captain, of Medford, Massachusetts. Swan made several voyages to West Africa between 1804 and 1823. He lost his life on March 31, 1823, when the brig *Hopestill* of Boston foundered on a return voyage from Africa. *References*: Samuel Swan, Jr., Letterbook, Peabody Museum of Salem, Mass.; George E. Brooks, ed., "A View of Sierra Leone *ca* 1815," *Sierra Leone Studies*, n.s. no. 13 (June 1960): 24–31; and George E. Brooks, "Samuel Swan's Letter Book: An American View of Sierra Leone and the Coast of Africa," *Sierra Leone Studies* n.s. no. 12 (December 1959): 245–59.

SWINGLE, CHARLES F(LETCHER) (1899-   ). Horticulturist, born May 13, 1899, in Manhattan, Kansas. Swingle graduated from Kansas State and Johns Hopkins universities. He was a commercial fruit and nursery grower in California until 1922 and nursery stock investigator for the Bureau of Plant Industry of the United States Department of Agriculture from 1922 to 1933. He led the Humbert-Swingle expedition to Madagascar in 1928 to collect rubber plants. He was later associate pomologist in the Soil Conservation Service from 1933 to 1935, horticulturist from 1935 to 1945, extension horticulturist in Wisconsin from 1947 to 1950, commercial strawberry grower in Wisconsin from 1950 to 1955, commercial fruit and nursery grower in California from 1955 to 1967, and manager of the Livingston Atmometer Company after 1967. *Reference*: *AMWS*.

T

"TAR BABY". The name given by State Department opponents of the Southern African policy adopted in 1969 by President Richard M. Nixon's administration as a result of a major review of the American policy toward Southern Africa (see National Security Study Memorandum (NSSM) 39*), because it would bind the United States to the white rule in Southern Africa. (The name refers to the "Uncle Remus" story by Joel Chandler Harris.) *Reference*: Anthony Lake, *The "Tar Baby" Option: American Policy Toward Southern Rhodesia* (New York, 1976), ch. 4.

TAUNT, EMORY H. (? –1891). Naval officer and commercial agent. Taunt was commissioned by the United States Navy in 1885 to explore the Congo Free State and to report on the commercial possibilities it offered. He made a round trip between Banana Point and Stanley Falls in the summer of 1885 and produced a report, *Journey of the River Congo* (U.S. Congress, Senate, Executive Document No. 77, 49th Congress, 2d Session, February 5, 1887). He took a leave of absence from the navy in 1886, and was principal agent of the Sanford Exploring Expedition* in the Congo from 1887 to 1889 and established several trading stations there. He became a commercial agent in the Congo in 1889. Died January 18, 1891, in Banana, Congo Free State. *References*: BCB 6; François Bontinck, *Aux Origines de l'État Indépendent du Congo: Documents Tirés d'Archives Américains* (Louvain, 1966), ch. 6.

TAYLOR, JAMES DEXTER (1876–1959). Missionary and philologist, born January 27, 1876, in Waltham, Massachusetts. Taylor graduated from Amherst College and Auburn Theological Seminary and was ordained in 1899. He was a missionary under the American Board of Commissioners for Foreign Missions (ABCFM)* in South Africa from 1899 until 1949. He first served in Natal and was later in charge of mission work in Johannesburg from 1927 until 1948. He made a new translation of the entire Bible into Zulu. He returned to the United States in 1948. He wrote *The American Board Mission in South Africa: A Sketch* *of Seventy-five Years* (Durban, 1911) and *One Hundred Years of the American Board Mission in South Africa 1835–1935* (n.p., 193-) and compiled and edited *Christianity and the Natives of South Africa: A Yearbook of South African Missions* (n.p., 1928?). Died February 11, 1959, in Newton Corner, Massachusetts. *References*: *Amherst*; and *SADNB*.

TAYLOR, MYRON (1873–1931). Missionary, born April 6, 1873, in Lapeer County, Michigan. Taylor was a missionary under the Brethren in Christ Foreign Missions* at Macha, Northern Rhodesia, from 1907 until his death. In 1920 he moved to Sikalongo, Northern Rhodesia. Mauled by a lion, he died September 16, 1931, at Sikalongo. His wife, **ADDA ENGLE TAYLOR** (1869–1960), niece of Jesse Engle,* was born December 4, 1869, in Bainbridge, Pennsylvania. Adda came to Southern Rhodesia in 1905 as a missionary under the Brethren in Christ Foreign Missions and was stationed in Mapane and Matopo until 1906, when, with Hanna Frances Davidson,* she helped establish the Macha station in Northern Rhodesia. She returned to the United States in 1932. Died August 2, 1960, in Harrisburg, Pennsylvania. *References*: *Engle*; and Martha M. Long, "Adda Engle Taylor," *Brethren in Christ History and Life* 7 (1984): 65–101.

TAYLOR, PRINCE A(LBERT), JR. (1907-   ). Clergyman, born January 27, 1907, in Hennesset, Oklahoma. Taylor graduated from Samuel Houston College and Gammon Theological Seminary. He served as a pastor in North Carolina and New York from 1931 to 1940, instructor and assistant to the president of Bennett College from 1930 to 1943, head of the department of Christian education and psychology at Gammon Theological Seminary from 1943 to 1948, and editor of *Central Christian Advocate* from 1948 to 1956. He was elected bishop in 1956 and served as Methodist bishop of Liberia from 1956 to 1964. He was later a bishop in the New Jersey area from 1964 to 1976. He wrote *The Life of My Years (Memoirs of a Former Methodist Bishop of Liberia)* (Nashville, Tenn., 1983). *References*: *Ebony*, February 1965; *EWM*; *WWA*; *WWBA*; and *WWE*.

TAYLOR, WILLIAM (1821–1902). Missionary, born May 2, 1821, in Rockbridge County, Virginia. Taylor became a preacher in 1842 and was ordained an elder in 1847. He was an evangelist in Georgetown, Washington, D.C.; missionary to California from 1849 to 1857; made evangelistic tours in New England, the Midwest and Canada from 1857 to 1862; and made a missionary tour to Australia and New Zealand from 1862 to 1866. He was a missionary in South Africa from 1866 to 1868. He again conducted evangelistic campaigns in England, the West Indies, Australia, and Ceylon from 1868 to 1870, and served in India from 1870 to 1875. He was elected missionary bishop of the Methodist Episcopal Church* in 1884 and served as a missionary bishop for Africa from 1884 to 1896, supervising missionary work in Liberia and establishing mission stations in the Congo, Angola, and Mozambique. He retired in 1896. He wrote *Christian Adventures in South Africa* (New York, 1867); *Africa Illustrated:*

Scenes from Daily Life on the Dark Continent from Photographs Secured in Africa by Bishop William Taylor, Dr. Emil Holub and the Missionary Super-intendents (New York, 1895); *The Flaming Torch in Darkest Africa* (New York, 1898); and *Story of My Life; an Account of What I Have Thought and Said and Done in My Ministry of More than Fifty-three Years in Christian Lands and among the Heathen*, ed. John C. Ridpath (New York, 1895). Died May 18, 1902, in Palo Alto, California. *References*: William Taylor Papers, Pacific School of Religion Library, Berkeley, Calif.; *ACAB*; *DAB*; *EWM*; *Leete*; *NCAB* 10:496; Charles W. Turner, "California's Taylor of Rockbridge: Bishop to the World," *Southern California Quarterly* 62 (1982): 229–38; and *WWWA*.

TEAGE, COLIN (? –1839). Colonist, born a slave in Virginia. Teage purchased himself and his family. He immigrated to Sierra Leone in 1821 and moved to Liberia in 1825. He became a prominent minister and engaged successfully in commerce. He became pastor of the Second Baptist Church in Monrovia in 1835. Died August 27, 1839, while returning from a visit to the United States. His son, **HILARY TEAGE** (ca. 1802–1853), was born a slave near Richmond, Virginia, immigrated to Sierra Leone with his parents in 1821, and moved to Liberia in 1825. Successful in commerce, he later became a Baptist minister. He edited the newspaper *Liberia Herald* from 1835 to 1847 and became Liberia's colonial secretary in 1835. He was one of the delegates to the Constitutional Convention of 1847 and drafted Liberia's Declaration of Independence. He was a senator in 1847–1848, attorney general in 1850–1851, and secretary of state in 1852–1853. Died May 21, 1853, in Monrovia. *References*: *African Repository* 29 (1853): 258, 316; *Davis*; *Huberich*; and *LC*.

TEMPELSMAN, MAURICE (1929-). Diamond trader, born in Belgium. Tempelsman fled with his family to New York at the outbreak of World War II. He studied at New York University and entered the family business, Leon Tempelsman and Son, diamond brokering, in New York City. He went to Africa in 1950 and began purchasing diamonds from African suppliers. He was the first buyer of Ghanaian diamonds and set up the first diamond cutting and polishing factory in Sierra Leone. He was in the Congo in the early 1960s, seeking and finding the inside track for future diamond and copper deals, and was adviser to several African heads of state. He converted Leon Tempelsman and Son into a diversified corporation and also became owner of American Coldset, a manufacturer of drill bits for oil wells. *References*: Louis Kraar, "Maurice Tempelsman's African Connections," *Fortune* 106 (November 15, 1982): 130–32; and Richard D. Mahoney, "United States Policy Toward the Congo 1960–1963," Ph.D. diss., Johns Hopkins University School of Advanced International Studies, 1980, ch. 7.

TEW, THOMAS (fl. 1692). Pirate, from Newport, Rhode Island. Tew sailed to Bermuda as a young man and was commissioned a privateer by the governor of Bermuda in 1692, but reverted to piracy. He was one of the founders of the pirate state of Libertalia in northern Madagascar. After making a fortune in Madagascar, he lived for many years in Rhode Island. Killed as a pirate somewhere in the Indian Ocean. *References*: Philip Gosse, *The Pirates' Who's Who* (Boston, 1924); and Addison B. C. Whipple, *Pirate: Rascals of the Spanish Main* (Garden City, N.Y., 1957), pp. 62–67.

THOMAS, CHARLES CHARRIER (1851–1878). Trader and hunter, born November 5, 1851, in Boston. Thomas was involved in the wool trade in Boston and went to Cape Town to establish a wholesale wool business. Being unsuccessful, he went to the interior on a trading expedition. He was the first American to settle in Southwest Africa in 1870 and was operating his own business in Walvis Bay in 1874. He established an ostrich breeding farm and traded in other goods. He went with Gerald McKiernan* in 1875 on an expedition to the north of Southwest Africa and reached Lake Ngami. Killed July 27, 1878, on the Okavango River, Southwest Africa. His brother, **JOHN LOUIS THOMAS** (1855- ?), a hunter, was born June 13, 1855, in Boston, and attended an agricultural college in Amherst, Massachusetts. He went to Walvis Bay in 1876 and trekked across Southwest Africa. He returned to the United States in 1879, later went to California, and disappeared in South America. *Reference*: *Tabler/ South West Africa*.

THOMAS, ELIZABETH MARSHALL. *See* MARSHALL, LAURENCE KENNEDY

THOMPSON, GEORGE (1817–1893). Missionary, born August 12, 1817, in Madison, New Jersey. Thompson attended Oberlin College and Mission Institute (Quincy, Ill.). He served a prison term from 1841 to 1846 because he helped some slaves escape. He was a missionary under the American Missionary Association* in Mende County, Sierra Leone, from 1848 until 1856. He returned to the United States in 1856 and was a missionary in Northern Michigan until 1879 when he settled in Oberlin, Ohio. He wrote *Africa in a Nutshell, for the Million; or, Light on the "Dark Continent"* (Oberlin, Ohio, 1881); *The Palm Land; or West Africa, Illustrated* (Cincinnati, 1858); *Thompson in Africa; or, an Account of the Missionary Labors, Sufferings, Travels, and Observations, of George Thompson, in Western Africa, at the Mendi Mission* (New York, 1852). Died February 4, 1893, in Oberlin, Ohio. *References*: George Thompson "Reminiscences," MS, Manuscripts Collection, Chicago Historical Society, Chicago; and *OAB*.

THOMSON, JAMES MADISON (ca. 1806–1838). Missionary educator, born in Demerara, British Guyana. Thomson was educated in England and then lived in New York City. He immigrated to Liberia in 1832. He served as secretary to James Hall* and became a teacher under the Domestic and Foreign Missionary Society of the Protestant Episcopal Church in the United States of America* in 1835. He started a mission school at Mount Vaughn in 1836, but was removed in 1838. Died in December 1838. His wife, **ELIZABETH MARS JOHNSON THOMSON** (1807–1864), educator, was born November 1807, in Connecticut, and immigrated to Liberia in 1830. She served with her husband as a teacher in the Mount Vaughn School. After his death, she returned to the United States, but was back in Liberia in 1842 and taught intermittently at Mount Vaughn until her death. Died April 26, 1864 at Mount Vaughn, Liberia. *Reference*: Randall K. Burkett, "Elizabeth Mars Johnson Thomson (1807–1864): A Research Note," *Historical Magazine of the Protestant Episcopal Church* 55 (1986): 21–31.

THORNTON, WYNES EDWIN (1872–1903). Deputy commissar and soldier born August 25, 1872, in Washington, D.C. Thornton was employed in the Department of the Treasury. In 1896 he signed an employment contract with the Congo Free State and went to the Congo in that year. He became commander of the military post of Banalia in the Arumwimi District in 1897, transferred in 1898 to the Stanley Falls District, and was posted to Bomili in 1901. His employment was terminated in 1902 and he returned to Europe, but was back in the Congo in 1903. Killed April 8, 1903, at Bendolet, Aruwimi-Nepoko, Congo Free State. *Reference*: BCB 5.

TICONDEROGA, **U.S.S.** Screw sloop of war. *Ticonderoga* embarked in November 1878 on a cruise around the world, with Commodore Robert W. Shufeldt* commanding. It was an expedition of a commercial nature, intended to expand existing trade relations and to establish new ones. She cruised along the coasts of Africa and through the Indian Ocean in 1878–1879. *References*: *DANFS*; and Kenneth J. Hagan, *American Gunboat Diplomacy and the Old Navy 1877–1889* (Westport, Conn., 1973), chs. 3–5.

TIMBERLAKE, CLARE H(AYES) (1907–1982). Diplomat, born October 29, 1907, in Jackson, Michigan. Timberlake graduated from the University of Michigan and studied at Harvard University. He entered the foreign service in 1930; was vice consul in Toronto, Buenos Aires, Zurich, Vigo, Spain, and Aden; consul in Aden; consul general in Bombay; and third secretary in Montevideo, Uruguay. He was desk officer in the Near Eastern Department from 1943 to 1945; assistant chief and chief of African Affairs from 1945 to 1947; counselor in New Delhi from 1950 to 1952; consul general in Hamburg from 1952 to 1955; counselor in Lima, Peru, from 1955 to 1957; minister-counselor in Buenos Aires in 1957 and in Bonn from 1958 to 1960. He was the first ambassador to the Congo in 1960–1961. He was later a special assistant to the undersecretary of

222

TISDEL, WILLIARD P.

state for political affairs, chair of the advisory staff of the Arms Control and Disarmament Agency, and member of the Foreign Service Board of Examiners until his retirement in 1970. Died February 22, 1982, in Bethesda, Maryland. *References*: *CB* 1961; *NYT*, February 25, 1982; *Washington Post*, February 24, 1982; and *WWA*.

TISDEL, WILLIARD P. (1843–1911). Businessman, born in Painesville, Lake County, Ohio. Tisdel served in the Civil War and then served as special agent of the Pacific Mail Steamship Company to the Central American Republics, Mexico, and Brazil. From 1884 to 1886 he served as special agent of the State Department to explore the commercial possibilities of the Congo, with special emphasis on determining promising markets for American products, but submitted negative reports. He was later commissioner to the Congo Free State. Died June 21, 1911, in Washington, D.C. *References*: François Bontinck, *Aux Origines de l'État Indépendent du Congo: Documents Tirés d'Archives Américaines* (Louvain, 1966), ch. 5; and *NYT*, June 22, 1911.

TJADER, (CHARLES) RICHARD (1869–1916). Big-game hunter, explorer, lecturer, and author, born April 21, 1869, in Karlskrona, Sweden. Tjader attended the theological seminary of Upsala, Sweden, and began evangelistic work in Sweden and Germany. He came to the United States in 1898 and helped organize the International Union Mission in New York in 1901. He led an expedition into British East Africa for the American Museum of Natural History in 1906–1907. After his return to the United States, he gave many illustrated lectures about his exploits, and wrote *The Big Game of Africa* (New York, 1919). Died December 27, 1916, in New York City. *References*: *NCAB* 17:144; and *NYT*, December 29, 1916.

TOPPENBERG, AKSEL VALDEMAR (1884–1957). Missionary, born February 29, 1884, in Aalborg, Denmark, and immigrated to the United States as a young man. Toppenberg graduated from Union College. He became a Seventh-Day Adventist missionary in Eritrea in 1909 and was transferred to Tanganyika in 1910, where he remained until 1917, when he returned to the United States. He went to Ethiopia again in 1921, moved to Uganda after the Italian occupation of Ethiopia, and served there until 1943. He came back to Eritrea in 1943, and finally to Southern Ethiopia where he served until 1952, when he returned to the United States. He wrote an autobiography, *Africa Has My Heart* (Mountain View, Calif., 1958). Died March 27, 1957, in Fullerton, California. *Reference*: *SDAE*.

TOTTEN, RALPH JAMES (1877–1949). Diplomat, born October 1, 1877, in Nashville, Tennessee. Totten was involved in railway and commercial business until 1907. He was consul at Puerto Plata, Dominican Republic, Maracaibo, Venezuela, Trieste, Austria, and Montevideo; consul general in Barcelona from

1922 to 1924; and member of the executive committee of the Foreign Service Personnel Board in 1925–1926. He headed a special mission to Ethiopia in 1926, was consul general in Cape Town from 1926 to 1930, minister resident in 1929–1930, and the first minister to South Africa from 1930 until his retirement in 1937. Died May 9, 1949. *Reference*: *WWWA*.

TOU, ERIK HANSEN (1857–1917). Missionary, born October 11, 1857, in Strand, Stavanger, Norway. Tou came to the United States in 1881 and graduated from Augsburg Seminary. He was missionary under the United Lutheran Church in America* and later under the Lutheran Free Church in Madagascar from 1889 until 1904. He was stationed at St. Augustine in 1889–1890 and in Manasoa from 1890 until 1903, establishing a school, a theological seminary, and two orphanages. He recorded his experiences in Norwegian in *Den Lutherske Frikires Hedningemission paa Madagascar* (Minneapolis, 1899). He returned to the United States in 1903; was pastor in Pukwana, South Dakota, from 1904 to 1909; and at Napoleon, North Dakota, from 1909 until his death. Died November 15, 1917, in Napoleon, North Dakota. *References*: *DAB*; and *WWPNL*.

TRADER HORN. First movie ever made outside the United States by any Hollywood company. Produced by Metro-Goldwyn-Mayer between 1929 and 1931 and directed by W. S. Van Dyke,* the movie was filmed on location in East Africa. *Reference*: Byron Riggan, "Damn the Crocodiles—Keep the Cameras Rolling!" *American Heritage* 19 (June 1968): 38–44, 100–103.

TSUMEB. A mining company in Namibia, it is a major extractor of base minerals, the largest private employer there, and the largest producer of lead and zinc in Africa. Tsumeb was controlled by two American companies which owned an estimated 65 percent of Tsumeb: Newmont Mining Corporation, incorporated in 1921 in Delaware, and American Metal Climax (AMAX), which was formed in 1951 from a merger between American Metal Company and Climax Molybdenum Company. AMAX sold its shares in Tsumeb in 1983. *Reference*: Reed Kramer and Tami Hulton, *Tsumeb: A Profile of United States Contribution to Underdevelopment in Namibia* (New York, 1973).

TURNBULL, COLIN M(ACMILLAN) (1924-   ). Anthropologist, born November 23, 1924, in Harrow, England. Turnbull served in the Royal Navy during World War II. He graduated from Oxford University and studied at the University of London and the Benares Hindu University (India). He stayed with Patrick Putnam* in the Belgian Congo in 1951 and returned to that area in 1954–1955 and from 1957 to 1959, studying the BaMbuti pygmies about whom he wrote *The Forest People* (New York, 1961), *Wayward Servants: The Two Worlds of the African Pygmies* (New York, 1965), and *The BaMbuti Pygmies* (New York, 1965). He came to the United States in 1959 and became a naturalized citizen. He was assistant curator of African ethnology at the American Museum of Natural

History from 1959 to 1966 and associate curator from 1965 to 1969. In 1964 and 1966 he conducted field work in Northeast Uganda and wrote *The Mountain People* (New York, 1972). He also wrote *The Lonely African* (New York, 1962), *Tradition and Change in African Tribal Life* (Cleveland, 1966), and *Man in Africa* (Garden City, N.Y., 1976). He was professor of anthropology at Hofstra University from 1969 to 1972 and later at Virginia Commonwealth University (Richmond, Va.) and George Washington University (Washington, D.C.). *References*: *AMWS*; *CA*; *CB* 1980; and *WWWA*.

TURNER, HENRY MCNEAL (1834–1915). Clergyman, born free, February 1, 1834, near Newberry, Abbeville County, South Carolina. In 1853 Turner was licensed to preach by the Methodist Episcopal Church, South,* and was a successful revivalist until 1857, when he settled in St. Louis. He joined the African Methodist Episcopal Church* in 1857, was a missionary in Baltimore, was ordained an elder in 1862, and was a pastor in Washington, D.C. He served as a chaplain during the Civil War. He moved to Georgia in 1866 and there built up the African Methodist Episcopal Church and the Republican Party, and served as state legislator in 1868. He later served as postmaster in Macon, Georgia; United States customs inspector and government detective; was a pastor in and near Savannah, Georgia, from 1872 to 1876; and manager of the African Methodist Episcopal Book Concern in Philadelphia from 1876 to 1888. He was a bishop for Georgia from 1888 to 1892 and later chancellor of Morris Brown College (later University) in Atlanta. He visited South and West Africa and introduced African Methodism there. He went to Sierra Leone in 1891 and established the church there and then in Liberia. He established African Methodism in Cape Town, South Africa, in 1898. He wrote *African Letters* (Nashville, Tenn., 1893). Died May 8, 1915, in Windsor, Ontario, Canada. *References*: Henry McNeal Turner Papers, Moorland-Spingran Research Center, Manuscript Division, Howard University, Washington, D.C.; *DAB*; *DANB*; *EWM*; *NCAB* 2:206; Edwin S. Redkey,'' Bishop Turner's African Dream,'' *JAH* 54 (1967): 271–90 (reprinted in *Black Apostles: Afro-American Clergy Confront the Twentieth Century*, ed. Randall K. Burkett and Richard Newman (Boston, 1978), pp. 227–46); Edwin S. Redkey, *Black Exodus: Black Nationalist and Back-to-Africa Movements, 1890–1910* (New Haven, Conn., 1969), chs. 2, 8; Edwin S. Redkey, "The Flowering of Black Nationalism: Henry McNeal Turner and Marcus Garvey," in *Key Issues in the Afro-American Experience* 2, ed. Nathan I. Huggins et al. (New York, 1971), 107–24; and *WWWA*.

TURNER, JAMES MILTON (1840–1915). Diplomat, born a slave May 16, 1840, in St. Louis, Missouri; his father bought his freedom in 1843. Turner graduated from Oberlin College and served during the Civil War. He taught in public schools in Kansas City from 1866 to 1871 and was second assistant state superintendent of schools in Missouri in 1870. He became a leading figure in Republican politics and was the first black to serve as minister resident and consul general in Liberia from 1871 to 1878. Died November 1, 1915 in Ardmore, Oklahoma. *References: Christmas; DAB;* and *DADH.*

TWAIN, MARK (1835–1910). Author and humorist, real name Samuel Langhorne Clemens, born November 30, 1835, in Florida, Missouri, and grew up in Hannibal, Missouri. Mark Twain was apprenticed to a printer at age twelve, worked at a newspaper, and was apprenticed to a steamboat pilot on the Mississippi River from 1856 to 1861. He moved to Nevada in 1861, where he worked on the Virginia City *Territorial Enterprise,* and to San Francisco in 1864, where he wrote for the *San Francisco Call* and other newspapers. He traveled in South Africa in 1896 and recounted his visit in *Following the Equator: A Journey Around the World* (Hartford, Conn., 1897). He later wrote *King Leopold's Soliloquy, a Defense of His Congo Rule* (Boston, 1905). Died April 21, 1910, in Redding, Connecticut. *References: DAB; NCAB* 6:24; Coleman Parsons, ''Mark Twain: Traveler in South Africa,'' *Mississippi Quarterly* 29 (1975–1976): 3–41; Coleman Parsons, ''Mark Twain: Clubman in South Africa,'' *New England Quarterly* 50 (1977): 234–54; and *SESA.*

TYLER, JOSIAH (1823–1895). Missionary, born July 9, 1823, in Hanover, New Hampshire. Tyler graduated from Amherst College and East Windsor Theological Seminary and was ordained in 1849. He became a missionary under the American Board of Commissioners for Foreign Missions (ABCFM)* in Natal, South Africa, in 1849. He was stationed among the Zulus at Esidumbeni, Natal, was in charge of the American Board Mission printing press from 1849 until 1871 and edited a monthly newspaper, *Ikwezi.* He returned to the United States in 1871, but came back to South Africa in 1873 and was stationed in Umsunduzi from 1874 until his retirement in 1889. He returned to the United States in 1889. He was an expert on Zulu law and custom and wrote *Forty Years among the Zulus* (Boston, 1891). Died December 20, 1895, in Asheville, North Carolina. *References: DSAB* 3; *EM; SADBN;* and *SESA.*

U

UNITED BRETHREN IN CHRIST, CHURCH OF THE: BOARD OF MISSIONS. Established in 1841 but remained inactive until 1855. It began missionary work in Sierra Leone in 1855, and the Mende Mission* was transferred to it by the American Missionary Association* in 1883. *References*: Emmett D. Cox, *The Church of the United Brethren in Christ in Sierra Leone* (South Pasadena, Calif., 1970); and *EMCM*.

UNITED CHRISTIAN MISSIONARY SOCIETY. Founded in 1920 to serve as the board of missions and Christian education of the Christian Churches (Disciples), as a result of a merger of the American Christian Missionary Society, the Christian Woman's Board of Missions, the Foreign Christian Missionary Society, and several other agencies. The Foreign Christian Missionary Society (founded in 1875) began missionary work in the Congo Free State in 1898, in South Africa in 1932, and in several other African states in the 1960s. Its work was assumed in 1973 by the Division of Overseas Ministries of the Christian Church (Disciples of Christ) in the United States and Canada. *References*: United Christian Missionary Society Archives, Disciples of Christ Historical Society, Nashville, Tenn.; *EMCM*; Robert G. Nelson, *Congo Crisis and Christian Mission* (St. Louis, 1961); Herbert Smith, *Fifty Years in Congo; Disciples of Christ at the Equator* (Indianapolis, 1949); and *TWTA*.

UNITED CHURCH BOARD FOR WORLD MINISTRIES. *See* AMERICAN BOARD OF COMMISSIONERS FOR FOREIGN MISSIONS.

UNITED LUTHERAN CHURCH IN AMERICA: BOARD OF FOREIGN MISSIONS. Organized in 1837 as the Foreign Missionary Society of the Evangelical German Churches (after 1842 Lutheran Churches) of the U.S.A., it became the Board of Foreign Missions in 1918. In 1869 it assumed missionary work in Liberia. It merged in 1962 with other Lutheran churches to form the Board of World Missions of the Lutheran Church in America, which was later renamed the Division for World Mission and Ecumenism. *References*: United Lutheran Church in America, Board of Foreign Missions Archives, Lutheran School of Theology, Chicago; Margaret V. Seebach, *Man in the Bush* (Baltimore, 1945); and Harold V. Whetstone, *Lutheran Mission in Liberia* (n.p., 1955).

UNITED MISSIONARY SOCIETY. The mission board of the United Missionary Church was organized in 1921 to unite and enlarge the foreign mission work of the church. The church sent its first missionaries to Nigeria in 1901 and began missionary work there in 1908 and in Sierra Leone in 1945. It merged in 1969 with Missionary Church Association to form the Division of Overseas Missions of the Missionary Church. *References*: United Missionary Church Archives, Bethel College Library, Mishawaka, Ind.; Everek R. Storms, *What God Has Wrought: The Story of the Foreign Missionary Efforts of the United Missionary Church* (Springfield, Ohio, 1948); and Everek R. Storms, *History of the United Missionary Church* (Elkhart, Ind., 1958).

UNITED PRESBYTERIAN CHURCH OF NORTH AMERICA: BOARD OF FOREIGN MISSIONS. Organized in 1866, it had its beginnings in the work of the Associate Reformed Presbyterian Church and the Associate Presbyterian Church, which merged in 1858. It began missionary work in Ethiopia in 1924. It also carried on missionary work in Kenya, Nyasaland, Mozambique, Nigeria, and Togo. It merged with the Board of Foreign Missions of the Presbyterian Church in the U.S.A.* in 1958 to form the Commission on Ecumenical Mission and Relations of the United Presbyterian Church in the U.S.A., which merged in 1983 with the Presbyterian Church in the United States to form the Presbyterian Church (USA). *Reference*: Walter N. Jamison, *The United Presbyterian Story: A Centennial Study 1858–1958* (Pittsburgh, 1958).

U.S. AFRICAN SQUADRON. As a result of the Anglo-American Treaty of 1842, the United States government created the African Squadron in 1843, and stationed it, mounting at least eighty guns, on the African coast to apprehend American slavers operating there. Due to obstructive attitudes of the secretaries of the navy, the squadron, never exceeding five vessels, was more involved in protecting and encouraging American trade that in suppressing the African slave trade. It only captured twenty-four slave ships. The ships were recalled in 1861 and it became part of the European Squadron in 1862. *References*: Alan R. Booth, "The United States African Squadron, 1843–1861," in *Boston University Papers in African History*, ed. Jeffrey Butler (Boston, 1964), pp. 77–117; George M. Brooke, Jr., "The Role of the United States Navy in the Suppression of the African Slave Trade," *American Neptune* 21 (1961): 28–41; and J. C. Furnas, "Patrolling the Middle Passage," *American Heritage* 9 (October 1958): 4–9, 101–2.

U.S. COMMISSION TO LIBERIA (1909). A commission sent to Liberia in 1909 by President William Howard Taft at Liberia's request, to investigate American interests and that of its citizens in Liberia. The members of the commission were Ronald P. Falkner, George Sale, and Emmett J. Scott.* The commission recommended that the United States government guarantee the independence and integrity of Liberia and should organize and supervise an adequate frontier force (see Liberian Frontier Force*). The report was published as Senate Executive Document No. 457 (61st Cong., 2d sess., Washington, D.C., 1910). *Reference*: Merle Curti and Kendall Birr, *Prelude to Point Four: American Technical Missions Overseas 1838–1938* (Madison, Wis., 1954), ch. 4.

V

VAN DYKE, W(OODBRIDGE) S(TRONG), 2ND (1889–1943). Film director, born in San Diego, California. Van Dyke went on the stage at the age of seven months and later began to appear in movies. He became assistant director to D. W. Griffith and then directed serials. He took a company to Africa, directed there "Trader Horn," and described his experiences in *Horning into Africa* (n.p., 1931). Died February 5, 1943, in Brentwood, California. *References*: Robert C. Cannon, *Van Dyke and the Mythical City, Hollywood* (Culver City, Calif., 1948); Richard Koszarski, *Hollywood Directors, 1914–1940* (New York, 1976), pp. 310–16; and *NYT*, February 6, 1943.

VEATCH, ARTHUR CLIFFORD (1878–1938). Geologist, born October 26, 1878, in Evansville, Indiana, and grew up in Rockport, Indiana. Veatch attended Indiana and Cornell universities. He was assistant state geologist of Louisiana from 1899 to 1902, professor of geology at Louisiana State University in 1902–1903, and field assistant of the United States Geological Survey from 1902 to 1910. He was chief geologist for the General Asphalt Company in Trinidad and Tobago from 1910 to 1913; in charge of foreign oil exploration for the engineering firm of S. Pearson and Sons, Limited, of London from 1913 to 1919; director of the exploration department of Sinclair Consolidated Oil Corporation from 1919 to 1928; and established his own consulting office in New York City in 1928. He did fieldwork in Africa and wrote *Evolution of the Congo Basin* (New York, 1935). Died December 24, 1938, in Port Washington, Long Island, New York. *References*: *Bulletin of the American Association of Petroleum Geologists* 23 (1939): 621–22; *DAB S2*; *GSA Proceedings* 1941, pp. 201–205; *IAB*; *NCAB* 29:164; and *WWWA*.

VEENSTRA, JOHANNA (1894–1933). Missionary, born April 19, 1894, in Paterson, New Jersey. Veenstra studied at the Union Missionary Training Institute (Brooklyn). A member of the Christian Reformed Church of North America, she was a missionary in the Sudan United Mission in Nigeria from 1920 to

1933. She was stationed at Ibi; at Lupwe, in Northern Nigeria, where she established a boarding school; and at Kwambai. She wrote *Pioneering for Christ in the Sudan* (Grand Rapids, Mich., 1926). Died April 9, 1933, in Vom, Nigeria. *References*: Henry Beets, *Johanna of Nigeria: Life and Labors of Johanna Veenstra S.U.M.* (Grand Rapids, Mich., 1937); and Winifred M. Pearce, *Johanna Veenstra* (London, 1957).

VENABLE, HENRY ISAAC (1811–1878). Missionary, born June 20, 1811, in Shelby County, Kentucky. Venable graduated from Clinton College (Ky.). He was a missionary under the American Board of Commissioners for Foreign Missions (ABCFM)* in South Africa from 1835 to 1839. He established a missionary station at Mosega, in the territory of the Zulu chieftain Mzilikazi, but abandoned it in 1836. He established a station at Hlangezwe in Zululand, near the Umhlatusi River, in 1837, but fled in 1838 after his station was destroyed by Zulus. He returned to the United States in 1839. Died May 20, 1878, in Paris, France. *References*: *DSAB* 2; *SESA*; and *Tabler/Natal*.

VERNAY, ARTHUR STANNARD (1876?–1960). Explorer and big-game hunter, born in Weymouth, England. Vernay came to the United States as a young man, but retained his British nationality. He founded the Vernay Galleries, an antiques gallery in New York City, and managed it until his retirement in 1941. He was a field associate at the American Museum of Natural History, headed several expeditions for the museum, and brought back thousands of specimens. He led the Vernay-Land expedition to the Kalahari Desert, Ngamiland, in 1930, and made an expedition to Nyasaland in 1946. Died October 25, 1960, in Nassau, the Bahamas. *References*: *New Yorker*, May 14, 1949; *NYT*, October 26, 1960; and *Times* (London), October 26, 1960.

VERNER, SAMUEL PHILLIPS (1873–1943). Missionary and explorer, born November 14, 1873, in Columbia, South Carolina. Verner graduated from the University of South Carolina and was ordained in 1895. He taught at Stillman Institute (Tuskaloosa, Ala.) from 1893 to 1895. He was a missionary under the Board of Foreign Missions of the Presbyterian Church in the United States* in the Congo Free State from 1895 to 1899 and served as business manager of the American Presbyterian Congo Mission (APCM)* in Luebo. He explored parts of the Kasai district from 1897 to 1899 and tried unsuccessfully to establish a mission station in Ndombe. He resigned from the mission, returned to the United States in 1899, and brought back numerous ethnological, geological, and zoological specimens which he gave the Smithsonian Institution. He wrote *Pioneering in Central Africa* (Richmond, Va., 1903) and an article on African pygmies in the August 1902 issue of *Atlantic Monthly*. He was general secretary of the American Congo Company,* and in 1907 headed an expedition for the American Congo Company* to set up a rubber gathering plantation near the Congo River. He later taught in Transylvania County, North Carolina, and was superintendent of the county school system. Died October 9, 1943, in Brevard, North Carolina. *References*: Samuel Phillips Verner Papers, South Carolina Library, University of South Carolina, Columbia, S.C.; John R. Crawford, "Pioneer African Missionary: Samuel Phillips Verner," *Journal of Presbyterian History* 60 (1982): 42–57; and *WWWA*.

VINCENT, FRANK (1848–1916). Traveler and author, born April 2, 1848, in Brooklyn, New York. Vincent attended Yale University. He began to travel in 1871 and made a systematic tour of the world betweeen 1871 and 1886. He explored the Congo Free State and wrote *Actual Africa: or, The Coming Continent: A Tour of Exploration* (New York, 1895). Died June 19, 1916, in Woodstock, New York. *References*: *ACAB*; *DAB*; and *WWWA*.

W

WALKER, WILLIAM (1808–1896). Missionary, born October 3, 1808, in Vershire, Vermont. Walker attended Middlebury College, graduated from Amherst College and Andover Theological Seminary, and was ordained in 1841. He served as missionary under the American Board of Commissioners for Foreign Missions (ABCFM),* stationed first in Cape Palmas, and later in Gabon from 1842 to 1871, and under the Board of Foreign Missions of the Presbyterian Church in the U.S.A.* in Gabon from 1879 to 1883. He served as pastor of the church at Baraka and head of a boys' boarding school. He was also vice commercial agent in Gabon. He converted the Mpongwe language to writing and translated parts of the Bible into this language. With Ira Preston* he made an exploration trip up the Ogowe River in 1854. He was later a pastor in Milton, Wisconsin. Died December 8, 1896, in Milton, Wisconsin. *References*: William Walker Papers, State Historical Society of Wisconsin, Madison, Wis.; *Amherst*; *AndoverTS*; and K. D. Patterson, "Early Knowledge of the Ogowe River and the American Explorations of 1854," *African Historical Studies* 5 (1972): 75–90.

WALLER, JOHN L(EWIS) (1850–1907). Lawyer, journalist, and consul, born a slave January 12, 1850, in New Madrid County, Missouri, and grew up in Inka (later Tama City), Iowa. Waller studied law and was admitted to the bar in 1877. He practiced law in Leavenworth and Lawrence, Kansas. He published a weekly newspaper, the *Western Recorder*, from 1882 to 1885, and was involved in the publication of the *American Citizen* in Topeka in 1888–1889. He was consul at Tamatave, Madagascar, from 1891 to 1894. He obtained a large land concession from the Malagasy government, intending to establish a colony. After the French invasion of Madagascar in 1894, Waller was arrested by the French authorities in 1895 and accused of breaking French postal regulations and transmitting military intelligence to the Malagasy. He was sentenced to twenty years of solitary confinement and shipped to France. He was released in 1896 but never succeeded in obtaining redress for his lost land concession. He was later

active in Kansas politics and was editor-in-chief of the *American Citizen* in
1896–1897. He also served in the Spanish-American War. Died October 13,
1907, in Mamaroneck, New York. *References*: Allison Blakely, "The John L.
Waller Affair, 1895–1896," *NHB* 37 (1974): 216–18; *DANB*; *NCAB* 5:195; R.
B. Woods, "Black American Press and the New Manifest Destiny: The Waller
Affair," *Phylon* 38 (1977): 24–34; and R. B. Woods, *A Black Odyssey: John
Lewis Waller and the Promise of American Life, 1878–1900* (Lawrence, Kans.,
1981).

WALTON, LESTER AGLAR (1882–1965). Diplomat and journalist, born
April 20, 1882, in St. Louis, Missouri. Walton graduated from Wilberforce
University. He was a reporter on the St. Louis *Globe-Democrat* and *Star-Times*,
drama editor of the New York *Age* from 1908 to 1920, director of Harlem's
Lafayette Theatre in 1917–1918, and associate editor of *Age* from 1932 to 1935.
He was minister to Liberia from 1935 to 1946. He negotiated several treaties
between the United States and Liberia, negotiated an agreement in 1941 au-
thorizing the landing of American troops on Liberian soil and giving the United
States the right to build an air base there, and negotiated an agreement in 1943
for the construction by the United States of a port in Liberia. He was adviser to
the Liberian delegate to the United Nations in 1948–1949. He later served with
the New York City Commission on Civil Rights until his retirement in 1964.
Died October 16, 1965, in New York City. *References*: Lester Aglar Walton
Papers, Schomburg Center for Research in Black Culture, New York Public
Library, New York City; *Christmas*; *DAB* S7; *NYT*, October 19, 1965; and
WWWA.

WARD, HENRY AUGUSTUS (1834–1906). Naturalist, born March 9, 1834,
in Rochester, New York. Ward attended Williams College and studied and
worked at Louis Agassiz's museum in Cambridge, Massachusetts. He studied
in Paris and made a tour of the Middle East in 1855, gathering fossils and
minerals. He made a collecting and exploration trip to West Africa from 1858
to 1860 and traveled in the Red Sea region in 1876–1877. He was professor of
natural history at the University of Rochester from 1861 to 1875 and established
Ward's Natural Science Establishment in Rochester, New York, in 1862. Killed
July 4, 1906, in an automobile accident in Buffalo, New York. *References*:
Henry A. Ward Papers, University of Rochester Library; *ACAB*; *DAB*; Sally G.
Kohlstedt, "Henry A. Ward: The Merchant Naturalist and American Museum
Development," *Journal of the Society for the Bibliography of Natural History*
9 (April 1978): 647–61; *NCAB* 28:169; Roswell H. Ward, *Henry A. Ward;
Museum Builder to America* (Rochester, 1948); and *WWWA*.

WARE, ENOCH R(ICHMOND) (1819–1875). Merchant, born January 2,
1819, in Winterport, Maine. Ware served as supercargo on a number of trading
voyages to West Africa. Subsequently he established his own mercantile house

in New York City and carried on extensive trade with West Africa. Died July 15, 1875, in Yonkers, New York. *References*: Enoch Richmond Ware Papers and diaries in private hands; Enoch Richmond Ware, "West African Trading Voyage: Diary of the Supercargo of the Brig 'Northumberland,' of Salem in 1844," *Yachting* 91 (March 1952): 45–47, 92–93; *Yachting* 91 (April 1952): 54–56, 102, 104; *Yachting* 91 (May 1952): 53–55, 84–85; George E. Brooks, Jr., "Enoch Richmond Ware: African Trader: 1839–1850: Years of Apprenticeship," *American Neptune* 30 (1970): 174–86, 229–48; Edward R. Ware, "Enoch Richmond Ware: Impressions by His Grandson," *American Neptune* 30 (1970): 167–73; and Edward R. Ware, "Health Hazards of the West African Trader, 1840–1870," *American Neptune* 27 (1967): 81–97.

WARING, COLSTON M. (ca. 1793–1834). Clergyman, merchant, and government official, born free in Virginia. Waring came to Liberia in 1823 and became one of the leading merchants of Liberia and pastor of the First Baptist Church in Monrovia. He was elected a member of the Colonial Council and vice agent and was acting administrator of the colony during 1828. He went on a missionary expedition to the interior in 1824, and extracts from his journal were published in the *African Repository*. *Reference*: *Huberich*.

WARNER, DANIEL BASHIEL (1815–1880). Colonist and government official, born free April 18, 1815, in Baltimore, Maryland. Warner immigrated to Liberia with his family in 1823. He entered the shipbuilding business and built several vessels. He was elected to the House of Representatives in 1847 and served as the first speaker of the house, secretary of state, and vice president. He was president of Liberia from 1864 to 1868. He was again vice president from 1879 until his death and also served as an agent of the American Colonization Society* in Monrovia. He wrote the words to Liberia's national anthem. Died December 1, 1880, in Monrovia. *Reference*: *African Repository* 57 (1881): 52.

WARNER, ESTHER SIETMANN (1910-   ). Artist and author, full name Esther Sietmann Warner Dendel, born February 2, 1910, in Laurel, Iowa. Warner graduated from Iowa State and Columbia universities. She lived in Liberia from 1941 to 1943. She wrote several autobiographical books: *New Song in a Strange Land* (Boston, 1948), *Seven Days to Lomaland* (Boston, 1954), and *The Crossing Fee: A Story of Life in Liberia* (Boston, 1968). She was ghost writer of Prince Modupe's *I Was A Savage* (New York, 1958) and wrote *African Fabric Crafts* (New York, 1974). *References*: Esther Sietmann Warner Papers, Special Collections, Mugar Memorial Library, Boston University, Boston; and *CA*.

WARRINER, RUEL CHAFFEE (1872–1934). Mining engineer, born January 11, 1872, in Montrose, Pennsylvania. Warriner graduated from Lehigh University. He was in the employ of the Lehigh Valley Coal Mining Company of

Hazelton, Pennsylvania, in 1896–1897. He came to the Witwatersrand, South
Africa, in 1897; was chief surveyor of the Crown Deep, Limited, from 1897 to
1900; assistant general manager of the Rand Mines from 1900 to 1903; and was
later manager of the Bonanza Gold Mining Company and the French Rand Gold
Mining Company and general manager of the Robinson Gold Mining Company.
He was dismissed in 1917 and became consulting engineer for the Central Mining
and Investment Corporation and vice president of several oil exploration com-
panies. He served with the British Aircraft Production Department during World
War I. Died July 1, 1934, in Johannesburg, South Africa. *References*: *NYT*,
July 3, 1934; and *SADNB*.

WASHBURN, HEZEKIAH M. (1884–1972). Missionary, born February 14,
1884, in Brooksville, Bracken County, Kentucky. Washburn attended Berea
College (Ky.) and graduated from Wheaton College and Louisville Presbyterian
Theological Seminary; he was ordained in 1912. He was a missionary under the
Board of Foreign Missions of the Presbyterian Church in the United States* in
the Belgian Congo from 1912 to 1949. He was stationed in Luebo in the Ibanche
station among the Bakuba tribe. In 1921 he was granted a lifetime seat in the
Bakuba king's tribal council. He returned to the United States in 1949 and served
as a pastor in Evington and Martinsville, Virginia, until 1957. Died July 19,
1972, in Martinsville, Virginia. His autobiography, *A Knight in the Congo:
God's Ambassador in Three Continents* (Bassett, Va., 1972) was published
posthumously. *References*: G. Kent, "How Hezzy Washburn Became a Congo
King," *Reader's Digest* 50 (May 1947): 111–14; and *Ministerial Directory of
the Presbyterian Church, U.S., 1861–1967* (Doraville, Ga., 1967).

WATERS, RICHARD P(ALMER) (1807–1887). Merchant and consul, born
September 29, 1807, in Salem, Massachusetts. Waters left school early, went
into business, and opened a store in Salem. He was the first consul in Zanzibar,
from 1837 until 1844, represented several Salem firms of Zanzibar and played
a dominant role in the local commercial scene. He returned to the United States
in 1844 and was a merchant in Salem and a farmer in North Beverly, Massachusetts. *References*: Richard P. Waters Papers and journals, Peabody Museum,
Salem; *Bulletin of the Essex Institute* 20 (1888): 174–91; and Philip Northway,
"Salem and the Zanzibar-East African Trade, 1825–1845: IV. Richard Palmer
Waters: First American Consul," *EIHC* 90 (1954): 261–73.

WEAVER, WILLIAM (ca. 1795–1852). Colonist. Weaver immigrated to Liberia from Petersburg, Virginia, in 1824. He supervised the establishment of
the settlement at Grand Bassa and founded the town of Edina. He was a member
of the Liberian Senate from 1847 to 1849. Died February 27, 1852, in Edina,
Liberia. *Reference*: *African Repository* 28 (1852): 242.

WEBB, FRANCIS ROPES (1833–1892). Sea captain, colonist, and government official, born March 27, 1833, in Salem, Massachusetts. Webb first went to sea in 1845 with his father. He served in the Union Navy during the Civil War. He made several voyages to Zanzibar and Arabia as master of the barque *Imaum*, in the employ of Benjamin West. He was later resident agent at Aden and Zanzibar for the house of John Bertram and consul in Zanzibar from 1869 to 1872. He was involved in the negotiations of a treaty for the suppression of the slave trade on the east coast of Africa, and assisted Henry Morton Stanley* in fitting out his first expedition. He went to Auckland, New Zealand, in 1881 as resident agent of Arnold, Hines & Company, and was consul there until 1891. Died July 11, 1892, at Chula Vista, California.

WEBB, HARRY HOWARD (1853–1939). Mining engineer, born August 15, 1853, in San Francisco. Webb graduated from the University of California and studied at the Royal School of Mines in London and the school of mines in Freiberg, Saxony, Germany. He worked in the mines in Nevada and was a mining engineer in Idaho and Montana. He became a consultant for the United Rhodesia Gold Fields Company in Northern Rhodesia in 1895, superintendent on the engineering staff of Consolidated Gold Fields of South Africa in 1896, and consulting engineer of that company and some of its affiliates from 1906 until 1916. He became a consulting engineer of Gold Fields American Development Company in 1917 and became involved in a syndicate to develop the borax deposits near Death Valley, California, in 1918. He retired in 1919. Died June 2, 1939, in Santa Barbara, California. *References*: *DAB* S2; and *NYT*, June 4, 1939.

WEBBER, HERBERT JOHN (1865–1946). Plant physiologist, born December 27, 1865, in Lawton, Michigan. Webber graduated from the University of Nebraska and Washington University (St. Louis). He was assistant pathologist in the United States Department of Agriculture in Eustis, Florida, from 1892 to 1897, doing citrus research. He transferred to Washington in 1897 and became physiologist in charge of the Laboratory of Plant Breeding in 1900. He was professor of plant biology at Cornell University in 1907–1908, head of the department of experimental plant biology there from 1908 to 1912, director of Cornell's Citrus Experiment Station from 1913 to 1929, and professor of subtropical horticulture at Cornell until 1936. He was special commissioner to study the citrus industry and agricultural research and education in the Union of South Africa in 1924–1925; his visit resulted in the founding of the Research Institute for Citrus and Subtropical Fruit at Nelspruit, Transvaal. Died January 18, 1946, in Riverside, California. *References*: Herbert John Webber Papers, University of California, Riverside, Library; *DAB* S4; Harry B. Humphrey, *Makers of North American Botany* (New York, 1961), pp. 260–62; *NCAB* 17:387; and *WWWA*.

WEBSTER, JOHN WHITE (1793–1850). University professor, born May 20, 1793, in Boston. Webster graduated from Harvard University and studied medicine in London. He visited the Azores in 1817–1818 and married Harriet Frederica Hickling, daughter of Thomas Hickling.* He did geological research in the Azores and wrote *A Description of the Island of St. Michael, Comprising an Account of Its Geological Structure; with Remarks on the Other Azores or Western Islands* (Boston, 1821). He taught chemistry at Harvard from 1824 to 1849. He became notorious for his murder of Dr. George Parkman, for which he was tried, convicted, and hanged, August 30, 1850, in Boston. *References*: *DAB*; *DAMB*; Robert Sullivan, *The Disappearance of Dr. Parkman* (Boston, 1971); Helen Thomson, *Murder at Harvard* (Boston, 1971); and *WWWA*.

WELLMAN, FREDERICK CREIGHTON (1871–1960). Medical missionary and author, born January 3, 1871, near Independence, Missouri. Wellman graduated from the Chicago Seminary and Kansas City Medical College and studied at the University of London. He was a missionary at the American Mission in Bihé, Angola, and remained there for nine years. He established two hospitals, explored parts of the interior and studied tropical diseases. In 1906 he described medicinal plants in Angola and how poisons were made. He was later professor of tropical medicine at Tulane University. Turning to art, he established schools of art in El Paso, Santa Fe, and Denver, and was dean of the College of Fine Arts at Denver University. Died September 3, 1960, in Chapel Hill, North Carolina. He wrote *Life Too Short: An Autobiography* (Philadelphia, 1943) under the pseudonym Cyril Kay-Scott. *References*: *CB* 1944; *NCAB* D:302; *NYT*, September 5, 1960; and *WWWA*.

WELMERS, WILLIAM E(VERT) (1916–). Missionary and educator, born April 4, 1916, in Orange City, Iowa. Welmers graduated from Hope College, Westminster Theological Seminary, and the University of Pennsylvania, and was ordained in 1943. He was a pastor in Philadelphia from 1943 to 1946 and a missionary in the Lutheran mission in Liberia from 1946 to 1948 and in 1954–1955. He was assistant and then associate professor of linguistics at Cornell University from 1950 to 1954, associate professor of linguistics and African languages at Kennedy School of Missions from 1955 to 1960, and professor of linguistics and African languages at the University of California at Los Angeles after 1960. He wrote *A Descriptive Grammar of Fanti* (Philadelphia, 1946), *Spoken Kpelle* (Monrovia, 1948), *African Language Structure* (Berkeley, Calif., 1973), and *A Grammar of Vai* (Berkeley, Calif., 1976). *References*: *CA*; *DAS*; and *WWA*.

WENGATZ, SUSAN (MOBERLY TALBOT) (1885–1930). Missionary, born January 29, 1885, in Coatesville, Indiana. Wengatz graduated from Taylor University. She was a missionary under the Board of Foreign Missions of the Methodist Episcopal Church in the U.S.A.* in Angola from 1910 to 1930. She was matron of a girls' boarding school in Quionga from 1911 to 1922 and later served at Malange. Bitten by a rabid dog, she died January 16, 1930, in Malange, Angola. Her husband, **JOHN C(HRISTIAN) WENGATZ** (1880-   ), a missionary, was born October 1880 in Steuben, New York. He graduated from Cazenovia Seminary and Taylor University and was a missionary under the Board of Foreign Missions of the Methodist Episcopal Church in Angola from 1910 until 1934, and in Liberia after 1934, first at Nana Kru and later at Grand Cess. He wrote *Miracles in Black: Missionary Experiences in the Wilds of Africa* (New York, 1938). *References*: Anna T. McPherson, *Forgotten Saints* (Grand Rapids, Mich., 1961), pp. 87–92; and Sadie L. Miller, comp., *In Jesus' Name: Memoirs of the Victorious Life and Triumphant Death of Susan Talbot Wengatz* (n.p., n.d.).

WESLEYAN METHODIST CHURCH OF AMERICA MISSIONARY SOCIETY. Established 1862, it began missionary work in Sierra Leone in 1889, in South Africa in 1910, in Swaziland in 1910, and later also in Northern Rhodesia, Southern Rhodesia, Mozambique, and Liberia. It was later renamed the Department of World Missions. *References*: Wesleyan Methodist Church of America Records, The Wesleyan Church Missionary Society Archives and Historical Society, Marion, Ind.; Charles W. Carter, *A Half Century of American Wesleyan Missions in West Africa* (Syracuse, N.Y., 1940); and George H. Clarke and Mary L. Clarke, *American Wesleyan Mission of Sierra Leone, W. Africa* (n.p., 191-?).

WHARTON, CONWAY TALIAFERRO (1890–1953). Missionary, born June 26, 1890, in Steel Creek, North Carolina. Wharton attended Southwestern Presbyterian University (Clarksville, Tenn.) and graduated from Austin College (Sherman, Texas) and Austin Theological Presbyterian Seminary (Texas); he was ordained in 1914. He was a missionary under the Board of Foreign Missions of the Presbyterian Church in the United States* and was a member of the American Presbyterian Congo Mission (APCM)* in Bushongo, Belgian Congo, from 1915 to 1928. He wrote *The Leopard Hunts Alone: The Life and Ways of the Savages of the Congo and How Christianity Was Welcomed by Them* (New York, 1927). He returned to the United States in 1928 and was a pastor in Sherman and Austin, Texas. He was again a missionary in Luebo, Belgian Congo, from 1944 to 1949, and was assigned to the Morrison Bible School in the Mutato station. He was a pastor in Ballinger, Texas, from 1950 until his death. Died December 3, 1953, in Ballinger, Texas. His wife, **ETHEL TAYLOR WHARTON** (1889-   ), was born September 1, 1889, in Butler, Missouri, and grew up in El Paso, Texas. She graduated from the University of Texas and taught Spanish. She was a missionary in the Belgian Congo from 1915 until 1928, when she returned to the United States because of ill health. She returned to the Belgian Congo in 1944 and served until 1949. She wrote *Led in Triumph: Sixty Years of Southern Presbyterian Missions in the Belgian Congo* (Nashville,

Tenn., 1952). *References*: *In Memory of Missionaries of the Presbyterian Church, U.S. who have Entered into Rest in the Years 1953–1955* (Nashville, Tenn., 1955); E. C. Scott, comp., *Ministerial Directory of the Presbyterian Church, U.S., 1861–1941* (Atlanta, 1950).

WHITE, STEWART EDWARD (1873–1946). Author, born March 12, 1873, in Grand Rapids, Michigan. White graduated from the University of Michigan and Columbia Law School. He worked as a trapper, lumberjack, and explorer and wrote about adventure and the outdoors. He spent much time in Africa, hunting big game. He explored German East Africa in 1913 and mapped that area. He wrote *African Camp Fires* (Garden City, N.Y., 1913), *The Leopard Woman* (Garden City, N.Y., 1912), *The Land of Footprints* (Garden City, N.Y., 1913), *The Rediscovered Country* (Garden City, N.Y., 1915), and *Simba* (Garden City, N.Y., 1918). He served in the army during World War I. He settled later in Santa Barbara, California. Died September 18, 1946, in San Francisco. *References*: *DAB* S4; *NCAB* 13:313, F:144; *NYT*, September 19, 1946; and *WWWA*.

WHITEHOUSE, WILLIAM FITZHUGH (1877–1955). Explorer, born September 6, 1877, in Elmhurst, Illinois. Whitehouse graduated from Yale University. He went on an exploring, map-making, and big-game hunting expedition in Somaliland, Abyssinia, British East Africa, and Uganda in 1899–1900, exploring lakes Rudolph and Stephanie. He explored Abyssinia in 1902 and described his travels in the September 1902 issue of *Scribner's* magazine. He was employed by the Guaranty Trust Company, New York, from 1900 to 1904; became a member of the New York Stock Exchange in 1904; partner in the investment firm of Shoemaker, Bates Company until 1911; and president of Jute Product, Inc., of New York City until his retirement. He was a pioneer of free ballooning after 1904 and served in the army in World War I. He was a state senator of Rhode Island from 1924 to 1928. Died May 27, 1955, in Newport, Rhode Island. *References*: *NYT*, May 28, 1955; and *WWWA*.

WILCOX, WILLIAM CULLEN (1850–1928). Missionary, born August 6, 1850, in Richfield, Ohio. Wilcox graduated from Oberlin College and Oberlin Theological Seminary and studied at Yale Divinity School, and was ordained in 1881. He was a missionary under the American Board of Commissioners for Foreign Missions (ABCFM)* from 1881 until 1910. He served at Mapumulu, Natal, Inhambane, Mozambique, again at Mapumulu, and later in the Groutville mission station in Umvoti, South Africa. He worked on the revision of the Zulu Bible until 1907. He then tried to establish a self-supporting native mission in South Africa and founded the Zulu Industrial Improvement Company at Ikeya, a real-estate venture that failed. He returned to the United States in 1917, worked on an assembly line in Detroit, and clerked in a book store in Los Angeles. He wrote *The Man from an African Jungle* (New York, 1925) and his memoirs, *Proud Endeavor: The Story of a Yankee on a Mission to South Africa*, comp.

and ed. Mark F. Wilcox (New York, 1962), which were published posthumously. Died January 26, 1928, in Bakersfield, California.

WILDER, GEORGE ALBERT (1855–1935). Missionary, son of Hyman Augustus Wilder,* born March 14, 1855, at the Adams Mission, Amanzimtoti, Natal, South Africa, and came to the United States in 1868. Wilder graduated from Williams College and Hartford Theological Seminary. He returned to South Africa in 1880 as a missionary under the American Board of Commissioners for Foreign Missions (ABCFM)* and served in the Zulu mission at Umtwalume. He established the East African Mission at Mt. Silinda, Rhodesia, in 1893. He retired in 1925 and wrote *The White African. The Story of Mafavuke, "Who Dies and Lives Again," as Told by Himself* (Bloomfield, N.J., 1933). Died December 28, 1935, in Glen Ridge, New Jersey. *Reference: Hewitt.*

WILDER, HYMAN AUGUSTUS (1822–1877). Missionary, born February 17, 1822, in Cornwall, Addison County, Vermont, and grew up in Millville, Orleans County, New York. Wilder graduated from Williams College and the East Windsor Seminary (Conn.), and was ordained in 1848. He was a missionary under the American Board of Commissioners for Foreign Missions (ABCFM)* in South Africa from 1849 until 1877. He established a mission station at Umtwalume in 1851, was a pioneer in industrial work for the Zulus, supervised the mission printing press, and was principal of the Adams Training School at Amanzimtoti until 1875. He returned to the United States in 1877. Died September 7, 1877, in Hartford, Connecticut. *References: DSAB* 4; *Hewitt*; and *SESA.*

WILES, V(IVIAN) MCKINLEY (1906–1970). Urologist, born July 31, 1906, in Barbados, British West Indies; brought to the United States in 1912 and grew up in Cambridge, Massachusetts. Wiles graduated from Andrews (Berrien, Mich.) and Loma Linda (Calif.) universities, and studied at New York University. He practiced medicine in New York City after 1939 and specialized in urology after 1952. He made many medical service trips to Africa after 1957 at his own expense, visiting hospitals and clinics in some twenty-two countries, treating patients, performing surgery, and making surveys of urological needs. In 1961, he became the first black to perform surgery at the Schweitzer Hospital in Lambarene, Gabon. Died March 22, 1970, in Riverside, the Bronx, New York. *References: NCAB* 55:451; and *NYT*, March 26, 1970.

WILLIAMS, ALPHEUS F(ULLER) (1874–1953). Mining engineer and executive, son of Gardner Fred Williams,* born June 21, 1874, in Oakland, California. Williams attended Cornell University and graduated from the University of California. He came to South Africa in 1899, was employed as assistant general manager of De Beers Consolidated Mines Limited of Kimberley from 1900 to 1904, succeeded his father as general manager of the company in 1905, and served until 1931. In 1931 he established a firm of structural engineers. He played an important part in the development of the St. John Ambulance in South Africa. He wrote *Diamond Deposits of German South West Africa* (Kimberley, 1914), *The Genesis of the Diamond* (London, 1932), and his memoirs, *Some Dreams Come True* (Cape Town, 1948). Died January 6, 1953, in Muizenberg, Cape, South Africa. *References*: *DSAB* 4; *NYT*, January 7, 1953; and *SADNB*.

WILLIAMS, ANTHONY D. (ca. 1799–1861). Colonist, born free in Virginia. Williams immigrated to Liberia in 1823. He was acting agent of the American Colonization Society* in 1830 and in 1832–1833 and agent from 1836 to 1839. He settled at Cape Palmas in 1841 and served as vice president of Liberia from 1851 to 1855. *Reference*: *Huberich*.

WILLIAMS, GARDNER FRED (1842–1922). Mining engineer, born March 14, 1842, in Saginaw, Michigan. Williams graduated from the College of California (later University of California) and studied at the Royal Mining Academy (Freiberg, Saxony, Germany). He was assayer of the mint in San Francisco in 1870–1871; mill superintendent in Pioche, Nevada, from 1871 to 1875; worked at various places in the West from 1875 to 1880; and was consultant for a New York exploration company in the West from 1880 to 1883. He went to South Africa in 1884 and was manager of the Transvaal Gold Exploration and Land Company in Pilgrim's Rest in Eastern Transvaal in 1884–1885. He was the first general manager of the De Beers Mining Company (later De Beers Consolidated Mines, Limited) from 1887 until 1905. He played an important part in the amalgamation of the diamond companies, was responsible for the institution of the open mines system for underground works, and improved the methods of working the mines. He retired in 1905. He wrote *The Diamond Mines of South Africa* (New York, 1902). He was active in the military operations during the siege of Kimberley in the South African War. Died August 22, 1922, in San Francisco. *References*: *DAB*; *DSAB* 4; *NCAB* 9:528; *SADNB*; and *WWWA*.

WILLIAMS, GEORGE WASHINGTON (1849–1891). Author, soldier and clergyman, born October 16, 1849, in Bedford Springs, Pennsylvania. Williams served in the Union Army during the Civil War, in the Mexican revolutionary army from 1865 to 1867, and in the Tenth Cavalry of the United States Army in 1867–1868. He attended Howard University and Wayland Seminary, graduated from Newton Theological Institution (Mass.), and was ordained in 1874. He was a pastor in Boston and Cincinnati from 1874 to 1877 and then studied law and was admitted to the bar. He went to the Congo Free State in 1890–1891 to write a series of articles for S. S. McClure and to report on the progress of the Congo railroad. He explored the Congo from the mouth of the Congo River to Stanley Falls and described the inhumane conditions existing there. He wrote *An Open Letter to Leopold II, King of the Belgians and Sovereign of the Independent State of Congo* (Stanley Falls, Congo Free State, 1890) and *A Report* *on the Proposed Congo Railway* (n.p., 1890?). Died August 2, 1891, in Blackpool, England. *References*: *ACAB*; *DAB*; *DANB*; *DLB*; John Hope Franklin, *George Washington Williams and Africa* (Washington, D.C., 1971); John Hope Franklin, *George Washington Williams: A Biography* (Chicago, 1985); *OAB*; and *WWWA*.

WILLIAMS, L. H. ("MIKE") (1926-). Soldier of fortune, born in San Antonio, Texas. Williams enlisted in the United States Army in 1942, was commissioned second lieutenant in 1948, was assigned to the 10th Special Forces in 1952, and served in Korea. He was discharged a captain in 1960. He joined the mercenaries led by Michael Hoar in Katanga in 1964, but was forced to leave when the United States government decided it did not want Americans fighting there. He went to Rhodesia in 1975 and joined the Rhodesian Armed Forces. He served in the 3 Protection Company at Mount Darwin, commanded the 5 Protection Company at Bulawayo, and in 1977 became second-in-command of the Grey's Scouts, Rhodesia's mounted infantry unit, which specialized in counterinsurgency activities. He returned to the United States in 1978. He wrote *Major Mike* (as told to Robin Moore; Westport, Conn., 1978). *Reference*: Jay Mallin and Robert K. Brown, *Merc: American Soldiers of Fortune* (New York, 1979), ch. 7.

WILLIAMS, WALTER B. (1868–1968). Missionary, born on the Isle of Wight. He was a missionary in Rio de Janiero, Brazil, under the British and Foreign Sailors' Society from 1892 to 1894. He came to the United States in 1894 and was a pastor in Minnesota and Washington from 1898 to 1905. He was a missionary under the Board of Foreign Missions of the Methodist Episcopal Church in the U.S.A.* in Africa from 1905 to 1933. He was stationed at Quiongua and Pungo Andongo, Angola, from 1905 to 1908. He was transferred to Liberia in 1908, served on the Kru coast, and helped to bring a peace settlement to the area following the Kru rebellion. He was stationed in Nana Kru as pastor, teacher, and district superintendent from 1913 until his retirement in 1933, when he returned to the United States. He wrote (with his wife) *Adventures with the Krus in West Africa* (New York, 1955). Died September 28, 1968, in St. Petersburg, Florida.

WILLIS, BAILEY (1857–1949). Geologist, born May 31, 1857. in Idlewild-on-Hudson, New York. Willis graduated from the Columbia School of Mines. He became a geologist for the Northern Pacific Railway in 1880 and explored Washington Territory. He was with the United States Geological Survey from 1882 to 1915, conducted geological exploration in China, helped the Argentine government establish a geological survey, and examined the geological features of Turkey in 1905. He was a professor of geology at Stanford University from 1915 to 1922 and became a consulting geological engineer in 1922. He was seismologist of the Carnegie Institute of Washington expedition to Palestine and

Cyprus in 1927 and was in Egypt in 1929. He explored the East African Rift and wrote *Living Africa: A Geologist's Wanderings through the Rift Valley* (New York, 1920), which is mostly autobiographical, and *East African Plateaus and Rift Valleys* (Washington, D.C., 1936). Died February 19, 1949, in Palo Alto, California. *References*: *BMNAS* 35 (1961): 333–50; *Bulletin of the Geological Society of America* 73 (1962): 55–72; *DAB* S4; *DSB*; *NCAB* 37:53; and *WWWA*.

WILSON, ALEXANDER ERWIN (1803–1841). Missionary, born December 11, 1803, in Mecklenburg County, North Carolina. Wilson graduated from the University of North Carolina and Union Theological Seminary of Virginia. He was a missionary under the American Board of Commissioners for Foreign Missions (ABCFM)* in South Africa from 1835 to 1838 and tried to establish a mission in the Transvaal. He returned to the United States in 1838 but went as a missionary to Liberia in 1839. Died October 13, 1841, at Fishtown, Cape Palmas, Liberia. His wife **MARY JANE (SMITHEY) WILSON** (1814–1836), was born in Richmond, Virginia, and accompanied her husband in 1834 to South Africa. Died at Moesga, in the Western Transvaal, the first white woman to die north of the Vaal River. *References*: *DSAB* 3; and *SADNB*.

WILSON, BENJAMIN F. (1838–1920). Physician, born in New Dartmouth, Massachusetts. Wilson practiced medicine in New Bedford, Massachusetts, and served as surgeon in the Union Navy during the Civil War. He went on a cruise on the whaler *Wainwright* in 1865 to regain his health, and left the ship in Anjouan (Johanna) in the Comoro Islands. He successfully treated the sultan of Anjouan and received in return a grant of land. He expanded his holdings, and his plantation became the second largest sugar cane plantation on the island. He later also engaged in the production of vanilla beans and coffee. He had difficulties with the Sultan of Anjouan from 1882 to 1884 and later with the French authorities who seized the Comoro Islands in 1886 and who tried to cancel Wilson's grants. Lengthy diplomatic negotiations had not solved the dispute by the time he died, although he continued to live on and operate his plantation. Died in Anjouan, the Comoro Islands. *Reference*: *The New Bedford* (Mass.) *Sunday Standard*, June 6, 1920.

WILSON, J(OHN) LEIGHTON (1809–1886). Missionary, born March 25, 1809, in Mount Clio, South Carolina. Wilson graduated from Union College and Columbia (now South Carolina) Seminary, studied at Andover Theological Seminary, and was ordained in 1833. He went on an exploring tour of West Africa in 1833–1834 and freed his slaves in 1834 and took them at his own expense to Liberia. He was a missionary under the American Board of Commissioners for Foreign Missions (ABCFM)* from 1834 until 1852. He founded a mission at Cape Palmas in 1834 and transferred it to Gabon in 1842. He traveled extensively, recorded the earliest investigation of the gorilla in its natural habitat, and wrote *Western Africa: Its History, Condition, and Prospects* (New

York, 1856). He compiled grammars and dictionaries of the Grebo and Mpongwe languages and translated parts of the Bible into the Mpongwe language. He returned to the United States in 1852. He was secretary of the Board of Foreign Missions of the Presbyterian Church* and editor of *Home and Foreign Record* from 1853 to 1861. During the Civil War he was in charge of the foreign missions of the Presbyterian Church in the Confederate States of America (later Presbyterian Church in the United States) from 1861 until 1885. He founded the *Missionary* in 1866 and was its editor until his death. Died July 13, 1886, in Mount Clio, South Carolina. *References*: ACAB; Henry H. Bucher, "John Leighton Wilson and the Mpongwe: The 'Spirit of 1776' in Mid-nineteenth Century Africa," *Journal of Presbyterian History* 54 (1976): 291–316; *DAB*; *NCAB* 21:226; and *WWWA*.

WILTSEE, ERNEST (ABRAM) (1863–1947). Mining engineer, born September 30, 1863, in Poughkeepsie, Dutchess County, New York. Wiltsee graduated from Columbia University School of Mines. He worked as a chemist in Braddock, Pennsylvania, and Pueblo and Denver, Colorado, until 1888; was assistant superintendent of a mine at Grass Valley, California, from 1888 to 1890; and manager of a mine at Homewardbound, California, from 1890 to 1892. He went to South Africa in 1892 as a mining manager for Barney Barnato and as an assistant to John Hays Hammond.* He was in charge of the Glencairn Mine and manager of the Geldenhuis Estate Mine at Johannesburg for the Consolidated Goldfields of South Africa. He became superintendent engineer for Consolidated Goldfields in 1895. He returned to the United States in 1896, engaged in various enterprises in California, Denver, and New York, and was later a consulting engineer in New York City. Died September 29, 1947, in Sacramento, California. *References*: Ernest Wiltsee Papers, Bancroft Library, University of California, Berkeley, Calif.; *NCAB* 14:388; and *San Francisco Chronicle*, December 17, 1947.

WINSHAW, WILLIAM CHARLES (1871–1966). Physician and wine-maker, born November 21, 1871, in Kentucky. Winshaw attended Tulane University Medical School. Winshaw supervised a shipment of mules from New Orleans to Koelenhof, near Stellenbosch, South Africa, in 1900. He then fought with the British Army during the South African War and was a medical officer to the colonial government in Cape Town. He leased a farm near Stellenbosch in 1904 and began to make wine, grape juice, and jam. The companies he established went bankrupt in 1920, but he was rehabilitated in 1924 and founded the Stellenbosch Farmers' Winery Limited (incorporated in 1950 as the Stellenbosch Farmers' Wine Trust), which became South Africa's largest wine-making firm. *Reference*: *Stellenbosch Three Centuries* (Stellenbosch, Cape Province, 1979).

WINSHIP, BLANTON (1869–1947). Army officer, born November 23, 1869, in Macon, Georgia. Winship graduated from Mercer University and the University of Georgia and practiced law in Macon from 1893 to 1898. He was commissioned first lieutenant in the United States Army in 1899, served in the Philippines, Cuba, and Mexico, and in France during World War I. He was a legal adviser to the government of the Philippines from 1928 to 1930 and judge advocate of the army from 1931 to 1933. He retired in 1933 with the rank of major general. He was special commissioner to Liberia and member of the League of Nations Commission on Liberia Affairs in 1933. He was governor of Puerto Rico from 1934 to 1939 and coordinator of the Inter-American Defense Board during World War II. Died October 9, 1947, in Washington, D.C. *References*: *DAB* S4; *NCAB* 37:246; *NYT*, October 10, 1947; *WAMB*; and *WWWA*.

WOLBACH, SIMEON BURT (1880–1954). Pathologist, born July 3, 1880, in Grand Island, Nebraska. Wolbach attended Lawrence Scientific School of Harvard University and graduated from its medical school. He was a member of the sleeping-sickness commission sent to Gambia in 1911. He was director of the research commission on typhus fever sent to Poland in 1920. He was assistant professor of bacteriology, associate professor of pathology and bacteriology, and professor of pathological anatomy at Harvard Medical School from 1910 until his retirement in 1947, and pathologist to Peter Bent Brigham, Children's, Infants, and Boston Lying-In hospitals and Free Hospital for Women in Boston until 1947. Died March 19, 1954, in Sudbury, Massachusetts. *References*: Simeon Burt Wolbach, "Diary of Expedition to Gambia, 1911," MS, Francis A. Contway Library of Medicine, Boston; *DAMB* 1984; *NCAB* 46:274; *NYT*, March 20, 1954; and *WWWA*.

WOLFF, HENRY ALBERT (1853–1933). Physician, born July 3, 1853, in Montreal, Quebec, Canada. Wolff graduated from Amherst College and Columbia University. He practiced medicine in South Africa from 1878 to 1896, in New York City from 1897 to 1900, and in California from 1900 until his death. He was state mineralogist to the Hova government in Madagascar in 1895–1896. He was surgeon major in the British Army during the Griqualand native rebellion in South Africa in 1878–1879. He resigned from the army to associate with Dr. Leander Starr Jameson in private practice. He was active in the Johannesburg Reform Committee (see Reform Committee), one of the leaders of the Jameson Raid in 1895–1896, and the only one to escape after the raid. Died October 30, 1933, in Pasadena, California. *Reference*: *Amherst*.

WOOD, CLINTON TYLER (1869–1932). Clergyman and educator, born January 15, 1869, in Carlisle, Ohio. Wood graduated from Princeton University and Princeton Theological Seminary. He studied at the University of Chicago and Kennedy School of Missions (Hartford, Conn.) and was ordained in 1898. He taught at Princeton Preparatory School from 1892 to 1895. He was principal of Missionary Training College in Wellington, Cape Province, South Africa, from 1898 to 1909, and professor of history there from 1898 to 1913. He was later professor of missions at the College of Wooster (Ohio), from 1912 to 1926. Died January 23, 1932, in Boston. *References*: *Wooster Daily Record*, January 25, 1932; and *WWWA*.

WOOD, HUBERT STEPHEN (ca. 1832–1921). Businessman and prospector, born in Philadelphia. Wood came to South Africa in 1861, occupied a farm in the Mount Currie area of Old Laager (now Kokstad) in East Griqualand from 1866 to 1871, and then went diamond prospecting in Kimberley and acquired a large fortune. He built the Royal Hotel at Kokstad in 1878 and established other hotels and bars as well as the first bank in Kokstad. He went to the gold diggings on the Witwatersrand in 1886, established American beer halls in Johannesburg, a hotel in Jeppe's Town in 1889, and an American restaurant in Johannesburg in 1892. These business ventures failed, and he returned to East Griqualand and farmed at Droevig. Died July 2, 1921, in Kokstad, South Africa. *Reference*: *DASB* 4.

WOODFORD, ETHELBERT GEORGE (1850–1923). Civil engineer, born July 12, 1850, at Cold Spring, Putnam County, New York, and grew up in London, England, until 1867 when he returned to the United States. He was machinist apprentice, was employed in a machine shop in Buffalo, New York, and in an iron works in New York City. He was a draftsman and assistant engineer in Callao, Peru, in 1871–1872, and was involved in the design and care of heavy machinery in Peru, Bolivia, and Chile until 1875. He came to South Africa in 1878 and worked in the Transvaal gold fields. He was acting town engineer in Kimberley, chief engineer of the mining board in 1878, and chief engineer at the Sterksbrown & Aliwal Railroad from 1883 to 1885. He returned to the United States in 1885 but was back in South Africa in 1887. He was first state mining engineer of the Transvaal Republic from 1888 to 1891 and largely developed its mining laws, but he quarreled with President Paul Kruger and was forced to leave. He prospected in Australia and Madagascar and returned to the United States in 1895. He was later consulting engineer in Denver, Colorado, and London, inspected mines in West Africa, returned to South Africa again in 1903 and located a rich diamond claim, but was back in the United States in 1907. Died November 9, 1923, in Seattle, Washington. *References*: *NCAB* 20:262; *NYT*, November 11, 1923; and *SADNB*.

WORK, ERNEST F(RANK) (1877–1957). Educator, born January 22, 1877, in Indiana County, Pennsylvania. Work graduated from Penn State Normal School and the University of Michigan. He became associate professor of political science at Muskingum College (New Concord, Ohio) in 1922, was registrar from 1923 to 1928, and professor of history from 1925 to 1946. At the suggestion of Ethiopians who had been his students, he was invited to Ethiopia by Emperor

Haile Selassie to organize its educational system. He served as adviser to the Ethiopian Ministry of Education and Fine Arts from 1932 to 1935 and helped to write the Constitution of Ethiopia. He wrote *Ethiopia: A Pawn in European Diplomacy* (New York, 1935). Died October 26, 1957, in New Concord, Ohio. *References*: Richard A. Caulk, "Ernest Work on Ethiopian Education," *Ethiopian Journal of Education* 8 (November 1975): 3–14; and *OAB*.

WRIGHT, RICHARD ROBERT, JR. (1878–1967). Clergyman, born April 16, 1878, in Cuthbert, Georgia. Wright graduated from Georgia State College and the universities of Chicago and Pennsylvania, and studied at the universities of Berlin and Leipzig. He was ordained an elder in 1901. He was a pastor in Elgin, Illinois; Chicago; and Conshohocken, Pennsylvania. He was editor of *The Christian Record* from 1909 to 1936 and president of Wilberforce University from 1932 to 1936. He was elected bishop in 1936 and served as bishop of the African Methodist Episcopal Church (AMEC)* in South Africa from 1936 until 1940. He founded a school of religion and a community clinic and built over fifty churches. He served in the United States after 1940 and was later senior bishop of the AMEC. He wrote *87 Years Behind the Black Curtain: An Autobiography* (Philadelphia, 1965). Died December 12, 1967, in Philadelphia. His wife, **CHARLOTTE CROGMAN WRIGHT** (1897–1959), wrote of her experiences in *Beneath the Southern Cross: The Story of an American Bishop's Wife in South Africa* (New York, 1955). *References*: *NYT*, December 14, 1967; and *Wright*.

WULSIN, FREDERICK (ROELKER) (1891–1961). Anthropologist, born July 8, 1891. Wulsin graduated from Harvard University. He traveled in East Africa and Madagascar in 1914–1915, forming a zoological collection for Harvard University's Museum of Comparative Zoology. He served in the army during World War I. He traveled in China, Mongolia, Central Asia, and Indochina from 1921 to 1924. He conducted an archaeological expedition to the Belgian Congo and French Equatorial Africa in 1927–1928 and wrote *An Archaeological Reconnaissance of the Shari Basin* (Cambridge, Mass., 1932) and *The Prehistorical Archaeology of Northwest Africa* (Cambridge, Mass., 1941). He was curator of anthropology at the University Museum of the University of Pennsylvania, served in the Office of the Quartermaster General during World War II, and was professor of anthropology at Tufts University from 1945 to 1958. Died February 26, 1961, in East Greenwich, Rhode Island. *References*: Frederick Wulsin, "Journal, 1914–1915," MS, Museum of Comparative Zoology Library, Harvard University; Frederick Wulsin Diaries and Photographs, 1927–1928, MS, Tozzer Library, Harvard University, Cambridge, Mass.; and *WWWA*.

Y

YATES, BEVERLY PAGE (ca. 1811- ?). Colonist, born free in Virginia. Yates immigrated to Liberia in 1829. He became active in Liberia's military affairs and was colonel of the First Regiment of Liberia Volunteers. He was associate justice of the Supreme Court in 1852, vice president in 1856, and commanding general of the Liberian Militia after 1873. *Reference: Richardson.*

YEATMAN, POPE (1861–1953). Mining engineer, born August 3, 1861, in St. Louis, Missouri. Yeatman graduated from Washington University (St. Louis). He was involved in mines in Missouri from 1888 to 1893. He went to South Africa in 1895, and was mining engineer for the Consolidated Gold Fields of South Africa, Limited, from 1895 to 1899, and manager of the Robinson Deep Gold Mining Company and the Simmer & Jack Gold Mining Company, Johannesburg. He was general manager and consulting engineer of the Randfontein Estates Gold Mining Company, Limited, in the Transvaal from 1899 to 1904. He returned to the United States in 1904, was chief engineer for the M. Guggenheim Sons' Company from 1906 to 1916, and helped to develop their interests in United States and Latin America. He directed the nonferrous metals department of the War Industries Board in World War I. He was later a private consulting engineer in New York City. He retired in 1943. Died December 5, 1953, in Chestnut Hill, Pennsylvania. *References: NCAB* 18:176; *NYT*, December 7, 1953; and *WWWA.*

YERBY, WILLIAM J(AMES) (1867–1950). Physician and consul, born September 22, 1867, in Old Town, Phillips County, Arkansas. Yerby graduated from Roger William University (Nashville, Tenn.) and Mehary Medical College (Nashville). He practiced medicine in Memphis, Tennessee, and was also engaged in publishing and printing from 1900 to 1906. He was consul in Sierra Leone from 1906 to 1915 and in Dakar, Senegal, from 1915 to 1925. He was later consul in La Rochelle, France; in Oporto, Portugal; and in Nantes, France;

until his retirement in 1932. Died July 3, 1950, in Chicago. *References*: *Christmas*; *NYT*, July 4, 1950; and *WWWA*.

YERGAN, MAX (1896–1975). Association official, born July 19, 1896, in Raleigh, North Carolina. Yergan graduated from Shaw and Howard universities. In 1915 he began his association with the Young Men's Christian Association (YMCA), went to India in 1916 as secretary of the International Committee of the YMCA, and was sent to East Africa in 1917 to supervise YMCA activities among African troops. He was senior secretary in South Africa from 1920 until 1936. He returned to the United States in 1936, organized the Council on African Affairs, and was its executive director. He wrote *Gold and Poverty in South Africa; a Study of Economic Organization and Standards of Living* (The Hague, 1939). Died April 11, 1975, in Mount Kisco, New York. *References*: Max Yergan Papers, Moorland-Spingarn Center, Manuscripts Division, Howard University, Washington, D.C.; *CB* 1948; and *NYT*, April 13, 1975.

YOUNG, CHARLES (1864–1922). Army officer, born March 12, 1864, near Mays Lick, Kentucky, and grew up in Ripley, Ohio. Young graduated from the United States Military Academy in 1889, was commissioned second lieutenant, and assigned to the 10th Cavalry. He served in Cuba during the Spanish-American War and in the Philippines from 1901 to 1903. He was military attaché in Haiti from 1904 to 1907 and in Liberia from 1912 to 1915. He helped organize the Liberian Frontier Force* and traveled all over Liberia, making maps. He was forced to retire from active duty in 1917, but was recalled in 1918, and was sent again to Liberia in 1919 as military adviser to the Liberian government. Died January 8, 1922, in Lagos, Nigeria, while on an inspection tour. *References*: *DANB*; and N. G. Heml, "Col. Charles Young: Pointman," *Crisis* 84 (1977): 173–76.

Chiefs of American Diplomatic Missions in Africa, 1863–1988

ABBREVIATIONS

AE/P	Ambassador Extraordinary and Plenipotentiary
CdA	Chargé d'Affaires
Comm	Commissioner
EE/MP	Envoy Extraordinary and Minister Plenipotentiary
MR/CG	Minister Resident and Consul General

Abbott, S. L. (1924-   ), AE/P Lesotho 1984–1987
Adair, E. Ross (1907-   ), AE/P Ethiopia 1971–1974
Adams, Alvin P. (1942-   ), AE/P Djibouti 1983–1985
Adams, Samuel Clifford, Jr. (1920-   ), AE/P Niger 1968–1969
Adams, Weston (1938-   ), AE/P Malawi 1984–1986
Aggrey, Orison Rudolph (1926-   ), AE/P Senegal and The Gambia 1973–1977
Anderson, Robert (1922-   ), AE/P Dahomey 1972–1974
Andrews, George Roberts (1932-   ), AE/P Mauritius 1983–1986
*Attwood, William (1919-   ), AE/P Guinea 1961–1963; AE/P Kenya 1964–1966
Bane, David Morgan (1915-   ), AE/P Gabon 1965–1969
Barrows, Leland Judd (1906-   ), AE/P Cameroon 1960–1966; AE/P Togo 1960–1961
Bartlett, Frederic Pearson (1909–1970), AE/P Malagasy Republic 1960–1962
Bellochi, Natale H. (1926-   ), AE/P Botswana 1985-
Beyer, Gordon Robert (1930-   ), AE/P Uganda 1980–1983
Bishop, James Keough (1938-   ), AE/P Niger 1979–1981
Black, Shirley Jane Temple (1928- `), AE/P Ghana 1974–1976
Blacken, John Dale (1930-   ), AE/P Guinea-Bissau 1986-
Blake, Robert Orris (1921-   ), AE/P Mali 1970–1973
*Blancké, Wilton Wendell (1908–1971), AE/P Central African Republic, Chad, and Gabon 1960–1961; AE/P Congo 1960–1963
Blane, John Propst (1929-   ), AE/P Rwanda 1982–1985; AE/P Chad 1985-
Bliss, Don Caroll (1897–1978), AE/P Ethiopia 1957–1960
Bogosian, Richard Wayne (1937-   ), AE/P Niger 1985-
Bolen, David Benjamin (1923-   ), AE/P Botswana, Lesotho and Swaziland 1974–1976
Borg, Parker W. (1939-   ), AE/P Mali 1981–1984

Bowdler, William Garton (1924-   ), AE/P South Africa 1975–1978

Boyatt, Thomas (1933-   ), AE/P Upper Volta 1978–1980

Bradford, William G. (1925-   ), AE/P Chad 1976–1979

Bray, Charles William III (1933-   ), AE/P Senegal 1981–1985

Brewer, William Dodd (1922-   ), AE/P Mauritius 1970–1973

Bridges, Peter Scott (1932-   ), AE/P Somalia 1984–1986

Brown, Ben Hill, Jr. (1914-   ), AE/P Liberia 1964–1969

Brown, Keith Lapham (1925-   ), AE/P Lesotho 1982–1983

Brown, Kenneth Lee (1936-   ), AE/P Congo 1981–1984

Brown, Lewis Dean (1920-   ), AE/P Senegal and The Gambia 1967–1970

Buckner, George Washington (1855-?), MR/CG Liberia 1913–1915

Bullington, James Richard (1940-   ), AE/P Burundi 1983–1986

Burdett, William Carter, Jr. (1918-   ), AE/P Malawi 1970–1974

Burns, John Howard (1913-   ), AE/P Central African Republic 1961–1963; AE/P Tanzania 1965–1969

Burroughs, John Andrews, Jr. (1936-   ), AE/P Malawi 1981–1984

Byrne, Patricia Mary (1925-   ), AE/P Mali 1976–1979

Byroade, Henry Alfred (1913-   ), AE/P South Africa 1956–1959

Caldwell, John Kenneth (1881–1982), MR/CG Ethiopia 1943; EE/MP Ethiopia 1943–1945

Calhoun, John Archibald (1918-   ), AE/P Chad 1961–1963

Carnahan, Albert Sidney Johnson (1897–1968), AE/P Sierra Leone 1961–1963

Carrington, Walter C. (1930-   ), AE/P Senegal 1980–1981

Carter, William Beverly, Jr. (1921–1982), AE/P Tanzania 1972–1975; AE/P Liberia 1976–1979

Casey, William Robert, Jr. (1944-   ), AE/P Niger 1982–1985

Chapin, Frederic Lincoln (1929-   ), AE/P Ethiopia 1966–1971

Childs, James Rives (1893–1988), AE/P Ethiopia 1951–1953

Clark, Alexander (1826–1891), MR/CG Liberia 1890–1891

Clark, Gilbert Edward (1917–1984), AE/P Mali 1968–1970; AE/P Senegal and The Gambia 1970–1973

Clark, Warren, Jr. (1936-   ), AE/P Gabon, 1987-

Clingerman, John Rufus (1931-   ), AE/P Lesotho 1979–1981

Cohen, Herman Jay (1932-   ), AE/P Senegal and The Gambia 1977–1980

Cole, Felix (1887–1969), EE/MP Ethiopia 1945–1947

Constable, Elinor Greer (1934-   ), AE/P Kenya 1986-

Constable, Peter Dalton (1932-   ), AE/P Zaire 1982–1984

Cook, Frances D. (1945-   ), AE/P Burundi 1980–1983

Cook, Mercer (1903-   ), AE/P Niger 1961–1964; AE/P Senegal 1964–1966; AE/P The Gambia 1965–1966

Cooke, Goodwin (1931-   ), AE/P Central African Empire 1978–1979

Corcoran, Thomas James (1920-   ), AE/P Burundi 1978–1980

Corrigan, Robert Foster (1914-   ), AE/P Rwanda 1971–1973

Corry, Andrew Vincent (1904–1981), AE/P Sierra Leone 1964–1967

Crigler, Trusten Frank (1935-   ), AE/P Rwanda 1976–1979; AE/P Somalia 1987-

Crosby, Oliver Sexsmith (1920-   ), AE/P Guinea 1977–1980

Crossland, John R. A. (1864–1950), MR/CG Liberia 1902–1903

Crowe, Philip Kingsland (1908–1976), AE/P South Africa 1959–1961

*Crum, William Demos (1859–1912), MR/CG Liberia 1910–1912

Curtis, James L. (1870–1917), MR/CG Liberia 1915–1917
Cutler, Walter Leon (1931-   ), AE/P Zaire 1975–1979
Cyr, Leo George (1909-   ), AE/P Rwanda 1966–1971
Dale, William Norris (1919-   ), AE/P Central African Republic 1973–1975
*Darlington, Charles Francis (1904–1986), AE/P Gabon 1961–1964
Davis, Allen Clayton (1927-   ), AE/P Guinea 1980–1983; AE/P Uganda 1983–1985
Dawson, Horace Greely, Jr. (1926-   ), AE/P Botswana 1979–1982
DeJarnette, Edmund T. (1938-   ), AE/P Central African Republic 1983–1986
Deming, Olcott Hawthorne (1910-   ), AE/P Uganda 1963–1966
De Pree, William Ames (1928-   ), AE/P Mozambique 1976–1980
de Vos, Peter Jon (1938-   ), AE/P Cape Verde and Guinea-Bissau 1980–1983; AE/P
    Mozambique 1983–1986
Dickinson, Dwight III (1916-   ), AE/P Togo 1970–1974
*Dudley, Edward Richard (1911-   ), EE/MP Liberia 1948–1949; AE/P Liberia 1949–
    1953
Dumont, Donald Albert (1911-   ), EE/MP Burundi 1962–1963; AE/P Burundi 1963–
    1966
Easum, Donald Boyd (1923-   ), AE/P Upper Volta 1971–1974; AE/P Nigeria 1975–
    1979
Edelman, Mark Leslie (1943-   ), AE/P Cameroon 1987-
Edmondson, William Brockway (1927-   ), AE/P South Africa 1978–1981
Egan, Wesley William, Jr. (1946-   ), AE/P Guinea-Bissau 1983–1985
Engert, Cornelius Van Hemert (1887–1985), MR/CG Ethiopia 1936
Engle, James Bruce (1919-   ), AE/P Dahomey, 1974–1976
Erhardt, John George (1889–1951), AE/P South Africa 1950–1951
Estes, Thomas Stuart (1913-   ), AE/P Upper Volta 1961–1966
Ferguson, Glenn Walker (1929-   ), AE/P Kenya 1966–1969
*Fergusson, Charles Vaughn, Jr. (1915–1981), AE/P Malagasy Republic 1962–1966
*Fergusson, Clarence Clyde, Jr. (1924–1983), AE/P Uganda 1970–1972
Ferriter, John Pierce (1938-   ), AE/P Djibouti 1985–1987
Fields, David C. (1937-   ), AE/P Central African Republic 1986-
Fischer, David Joseph (1939-   ), AE/P Seychelles 1982–1985
Flake, Wilson Clark (1906–1977), AE/P Ghana 1957–1960
Francis, William Treyanne (1870–1929), MR/CG Liberia 1927–1929
Frechette, Myles Robert René (1936-   ), AE/P Cameroon 1983–1987
Fritts, Robert Eugene (1934-   ), AE/P Rwanda 1974–1976; AE/P Ghana 1983–1986
Funkhouser, Richard Edgar (1917-   ), AE/P Gabon 1969–1970
Gallman, Waldemar John (1899–1980), AE/P South Africa 1951–1954
Gammon, Samuel Rhea III (1924-   ), AE/P Mauritius 1978–1980
*Garnet, Henry Highland (1815–1882), MR/CG Liberia 1881–1882
Gilstrap, Samuel Patrick (1907-   ), AE/P Malawi 1964–1965
*Godley, George McMurtie (1917-   ), AE/P Congo 1964–1966
Good, Robert Crocker (1924–1984), AE/P Zambia 1965–1968
Gordon, Robert Charles Frost (1920-   ), AE/P Mauritius 1980–1983
Graham, Pierre Robert (1922-   ), AE/P Upper Volta 1974–1978
Grove, Brandon Hambright, Jr. (1929-   ), AE/P Zaire 1984–1987
*Gullion, Edmund Asbury (1913-   ), AE/P Congo 1961–1964
Hadsel, Fred Latimer (1916-   ), AE/P Somalia 1969–1971; AE/P Ghana 1971–1974

Hall, William O. (1914–1977), AE/P Ethiopia 1967–1971

Handley, William Jules (1918–1979), AE/P Mali 1961–1964

Handyside, Holsey Gates (1927-   ), AE/P Mauritania 1975–1977

*Hanson, Abraham (1818–1866), Comm/CG Liberia 1864–1866

Hardy, Alan M. (1934-   ), AE/P Equatorial Guinea 1981–1984

Hare, Paul Julian (1937-   ), AE/P Zambia 1985-

Harrop, William Caldwell (1929-   ), AE/P Guinea 1975–1977; AE/P Kenya & Seychelles 1980–1983; AE/P Zaire 1987-

Healy, Theresa Ann (1932-   ), AE/P Sierra Leone 1980–1983

*Heard, William Henry (1850–1937), MR/CG Liberia 1895–1898

Heck, Louis Douglas (1918-   ), AE/P Niger 1974–1976

Hennemeyer, Robert Thomas (1925-   ), AE/P The Gambia 1984–1986

Hicks, Irvin (1938-   ), AE/P Seychelles 1985–1987

Hinton, Deane Roesch (1923-   ), AE/P Zaire 1974–1975

Hoffacker, Roscoe Lewis (1923-   ), AE/P Cameroon and Equatorial Guinea 1969–1972

Holcomb, Thomas, Jr. (1879–1965), EE/MP South Africa 1944–1948

Holloway, Anne Forrester (1941-   ), AE/P Mali 1979–1981

*Hood, Solomon Porter (1853–1943), MR/CG Liberia 1922–1926

*Hopkins, Moses Aaron (1846–1886), MR/CG Liberia 1885–1886

Horan, Harold Eugene (1927-   ), AE/P Malawi 1978–1980

Horan, Hume Alexander (1934-   ), AE/P Cameroon and Equatorial Guinea 1980–1983

Horowitz, Herbert Eugene (1930-   ), AE/P Gambia 1986-

Houdek, Robert G. (1940-   ), AE/P Uganda 1985-

Hummel, Arthur William, Jr. (1920-   ), AE/P Ethiopia 1975–1976

Hurd, John Gavin (1914-   ), AE/P South Africa 1970–1975

James, Charles A. (1922-   ), AE/P Niger 1976–1979

*Johnson, Joseph Lowery (1874–1945), MR/CG Liberia 1918–1922

Johnson, Marilyn Priscilla (1922-   ), AE/P Togo 1978–1981

Jones, Marshall Paul (1915–1985), AE/P Malawi 1965–1970

Jones, Richard Lee (1893–1975), AE/P Liberia 1955–1959

Kaiser, Philip Mayer (1913-   ), AE/P Mauritania 1961–1964, AE/P Senegal 1961–1964

Keating, Robert Brendon (1924-   ), AE/P Madagascar and Comoros Islands 1983–1986

Keeley, Robert Vossler (1929-   ), AE/P Mauritius 1976–1978; AE/P Zimbabwe 1980–1984

Keena, Leo John (1878–1967), EE/MP South Africa 1937–1942

King, David Sjodahl (1917-   ), AE/P Malagasy Republic 1967–1969; AE/P Mauritius 1968–1969

Kirk, Roger (1930-   ), AE/P Somalia 1973–1975

Knox, Clinton Everett (1908–1980), AE/P Dahomey 1964–1969

Koren, Henry Lloyd Thornell (1911-   ), AE/P Congo 1964–1965

Korn, David A. (1935-   ), AE/P Togo 1986-

Korry, Edward Malcolm (1922-   ), AE/P Ethiopia 1963–1967

Kryza, Elmer Gregory (1922-   ), AE/P Mauritania 1977–1980

Kux, Dennis Henry (1931-   ), AE/P Ivory Coast 1986-

Lamm, Donald Wakeham (1914-   ), CdA Ghana 1957

*Lanier, Raphael O'Hara (1900–1962), EE/MP Liberia 1946–1948

LeMelle, Wilbert John (1931-   ), AE/P Kenya and Seychelles 1977–1980

Leonhart, William (1919-   ), AE/P Tanganyika 1962–1965

Lewis, Arthur Winston (1926-), AE/P Sierra Leone 1983-

Lewis, Geoffrey Whitney (1910-), AE/P Mauritania 1965–1967; AE/P Central African Republic 1967–1970

Linehan, John Andrew, Jr. (1924-), AE/P Sierra Leone 1977–1980

Little, Edward Southard (1918-), AE/P Chad 1974–1976

*Locker, Jesse Dwight (1891–1955), AE/P Liberia 1953–1955

Loeb, James Isaac, Jr. (1908-), AE/P Guinea 1963–1965

Looram, Matthew James, Jr. (1921-), AE/P Dahomey 1969–1971; AE/P Somalia 1972–1973

Loughran, John Lewis (1921-), AE/P Somalia 1975–1978

Low, Stephen (1927-), AE/P Zambia 1976–1979; AE/P Nigeria 1979–1981

Lukens, Alan Wood (1924-), AE/P Congo 1984–1987

Lupo, Samuel Eldred (1933-), AE/P Guinea 1987-

Lyman, Princeton N. (1935-), AE/P Nigeria 1986-

Lynch, Andrew Green (1902–1966), AE/P Somalia 1960–1962

Lynch, Patricia Gates (1926-), AE/P Madagascar and the Comoros 1986-

Lyne, Stephen Richard (1935-), AE/P Ghana 1987-

*Lyon, Ernest (1860–1938), MR/CG Liberia 1903–1910

McBride, Robert Henry (1918–1983), AE/P Congo 1967–1969

McClelland, Roswell Dunlop (1914-), AE/P Niger 1970–1973

McCoy, William D. (1853–1893), MR/CG Liberia 1892–1893

McElhiney, Thomas Watkins (1919-), AE/P Ghana 1968–1971

McGuire, Ralph Jack (1920-), AE/P Mali 1973–1976

McIlvaine, Robinson (1913-), AE/P Dahomey 1961–1964; AE/P Guinea 1966–1969; AE/P Kenya 1969–1973

McKesson, John Alexander III (1922-), AE/P Gabon 1970–1975

McNamara, Francis Terry (1927-), AE/P Gabon and São Tomé and Principe 1981–1984

*MacVeagh, Lincoln (1890–1972), EE/MP South Africa 1942–1943

*Mahoney, William Patrick, Jr. (1916-), AE/P Ghana 1962–1965

Maino, Theodore C. (1913-), AE/P Botswana 1982–1985

Manfull, Melvin Lawrence (1919-), AE/P Central African Republic 1970–1972; AE/P Liberia 1972–1975

Manhard, Philip Wallace (1921-), AE/P Mauritius 1974–1976

Mark, David Everett (1923-), AE/P Burundi 1974–1977

Marks, Edward (1934-), AE/P Cape Verde and Guinea-Bissau 1977–1980

Marshall, Anthony Dryden (1924-), AE/P Malagasy Republic 1969–1971; AE/P Kenya 1973–1977; AE/P Seychelles 1976–1977

Matheron, Richard Cavins (1927-), AE/P Swaziland 1979–1982

Mathews, Elbert George (1910–1977), AE/P Liberia 1959–1962; AE/P Nigeria 1964–1969

*Melady, Thomas Patrick (1927-), AE/P Burundi 1969–1972; Uganda 1972–1973

Melone, Harry Roberts, Jr. (1928-), AE/P Rwanda 1979–1982

Mendenhall, Joseph Abraham (1920-), AE/P Malagasy Republic 1972–1975

Merrell, George Robert (1898–1962), EE/MP Ethiopia 1947–1949; AE/P Ethiopia 1949–1951

Miller, David Charles, Jr. (1942-), AE/P Tanzania 1981–1984; AE/P Zimbabwe 1984–1986

Miller, Robert Hopkins (1927-), AE/P Ivory Coast 1983–1986
Miner, Robert Graham (1911-), AE/P Sierra Leone 1967–1971
Moffat, Jay P. (1932-), AE/P Chad 1983–1985
Moore, Charles Robert (1915-), AE/P Mali 1965–1968; AE/P Cameroon 1972–1975;
  AE/P Equatorial Guinea 1972–1975
Moose, George E. (1944-), AE/P Benin 1983–1986; AE/P Senegal 1988-
Moran, James B. (1924-), AE/P Seychelles 1987-
Morgan, George Allen (1905-), AE/P Ivory Coast 1965–1969
Morris, Brewster Hilliard (1909-), AE/P Chad 1963–1967
*Morrow, John Howard (1910-), AE/P Guinea 1959–1961
Mulcahy, Edward William (1921-), AE/P Chad 1972–1974
Murphy, Richard William (1929-), AE/P Mauritania 1971–1974
Neher, Leonardo (1922-), AE/P Burkina Faso 1984–1987
Nelson, Charles Joseph (1920-), AE/P Botswana, Lesotho and Swaziland 1971–1974
Nelson, Harvey Frans, Jr. (1924-), AE/P Swaziland 1985-
Nickel, Herman W. (1928-), AE/P South Africa 1982–1986
Norland, Donald Richard (1924-), AE/P Botswana, Lesotho, and Swaziland 1976–
  1979; AE/P Chad 1979–1980
Norris, Chester E., Jr. (1927-), AE/P Equatorial Guinea 1988-
North, Jerrold Martin (1931-), AE/P Djibouti 1980–1982
Oakley, Robert Bigger (1934-), AE/P Zaire 1979–1982; AE/P Somalia 1982–1984
Olson, Clinton Louis (1916-), AE/P Sierra Leone 1972–1974
Palmer, Joseph II (1914-), AE/P Nigeria 1960–1964
Palmer, Ronald DeWayne (1932-), AE/P Togo 1976–1978; AE/P Mauritius 1986-
Payton, Robert Lewis (1926-), AE/P Cameroon 1967–1969
Peck, Edward Lionel (1929-), AE/P Mauritania 1982–1985
Penner, Vernon Dubois, Jr. (1939-), AE/P Cape Verde 1986-
Perkins, Edward Joseph (1928-), AE/P Liberia 1985–1986; AE/P South Africa 1986-
Perry, Cynthia S. (1928-), AE/P Sierra Leone 1986-
Petterson, Donald K. (1930-), AE/P Somalia 1978–1982; AE/P Tanzania 1986-
*Philip, (Herman) Hoffman (1872–1951), MR/CG Abyssinia 1908–1910
Phillips, James Daniel (1933-), AE/P Burundi 1986-
Phinney, Robert H. (1921-), AE/P Swaziland 1982–1984
Pickering, Thomas Reeve (1931-), AE/P Nigeria 1981–1983
Piper, Larry Gordon (1928-), AE/P The Gambia 1980–1982
Platt, Nicholas (1936-), AE/P Zambia 1982–1984
Poullada, Leon Baqueiro (1913-), AE/P Togo 1961–1964
Pringle, Robert Maxwell (1936-), AE/P Mali 1987
Pugh, Robert L. (1921-), AE/P Mauritania 1985-
Quainton, Anthony Cecil Eden (1934-), AE/P Central African Republic 1976–1978
Rawlings, James Wilson (1929-), AE/P Zimbabwe 1986-
Rawls, Nancy Vivian (1926–1985), AE/P Togo 1974–1976; AE/P Ivory Coast 1980–
  1983
Reams, Robert Borden (1904-), AE/P Dahomey, Niger and Upper Volta 1960–1961;
  AE/P Ivory Coast 1960–1962
Reinhardt, John Edward (1920-), AE/P Nigeria 1971–1975
Renchard, George Willmot (1907–1982), AE/P Burundi 1968–1969
Rhetts, Charles Edward (1910–1971), AE/P Liberia 1962–1964

Richards, Arthur Lincoln (1907-), AE/P Ethiopia 1960–1962

Rivkin, William Robert (1919–1967), AE/P Senegal and The Gambia 1966–1967

Roberts, Owen W. (1924-), AE/P Togo 1984–1986

Rondon, Fernando Enrique (1936-), AE/P Madagascar and Comoros Islands 1980–1983

Root, John Frick (1918-), AE/P Ivory Coast 1969–1974

Rosenthal, James D. (1932-), AE/P Guinea 1983–1986

Ross, Claude George Anthony (1917-), AE/P Central African Republic 1963–1967; AE/P Tanzania 1969–1972

Rountree, William Manning (1917-), AE/P South Africa 1965–1970

Ruddy, Francis Stephen (1937-), AE/P Equatorial Guinea 1984–1988

Russell, Francis Henry (1904-), AE/P Ghana 1960

Rutter, Peter (1915-), CdA Ghana 1957

Ryan, Robert J., Jr. (1939-), AE/P Mali 1982–1987

Ryan, Robert Joseph (1914-), AE/P Niger 1964–1968

Samuels, Michael Anthony (1939-), AE/P Sierra Leone 1974–1977

Satterthwaite, Joseph Charles (1900-), AE/P South Africa 1961–1965

Schaufele, William Everett, Jr. (1923-), AE/P Upper Volta 1969–1971

*Seys, John (1799–1872), MR/CG Liberia 1866–1870

Sherer, Albert William, Jr. (1916-), AE/P Togo 1967–1970; AE/P Equatorial Guinea 1968–1969; AE/P Guinea 1970–1971

Shinn, David H. (1940-), AE/P Burkina Faso 1987-

Shirley, John William (1931-), AE/P Tanzania 1984-

Shurtleff, Leonard G. (1940-), AE/P Congo 1987-

Simonson, Joseph (1904–1985), AE/P Ethiopia 1953–1957

*Skinner, Elliott Percival (1924-), AE/P Upper Volta 1966–1969

Smalley, Robert M. (1925-), AE/P Lesotho 1987-

*Smith, Ezekiel Ezra (1852–1933), MR/CG Liberia 1888–1890

Smith, Owen Lun West (1851-?), MR/CG Liberia 1898–1902

Smith, Robert Powell (1929-), AE/P Ghana 1976–1979; AE/P Liberia 1979–1981

Smith, Robert Solwin (1924-), AE/P Ivory Coast 1974–1976

Smith, Thomas W. M. (1930-), AE/P Ghana 1979–1983; AE/P Nigeria 1984-

*Smyth, John Henry (1844–1908), MR/CG Liberia 1878–1881, 1882–1885

Smythe, Mabel Murphy (1918-), AE/P Cameroon 1977–1980; AE/P Equatorial Guinea 1979–1980

*Southard, Addison E. (1884–1970), MR/CG Ethiopia 1927–1934

Spain, James William (1926-), AE/P Tanzania 1975–1979

Spearman, Leonard H. O., Sr. (1929-), AE/P Rwanda 1988-

Spiro, Herbert John (1924-), AE/P Cameroon and Equatorial Guinea 1975–1977

Stadtler, Walter Edward (1936-), AE/P Benin 1986-

Stearns, Monteagle (1924-), AE/P Ivory Coast 1976–1979

Stebbins, Henry Endicott (1905–1973), AE/P Uganda 1966–1969

Steigman, Andrew Lee (1933-), AE/P Gabon 1975–1977; AE/P São Tomé and Principe 1975–1977

Stevenson, Robert Ayer (1918-), AE/P Malawi 1974–1978

Swing, William Lacy (1934-), AE/P Congo 1979–1981; AE/P Liberia 1981–1985

Taylor, Charles Henry James (1857–1898), MR/CG Liberia 1887

Thomas, Gerald Eustis (1929-), AE/P Kenya 1983–1986

Thurston, Raymond LeRoy (1913–1981), AE/P Somalia 1965–1968

Tienken, Arthur T. (1922-   ), AE/P Gabon and São Tomé and Principe 1978–1981

*Timberlake, Clare Hayes (1907–1982), AE/P Congo 1960–1961

Todman, Terence Alphonso (1926-   ), AE/P Chad 1969–1972; AE/P Guinea 1972–1975

Torbert, Horace Gates, Jr. (1911-   ), AE/P Somalia 1962–1965

*Totten, Ralph James (1877–1949), MR/CG South Africa 1929–1930; EE/MP South Africa 1930–1937

Troxel, Oliver Leonard, Jr. (1919-   ), AE/P Zambia 1969–1972

Trueheart, William Clyde (1918-   ), AE/P Nigeria 1969–1971

*Turner, James Milton (1840–1915), MR/ CG Liberia 1871–1878

Upston, John Edwin (1935-   ), AE/P Rwanda 1986–1987

Vance, Sheldon Baird (1917-   ), AE/P Chad 1967–1969; AE/P Congo 1969–1974

Viets, Richard Noyes (1930-   ), AE/P Tanzania 1979–1981

Villard, Henry Serrano (1900-   ), AE/P Senegal 1960–1961; AE/P Mauritania 1960–1961

Wailes, Edward Thompson (1903–1969), AE/P South Africa 1954–1956

Walker, Howard Kent (1935-   ), AE/P Togo 1982–1985

Walker, Julius Waring, Jr. (1927-   ), AE/P Upper Volta 1981–1984

Walker, Lannon (1936-   ), AE/P Senegal 1985–1988

*Walton, Lester Aglar (1882–1965), EE/MP Liberia 1935–1945

Wells, Melissa Foelsch (1932-   ), AE/P Cape Verde and Guinea-Bissau 1976–1977; AE/P Mozambique 1987-

Westerfield, Samuel Zazachilds, Jr. (1919–1972), AE/P Liberia 1969–1972

Wilkowski, Jean Mary (1919-   ), AE/P Zambia 1972–1976

Williams, Franklin Hall (1917-   ), AE/P Ghana 1965–1968

Williamson, Larry C. (1930-   ), AE/P Gabon and São Tomé and Principe 1984–1987

Wine, James Wilmer (1918-   ), AE/P Ivory Coast 1962–1965

Winship, North (1885–1968), EE/MP South Africa 1948–1949; AE/P South Africa 1949

Wisner, Frank G. II (1938-   ), AE/P Zambia 1979–1982

Withers, Charles Dudley (1916-   ), AE/P Rwanda 1963–1965

Witman, William II (1914–1978), AE/P Togo 1964–1967

Woodruff, Arthur H. (1928-   ), AE/P Central African Republic 1981–1983

Wright, Thomas Kenneth (1908-   ), AE/P Mali 1960–1961

Yates, John Melvin (1939-   ), AE/P Cape Verde 1983–1986

Yost, Robert Lloyd (1922-   ), AE/P Burundi 1972–1974

List of Individuals by Profession and Occupation

ADVENTURERS. *See* **EXPLORERS**

AGRICULTURISTS

Alvord, Emory Delmont
Barrett, Otis Warren
Bell, William Clark
Calloway, James Nathan
Hoffman, John Wesley
Shantz, Homer Leroy

ANTHROPOLOGISTS

Bascom, William Russel
Benedict, Burton
Bohannan, Laura M. Smith
Bohannan, Paul James
Childs, Gladwyn Murray
Codere, Helen Frances
Colson, Elizabeth Florence
DeVore, Irven Boyd
Edel, May Mandelbaum
Fallers, Lloyd Ashton
Goldschmidt, Walter Rochs
Hall, Henry Usher
Hambly, Wilfrid Dyson
Hammond, Peter Boyd
Harley, George Way
Herskovits, Frances Shapiro
Herskovits, Melville Jean
Johanson, Donald Carl
Johnson, Amandus
Lee, Richard Borshay
Linton, Ralph
Loeb, Edwin Meyer

Marshall, Laurence Kennedy
Marshall, Lorna Jean McLean
Miner, Horace Mitchell
Putnam, Patrick Tracy Lowell
Robeson, Eslanda Cardozo
Schwab, George
Skinner, Elliott Percival
Starr, Frederick
Thomas, Elizabeth Marshall
Turnbull, Colin Macmillan
Wulsin, Frederick Roelker

ARMY OFFICERS. *See* **SOLDIERS**

ART EXPERTS

Gebaver, Paul
Head, Matthew

ART PATRONS

Frick, Childs

ARTISTS

Clayton, Ida May
Dugmore, Arthur Radclyffe
Feeling, Thomas
Fuertes, Louis Agassiz
Leigh, William Robinson
Mott-Smith, May
Putnam, Anne Eisner
Warner, Esther Sietmann

ASSOCIATION OFFICIALS

Mott, John Raleigh
Yergan, Max

ASTRONOMERS

Alden, Harold Lee
Bailey, Solon Irving
Loomis, Eben Jenks

AUTHORS

Akeley, Delia Denning
Bacon, David Francis
Barnes, James
Bradley, Mary Wilhelmina Hastings
Browne, John Ross
Chamberlain, George Agnew
Cullen, Lucy Pope
Du Bois, Shirley Lola Graham McCanns
Du Bois, William Edward Burghardt
Dye, Eva Nichols
Ellis, George Washington
French-Sheldon, May
Garner, Richard Lynch
Geil, William Edgar
Harley, Winifred Frances Jewell
Head, Matthew
Hemingway, Ernest Miller
Hubbard, Margaret Carson
Hubbard, Wynant Davis
Johnson, Osa Helen
Kirkland, Caroline
Lacy, Leslie Alexander
MacCreagh, Gordon
Mackenzie, Jean Kenyon
Mayfield, Julian
Powell, Edward Alexander
Robeson, Eslanda Cardozo
Rogers, Joel Augustus
Ruark, Robert Chester
Seabrook, William Buehler
Simonton, Ida Vera
Stallings, Laurence Tucker
Stevens, Thomas
Tjader, Charles Richard
Twain, Mark
Vincent, Frank
Warner, Esther Sietmann
Wellman, Frederick Creighton
White, Stewart Edward
Williams, George Washington

AVIATORS

Julian, Hubert Fauntleroy
Light, Richard Upjohn
Robinson, John C.

BACTERIOLOGISTS

Poindexter, Hindrus Augustus

BANKERS

Blowers, George Albert

BIG-GAME HUNTERS. *See* HUNTERS

BLACK LEADERS

Cuffe, Paul
Delany, Martin Robinson
Du Bois, William Edward Burghardt
Turner, Henry McNeal
Williams, George Washington

BLACKSMITHS

Alexander, Daniel Robert

BOTANISTS

Baldwin, John Thomas, Jr.
Brass, Leonard John
Collins, Guy N.
Cook, Orator Fuller
Sauer, Jonathan Deininger
Shantz, Homer Leroy
Stoneman, Bertha
Webber, Herbert John

BUSINESSMEN

Brooks, Berry Boswell, Jr.
Ellis, William Henry
Engelhard, Charles William, Jr.
Gibbs, Mifflin Wistar
Irwin, David Duryea
Mitchell, Charles Edward
Schlesinger, Isidore William
Smith, Albert E.
Streeter, Daniel Willard
Tempelsman, Maurice
Tisdel, Williard P.
Wood, Hubert Stephen

CARTOONISTS

Baldridge, Cyrus Leroy
McCutcheon, John Tinney

CLERGYMEN

Alleyne, Cameron Chesterfield
Bacon, Samuel
Burgess, Ebenezer
Campbell, Robert Erskine
Coan, Josephus Roosevelt
Coker, Daniel
Coppin, Levi Jenkins
Crummell, Alexander
Durning, Dennis Vincent
Finley, Josiah F. C.
Flickinger, Daniel Krumbler
Garnet, Henry Highland
George, David
Gurley, Ralph Randolph
Hanson, Abraham
Harris, Bravid Washington
Hartzell, Joseph Crane
Heard, William Henry
Hopkins, Moses Aaron
Johnson, Eben Samuel
Lyon, Ernest
McGeough, Joseph F.
Noser, Adolph Alexander
Overs, Walter Henry
Payne, John
Penick, Charles Clifton
Rainsford, William Stephen
Robinson, James Herman
Rudin, John James
Savage, Thomas Staughton
Scott, Isaiah Benjamin
Sims, David Henry
Smith, Charles Spencer
Smith, Ezekiel Ezra
Stauffer, Elam Weidman
Taylor, Prince Albert, Jr.
Turner, Henry McNeal
Waring, Colston M.
Williams, George Washington
Wood, Clinton Tyler
Wright, Richard Robert, Jr.

COACH PROPRIETORS

Cobb, Freeman

COLONIAL AGENTS

Ashmun, Jehudi
Ayres, Eli
Bacon, Ephraim
Burgess, Ebenezer
Coker, Daniel
Hall, James
McGill, George R.
McGill, Samuel F.
Mechlin, Joseph, Jr.
Randall, Richard

COLONISTS

Anderson, William Spencer
Benedict, Samuel
Benson, Stephen Allen
Brander, Nathaniel
Buchanan, Thomas
Campbell, Robert
Drayton, Boston J.
Harris, Sion
Heany, Maurice
Johnson, Elijah
Long, Tex
Newport, Matilda
Payne, James Spriggs
Roberts, Joseph Jenkins
Roye, Edward James
Russwurm, John Brown
Sherman, Reginald A.
Skipwith, Peyton
Smith, James Skivring
Teage, Colin
Teage, Hilary
Warner, Daniel Bashiel
Weaver, William
Webb, Francis Ropes
Williams, Anthony D.
Yates, Beverly Page

COLONIZATIONISTS

Cuffe, Paul
Dean(e), Harry Foster
Delany, Martin Robinson

COMMERCIAL AGENTS. *See*
DIPLOMATS

COMPANY DIRECTORS

Honnold, William Lincoln
Robins, Lord Ellis

CONSULS. *See* **DIPLOMATS**

CORRESPONDENTS. *See*
JOURNALISTS

DIPLOMATS

Attwood, William
Blancké, Wilton Wendell
Chamberlain, George Agnew
Chase, Isaac
Clark, Reed Page
Crum, William Demos
Dabney, Charles William
Dabney, John Bass
Dabney, Samuel Wyllys
Dabney, William Henry
Darlington, Charles Francis
Dudley, Edward Richard
Duggan, William Redman
Fergusson, Clarence Clyde, Jr.
Garnet, Henry Highland
Gibbs, Mifflin Wistar
Godley, George McMurtie
Gullion, Edmund Asbury
Hanson, Abraham
Hathorne, William Hollingsworth
Hay, Adelbert Stone
Heard, William Henry
Hickling, Thomas
Hodges, Samuel
Hollis, George Fearing
Hollis, William Stanley
Holmes, Gideon Skull
Hood, Solomon Porter
Hopkins, Moses Aaron
Hubbard, Margaret Carson
Huckins, Daniel Montgomery
Hunt, William Henry
Johnson, Joseph Lowery
Lanier, Raphael O'Hara
Locker, Jesse Dwight
Lugenbeel, James Washington

Lyon, Ernest
MacVeagh, Lincoln
Mahoney, William Patrick, Jr.
Melady, Thomas Patrick
Mitchell, Charles Edward
Mohun, Richard Dorsey Loraine
Morrow, John Howard
Philip, Herman Hoffman
Pike, Nicholas
Pinney, John B.
Roberts, Edmund
Robinson, William W.
Ropes, Edward Dehonde, Sr.
Ropes, Edward Dehonde, Jr.
Seys, John
Skinner, Elliott Percival
Skinner, Robert Peet
Slocum, Clarence Rice
Smith, Ezekiel Ezra
Smyth, John Henry
Southard, Addison E.
Strickland, Peter
Taunt, Emory H.
Timberlake, Clare Hayes
Tisdel, Williard P.
Totten, Ralph James
Turner, James Milton
Waller, John Lewis
Walton, Lester Aglar
Waters, Richard P.
Yerby, William James

ECOLOGISTS

Cowles, Raymond Bridgman

ECONOMISTS

Dean, William Henry, Jr.
Dunaway, John Allder
Kemmerer, Edwin Walter
Luther, Ernest W.

EDUCATORS

Bliss, Anna Elvira
Buell, Raymond Leslie
Coan, Josephus Roosevelt
Crummell, Alexander
Du Bois, William Edward
   Burghardt
Ferguson, Abbie Park

Fergusson, Clarence Clyde, Jr.
Freeman, Martin Henry
Furbay, John Harvey
Gilson, Hannah Juliette
Gordon, Nora Antonia
Hood, Solomon Porter
Johnson, Charles Spurgeon
Lanier, Raphael O'Hara
McGill, George R.
Melady, Thomas Patrick
Morrow, John Howard
Nau, Henry
Roberts, Joseph Jenkins
Scott, Emmett Jay
Sibley, James Longstreet
Stewart, Thomas McCants
Stoneman, Bertha
Thomson, Elizabeth Mars Johnson
Thomson, James Madison
Webster, John White
Welmers, William Evert
Wood, Clinton Tyler
Work, Ernest Frank

ENGINEERS. *See also* **MINING ENGINEERS**

Labram, George
Park, Walter E.
Roberts, Leo Bond
Robeson, Anthony Maurice
Seymour, Louis Irving
Storke, Arthur Ditchfield
Woodford, Ethelbert George

ENTOMOLOGISTS

Cooley, Robert Allen
Lounsbury, Charles Pugsley
Mally, Charles William
Mann, William M.

ETHNOMUSICOLOGISTS

Boulton, Laura Theresa Craytor
Merriam, Alan Parkhurst

EVANGELISTS

Lake, John Graham
Smith, Amanda Berry

EXPATRIATES

Lacy, Leslie Alexander
Mayfield, Julian
Sutherland, William H.

EXPLORERS. *See also* **TRAVELERS**

Abbott, William Louis
Akeley, Carl Ethan
Akeley, Delia Denning
Akeley, Mary Lee Jobe
Anderson, Benjamin Joseph Knight
Baum, James Edwin
Bigelow, Harry Augustus
Bridgman, Herbert Lawrence
Burnham, Frederick Russell
Chaillé-Long, Charles
Chanler, William Astor
Du Chaillu, Paul Belloni
French-Sheldon, May
Geil, William Edgar
Hoefler, Paul Louis
Johnson, Martin Elmer
Johnson, Osa Helen Leighy
Julian, Herbert Fauntleroy
Morden, William James
Mott-Smith, May
Rainey, Paul James
Rand, Austin Loomer
Roberts, Leo Bond
Scull, Guy Hamilton
Shufeldt, Mason Abercrombie
Smith, Arthur Donaldson
Stanley, Henry Morton
Tjader, Charles Richard
Vernay, Arthur Stannard
Verner, Samuel Phillips
Whitehouse, William Fitzhugh

EXPLOSIVES EXPERTS

Quinan, Kenneth Bingham
Quinan, William Russell

FILM PRODUCERS

Hoefler, Paul Louis
Hubbard, Wynant Davis
Johnson, Martin Elmer
Johnson, Osa Helen Leighy

FINANCIAL ADVISERS

Colson, Everett Andrew
De La Rue, Sidney
Loomis, John

FINANCIERS

McMurdo, Edward or Edwin
Mein, William Wallace
Robins, Lord Ellis

GEOGRAPHERS

Hance, William Adams
Light, Richard Upjohn
Sauer, Jonathan Deininger

GEOLOGISTS

Becker, George Ferdinand
Billings, Katharine Stevens
  (Fowler-Lunn)
Curtis, Joseph Story
Hatfield, Willis Charles
Shaler, Millard King
Veatch, Arthur Clifford
Willis, Bailey

GOVERNMENT OFFICIALS

Bacon, Ephraim
Bane, Howard T.
Chesham, Marion Caher Donoghue
  Edwards
Crum, William Demos
Darlington, Charles Francis
Cuyler, Jacob Glen
De La Rue, Sidney
Devlin, Lawrence Raymond
Henze, Paul Bernard
McGill, George R.
McGill, Samuel F.
Mechlin, Joseph, Jr.
Payne, James Spriggs
Priest, James M.
Roberts, Joseph Jenkins
Roosevelt, Theodore
Roye, Edward James
Russwurm, John Brown
Scott, Emmett Jay
Sears, Philip Mason
Sherman, Reginald A.
Spencer, John Hathaway
Stockwell, John
Teage, Hilary
Waring, Colston M.
Warner, Daniel Bashiel
Webb, Francis Ropes

HERPETOLOGISTS

Loveridge, Arthur
Stewart, Margaret McBride

HISTORIANS

Du Bois, William Edward
  Burghardt
Johnson, Amandus

HORTICULTURISTS

Davis, Rees Alfred
Swingle, Charles Fletcher

HUNTERS

Akeley, Delia Denning
Bigelow, Harry Augustus
Boyce, William Dickson
Bradley, Herbert Edwin
Brooks, Berry Boswell, Jr.
Crile, George Washington
Hubbard, Wynant Davis
Jones, Charles Jesse
Klein, Alfred J.
McKiernan, Gerald
Moore, Henry Clay
Morden, William James
Rainey, Paul James
Rainsford, William Stephen
Render(s), Adam
Roosevelt, Theodore
Ruark, Robert Chester
Said, William Prestly
Simson, Leslie
Snow, Henry Adelbert
Streeter, Daniel Willard
Thomas, Charles Charrier
Thomas, John Louis
Tjader, Charles Richard
Vernay, Arthur Stannard

ILLUSTRATORS

Baldridge, Cyrus Leroy
Feeling, Thomas

INVENTORS

Babe, Jerome L.

JOURNALISTS

Attwood, William
Bradley, Mary Wilhelmina Hastings

Baum, James Edwin
Carpenter, Frank George
Davis, Richard Harding
Farson, James Negley
Gunther, John
Hillegas, Howard Clemens
Hoefler, Paul Louis
Howland, Frederick Hoppin
Hubbard, Margaret Carson
Ralph, Julian
Rogers, Joel Augustus
Ruark, Robert Chester
Schuyler, George Samuel
Scull, Guy Hamilton
Stallings, Laurence Tucker
Stanley, Henry Morton
Stevens, Thomas
Waller, John Louis
Walton, Lester Aglar

JURISTS

Dudley, Edward Richard
Pringle, Benjamin

LABOR LEADERS

Matthews, Thomas

LAWYERS

Bradley, Herbert Edwin
Fergusson, Clarence Clyde, Jr.
Gibbs, Mifflin Wistar
Locker, Jesse Dwight
Mahoney, William Patrick, Jr.
Pringle, Benjamin
Rideout, Conrad A.
Smyth, John Henry
Stewart, Thomas McCants
Waller, John Lewis

LECTURERS

French-Sheldon, May
Lacy, Leslie Alexander
Simonton, Ida Vera
Tjader, Charles Richard

LEGAL ADVISERS

Rideout, Conrad A.
Spencer, John Hathaway

LIBRARIANS

Ferguson, Milton James

LINGUISTS

Chatelain, Héli

MAP MAKERS

Roberts, Leo Bond

MATHEMATICIANS

Loomis, Eben Jenks

MEDICAL MISSIONARIES. *See also* MISSIONARIES; PHYSICIANS and SURGEONS

Adams, Newton
Becker, Carl K.
Bergsma, Stuart
Biddle, Harry Nicholas
Boone, Clinton Caldwell
Bridgman, Burt Nichols
Buck, Theresa Robinson
Carlson, Paul Earle
Cushman, Mary Floyd
Davis, William Ellsworth
Dye, Royal J.
Dyrnes, Johannes Olsen
Ennis, Merlin Walter
Fleming, Lulu Cecilia
Ford, Henry Alexander
Gribble, Florence Alma Newberry
Gurney, Samuel
Harley, George Way
Hurlburt, Elizabeth Morse
Johnson, Silas Franklin
Johnson, Titus M.
Kersey, Ruth May
Lambie, Thomas Alexander
Lockett, Basil Lee
Lynch, Franklin Pierce
Mabie, Catherine Louise Roe
McCord, James Bennett
McMillan, Aaron Manasses
Nassau, Robert Hamill
Pearson, Ernest B.
Poole, Mark Keller
Snyder, Dewitt Clinton
Springer, Helen Emily
  Chapman
Steidel, Florence
Wellman, Frederick Creighton

MERCHANTS

Bickham, Martin
Chase, Isaac
Cotheal, Alexander Isaac
Cuffe, Paul
Dabney, Charles William
Dabney, John Bass
Dabney, Samuel Wyllys
Dabney, William Henry
Hall, George
Hickling, Thomas
Hodges, Samuel
Holmes, Gideon Skull
Huckins, Daniel Montgomery
Lawlin, Richard E.
McKiernan, Gerald
Masury, Samuel Richard
Osgood, John Felt
Roberts, Edmund
Ropes, Edward Dehonde, Sr.
Ropes, Edward Dehonde, Jr.
Roye, Edward James
Sparhawk, Augustus
Strickland, Peter
Taunt, Emory H.
Tempelsman, Maurice
Thomas, Charles Charrier
Tisdel, Williard P.
Ware, Enoch Richmond
Waring, Colston M.
Waters, Richard P.

METALLURGISTS

Butters, Charles

MICROBIOLOGISTS

Noguchi, Hideyo

MINERS

Babe, Jerome L.
Hall, George
Ramsay, William J.

MINING ENGINEERS

Ball, Sydney Hobart
Boise, Charles Watson
Butters, Charles
Catlin, Robert Mayo
Davis, Carl Raymond

De Crano, Edmund Gerard
Dickinson, Harold Thomas
Hammond, John Hays
Honnold, William Lincoln
Horner, Preston King
Jennings, James Hennen
Labram, George
Mein, Thomas
Mein, William Wallace
Mitchell, Lebbens H.
Munroe, Harold Simonds
Parker, Russell Jonathan
Selby, Paul
Simson, Leslie
Smith, Hamilton
Starr, George William
Storke, Arthur Ditchfield
Warriner, Ruel Chaffee
Webb, Harry Howard
Williams, Alpheus Fuller
Williams, Gardner Fred
Wiltsee, Ernest Abram
Yeatman, Pope

MINING EXECUTIVES

Christie, Lansdell Kisner
Honnold, William Lincoln
Irwin, David Duryea
Storke, Arthur Ditchfield
Williams, Alpheus Fuller

MISSIONARIES. *See also* MEDICAL MISSIONARIES; PHYSICIANS and SURGEONS

Agnew, George Harry
Allen, Frances Grace
Alvord, Emory Delmont
Anderson, George Nathanael
Anderson, Vernon Andy
Anderson, William Harrison
Armitage, Frank Benjamin
Bailey, Albert William
Barron, Edward Winston
Bedinger, Robert Dabney
Bell, William Clark
Bender, Carl Jacob
Best, Jacob
Booth, Newell Snow
Bowen, Thomas Jefferson

Branch, Thomas H.
Bridgman, Frederick Brainerd
Bridgman, Henry Martyn
Bridgman, Laura Brainerd
  Nichols
Bryant, James Churchill
Burgess, Andrew Severance
Burns, Francis
Bushnell, Albert
Camphor, Alexander Priestly
Carey [Cary], Lott
Carpenter, George Wayland
Cartwright, Andrew
Champion, George
Chatelain, Héli
Cheek, Landon N.
Childs, Gladwyn Murray
Clark, Walter Halsey
Clarke, George Hobson
Clarke, Mary Lane
Clarke, Roger
Clarke, William Henry
Cockerill, Walter Benjamin
Coles, John J.
Coles, Samuel Bracey
Colley, William W.
Coppin, Levi Jenkins
Cox, Melville Beveridge
Crummell, Alexander
Danielson, Elmer Reinhold
David, William Joshua
Davidson, Hannah Frances
Day, David Alexander
DeLaney, Emma B.
DeYampert, Lillian May
  Thomas
Dodge, Ralph Edward
Duff, Clarence Walker
Edmiston, Althea Brown
Edwards, Mary Kelly
Ehnes, Morris Wellington
Eldred, Robert Ray
Engle, Jesse M.
Faris, Ellsworth
Fearing, Maria
Ferguson, George Reid
Ferguson, Samuel David
Forsberg, Malcolm

Fraser, Melvin
Frederick, John Richard
Gebauer, Paul
George, Eliza Davis
Girouard, Paul Joseph
Gomer, Joseph
Good, Adolphus Clemens
Goodenough, Herbert Delos
Gordon, Nora Antonia
Gorham, Sarah J.
Gribble, James S.
Grout, Aldin
Grout, Lewis
Gunderson, Adolphus Eugene
Haas, William Clarence
Haigh, Lawrence Benjamin
Hanson, Herbert Martin
Harris, Bravid Washington
Haven, Jesse
Helser, Albert David
Hensey, Andrew Fitch
Hogstad, John [Johan] Peter
Holton, Calvin
Hotchkiss, Willis Ray
Hult, Ralph D.
Hurlburt, Charles Erwin
Ireland, William
Jerstad, Jakob Berntsen
Jobson, Orville Deville
Johnson, Victor Eugene
Jones, Edward
Jones, Robert Llewellyn
Kellersberger, Julia Lake
  Skinner
Kelly, John
Kelly, Lorena
Keys, Pliny Whittier
Krug, Adolph Nicholas
Kulp, Harold Stover
Lapsley, Samuel Norvell
Lindley, Daniel
McCauley, Vincent J.
McDowell, Henry Curtis
MacKenzie, Jean Kenyon
Martin, Motte
Milligan, Robert Henry
Mills, Samuel John, Jr.
Moe, Petra Mallena

Morrison, William McCutchan
Myers, Estella Catherine
Nau, Henry
Officer, Morris
Parham, Catherine
Paull, George
Perry, May
Phillips, Ray Edmund
Pinney, John B.
Pixley, Stephen Clapp
Preston, Ira Mills
Priest, James M.
Raymond, William
Reading, Joseph Hankinson
Reed, George Clinton
Rees, Emory J.
Richards, Erwin Hart
Robbins, Elijah
Roberts, George Arthur
Roberts, John Wright
Rogers, Joel C.
Rood, David
Roseberry, Robert Sherman
Ross, Emory
Sadler, George Washington
Sanders, William Henry
Savage, Thomas Staughton
Schmelzenbach, Elmer
Schmelzenbach, Harmon F.
Schwab, George
Scott, Peter Cameron
Seys, John
Sheppard, Lucy Gantt
Sheppard, William Henry
Smith, Amanda Berry
Smith, Charles Edwin
Smith, Charles Eugene
Smith, Herbert
Springer, John McKendree
Stauffacher, John
Stauffer, Elam Weidman
Stone, Seth Bradley
Taylor, Adda Engle
Taylor, James Dexter
Taylor, Myron
Taylor, William
Thompson, George
Thomson, Elizabeth Mars Johnson

Thomson, James Madison
Toppenberg, Aksel Valdemar
Tou, Erik Hansen
Tyler, Josiah
Veenstra, Johanna
Venable, Henry Isaac
Verner, Samuel Phillips
Walker, William
Washburn, Hezekiah M.
Welmers, William Evert
Wengatz, John Christian
Wengatz, Susan Moberly Talbot
Wharton, Conway Taliaferro
Wharton, Ethel Taylor
Wilcox, William Cullen
Wilder, George Albert
Wilder, Hyman Augustus
Williams, Walter B.
Wilson, Alexander Erwin
Wilson, John Leighton

MOTION PICTURE DIRECTORS

Hubbard, Margaret Carson
Van Dyke, Woodbridge Strong,
    2nd

MOTION PICTURE PHOTOGRAPHERS

Dickson, William Kennedy Laurie
Rainey, Paul James
Smith, Albert E.

NATURALISTS

Abbott, William Louis
Akeley, Carl Ethan
Allen, Glover Merrill
Brown, William Harvey
Clark, James Lippitt
Cooke, Caleb
Cowles, Raymond Bridgman
Fuertes, Louis Agassiz
Garner, Richard Lynch
Good, Adolphus Clemens
Heller, Edmund
Lang, Herbert Otto Henry
Mearns, Edgar Alexander
Pike, Nicholas
Putnam, Patrick Tracy Lowell
Savage, Thomas Staughton

Snow, Henry Adelbert
Ward, Henry Augustus

NAVAL OFFICERS

Bridge, Horatio
Foote, Andrew Hull
Glassford, William Alexander, 2nd
Lynch, William Francis
Perry, Matthew Calbraith
Shufeldt, Mason Abercrombie
Shufeldt, Robert Wilson
Stockton, Robert Field
Taunt, Emory H.

NEWSPAPER PUBLISHERS

Boyce, William Dickson
Bridgman, Herbert Lawrence

ORNITHOLOGISTS

Bailey, Alfred Marshall
Boulton, Wolfrid Rudyerd
Chapin, James Paul
Friedmann, Herbert

PALEONTOLOGISTS

Frick, Childs
Gregory, William King

PHILANTHROPISTS

Chesham, Marion Caher Donoghue Edwards

PHOTOGRAPHERS

Akeley, Mary Lee Jobe
Carpenter, Frank George
Dugmore, Arthur Radclyffe
Elisofon, Eliot
Elliott, Arthur
Johnson, Martin Elmer
Johnson, Osa Helen Leighy
Light, Mary
Selby, Paul

PHYSICIANS and SURGEONS. See also MEDICAL MISSIONARIES; MISSIONARIES

Ayres, Eli
Bacon, David Francis
Bergsma, Stuart
Campbell, Guy Gibson

Crile, George Washington
Darling, Samuel Taylor
Gorgas, William Crawford
Hall, James
Johnson, Titus M.
Light, Richard Upjohn
Lugenbeel, James Washington
Mearns, Edward Alexander
Mechlin, Joseph, Jr.
Noble, Robert Ernest
Orenstein, Alexander Jeremiah
Pearce, Louise
Randall, Richard
Smith, Arthur Donaldson
Smith, James Skivring
Strong, Richard Pearson
Wiles, Vivian McKinley
Wilson, Benjamin F.
Wolbach, Simeon Burt
Wolff, Henry Albert
Yerby, William James

PIONEERS. See COLONISTS

PIRATES

Tew, Thomas

PLANT GEOGRAPHERS

Sauer, Jonathan Deininger

POACHERS

Ro(d)gers, James Wood

POLITICIANS

Gibbs, Mifflin Wistar

PRIMATOLOGISTS

Fossey, Dian

PRINTERS

James, Benjamin Van Renssalaer

PROSPECTORS

Moore, Henry Clay
Render(s), Adam
Wood, Hubert Stephen

PSYCHOLOGISTS

Bingham, Harold Clyde
Nissen, Henry Wieghorst

PUBLICISTS

Buell, Raymond Leslie

RABBIS
Ford, Arnold Josiah

REPORTERS. *See* JOURNALISTS

SCOUTS
Burnham, Frederick Russell

SEA CAPTAINS
Carnes, Joshua A.
Cleveland, Richard Jeffrey
Dean(e), Harry Foster
Drake, Philip
Harrington, Edward
Hathorne, William
  Hollingsworth
Holmes, Gideon Skull
Lambert, Jonathan
Lawlin, Richard E.
Morrell, Benjamin
Putnam, Horace B.
Rogers, Thomas
Stout, Benjamin
Swan, Samuel, Jr.
Webb, Francis Ropes

SETTLERS
Barns, Thomas Alexander
Brown, William Harvey
Cuyler, Jacob Glen
Heany, Maurice
Long, Tex
McMillan, William Northrup
Sewall, William Gilman
Wilson, Benjamin F.

SHIP OWNERS
Cuffe, Paul

SHOWMEN
Farini, Gilarmi (Guillermo)
  Antonio

SLAVE TRADERS
Dewolf, James
Drake, Philip
Scott, George

SOCIOLOGISTS
Butterfield, Kenyon Leech
Coulter, Charles Wellsley

Ellis, George Washington
Faris, Ellsworth
Johnson, Charles Spurgeon
Jones, Thomas Jesse
Ross, Edward Alsworth

SOIL CONSERVATIONISTS
Bennett, Hugh Hammond
Marbut, Curtis Fletcher

SOLDIERS
Blake, John Y. Filmore
Brown, William Harvey
Burke, Lindsay Gaines
Burnham, Frederick Russell
Chaillé-Long, Charles
Cuylere, Jacob Glen
Gorgas, William Crawford
Heany, Maurice
Long, Tex
McMurdo, Edward or Edwin
Melen, Nels
Mohun, Richard Dorsey
  Loraine
Robins, Lord Ellis
Sherman, Reginald A.
Thornton, Wynes Edwin
Williams, George Washington
Williams, L. H.
Winship, Blanton
Young, Charles

SURVEYORS
Anderson, Benjamin Joseph
  Knight

TAXIDERMISTS
Akeley, Carl Ethan
Clark, James Lippitt

TELEVISION FILM DIRECTORS
Denis, Armand

TELEVISION PROGRAM DIRECTORS
Du Bois, Shirley Lola Graham
  McCanns

TRADERS. *See* MERCHANTS

TRAVELERS

Barns, Thomas Alexander
Bradley, Herbert Edwin
Bradley, Mary Wilhelmina
  Hastings
Browne, John Ross
Carpenter, Frank George
Farini, Gilarmi (Guillermo)
  Antonio
MacCreagh, Gordon
Powell, Edward Alexander
Roosevelt, Theodore
Simonton, Ida Vera
Streeter, Daniel Willard
Vincent, Frank

WINE MAKERS

Winshaw, William Charles

WRITERS. *See* AUTHORS

ZOOLOGISTS

Carter, Thomas Donald
Elliot, Daniel Giroud
Jolly, Alison Bishop
Loring, John Alden
McGregor, James Howard
Mann, William M.
Osgood, Wilfred Hudson
Rand, Austin Loomer
Raven, Henry Cushier
Schaller, George Beals

Bibliographical Essay

In his article, " 'Non-benign Neglect': The United States and Black Africa in the Twentieth Century," in *American Foreign Relations: A Historiographical Review*, ed. Gerald K. Haines and J. Samuel Walker (Westport, Conn.: Greenwood Press, 1981), pp. 271–92, Thomas J. Noer reviewed the literature on U.S. relations with Africa. The *Guide to American Foreign Relations Since 1700*, ed. Richard D. Burns (Santa Barbara, Calif.: ABC-Clio, 1983), especially chapters 18 and 37, is more selective. *American-Southern African Relations: Bibliographic Essays*, ed. Mohamed El-Khawas and Francis Kornegay, Jr. (Westport, Conn.: Greenwood Press, 1975) and C. Tsehloane Keto, *American-Southern African Relations, 1784–1980: Review and Select Bibliography* (Athens: Ohio University Center for International Studies, Africa Studies Program, 1985) are specialized. Bibliography of materials dealing with the various African countries can be found in the volumes of the *African Historical Dictionaries* (Metuchen, N.J.: Scarecrow Press, 1974-), series.

Doctoral dissertations are recorded in Michael Sims and Alfred Kagan, *American and Canadian Doctoral Dissertations and Master's Theses on Africa 1886–1974* (Waltham, Mass.: African Studies Association, Brandeis University, 1976).

Several full-scale surveys of American relations with Africa exist. They include Eric Rosenthal, *Stars and Stripes in Africa*, new rev. ed. (Cape Town: National Books, 1968); Edward Chester, *Clash of Titans: Africa and U.S. Foreign Policy* (Maryknoll, N.Y.: Orbis Books, 1974); Russell W. Howe, *Along the Africa Shore: An Historic Review of Two Centuries of U.S.-African Relations* (New York: Barnes & Noble, 1975); and Peter Duignan and L. H. Gann, *The United States and Africa: A History* (New York: Cambridge University Press, 1984). They all contain bibliographies. Books dealing with specific periods of time include Michael McCarthy, *Dark Continent: Africa as Seen by Americans* (Westport, Conn.: Greenwood Press, 1983); Edward McKinley, *The Lure of Africa: American Interests in Tropical Africa, 1919–1939* (Indianapolis: Bobbs-Merrill, 1974); Thomas J. Noer, *Cold War and Black Liberation: The United States and White Rule in Africa, 1948–1968* (Columbia: University of Missouri Press, 1985); and Henry F. Jackson, *From the Congo to Soweto: U.S. Foreign Policy toward Africa Since 1960* (New York: W. Morrow, 1982).

The majority of books on the United States and Africa deal with U.S. foreign policy toward Africa: *The United States and Africa*, ed. Walter Goldschmidt (New York: Columbia University Press, 1958); Rupert Emerson, *Africa and the United States Foreign*

Policy (Englewood Cliffs, N.J.: Prentice-Hall, 1967); *U.S. Policy Toward Africa*, ed. Frederick S. Arkhurst (New York: Praeger, 1975); *Africa and the United States: Vital Interests*, ed. Jennifer S. Whitaker (New York: New York University Press, 1978); Robert M. Price, *U.S. Foreign Policy in Sub-Saharan Africa: National Interest and Global Strategy* (Berkeley: University of California Press, 1978); Helen A. Kitchen, *U.S. Interests in Africa* (New York: Praeger, 1983); David A. Dickman, *United States Foreign Policy Towards Sub-Saharan Africa* (Lanham, Md.: University Press of America, 1985); *African Crisis Areas and U.S. Foreign Policy*, ed. Gerald J. Bender et al. (Berkeley: University of California Press, 1985); *Beyond Constructive Engagement: United States Foreign Policy toward Africa*, ed. Elliott P. Skinner (New York: Paragon House, 1986).

Daniel P. Mannix and Malcolm Cowley, *Black Cargoes: A History of the Atlantic Slave Trade, 1518–1865* (New York: Viking Press, 1962); James A. Rawley, *The Transatlantic Slave Trade: A History* (New York: Norton, 1981); Jay Coughtry, *The Notorius Triangle: Rhode Island and the African Slave Trade, 1700–1807* (Philadelphia: Temple University Press, 1981); and Warren S. Howard, *American Slavers and the Federal Law* (Berkeley: University of California Press, 1963), all deal with the American slave trade with Africa. Cyrus T. Brady, *Commerce and Conquest in East Africa, with Particular Reference to Salem Trade with Zanzibar* (Salem, Mass.: Essex Institute, 1950); George E. Brooks, Jr., *Yankee Traders, Old Coasters and African Middlemen: A History of American Legitimate Trade with West Africa in the Nineteenth Century* (Boston: Boston University Press, 1970); and Norman R. Bennett and George E. Brooks, Jr., eds., *New England Merchants in Africa: A History Through Documents, 1802–1865* (Boston: Boston University Press, 1965) all deal with the legitimate trade.

The more important books dealing with black immigration to Africa and back-to-Africa movements are Floyd J. Miller, *The Search for Black Nationality: Black Emigration and Colonization 1787–1863* (Urbana: University of Illinois Press, 1975); Edwin S. Redkey, *Black Exodus: Black Nationalist and Back to Africa Movements, 1890–1910* (New Haven, Conn.: Yale University Press, 1969); Wilson J. Moses, *The Golden Age of Black Nationalism, 1850–1925* (Hamden, Conn.: Shoestring Press, 1978); *Africa as Seen by American Negroes*, ed. John A. Davis (Paris: Presence Africaine, 1958); *Afro-Americans and Africa: Black Nationalism at the Crossroads*, comp. William B. Heimrich (Westport, Conn.: Greenwood Press, 1977); *Apropos of Africa: Sentiments of Negro Leaders on Africa from the 1800's to the 1950's*, comp. Adelaide C. Hill and Martin Kilson (London: Cass, 1969); Sylvia M. Jacobs, *The African Nexus: Black American Perspectives on the European Partitioning of Africa, 1880–1920* (Westport, Conn.: Greenwood Press, 1981); Robert G. Weisbord, *Ebony Kinship: Africa, Africans, and the Afro-Americans* (Westport, Conn.: Greenwood Press, 1973).

Several studies of United States relations with specific countries of Africa have been written:

Cameroon: Peter Agbor-Tabi, *U.S. Bilateral Assistance in Africa: The Case of Cameroon* (Lanham, Md.: University Press of America, 1984).

Congo: Madeleine G. Kalb, *The Congo Cables: The Cold War in Africa—from Eisenhower to Kennedy* (New York: Macmillan, 1982); Richard D. Mahoney, *JFK: Ordeal in Africa* (New York: Oxford University Press, 1983); Stephen R. Weissman, *American Foreign Policy in the Congo 1960–1964* (Ithaca, N.Y.: Cornell University Press, 1974).

Ethiopia: Brice Harris, Jr., *The United States and the Italo-Ethiopian Crisis* (Stanford, Calif.: Stanford University Press, 1964); Harold G. Marcus, *Ethiopia, Great Britain, and the United States, 1941–1974: The Politics of Empire* (Berkeley: University of California Press, 1983).

Liberia: Robert E. Anderson, *Liberia: America's African Friend* (Chapel Hill: University of North Carolina Press, 1952); Raymond W. Bixler, *The Foreign Policy of the United States in Liberia* (New York: Pageant Press, 1957); Tom W. Shick, *"Behold the Promised Land": A History of Afro-American Settler Society in Nineteenth-Century Liberia* (Baltimore: Johns Hopkins University Press, 1980); Hassan B. Sisay, *Big Powers and Small Nations: A Case Study of United States-Liberian Relations* (Lanham, Md.: University Press of America, 1985); Elizabeth Harris, *African and American Values: Liberia and West Africa* (Lanham, Md.: University Press of America, 1985); I. K. Sundiata, *Black Scandal: America and the Liberian Labor Crisis, 1929–1936* (Philadelphia: Institute for the Study of Human Issues, 1980).

Madagascar: G. Michael Razi, *Malgaches et Américains: Relations Commerciales et Diplomatiques au XIXème Siècle* (Antananarivo?: Agence d'Information des Etats-Unis, 1981?).

Mauritius: *Early American Trade with Mauritius*, ed. Auguste Toussaint (Port Louis, Mauritius: Esclapan, 1954).

Namibia: Allan D. Cooper, *U.S. Economic Power and Political Influence in Namibia, 1700–1982* (Boulder, Colo.: Westview Press, 1982).

Nigeria: Bassoy E. Ate, *Decolonization and Dependence: The Development of Nigerian-U.S. Relations, 1960–1984* (Boulder, Colo.: Westview Press, 1987).

Rhodesia: Anthony Lake, *The "Tar Baby" Option: American Policy Toward Southern Rhodesia* (New York: Columbia University Press, 1973).

South Africa: Allan R. Booth, *United States Experience in South Africa, 1784–1870* (Capetown: A. A. Balkema, 1978); John H. Ferguson, *American Diplomacy and the Boer War* (Philadelphia: University of Pennsylvania Press, 1939); Thomas J. Noer, *Briton, Boer, and Yankee: The United States and South Africa, 1870–1914* (Kent, Ohio: Kent State University Press, 1978); *Business in the Shadow of Apartheid: U.S. Firms in South Africa*, ed. Jonathan Leape et al. (Lexington, Mass.: Lexington Books, 1985); Barbara Rogers, *White Wealth and Black Poverty: American Investments in Southern Africa* (Westport, Conn.: Greenwood Press, 1976); *U.S. Military Involvement in Southern Africa*, ed. Western Massachusetts Association of Concerned African Scholars (Boston: South End Press, 1978); Desaix B. Myers III et al., *U.S. Business in South Africa: The Economic, Political and Moral Issues* (Bloomington: Indiana University Press, 1980); *American Policy in Southern Africa: The Stakes and the Stance*, 2d ed., ed. Rene Lemarchand (Washington, D.C.: University Press of America, 1981); *The American People and South Africa: Publics, Elites and the Policy-making Process* (Lexington, Mass.: Lexington Books, 1981); Richard E. Bissell, *South Africa and the United States: The Erosion of an Influential Relationship* (New York: Praeger, 1982); Kevin Danaher, *In Whose Interest? A Guide to U.S.-South Africa Relations* (Washington, D.C.: Institute for Policy Studies, 1984); Ann Seidman and Neva Seidman, *South Africa and U.S. Multinational Corporations* (Westport, Conn.: Lawrence Hill, 1978); Kevin Danaher, *The Political Economy of U.S. Policy Toward South Africa* (Boulder, Colo.: Westview Press, 1985); Christopher Coker, *The United States and South Africa, 1968–1985: Constructive Engagement and Its Critics* (Durham, N.C.: Duke University Press, 1986); H. E. Newsum and Olayiwola Abegunrin, *United States Foreign Policy Towards Southern Africa: Andrew Young and Beyond* (New York: St. Martin's Press, 1987); Vincent Victor Razis, *The American Connection: The Influence of United States Business on South Africa* (New York: St.

Martin's Press, 1986); Ann Seidman, *The Roots of Crisis in Southern Africa* (Trenton, N.J.: Africa World Press, 1985).

Western Sahara: Leo Kamil, *Fueling the Fire: U.S. Policy and the Western Sahara Conflict* (Trenton, N.J.: The Red Sea Press, 1986).

The literature on the part played by missionaries and missionary societies is extensive. Kenneth S. Latourette, *History of the Expansion of Christianity*, Vols. 5 and 7 (New York: Harper & Brothers, 1937–1945); Sylvia M. Jacobs, ed., *Black Americans and the Missionary Movement in Africa* (Westport, Conn.: Greenwood Press, 1982); Walter L. Williams, *Black Americans and the Evangelization of Africa 1877–1900* (Madison: University of Wisconsin Press, 1982); and J. Mutero Chirenje, *Ethiopianism and Afro-Americans in Southern Africa, 1883–1916* (Baton Rouge: Louisiana State University Press, 1987).

Mira Wilkins, *The Maturing of Multinational Enterprise: American Business Abroad from 1914 to 1970* (Cambridge, Mass.: Harvard University Press, 1974) provides a general survey of American business expansion abroad, and Merle Curti, *American Philanthropy Abroad: A History* (New Brunswick, N.J.: Rutgers University Press, 1963) provides a survey of philanthropic aid.

Index

Putnam, Patrick Tracy Lowell, *174*, 223
Pygmies, 27, 90, 174, 223

Quessua, 67
Quinan, Kenneth Bingham, *175*
Quinan, William Russell, *175*

Rafai, 99
Rainbow, *177*
Rainey, Paul James, 106, *177*
Rainsford, William Stephen, *177*
Ralph, Julian, *178*
Ramsay, William J., *178*
Rand, Austin Loomer, *178*
Randall, Richard, *178–79*
Rand Central Ore Reduction Company, 35
Randfontein Estates Gold Mining Company, 251
Rand Mines, 60, 77, 162–64, 197, 237
Raven, Henry Cushier, 94, *179*
Raymond, William, 150, *179*
Reading, Joseph Hankinson, *179*
Reagan, Ronald, 52
Reed, George Clinton, *179–80*
Rees, Emory J., *180*
Reform Committee, 35, 57, 101, *180*, 248
Render(s), Adam, *180*
Reunion, 2
Rhodes, Cecil, 62, 64, 101, 154
Rhodesia. *See* Northern Rhodesia; Southern Rhodesia
Rhodesia Congo Border Concessions, 104, 112
Rhodes-Livingstone Institute, 51
Rhokana Corporation, 156
Richards, Erwin Hart, *180–81*
Rideout, Conrad A., *181*
Rio Muni, 129, 166
Roan Antelope Copper Mines, 118, 213
Robbins, Elijah, *181*
Roberts, Edmund, *181–82*
Roberts, Frederick, 178
Roberts, George Arthur, *182*
Roberts, John Wright, *182*
Roberts, Joseph Jenkins, *182*, 189
Roberts, Leo Bond, *182–83*

Roberts Field, *183*
Robeson, Anthony Maurice, *183*
Robeson, Eslanda Cardozo, *183*
Robins, Lord (Ellis Robins), *183–84*
Robinson, James Herman, 55, *184*
Robinson, John C., 125, *184–85*
Robinson, William W., *185*
Robinson Chlorination Works, 149
Robinson Deep Gold Mining Company, 149, 197, 238, 251
Ro(d)gers, James Wood, *185*
Rogers, Joel Augustus, *185*
Rogers, Joel C., *185–86*
Rogers, Thomas, *186*
Rood, David, *186*
Roosevelt, Theodore, 106, 137, 142, 149, *186*
Ropes, Edward Dehonde, Sr., *186–87*
Ropes, Edward Dehonde, Jr., *187*
Roseberry, Robert Sherman, *187*
Ross, Edward Alsworth, *187*
Ross, Emory, *188*
Roye, Edward James, *188*, 200, 205
Ruanda-Burundi, 86, 151
Ruark, Robert Chester, *188–89*
Rubber, 82–83
Rudin, John James, *189*
Rudolph, Lake, 204, 242
Ruhengeri, 85
Russwurm, John Brown, 143, *189*
Ruth, 132
Ruwenzori, 211
Rwanda, 49–50, 85, 167, 171
Ryan, Thomas Fortune, 8

Saba Saba, 144
Sabi Game Reserve, 197
Sachikela, 44
Sadler, George Washington, *191*
Said, William Prestley, *191*
St. Augustine, 119
St. Helena, 138
Saint John River, 18
St. Michael, 109, 115
St. Paul River, 10–12, 63, 163
Sale, George, 229
Salisbury, 31, 67, 97
Sally II, 21

Verner, Samuel Phillips, *232–33*
Victoria, Lake, 79
Victoria Falls and Transvaal Power Company, 183
Vihiga, 180
Vincent, Frank, *233*
Virginia, 197
Virunga Mountains, 85, 193
Vissering, Gerard, 128
Vivi, 208
Vohimari, 119
Volta River, 34
Vom, 231

Wakan Airport, 92
Walker, William, 172, *235*
Wälläga, 132
Waller, John Lewis, *235–36*
Walton, Lester Aglar, *236*
Walvis Bay, 144, 220
Wanga, 24
Ward, Henry Augustus, *236*
Ware, Enoch Richmond, *236–37*
Waring, Colston M., *237*
Warner, Daniel Bashiel, *237*
Warner, Esther Sietmann, *237*
Warriner, Ruel Chaffee, *237–38*
Washburn, Hezekiah M., *238*
Wasolo, 39
Waters, Richard Palmer, *238*
Weaver, William, *238*
Webb, Francis Ropes, *239*
Webb, Harry Howard, *239*
Webber, Herbert John, *239*
Webster, John White, *240*
Wellington, 23, 81, 213, 249
Wellman, Frederick Creighton, *240*
Welmers, William Evert, *240*
Wema, 62
Wembo Nyama, 128
Wengatz, John Chrsitian, *241*
Wengatz, Susan Moberly Talbot, *240–41*
Werner, Beit and Company, 119
Wesleyan Methodist Church of America Missionary Society, 47, *241*
West Africa, 2, 15, 34, 39, 100, 102, 106, 125, 129, 152, 159, 161–62, 166,

173, 179, 184, 194–96, 198, 204, 214, 216, 224, 236–37
Wharton, Conway Taliaferro, *241–42*
Wharton, Ethel Taylor, *241–42*
White, Stewart Edward, *242*
Whitehouse, William Fitzhugh, *242*
White Plains, 121
Wilberforce Institute, 49
Wilcox, William Cullen, *242–43*
Wilder, George Albert, *243*
Wilder, Hyman Augustus, *243*
Wiles, Vivian McKinley, *243*
Williams, Alpheus Fuller, *243–44*
Williams, Anthony D., *244*
Williams, Gardner Fred, *244*
Williams, George Washington, *244–45*
Williams, L. H., *245*
Williams, Walter B., *245*
Willis, Bailey, *245–46*
Wilson, Alexander Erwin, *246*
Wilson, Benjamin F., *246*
Wilson, John Leighton, *246–47*
Wilson, Mary Jane Smithey, *246*
Wiltsee, Ernest Abram, *247*
Wine making, 247
Winshaw, William Charles, *247–48*
Winship, Blanton, *248*
Witwatersrand, 18, 23, 57, 94, 119, 149, 197, 205, 249
Wolbach, Simeon Burt, *248*
Wolff, Henry Albert, *248*
Woman's Missionary Union, 168
Wood, Clinton Tyler, *248–49*
Wood, Hubert Stephen, *249*
Woodford, Ethelbert George, *249*
Work, Ernest Frank, *249–50*
Wright, Charlotte Crogman, *250*
Wright, Richard Robert, Jr., *250*
Wulsin, Frederick Roelker, *250*

Yale University, 5
Yatenga, 101
Yates, Beverly Page, *251*
Yellow fever, 162–63
Yerby, William James, *251–52*
Yergan, Max, *252*
YMWB. *See* Young Missionnary Workers' Band

About the Author

DAVID SHAVIT is Associate Professor of Library and Information Studies at Northern Illinois University. He is the author of *The Politics of Public Librarianship* (Greenwood Press, 1986) and *The United States in the Middle East: A Historical Dictionary* (Greenwood Press, 1988). His articles have appeared in such journals as *The Journal of Library History, Library Journal,* and *Public Library Quarterly.*